General Washington and the Jack Ass

and other American Characters, in Portrait

By J. H. Powell

RICHARD RUSH, *Republican Diplomat*

BRING OUT YOUR DEAD: *The Great Plague of Yellow Fever in Philadelphia in 1793*

THE BOOKS OF A NEW NATION: *United States Government Publications, 1774–1814*

THE UNITED STATES OF AMERICA in the 1790's. This map, engraved by B. Tanner "from an entire original drawing," was published by Charles Smith, a bookseller, stationer and sort of hack writer of New York. The "entire original drawing" was obviously made after June, 1792 when Kentucky became a state (with its boundary at the Big Sandy, as the artist knew, though he had only the vaguest notion where the Big Sandy ran) but before June, 1796 when Tennessee entered the union.

(Reproduced by permission of The Huntington
Library, San Marino, California.)

General Washington and the Jack Ass

and other American Characters, in Portrait

J. H. Powell

Thomas Yoseloff
South Brunswick • New York • London

Thomas Yoseloff, Publisher
Cranbury, New Jersey 08512

Thomas Yoseloff Ltd
108 New Bond Street
London W. 1, England

SBN 498–06808–0
Printed in the United States of America

For

Julian and Grace Boyd

Contents

List of Illustrations

(The writer is particularly grateful to Marian Carson of Philadelphia for help in planning the illustrations. A special thanks is due, also, to the artist Isa Barnett for permission to reproduce on the jacket-cover portions of his lively painting, "The Grand Federal Procession, Philadelphia, July Fourth, 1788.")

American Characters, in Portrait

1

Philadelphia Lawyer

The way you went from Philadelphia to New York in 1735 was this:

You called in at a tavern at Second and Mulberry streets—Mulberry would not be "Arch" street for two generations yet—where you booked a seat in the next Bordentown coach, and you tried to find out when it was expected to leave. Regular service, in spite of confident announcements in the press, was something you didn't count on. If you were a person of standing and good for a sixpence hard money, a tavern callboy would come to your house before dawn to rout you out.

The coach was high off the ground, almost as high as a man in the saddle and fully as hard as a saddle to mount into. You put the ball of one foot gingerly on a tiny step, none too securely attached; you dared not trust it with all your weight. You grasped the door posts and hauled yourself as swiftly as you could into the coach with both hands. Seats faced each other; they were shallow for your buttocks, and not at all wide. Two people side-by-side on each quite filled the interior space. You bounced against your fellow passenger at every turn of the wheels. The coach was a lumbering craft: it swayed and pitched and tossed on its springs; the axles creaked; you held tight to a leather strap for safety. A flask of spirits made the trip easier. The cushion you perched on was a thin straw-tick covering a hard wooden bench. Those benches canted forward, your weight was on your feet. After an hour in the coach, it was your legs that were tired.

13

The route took you up crowded cobbled streets, across Pegg's Run on a narrow high-arched bridge—"kiss-me-quick," people said, "thank-you-ma'am" as their stomachs settled back. By and by houses were fewer, cobblestones ceased, the post-road smoothed out, your coachman high on his swaying box could even gallop his horses now and then between villages, inns, crossroads out in the county. Kensington was a stop, and The Jolly Post Boy at Frankford—your coachman was not the post, but he was an "opportunity" for private letters to be conveyed for a fee. Above Frankford came hills to labor up and rattle down, creeks to ford, Pennypack, Poquessing, at last Neshaminy. If water was running high in the creeks, a route further inland had to be chosen. That choice of route determined which ferry you used to cross the Delaware, whether Burlington or further up river near Bordentown. Ferries were beamy river craft, with sails, oars, and poles. If airs were light or the winds against you, the downward current at ebb, the upward tide at flow might keep you in the river a long and tedious while. If the coach and team crossed with you—often they did—loading that coach on board the ferry and managing the horses took skilled experienced men, and patience a'plenty. This was the first great problem of the trip: crossing the Delaware.

At Bordentown, you could get a bed at the Inn, take dinner and ale in the Ordinary, book passage in the next day's coach for Elizabeth. If it ran next day. This was an easier ride, the long level stretch across Jersey—"East Jersey," people still called it. They called the road "The King's Way." There were more creeks to wade through and rivers to ferry: the Raritan, the Rahway, cranberry bogs and brooding forests to pass. There were frequent farms; this was a well-peopled land. But still the journey was risky, tales of robbers, highwaymen, gangs of thugs prepared you for danger. Unfortunately they did not always prepare you for legal robbery: the exactions of ferryboatmen, extortionate charges at inns and taverns, local tolls that were scarcely more than blackmail. Elizabeth Town was a whole city thriving on the helplessness of travelers and their needs. You stayed overnight at one of the several good inns, you higgled at the dock for your passage. Here was the second great problem of the trip: the voyage to New York. It was a long sail, down the narrow Kill van Kull to the lower water of Upper Bay, clear up the length of Upper Bay to Manhattan Island where you tied up at the ferry stairs inside Leisler's Half-Moon at Battery Castle, or at one of the private wharves of the city. If the wind was slack, you might lie the whole day in stays. If it was northerly, you could tack back and forth without end. Or Upper Bay could be rough, sometimes too rough for the pinks and shallops of ferrymen. You could find yourself carried back again to Elizabeth. But if your luck held, you sailed from Elizabeth to New York in a few hours.

Now this was the way you made the journey, if you had enough money.

If you didn't, if you rode your own horse, you made sure to travel with the coach, or with others, for protection. If you were a poor man, you walked— and you begged or worked your way across the ferries. Or you prevailed upon a drover hauling goods to take you with him as a helper; perhaps he would pay the ferry if you stood at the horses' heads to keep them quiet on the river, or cleaned up the boat after them. If you were a rich man, with a strong back and energetic, you could drive your own "chair," a two-wheeler surmounted by a canopy to shade you from the sun. A chair gave you a rough jouncing ride; it was a young man's sporting vehicle. You ate the coach's dust all the way, but you whipped up to get to the Inn first in mid-afternoon to snatch the best place. And you fought to get your horse and chair secured on the ferries.

It was a hard journey. There was nothing pleasant about it. Yet roads were often crowded, for even then we were a traveling people, every trip filled with incident. Even then New Jersey was a highway to the sea.

Mr. Andrew Hamilton was a very rich man. He owned his own private carriage, a notable circumstance. Only seven men in the entire Province of Pennsylvania owned their own private four-wheeled carriages. There was one more, an eighth, but the Province owned it: the State Coach used by the Governor. Mr. Hamilton, Speaker of the Pennsylvania Assembly— "Mr Speaker" he was called at home—for all his Scottish good sense never-theless always maintained a certain elegance. It was one of the perquisites of marrying a rich widow. For all his Scottish toughness and vigor, he was frail, and no longer young. His coachman would have to carry a groom along to help manage the team on those river boats, that Upper Bay sloop. It would be exhausting, this trip. But he had to make it. James Alexander had sent for him.

He had made it before, and many other journeys, north and south through the woods and farmsteads, over rivers and bays, up and down the land and waters of these middle colonies in America. He could follow the stage. *"As you see,"* Mr. Hamilton said, *"I labour under the weight of many years, and am borne down with great infirmities of body; yet old and weak as I am, I should think it my duty, if required, to go to the utmost part of the land where my service could be of any use. . . ."*

Now exactly how many those years were, which weighed down on Mr. Hamilton, we do not know for certain. We only know what he said. He was far from home, a Philadelphian speaking to a New York jury, twelve men who had never seen him before. He could say pretty much what he liked. Above him sat a young and angry Chief Justice: making himself appear to be old and weak could be a contrast, an effect for the jury, a trick in the sharp game of pleading.

Like most tricks it was risky, for Mr. Hamilton was far from being the oldest man in the room. We have some reason for believing he was born in the year 1676. If so, he was fifty-nine in 1735, this ninth year of George II. Fifty-nine was scarcely a remarkably old age. His opponent in this cause was Richard Bradley, King's Attorney General in New York, "Mr. Attorney" he was called in court. The number of years Mr. Attorney labored under was not much short of seventy-five. At least, old Mr. Bradley had been at Cambridge University fully fifty-eight years before, in 1677–78, when Mr. Hamilton had been a mere infant. If by speaking of his age and frailties Hamilton intended the jury to think him older than Bradley, pitiable and valiant for his "great infirmities of body," he must have been doing some lawyer's playacting.

He did it superbly. Andrew Hamilton started his own legend, in the Zenger trial. That legend grew in his lifetime; he did nothing to dispel it. Legend has grown about him ever since. By now it is part of history, and cherished lore, the most-often-told story of American law before the Revolution, the tale of "The Philadelphia Lawyer"—how he traveled full of years to New York ("at his own expense," people always say), pled the cause of the poor immigrant printer John Peter Zenger before an awesome tribunal, by his matchless logic and eloquence "foiled the sophistry of the royalist court, aroused the jury to defy the judge," won acquittal for Zenger, the huzzahs of New York, and by the brilliance of his pleading established Freedom of the Press in America—forever, people add.

Lawyers, particularly, love to tell the story. Lawyers are innocent historians. It is the drama in the courtroom they dwell on: Mr. Hamilton's undoubted skill, his easy urbanity, the thrill of his daring, the delight of his wit, the eloquent simplicity of his language, the rhythms of his voice heard clear as a bell from the printed page. Now these things are all there. Certainly his performance that hot summer's day is a moment of grandeur, preserved for us in all its stately measures. But it is preserved for us, by Mr. Hamilton's most enthusiastic admirers—specifically, by those for whom he won his case. Historians must not be innocent. Confronted by evidence so partisan, so entirely one-sided, the historian must be on his guard at every point. He must begin by separating fact from legend.

It is legend, that Zenger was poor. He was remarkably well supported in his printing business by the most powerful group of public men who had ever established a newspaper in an American colony. Shortly before his arrest he moved from his modest place in Smith Street to a more commodious dwelling and shop, "in Broad street, near the Upper End of the Long Bridge." True enough, he was an immigrant, but being an immigrant was no disadvantage in this polyglot town of immigrants, New York.

It is legend, that this trial established Freedom of the Press. The Zenger case established neither law nor precedent in America. Authorities continued to bring libel suits against printers for years afterwards. There was no place in the empire where the press was what we call free. The press was something governments controlled. In England, printers would continue till the 1770's to be prosecuted for publishing Parliamentary debates. In Virginia only one printer existed till 1766, and he was scrupulous never to publish anything "disagreeable to the governor," for fear of losing his public printing contracts. In Massachusetts printers were accustomed to securing in advance permission for anything they published; Commodore Sir Charles Knowles brought a libel suit against Dr. William Douglass of Boston for calling him in print a low place-holder, a coward, and a petty tyrant. The case was heard in Massachusetts courts three separate times in 1748–49 (fourteen years after Zenger), was appealed by Sir Charles to King in Council, was dropped only when Sir Charles received the lucrative appointment to be Governor of Jamaica. In New York as late as 1757, twenty-two years after Zenger, a printer would be prosecuted for printing the public proceedings of the Assembly—and found guilty. Freedom of the Press would true enough come to America, but later, by other routes, other men, in other times.

It is legend, that Andrew Hamilton was a venerable antique famous everywhere when he made his celebrated trip to New York; legend, that his entrance into the court room created a sensation, that court, bar and spectators recognized him as the leading attorney-at-law on the American mainland. He was not that. No one was. There was no American bar, there were thirteen separate colonial bars, each with direct channels of appeal to Westminster, but with no formal and scarcely any informal relationship one to the other. Fame did not run that way, across colonial boundaries. Except to his Scottish friend James Alexander, and that other Scot Cadwalader Colden who had formerly practiced medicine in Philadelphia, Mr. Hamilton was virtually unknown in New York. This very trip was the episode that would eventually spread his fame, this plea to the jury August 4, 1735. It was *after* his day (thirty years after) that the whole empire would come to know the name Andrew Hamilton.

In 1735 his fame, such as it was, lay entirely confined within the two colonies of the Penn Proprietaries, Pennsylvania and Delaware. It was the fame of a political leader, not that of a practicing lawyer. True enough, when he died in 1741 his grateful young friend Benjamin Franklin, whom he had mightily assisted with printing contracts, remarked on his local prominence as a lawyer. Franklin wrote, "He was long at the Top of his Profession here . . ." But that meant little or nothing; this was 1741. Pennsylvania's legal profession was a tiny thing; there were only two lawyers in the province, Kinsey and Assheton, who could claim some training and formal schooling. Judges and chief justices except for those two were laymen, not lawyers.

The reason was peculiar to Pennsylvania. Quakers heartily disapproved of worldly litigation—of this business of going to law. They settled their worldly disputes by arbitration, if they could. When they couldn't, they resorted to courts, but not for gain. To serve another man as attorney was a Christian's duty, Quakers believed. For anyone to take money or rewards for doing such a duty had actually been against the laws of the province for the first forty years of its history. Not until 1722, only thirteen years before Zenger's case, had Pennsylvania repealed its first statutes and made legal the practice of law. In thirteen scant years, no professional attitudes or traditions had developed. The bar of Philadelphia was new, and primitive, in striking contrast to the large, much older, certainly much more learned and now even organized professional bar of New York City. Mr. Hamilton had actually pled very few cases at any bar, since his arrival in Philadelphia twenty years before. When he did, he pled as attorney for the Penns, or the Province.

And not, if the truth must be told, with formal training behind him. Mr. Hamilton had taught himself law—and here another legend must yield to fact. In his time, barristers from the Inns of Court were beginning to appear at the bars of the middle colonies. The strong impulses and best efforts of these skilled professionals newly come from London, were to make colonial practice match English, to introduce correct pleadings and sound Common Law principles into the primitive, amateurish, often haphazard jurisprudence of colonial courts. Mr. Hamilton, like James Alexander, had no English background of study or pleading. He was a lawyer self-taught, from hand-books and random texts; his entire experience had been in those very innovating, unlearned, rudimentary, informal courts of rural colonial counties, as remote from Westminster as it was possible in this empire to get. If young Chief Justice DeLancey in Zenger's trial represented the best learning and training of the law, Mr. Hamilton represented the old-fashioned way of the American colonies, of ignoring British precedents, pursuing reason or feelings rather than rules.

And so, of course, did the jury.

When he was a young Scottish immigrant down in Accomac on the isolated Eastern Shore of Virginia, Andrew Hamilton had been willed a library of law texts by the busy Presbyterian divine, the Rev. Francis Mackemie. He was admitted to practice in innocent Eastern Shore bars, he made his way gradually northward into Maryland accumulating wealth by marriage (and by other means not always well thought of; William Byrd of Westover found him owning a certain plantation, said he was "a man of bad character, and he got the estate nobody knows how")—and accumulating a reputation in county courts. The habit of study was certainly on him; he sought books wherever he could, there is no doubt he studied avidly and well. James

Logan, the Penns' resident Secretary in Philadelphia, hired him for a suit in Sussex county, Delaware. Their opponent, Logan wrote William Penn, "was baffled at the Court by the Dexterity of our Lawyer's Management, without bringing the matter to Trial."

That was in 1714. All the years afterwards, Logan's words remained Mr. Hamilton's measure. Dexterity, cleverness, shrewd insight in dealing with people were qualities the rugged Scot had in abundance. But those were qualities far different from professional commitment to English forms of pleading, different from the learning in the law so prized at the New York bar.

And his pleading that day in 1735 for Zenger did nothing to make people think him a legal *savant*. They thought him a superb public orator, a magnificent presence, a dextrous person, but a rebel against the law, an opponent of the law's knowledge and skills. When he finished his remarkable speech, the scholarly Chief Justice found it necessary to rebuke him mildly; Mr. Attorney Bradley observed that he "had gone very much out of the way, and had made himself and the people very merry," but the cases he cited had not been to the point. And his friend Alexander, in whose place he was standing, at whose request he had come, Alexander the most painstaking of legal scholars, found it necessary to apologize publicly for Mr. Hamilton's unlearned, unprofessional pleading:

". . . when the defendant is innocent and unjustly prosecuted," Alexander wrote, "his counsel may, nay ought to, take all advantages and use every stratagem that his skill, art, and learning can furnish him with. This last was the case of Zenger at New York, as appears by the printed trial and the verdict of the jury. It was a popular cause. The liberty of the press in that Province depended on it. On such occasions the dry rules of strict pleading are never observed. The counsel for the defendant sometimes argues from the known principles of law, then raises doubts and difficulties to confound his antagonist, now applies himself to the affections, and chiefly endeavours to raise the passions. Zenger's defense is to be considered in all those different lights."

And in the light of character. For what is not legend, what is crystal clear and certainly truth, is the record that has come down to us—a record of astonishing immediacy in which individuals of the past take on shapes and features and qualities, become fleshed and vivid, not the larger-than-lifesize heroes of legend but persons of human dimensions, irresistibly our contemporaries. For all it is biased, for all it has been much tampered with, this record is convincing. You cannot doubt these were Mr. Hamilton's actual words; you cannot miss his singularly powerful personality. The reporter (whoever he was; we have no way of knowing, though it may have been Alexander himself) seems surprised at what he records, the audacity of it, almost the impossibility that Hamilton should prevail over the jury, persuade the twelve men to render, at no little risk to themselves, a verdict against the law, against the facts, against instructions. And against the government.

The bulky packet from James Alexander with its urgent news and its call for help, reached Mr. Hamilton the last days of July. By an entirely improbable chance it came at a moment when he was unexpectedly free. Zenger's trial was set for August 4. Any other year, Speaker Hamilton would have had to say *no* to his friend Alexander, for early August was always the time for his Pennsylvania Assembly to meet, in one of its four regular sessions between October elections. But this summer of 1735 was different. Five years now, Mr. Hamilton had been pushing ahead with a big expensive project he particularly cherished: the construction of a fine commodious State House for the government of the Province of Pennsylvania. Mr. Speaker was heartily tired of his Assembly having to meet for its sessions in taverns, or some dilapidated vacant residence. The State House project had proved monstrously difficult and bitterly controversial, but finally the builders had actually made progress. Roof, walls, and floors were finished, several "raisings" had been celebrated, at last Mr. Hamilton could hope they might soon make an end of it. In April he had ventured to promise the members of Assembly that if they would agree to postpone their regular summer session for as long as one month, they would probably be able when they did come together to meet in their handsome new quarters, for the first time. Instead of August 1, therefore, the Assembly had adjourned till September 15. And now Hamilton knew the adjournment would hold, because the Governor had been forced to call a special session for two weeks in June, and he certainly would not dare impose upon the members again.

That special session had been necessary because of Maryland affairs. Lord Baltimore had petitioned the crown claiming *he* not the Penns owned The Three Lower Counties on Delaware (as Delaware was then called). The Pennsylvania Assembly of course had to respond, defending the Penns, and Mr. Speaker had been very busy those two June weeks on high serious matters. He also took advantage of the opportunity, and of the rare spirit of unity among the members, to clear up two minor pieces of business: he wrote for Assembly an extremely complex and difficult statute confirming the sale by Proprietors and quieting title of a manor of 14,000 acres (John Penn needed the money); and he had an order agreed to, "That the two old Houses next opposite to the State-house (one being the House where the Assembly now sits) be demolished, and the Materials thereof be disposed of to the best Advantage . . ." Now with the shabby old residences gone the builders would have to finish the new State House, for sure, by September 15.

The special session concluded June 25. After that, July and August stretched ahead for Mr. Hamilton with no duties save routine ones, easy familiar tasks. His provincial offices rarely pressed him hard in summer. They were as numerous as ever: right now, in addition to being Speaker he was Trustee of the General Loan Office, Judge of the Orphans' Court, Recorder of Philadelphia, and Judge of Common Pleas. He was accustomed to them all, and nothing very serious was afoot. Except, of course, the business of putting chancery jurisdiction in Pennsylvania on a correct basis, and transmitting funds to the Provincial Agent in London, and urging workmen to greater efforts every day at the State House, and enforcing the new Poor Relief Act about waifs and strays in the Province, and preparing for October's elections . . .

In Assembly, he was in fairly good case. His son James, and his new son-in-law William Allen, were both coming on well at his direction. Just as Bucks County always returned him, so he had arranged a safe seat for James from Lancaster County, and for William Allen from Philadelphia. Young Allen was already Grand Master of Masons; now he was seeking election as Mayor of Philadelphia, which promised agreeably to enlarge Mr. Hamilton's already dominant sphere of influence.

His bitterest enemies had been remarkably quiet lately. There were still attacks, of course, still crackling scurrilities against him in Bradford's paper. Paragraph writers loved to portray him as the great Gargantua of self-love, self-esteem. They picked up his every word. Recently he had observed in a letter that in spite of his age his eyesight was still keen. One writer pictured him crying out in Assembly,

> 'Tis *I*, 'tis *I*, 'tis *I* alone
> Can Mountains move, and reach the Moon,
> And see as well as Twenty-one!

Mr. Hamilton was "Catiline" in the press, or "tyrant," "Sejanus *Redivivus*," "this Potent Revealer of politic mysteries." The first book against him had been called *The Life and Character of a Strange He-Monster*. The latest was a screed purporting to prove he had cheated the Widow Richardson out of her lands. He hadn't, of course. But there was no use in saying so.

There was never any use in answering attacks. Pennsylvania politics was a rough game without rules, violent, full of passionate angers. Mr. Speaker expected to be unpopular. Those he had defeated reviled him, and he was perfectly aware those at the top of the pile would never accept him as one of them. After twenty years, Andrew Hamilton was still an outsider in Philadelphia. To the great men, the famous men, Pennsylvania's imposing inner circle of Welsh and English Quakers—to Jonathan Dickinson, Lawrence Growden, to William Penn's own trustees ("the triumvirate") Isaac

Norris, Edward Penington, Samuel Carpenter—Hamilton ever remained an alien Scot, a worldly man who refused to move in Meeting. And he was that most unacceptable of all persons, a Deist. He attended no church, made no concessions to convention, he talked thoughtfully of knowledge and nature and Newton's new science as the way to apprehend God. James Logan, Secretary of the Province, was certainly glad of his support, the Proprietary family were sometimes grateful, once to the extent of presenting him 153 acres of land on the very edge of the city as a personal gift. But they could never consider such sort as he, as one who belonged.

Hamilton had to make his own way, his own place. He had come to Philadelphia a man nearly forty. In his fifties, he finally succeeded in domi-nating the Assembly. Not the government, not the Proprietors, the Governor, the Council, the courts—but the House of Representatives, the branch elected by the freemen, and by a provision (probably an accidental, un-intended provision) of the Charter of 1701, the branch possessed of the sole privilege of legislating for the Province. His domination was hard won. He had won it in the midst of popular discontents and surly risings, by organizing freeholders at election, securing their votes for himself and a few respectable associates, by building a political following. Gradually the older leaders died off, David Lloyd in 1731, Isaac Norris just this June of 1735, unexpectedly. Hamilton, now at the end of his fifties, could feel his victory nearly complete.

Pennsylvania was different, because of him. Before Hamilton, government had been torn with antagonisms, Governor and Council of one mind, the elected Assembly under Lloyd's leadership of another, Secretary Logan the Proprietor's servant frequently caught between. The bustle and frowardness of the popular Assembly had been Logan's cross, and his torment. But once Hamilton had won control, antagonisms slacked off, difficulties abated, a measure of harmony came to the government, prosperity came to Pennsyl-vania.

For Speaker Hamilton was undoubtedly "William Penn the Old Pro-prietor's" man. He was none of your mobbish levellers, a Keithite bent on seizing power. Nor was he a factional Quaker like Lloyd, opposed to Penn and his descendants, plotting with the Fords against them. He was indepen-dent, he could never be swayed by influence or preferment, he was consistent, and steady. Long ago, he had read Penn's Charter of Privileges of 1701—how he found a copy to read is a mystery; perhaps James Logan let him see the government's transcript—and into his Scottish mind had sprung a vision. He abandoned his law practice, his Assembly seat, and his public career in Maryland; with Logan's encouragement he removed to Philadelphia.

The vision Andrew Hamilton had seen was that William Penn's Charter gave to Pennsylvania the freest constitution of government ever known in the world. *"It was Love of Liberty first drew me here,"* he would say. The word liberty was always on his tongue. *"The loss of liberty to a generous mind is worse than death."* *"The man, who loves his country, prefers its liberty to all other considerations; well knowing that, without liberty, life is a misery."*

Now mountebanks talk of liberty, and fools, and demagogues to abuse the public mind. It is a threadbare word on noisy tongues. But so do statesmen talk of it, and lawyers, and Scotsmen who dream. Hamilton charged it with meanings—the special meanings William Penn had given it in 1682, and '83, and in his final Charter of 1701. "Any government is free to the people under it, where the laws rule, and the people are a party to those laws," Penn had said. "We must *give* the liberties we *ask* . . ." "We put the power in the people." The opening words of Penn's First Frame of '82 were apt for cutting in stone: "Government seems to me a part of religion itself, a thing sacred in its institutions and end." To the inhabitants Penn had written, "You shall be governed by laws of your own making."

For twenty years, Hamilton had applied those words, and all the principles of Penn's Charters, to every transaction of his public life. He applied them in legislative battles, in contests against governors and councils, against Assemblymen, even against Secretary Logan and the Proprietors themselves when the sons of William Penn found their father's grants of rights too permissive for their needs. If the records of the Philadelphia County courts still existed, we might see how he applied them in the law.

He applied them, not as a practicing professional lawyer but as a man in public office. Under the old laws, there were no practicing professional lawyers when he came in 1714 to Philadelphia's unpaid, amateur bar. Law was an avocation, not a way to wealth. Mr. Hamilton's wealth remained for a long while his 900 acres on the Chester River in Maryland, the £200 sterling and 7,000 pounds of tobacco he got by selling his plantation down in Accomac, and such lands as he acquired in Pennsylvania. But the law became his life, at least the public part of Pennsylvania's law, dealing with Proprietary lands and citizens' rights.

He arranged it so. Apparently he was persuaded to arrange it, in 1713, because James Logan in his turn saw a vision. Logan was in his hardest times, as Secretary. William Penn Lord Proprietor had suffered a massive seizure, he was in pitiable condition, his mind was nearly gone. His wife Hannah Callowhill Penn was conducting Pennsylvania's governance with a firm hand, but she had no funds, and surely the eternal suits and disputes with Lord Baltimore would wax hotter now in the Proprietor's disability. And in Philadelphia Logan was plagued with opponents. The Assembly was ever higher against him, thoroughly anti-Proprietary; David Lloyd drafted bills and pled causes with a keen lawyer's devilish skill. One other lawyer in the Province was Lloyd's equal, Robert Assheton, a cousin of William Penn. Logan had taken Assheton into the Council, where he could draft bills for Governor and Council in opposition to Lloyd's Assembly acts, and where he could plead the Proprietary cause. But Assheton alone was far from enough. He was "Mr. Penn's stiff friend, and had stickl'd for him," but only Logan of all the councillors would vote with him. The Secretary needed able lawyers, shrewd, knowledgable men. So did the Proprietrix. But the severe Quaker laws against professional practice, of course, prevented any coming to the province.

If none would come of their own accord, Logan would have to persuade them—and that is evidently what he did. To snatch an important Maryland attorney right out of Maryland would render Lord Baltimore by that much the poorer. Mr. Hamilton's practice was considerable in Maryland; it included cases before the Provincial Council, and recently he was turning up more and more often in Kent County, Delaware, as counsel. For a certainty Logan talked with him in Philadelphia at the end of the year 1712 when he hired him to represent the Penns in Sussex County, Delaware; for a guess he explained to Hamilton just how it could be arranged that a man might make a better living and rise higher in Pennsylvania where lawyers were not allowed to take a fee, than in Maryland where they were. The Scotsman evidently listened.

In February, Hamilton won the case for the Penns in Sussex County, Delaware; in March, he sold his plantation in Accomac; in September, he sailed for London. He sailed with a letter in his pouch from James Logan to Hannah Penn, which he was to present to the Proprietrix in person. It was a pleasant letter; Logan even made one of his Friendly little jokes: "This comes by one Andrew Hamilton . . . an Ingenious man, and, for a Lawyer, I believe, a very honest one . . ."

And in London, Hamilton became a barrister. This must have been his errand; he stayed only long enough for that single accomplishment, he was quickly back in the colonies where he rented a house at Third and Chestnut Streets in Philadelphia. And this single errand must have been what Logan and the Proprietrix had planned for him. The only reason for a successful colonial lawyer to become a barrister was additional prestige in courts, especially royal courts, and in appeals on the record from colonial courts to England. A barrister would be more eligible for legal or judicial office than a mere lawyer admitted to the bar. The crown would be more pleased with the Penn family if they appointed a barrister to office in their Province, and more impressed with his pleadings. And in Pennsylvania the only income an attorney could make was the salary of an office.

On January 27, 1713/14, Andrew Hamilton enrolled himself as a member of Gray's Inn. Two weeks later he was called "per favor" to the bar. It was an expensive formality, of little substantive meaning but in Queen Anne's time of considerable significance. The Inns of Court had stopped teaching long ago, had even ceased their ancient mootings and boltings. But the Inns were still the only granters of the degree Barrister-At-Law, and the most familiar, most ordinary course for a young man to be called to the bar was still for him to enroll in one of the several Inns, reside there for twelve terms (three to four years), do his studying by attending courts and parliaments and working in some lawyer's office or on his own under some clerk's direction, appear a stated number of times each term for dinner in the Great Hall of his Inn, perform a number of "exercises" during the confusion of the company at dinner—the young hopeful would advance to the High Table, catch the eye of some well-disposed senior barrister, and commence (as best he could with no one listening) the formal presentation of a case: "*A is seized in the fief of Blackacre . . .*" Finally, he would petition to be called, the governing body of his Inn would set him some kind of examination, though this too had become the merest formality; then he would be admitted.

An older man, a man presumably already proved in the law, could get round this lengthy and rather ridiculous procedure by seeking admission *per favor:* he made the right connections, paid a whopping big fee in lieu of eating the required number of dinners, went once to dinner in the Hall. Someone was appointed to examine him, again no more than an accommodation; then he was certified "Utter Barrister-At-Law." His certificate was good wherever in the world Her Majesty's courts held, and good for his lifetime. In the American colonies, a barrister of the Inns would be at once licensed to practice, or in some colonies (New York among them) would be welcomed into any court, on any cause, without the formality of a license.

Admission *per favor* meant prestige, and rank, and honor, and a certain authority. Indeed, it meant everything regular admission meant, except knowledge of the law. Real barristers, those who had actually done their arduous studies, held admission *per favor* in something near disdain. Yet it was a sensible thing for an older man to seek, even at the high cost. That Andrew Hamilton took it in 1713/14, then removed to Philadelphia where he received preferment suitable to a barrister, cannot have been a sequence unplanned. On August 23, 1717, the Scotsman from the Eastern Shore was named "Attorney General, or Clerk of the Crown" for Pennsylvania. Thus it was that Logan gained a Proprietor's man in government to stand between Council and Assembly, and plead in Proprietary courts; Hannah Penn gained a barrister in authoritative position to plead in royal courts against Lord Baltimore's petitions; and Pennsylvania gained a new leader from the outside, unconnected with any of the troubling busy factions.

As Attorney General, Hamilton displayed remarkable vigor. The Assembly voted him a salary of £40 (the governor was then getting £200). They soon raised it to £60 when they saw how effective his work was: bringing criminals to speedy trial, revising all the laws passed since the beginning, publishing them in a complete edition, writing new statutes for Assembly to pass: *An Act for the Advancement of Justice, and the more certain Administration thereof; An Act for punishing Accessaries to Felony . . . for directing how petty Offenses shall be punished . . . for the more effectual Recovery of debts due from Foreigners, and Persons absconding . . .* The Assembly was suddenly very busy, on law codes and jurisprudence: "A motion being made, and the Question put, that the Salary allowed the present Attorney-General, *Andrew Hamilton,* for this Year, be augmented? *Passed in the Affirmative.*"

Several years he remained "Mr. Attorney" for the Province, legal servant of the Proprietors. Once again he went to England, an extended trip this time on Penn family business. But Pennsylvania was a fluid place, swiftly changing: shiploads of immigrants came every year; in 1722 law practice was made legal; after William Penn's death the young Proprietors altered their father's original policies, became difficult for Mr. Hamilton to serve. He resigned as Attorney General, began to take private clients, found himself named or elected to lesser positions: Prothonotary of the Supreme Court, Recorder of Philadelphia, some years Sheriff, later Judge of Vice-Admiralty. In his work as practicing lawyer, he rarely pled in courts; rather he preferred to arrange private settlements. He was particularly noted for this, locally; and apparently he was financially successful, for he refrained from collecting the salaries or fees due him in his various offices, a practice not universal among Scotsmen. And in politics he began his remarkable Assembly career. In 1727 he was elected for Bucks County; from 1729 on (except for one year) he was Speaker, and certainly the dominating member.

And as Mr. Speaker, his rôle in the Province became far different from his first career as Mr. Attorney. It was not that he changed his principles; Logan changed, and the Penns. Mr. Hamilton remained what he had started, champion of Penn's Charter of Privileges. Curiously his championship of the Charter separated him from the Secretary, and from the high leadership of Pennsylvania. For in actual fact, neither Penn himself as long as he was in health, nor his wife in the years of his incapacity, nor his sons afterwards, nor his servant Logan nor his principal Quaker followers and trustees, liked that final Charter of 1701. In England, Penn before he was stricken hoped to surrender the Province to the crown, that he might pay his debts. (*"O Pennsylvania! what hast thou cost me?"* Penn wrote. *"Above thirty thousand pounds more than I ever got by it, two hazardous and most fatiguing voyages, my straits and slavery here, and my child's soul almost . . ."*) His sons the three Lords Proprietor continued to seek some such profitable surrender, and in Pennsylvania their servants in the government sought to extract all the money they could and suppress all the political unrest, in order to pave the way for an accommodation. Isaac Norris and others of the Council tried to ignore the Charter of 1701—indeed did ignore it, for even after it was granted the Council went right on legislating. And James Logan, loyal steadfast Logan, strove to change its provisions. Penn had not really intended to take legislative power from the Council, vest it in the representatives alone, create a one-house legislature, Logan said. This was "a practice not followed in any other colony." Exactly because it was a practice not followed in any other colony, Hamilton revered the Charter, prized its grants of liberty, held it as a constitution granted to the people, a contract fundamental in its parts, irrevocable even by those who had granted it. In Assembly, this Scottish outsider, this Deistical *arriviste,* found himself contending *for* the Charter, *against* the Quaker leaders, the Council, the Governor, Friend Logan, Friend Norris, against the very men who had fashioned The Holy Experiment.

He turned Penn's words and his principles against those who had been closest to Penn. And he had the mass of new-arrived immigrants on his side. As Pennsylvania grew with non-Quakers from the Old World, affairs slipped from the grasp of the tiny Friendly establishment into the hands of Assembly and the freehold electors, because of that very Charter grant of 1701 which Penn had intended (if at all) to be a concession to his own Friendly people. Mr. Hamilton never missed a chance to refer to "the religious and civil Liberties we possess" and "the many benefits bestowed" by the Charter. When he became Speaker, he altered the formula of his parliamentary address to the Governor at the opening of each session (formally claiming the rights of the house as the just rights of freemen) by adding the words: "just Rights of the Freemen of *Pennsylvania,* derived and confirmed to them by their Charter of Privileges . . . "

It is said Magna Charta owes more to Edward Coke of the seventeenth century, than to the Runnymede barons of the thirteenth. Just so, Penn's celebrated Charter of Privileges of 1701 owed more to its champion than to its author. Hamilton was first among the inheritors who brought Penn's Charter to active and functioning life, and made it fundamental law. And brought it out of obscurity. The Charter, when first granted October 28, 1701, had been "distinctly read in Assembly," but oddly it had never been printed. People at large had no notion what it said, and even representatives in Assembly were not sure. When constitutional crises arose the representatives would have to order, *"The Charter of Privileges be read."* And the whole long document would be intoned aloud by the Clerk, if the Secretary would lend it to him for reading. Finally after twenty-five years, in the midst of sharp factional bitterness of 1726, it was published—eight folio pages from the press of Samuel Keimer, with the wrong date, and regrettable errors; but at least for a few pennies citizens could read the famous constitution under which they were governed. Hamilton had a principal part in that printing, and next year, 1727, it was he who extracted from the Governor "an exemplified Copy of the Charter of Privileges, under the Great Seal of this Province," that would lie in the House of Representatives so the Assembly would have its own copy of the fundamental law.

This Charter of Privileges, granting liberty of conscience to all people, the rights of citizenship to all Christians, and vesting all powers of legislation in elected representatives of the people, made Pennsylvania, as Mr. Hamilton viewed his world, superior to all other colonies anywhere in the empire, superior in the freedom of her citizens even to England itself. *"The Liberties and Privileges we derive by the Charter, granted to the People of this Province, by our late honourable Proprietary, cannot fail of exciting in every good Man a strong Desire of seeing his Descendants here . . ."*

This was his cause—William Penn's Charter of Privileges, and Pennsylvania's civil liberties. He said so every session, as he opposed "Men who have acted in such a Manner as if they utterly disregarded all those inestimable Privileges . . ." He repeated it on every occasion when he "struggled with those Men, in order to rescue the Constitution out of their Hands, which thro' their Mistakes (*if they really were Mistakes*) was often brought on the Brink of Destruction. . . ."

He would say so again in the Zenger trial, to New Yorkers, this August. It was what he must say, the one thing in his life significant to be said: *"Blessed be God, I live in a government where liberty is well understood, and freely enjoyed . . . "*

The news in James Alexander's letter was a lawyer's nightmare, a hotchpotch of animus, accusations, bitterness, and strife. Mr. Hamilton had to separate facts from the overheated pottage, isolate what was relevant from what was merely regrettable, discern exactly how things stood with the client Zenger. He had to do it swiftly. Alexander's letter came late in July, "a few days before I left home . . ." He had precious little time for preparation. Preparation is the lawyer's only hope.

By now the printer Zenger had been eight months in jail, charged with seditious libel. Certainly that was relevant. His counsel had been disbarred; they were asking Mr. Hamilton to appear in their place, sending him instructions quite as solicitors instructed a barrister. That was relevant. It left him free to decide on his plea, and his pleading; he would determine the defense as counsel of record. But how much of the rest of Alexander's news related to this particular case? To this prisoner, thus charged?

William Cosby, "Captain-General and Governor-in-Chief of the Provinces of New York, New Jersey and Territories thereon depending, in America, Vice-Admiral of the same, and Colonel in His Majesty's Army"—Governor Cosby might be a detestable person, venal and thievish, as Tories said he was. That would be nothing unusual. Colonial governors were frequently detestable persons, in the Duke of Newcastle's detestable administration. To Hamilton, as to James Alexander, any Whig was likely to be venal and thievish. Perhaps Cosby had actually been guilty of extortion, as rumor charged, when he was Governor of Minorca before coming to New York; that had nothing to do with Zenger's plight. Perhaps he had snarled boorishly when the legislature voted him a salary of only £1,500 (more by a third than Pennsylvania's Governor was now paid) and gratuity of only £750 (never granted at all in Pennsylvania). The snarl may have made him unpopular, but it would not get Zenger out of jail. Snarls were not constitutional matters.

Cosby was described as "about 45 and Gay . . . has the Earl of Halifax's sister for his wife, 2 daughters almost women and a son." Mr. Hamilton's only previous dealing with him had turned out well enough. It was just last winter: the Speaker by a series of improbable chances had personally apprehended a gang of Irish counterfeiters. They were "Livers in the Jerseys" though they pushed their bad bills in Philadelphia, and in The Three Lower Counties on Delaware. When they fled back across the river to their refuge in Salem, West Jersey, the redoubtable Hamilton pursued them till they holed up in a farm house. There he found a great quantity of their false bills concealed in a haystack. He routed out a constable, had "the Irish saints and scholars" arrested. But a Jersey magistrate set them free on bail. Mr. Hamilton refused to be bilked of his prize: he sent a rider galloping up The King's Way 150 miles clear to New York for a governor's warrant, Cosby sent it back at once, properly executed, Mr. Hamilton contrived to secure the adventurers again and transport them to a Delaware jail. For all he knew from this, Governor Cosby was efficient and brisk, as an army colonel should be. Taking those counterfeiters had been a stroke of the first importance. It had rescued the currencies of two Provinces, everyone said. Mr. Hamilton went to New Castle himself in March, to prosecute the criminals in The Lower Counties court, and see that they were found guilty. His Pennsylvania Assembly voted him a special fee of £41–10s–5d for the pains he had taken.

Yet obviously Cosby had turned James Alexander against him, and a host of people in New York and the Jerseys. Though he followed twenty years of good government under three excellent governors—Hunter, Burnet, Montgomerie—twenty years which had quieted faction, softened rivalries and angers in this powder keg New York, it had taken Cosby only a few months to reawaken every bitterness, rough-sand antagonisms, stir hot and high the stew of faction again. He had chosen favorites for place and power, built a governor's party, and of course by his favors to a few had angered the many left on the outside. Those many had coalesced into an opposition; Alexander was their leader.

The furious political animosities of New York were not Mr. Hamilton's concern, nor did he have time to consider his position regarding them. He had confidence in James Alexander, must accept his word for how things stood. His word was, that Colonel Cosby had astonished the people by his actions, had behaved like a despot, destroyed freedoms of the constitution (if, as Mr. Hamilton might observe, royal governments could be said to have a constitution). Most of all, it appeared, the opposition detested his avarice, his evident greediness for money. Councillor Rip Van Dam, relic of the old Dutch aristocracy, had served as Acting-Governor after Montgomerie's death before the new appointee appeared. Cosby as soon as he came seized every chance, even the most unlikely ones, to improve his fortune. He appointed his small son Billy to a lucrative sinecure, Secretary of New Jersey. And he demanded one-half of all fees Mynheer Van Dam had collected as Acting-Governor. Both were entirely legal acts. Cosby displayed a royal warrant from King George himself stating half the fees were to be his. Van Dam indignantly refused to pay, unless the Governor made over to *him* one-half the fees *he* had collected while still in London. This would be a very large sum indeed, something over £3,000. Cosby had no intention of parting with it. But he determined still to have his way, and he decided to sue Van Dam to recover his half. Before a jury, of course, he could scarcely hope for a favorable one-sided hearing. It would have to be a suit in equity, without a jury. But as Governor, Cosby himself was Chancellor. He could scarcely bring an action in his own behalf, before himself. Even under Newcastle's Whigs, the House of Lords would never allow that.

He could, however, as Chancellor and Governor, create a new equity court. He did: he issued an order that the Supreme Court of New York would sit in terms as a Court of Exchequer, and he directed Mr. Attorney Bradley to bring a bill against Mynheer Van Dam in the King's name. Van Dam engaged James Alexander and William Smith for his counsel; they pled the Supreme Court held no such jurisdiction, that Cosby's order constituting the Court of Exchequer was not legal. And they won. Old Chief Justice Lewis Morris, of Alexander's party, ruled in their favor. John Peter Zenger, without official authorization from anybody, printed two books reporting the Supreme Court proceedings: one contained the arguments of Alexander and Smith against the Governor's new court, the other the opinion of Chief Justice Morris supporting the two lawyers' position. The latter went through three printings at once. The former was issued with an addendum by Van Dam: "for obtaining equal justice of His Excellency William Cosby, Esq." The case was a sensation, and so were the books—not from any general popularity attaching to Rip Van Dam, who was one of the wealthiest of the imperially wealthy patroons, nor the brilliant old Morris, Councillor and great landholder in New Jersey and manor holder in the Bronx; but rather from the vigorous pleadings by James Alexander against a Star Chamber court, and his attacks on the Governor for unprecedented prerogative acts.

Cosby's reply was abruptly to remove Lewis Morris from the Chief Justiceship. It was within his power, but he made two technical errors when he did it: he failed to have the Council join him in the action (there is no evidence Council refused, only that they were not asked to consent to the removal), and he appointed his new Chief Justice James DeLancey and his puisne justice Frederick Philipse "for and during our will and pleasure" instead of "during good behaviour," which would have meant for life, and would have been the correct legal appointment. They were no more than technical errors, the Governor had been imperfectly advised; he could correct the mistakes at any moment.

James DeLancey was a young man, in his thirties, and he was the first native-born New Yorker to be Chief Justice. He was thoroughly well-educated for the post, a product of Eton College and Cambridge University, and after the proper number of years' study a barrister of Lincoln's Inn. There is no doubt he was learned in the law. The case was heard again; in a tightly reasoned charge packed with precedents and citations, DeLancey defended the equity jurisdiction of the Supreme Court sitting as Court of Exchequer. Mynheer Van Dam was hailed once more to the bar.

This time, Van Dam refused to plead. Now James Alexander could have bade him stand mute; or he could have applied for appeal to the Privy Council to determine the jurisdictional question. But when he tried that, De Lancey refused to sit as Chief Justice to grant an appeal. He was sitting as Chief Baron, he said, or Vice-Chancellor. This was the equity side of Exchequer court: the Governor's fees were a matter of the King's revenue. Mr. Attorney was acting for the King. Whereupon in the King's name Mr. Attorney ordered Van Dam to answer in person the question, how do you plead? Van Dam announced he would answer no questions at all, for this court was improperly constituted, at which Attorney General Bradley produced, as if by sleight-of-hand, a Governor's commission of rebellion against him.

It was a surprising move: it had never been used in Mr. Hamilton's time in America; it was a process almost unknown in the colonies. A commission of rebellion meant, that if he did not yield himself to the Governor's jurisdiction and direction, all Mynheer Van Dam's extensive properties and estate would be forfeit to the crown. And Mr. Bradley was in earnest. He promptly commenced process to seize everything Rip Van Dam owned. But he used two witnesses who lied; their perjury was found out, his execution of process fell apart.

Now Richard Bradley undoubtedly used those two witnesses in perfectly good faith. It was not he who suborned the perjury; it turned out to be an individual named Queen Marsh. As he pored through this record, Mr. Hamilton could recognize too much was at stake, Van Dam's holdings too vast, for anyone to imagine an experienced man like old Bradley trying to seize them on foul trickery or perjured testimony. Certainly young James DeLancey would never tolerate such dishonesty in his new position, his new court. And Governor Cosby may have been innocent as well—an impatient military man, unskilled in the law, dependent on others. It looked as if he had been imposed upon once more, by unscrupling subordinates seeking to do his will at any cost. Even Whiggish corruption usually drew the line somewhere. But the episode of the suborned witnesses was used to damn Cosby, when people learned of it from his opponents. Certainly as Governor he had signed that commission of rebellion. Certainly his enemies could represent him to New Yorkers as a Governor who had corrupted power and place to try to grasp for himself one of the largest estates in the colony.

Another subordinate soon made him look even worse. As High Sheriff of Westchester County, Nicholas Cooper had the job of supervising elections. Old Lewis Morris, by now seething with indignation, lived mostly in New Jersey where he was Councillor. But he also had his Westchester estate "Morrisania," and he decided to stand for a special election to the New York Assembly, thus winning a seat in the lower house from which he could strike back at Cosby. Some of his neighborhood supporters were Quakers. Sheriff Cooper, the Governor's man, demanded every freeholder as he presented himself at the polls swear a solemn oath that he owned land and was entitled to vote. Quakers, of course, for religious reasons would swear no oath at all, of any kind—as the Sheriff well knew. And when each Friend in turn refused Cooper disfranchised him, thirty-eight of them in all. It was not illegal; no law in New York protected Quakers. Neither was it effective, for Morris (far more skilled than Cosby or Sheriff Cooper at controlling elections) won his seat anyway. But it certainly an offense against custom; an affront to well-known, well-respected freeholders; and a threat to the very processes of free elections.

In all likelihood Governor Cosby had nothing to do with disfranchising the Quakers. Probably he learned of Sheriff Cooper's high-handedness only afterwards, when everyone else was talking about it. Plainly he did not approve what Cooper had done, for in a short time he issued an executive order that the Quakers' "I affirm" would henceforth be accepted in elections, in place of the world's peoples' "I do swear." But as Governor, he could be blamed. Now his opponents condemned him as a man who had corrupted place and power to deny the franchise.

It was after this election, and after the perjured witnesses episode, that

James Alexander, William Smith, Lewis Morris, Rip Van Dam and a number of others opposed to the Whiggish Governor, prevailed upon John Peter Zenger to start a second newspaper in New York. Bradford's *New York Gazette* was the only paper, and it was the official one. William Bradford proudly styled himself "Printer to the King's most excellent Majesty for the Colony of New York." Bradford published everything DeLancey said or wrote, all Cosby's proclamations, everything the government handed him to print, but no word of criticism, nothing distressful to administration, indeed nothing about administration at all unless the government *had* handed it to him with directions to print it. James Alexander wanted a voice of his own, to say things very distressful indeed to administration. The first number of Zenger's *New York Weekly Journal. Containing the Freshest Advices, Foreign and Domestick* appeared on Monday, November 5, 1733. Zenger must have been uncommonly hurried, for he made mistakes any conscientious printer would regret. His dateline in the first issue read "Munday" for Monday, "October 5" for November 5.

From that number on, every Monday the *Weekly Journal* delighted New Yorkers and aroused them, with thinly veiled unsigned attacks upon the Governor and all his people. In the guise of conversations reported, letters received, even news of animals strayed or stolen, Cosby was blamed personally (though never named) for every act of corruption or injustice committed by anyone in New York. We have seen men's deeds to property destroyed, the *Journal* proclaimed, an allusion to Cosby's voiding a Mohawk Indian grant to Albany traders. We have seen judges arbitrarily removed. New courts are erected without the concurrence of Assembly, courts of equity in which trials by jury can be taken away "when a Governour pleases." Men of known estates have been denied their votes, contrary to—the *Journal* did not say "to law," but used a careful phrase, a lawyer's precise phrase—"contrary to the received practice, the best expositor of any law." "Who is there . . . that can call any Thing his own or enjoy any Liberty larger than those in the Administration will condescend to let them do?" ". . . the People of this City and Province think as matters now stand that their liberties and properties are precarious, and that slavery is like to be intailed on them and their Posterity . . ." All men were obliged to depend upon "the Smiles or Frowns of a Governour, both which ought equally to be despised" when the interest of the country is at stake.

Now the law was perfectly clear, and perfectly sensible: peace and good order demanded respect for government. Any man who published something scandalous, virulent, or discreditable about a governor, who defamed, traduced, or vilified a public official in order to stir up the people against him, was committing a crime. The crime was the wicked intent, the malice in the heart of the man who published it, the purpose of stirring people to unrest, mistrust, discontent. Such a publication, originating in such malice of mind, would move people to sedition, riot, and uprising. *Libel* was a defaming publication. *Seditious* libel was a defaming publication designed to incite people to resistance, even insurrection, against lawful authority.

A good citizen strove to spread respect for law, and for government. Only a bad citizen, bent on evil, would seek to expose public persons to public contempt. If a man had actually been injured by acts of govenors, the law provided him ample remedies, numerous actions for redress, for making things right, securing justice. What it did not provide him was the privilege of arousing those who had not been injured, arousing the whole community to distrust, resistance and sedition.

It was any governor's sworn duty to put down sedition, to preserve peace, confidence and good order. He certainly had the power to stop seditious libels at once when they appeared. And he could stop them even if everything said to his scandal were true. Indeed, the law had long held that maliciously, wickedly publishing the truth about a public man was a worse crime than publishing a lie. "The greater the truth, the greater the libel"— it was an old legal tag. This too was reasonable, for a governor injured by a lie could disprove the lie and thus expose his traducer, but a governor injured by the truth, published in malice for the purpose of injuring, had no chance of winning back public confidence, except the thin chance of exposing the malice. It might be quite true that a public man's sister was a whore, convicted as a public prostitute, but to publish that truth for the purpose of bringing contempt upon the public man, exposing him to contumely, stirring a rising-up against him, was seditious libel and worse in degree than if the whole story were a lie.

The opinion of a Chief Justice in a docketed case was certainly a very public matter, publicly delivered and publicly received. Yet Zenger could have been prosecuted for printing and publishing Chief Justice Morris' opinion in Van Dam's case—if it appeared that he had published it in malice, with the intent of discrediting the Governor with the people. And the fact he published it without official order or permission would have gone a long way toward showing that very intent. This was the law.

It was a law rarely used in the colonies. The case of William Bradford in Philadelphia went way back to 1693, and had nothing in it applicable to Zenger's case that Mr. Hamilton could use—not even the coincidence that the same William Bradford was now official printer in New York, Zenger's former employer and present rival. Governors and public men were always being attacked in the public press, violently, heatedly, with richly colorful invective. Mostly they ignored it. But Whigs in England had been prosecuting writers and printers, of late. Chief Justice Holt had converted seditious libel into a Whiggish political instrument. The law existed, available to any governor who wished to seize weapons rather than steel himself to patience.

As Zenger week after week printed in his *Journal* things Lewis Morris wrote, and James Alexander and Smith and others of his backers, he was surely courting prosecution, and surely he knew it. Surely Alexander knew it too, and courted it on purpose. Zenger's *Journal* was a partisan creation, meant for a daring political challenge. Any libel must be a jury trial. The *Journal* was rousing readers to Alexander's cause, strengthening the feeling against the Governor, spreading among the people enthusiasm for political opposition—among the very people from whom the jury would have to be drawn.

Its effect was immediate. Only ten weekly issues of the *Journal* had appeared, when Chief Justice DeLancey charged "the Gentlemen of the Grand-Jury for the City and County of New-York" to investigate certain libels being printed and circulated. Bradford published DeLancey's *Charge;* it was an official document. Zenger in answer brought out an eighteen-page folio pamphlet, *Some Observations on the Charge given by the Honourable James DeLancey, Esq.,* with his imprint: "New York: Printed and sold by John Peter Zenger. Price 1s." The gentlemen of the grand jury serenely reported they could find no libels being printed.

Plainly, Alexander had captured the city and county of New York. Here was his major strength, and the grand jury's refusal came near being a license to libel. In the next eight months, the next thirty-six issues of Zenger's newspaper emitted ever stronger and bolder stuff. Alexander's new voice became the loudest voice in New York. And apart from his *Weekly Journal,* Zenger drew pamphlets, broadsides, separates, and singleleafs from his press. To every official publication from Bradford he contrived to issue something in response. Against James Alexander, Councillor Francis Harrison wrote a personal attack, and a Council committee issued a report questioning his conduct. Zenger countered with two pamphlets of Van Dam's (one was reprinted in Boston; New York's swelling political struggle was making news elsewhere) and with Alexander's own *The Vindication. Of James Alexander . . . from matters charged and suggested . . . in two pamphlets lately published . . .* On the title of this twenty-two page folio, the printer placed his new and fuller imprint, for this was the moment in his unaccustomed prosperity when he moved from Smith Street, and wished to tell his customers so: "Printed by John Peter Zenger, and to be sold by him at his House in Broad Street, near the Upper End of the Long Bridge, in New York."* Usually he was much briefer. The pseudonymous *Reply to the*

---

* And regrettably, he made his usual errors. His imprint gave the date "1733" where he meant 1734. The year began in those days, not on January 1 but on March 25, and frequently books published in the months January, February, and March have been

Speech of Governor Cosby. By Sydney bore his customary "New York, Printed by John Peter Zenger." But nowadays his most dangerous work, charged with electrical sparks and political fire, sensibly bore no imprint at all. *A Letter from a Gentleman in New York,* signed "P.P.," had for a colophon the mysterious legend "America: Printed in the year 1733," but even this pallid concealment was too risky for the lawyers behind Zenger's enterprise. Entirely without any kind of printer's identification was the safest way, and that is the way *Damon and Alexis. A Pastoral* appeared, and *A Copy of a Letter from James Jackson . . . to his friend in Ireland,* and a broadside with forty lines of verse headed *Ridentem Dicere Verum Quid Vetat,** and others. Any printer of libellous matter is well advised to withhold his imprint, so no one can prove to a jury it was he who printed or published it.

At the end of eight months, an election of local magistrates was approaching in the now thoroughly aroused city. With no imprint, Zenger published a four-page piece, *Two Letters on Election of Aldermen,* purporting to be written by one "Timothy Wheelwright." And on the eve of the voting he brought out the work which finally moved the Whigs to take action. Likewise without imprint, apparently spread about the city furtively rather than offered for sale, it was a quarto singleleaf bearing two poems, *A SONG made upon the election of new magistrates for this city,* and *A Song made upon the foregoing occasion.*

Whoever wrote these *Election Songs* had abandoned caution, or any care for the common law of libel. If Cosby's advisers were lying in wait for a chance to prosecute, they had it now. Not that the *Songs* were astonishingly virulent; Mr. Hamilton had seen much worse. His own enemies had used more picturesque language reviling him in the press, and older, more patient governors of New York could have shown Cosby far more savage songs than these. The Earl of Bellomont had heard himself called the "grand Ringleader" of a "hellish Tribe . . . great by his Title   Vile in every action." Governor John Nanfan had been slandered immoderately, "a fawning sychophant . . . a Crafty Knave deliver'd from a jayle To be a Statesman   here," and

> . . . proud as Lucifer tho poor as job
> greedy as Cibernis mercilesse as the mob
> Fierce as a Lyon in's Judiciall Chair
> But when he's out as Timorous as a hare . . .

---

mis-dated in our later years, after the calendar reform of 1752. But some of *The Vindication* deals with transactions of April, so there can be no doubt of the error in the imprint. Cosby was admittedly a wretched governor; unfortunately we must observe that Zenger was a pretty shoddy craftsman as a printer.

* The line is from the first *Satire* of Horace, i, 24. We could translate it "Who says laughter can't tell the truth?"

Even Robert Hunter, agreeable, firm, pacific Hunter—"You have governed well and wisely, like a prudent Magistrate, like an affectionate Parent," the Assembly told Hunter, after ten years—even Hunter could write his friend Dean Swift, from turbulent New York, "I am used like a dog . . ."

None of these had turned to the law to suppress libels. They had accepted the harsh terms of the political game. But Cosby was no Robert Hunter. And these two *Election Songs* did actually fulfill the prescription for seditious libel, if he wished to invoke the law. The Governor was in no way party to the election of city aldermen; the *Songs* could have no other purpose for dragging him in than to foment mistrust of him, discredit him, stir up the people against him. The anonymous writer could claim no injury, no interest affected; therefore presumably he could have had no other motive than that "express malice" the law deplored. The *Songs* named the Govenor specifically; they threatened him:

No governor can order us
  To bend the knee to him.
If he does the Blunderbuss
  Can make his glory dim.
They say the devil dwells in Hell
  And Cosby, too, might just as well——

vilified him:

We'll vote against the cowardly crew,
  And boldly face the worst
That the despot dares to do.
  He knows he stands accurst——

held him up to public contumely:

Cosby knows the jig is up,
  Vict'ry is in the air——

and disgrace:

Come on, brave boys, let us be brave
  For liberty and law;
Boldly despise the haughty knave
  That would keep us in awe——

and sought to induce violence and risings against him:

Tho' pettyfogging knaves deny
  Us rights of Englishmen;
We'll make the scoundrel rascals fly
  And ne'er return again.

This was no complaint of a subject injured by a public act; this was a traducing of the Governor's character, a gratuitous attempt to alienate citizens from their government, an insult calculated to inflame citizens against authority. James Alexander by now must have thought himself in strong case indeed, to dare such stuff in print. And he must have thought Cosby helpless.

As to that, Mr. Hamilton could see, Cosby was pretty much helpless, except for the courts. In royal colonies the courts were not independent branches of government, but parts of the Governor's encompassing office; quite as in England (in older times) all justice had proceeded from the sovereign. Courts acted on the Governor's order, though they had to act in proper legal fashion, for appeals could be taken to Westminster. Only through his courts could a governor protect himself (and, as he would say, protect the King) from slanderous publications.

All the information Mr. Hamilton had in his packet from James Alexander was partisan, factional; all of it from the Governor's enemies. In politics there was ever the need of a scapegoat. Between the lines Mr. Hamilton could discern other issues, the enforcement of the Navigation Acts against shippers who would rather have them ignored, the jealousies of those removed from office. He could also discern that plenty of men of honor, importance, place and power supported the Governor, adhered to his party. Certainly James Alexander had won an imposing following in the city, had captured the city offices in this election. He had ascended to such confidence as to launch this fusillade of vulgar abuse from Zenger's press—against a scapegoat, a single man he would make the symbol of all those he opposed in New York. But he was taking on a lot. Royal government with its establishment, its licensed monopolists of trade and services and fees, its archives and records and all the sanctions implicit in the Great Seal, was a massive company. It would be a critical confrontation for his friend Alexander. The stakes, Mr. Hamilton realized, were far greater than Zenger's fate. The stakes were the commerce and wealth of the province of New York.

After the *Election Songs,* Governor Cosby resolved to suffer no more insults to be heard. His resolution was timely, as he consulted his own self-interest, which William Cosby could be relied upon to do. For Lewis Morris had gone to England to represent to Parliament and the Board of Trade the light in which he viewed the Governor's various acts, and of all circumstances this was the most disturbing to Cosby. It was one thing to remain tolerant of scandalous vituperation in a colonial city far from Westminster. It was quite another to know your chief enemy was actually in person before the Privy Council, making charges you had no chance to answer. Governors even better connected than William Cosby had been injured when angry citizens had taken sail for England.

In the voluminous record before him, Mr. Hamilton could trace Cosby's successive steps to bring his enemies to account for their spate of libels. On October 15, Chief Justice DeLancey once more addressed the grand jury. His language was temperate; he meant to be persuasive: "The words in the song court outright violence against the King's government . . . abusive, insolent, and mischievous. . . . Our best people are being libeled . . . an endeavor is being made, to trample on all order and government . . . all this must end in sedition. . . ." The jury would have to indict the offender: "If you, gentlemen, do not act, you may well consider that your failure to do so will result in violent disturbances of the public peace. The fault will be at your door."

The gentlemen of the grand jury in good conscience and fidelity to their oaths could no longer pretend to be ignorant of what everyone knew. But they could remove the fault from their door, and with a merry solemnity lay it at the Governor's. They reported that they had indeed discovered certain pernicious libels being printed and circulated, and they "requested" the Governor to issue a proclamation for the discovery of the offenders. This could not have been what Cosby wished. There would be something a little foolish about an official proclamation concerning two songs. The Governor would scarcely show to best advantage. And by their "request" the gentlemen had ensured that if anyone was to be named, it would be the Governor, not the grand jury, who named him. This would still leave the grand jury the chance, if someone were brought before them, to refuse to indict.

Two days later the Council, apparently without Cosby's knowledge even though his name was used, sent a proposal to the Assembly for a joint resolution, ordering four numbers of Zenger's *Journal* to be burnt by the Public Hangman. The Assembly coolly laid Council's resolution on the table. Council waited two weeks, then on November 2 ordered the Mayor and aldermen of the city to do the burning. They had to order someone, for Council had no executioner of their own. The Public Hangman acted only on order of the whole legislature (that is, Governor, Council, and Assembly) and on proper warrants reciting court actions. The Mayor and aldermen had a lesser officer in their employ, the Public Whipper of the city. But Council's order, addressed to them, was an act of Council alone, and had no more authority than a private letter from friends. The Quarter Sessions Court refused to enter it on its docket as an official act, and the Mayor and aldermen—in no way obliged to be servants to the Council, and certainly not friends—sent no reply. Neither did they send the Public Whipper. The councillors found themselves looking ridiculous; they had ordered a burning they could find no way of carrying out. Apparently they could not prevail even upon the Sheriff to conduct the ceremony. Ultimately, the Sheriff did send them one of his Negro slaves, and it was that humble individual who stood on the parade at the Fort, with no one but a few soldiers of the garrison looking on, and solemnly consigned four numbers of Zenger's *Weekly Journal* to the flames. The councillors themselves failed to turn up to witness their fiasco.

Cosby, meanwhile, was obliged by the grand jury's sly "request" to issue his proclamation. He issued two, on the same day, November 6. Bradford printed them in his best formal broadside style, they were read aloud and posted at the usual places about the city. One offered £20 reward to anyone who would reveal the name of the "ill-minded and disaffected" person who had written the two *Election Songs*. The other offered £50 to anyone who would come forward with the names of the authors of "scandalous, virulent, false and seditious reflections" which had been appearing in the *New York Weekly Journal.* These reflections, the Governor proclaimed, brought discredit not only upon "the whole legislature, in general" and "the most considerable persons in the most distinguished stations in this province, but also upon His Majesty's lawful and rightful government, and just prerogative." He pronounced they were "contrived by the wicked authors of them, not only to create jealousies, discontents and animosities in the minds of His Majesty's liege people of this province, to the subversion of the peace and tranquility thereof, but to alienate their affections from the best of kings, and raise factions, tumults and sedition among them." He described the scandalous writings as having appeared in many issues of the *Journal* "but more particularly those numbered 7, 47, 48, and 49" which were the very issues Council had ordered burned, and though that burning was a dubious affair still those numbers had in some sort been proceeded against at law, and therefore at law they no longer existed. Obviously, Cosby and his Council had not been acting in concert.

The clear purpose of the proclamations was to unmask the authors, not to prosecute Zenger the mere printer and publisher. Certainly Zenger was offensive to administration: young Chief Jusice DeLancey met him on the street one Sunday in October, and raged at him fiercely in a most unjudicial manner. But prosecuting Zenger would not stop James Alexander's loudest public voice, it would not defeat the opposition, show them up for libellers, help administration recapture the Assembly. Cosby was casting his sling for the real leaders and caballers. In effect his proclamations said, tell me who these wicked authors are, and Zenger I'll not bother with.

Who the wicked authors were, was of course well-known to everyone, including the Governor. A town of 8,500 does not keep major secrets, nor very many minor ones. Yet not a soul came forward to give legal evidence and proof against them, and claim the reward. It was something surprising: £70 was a considerable sum. It had been more than a year's salary for Mr. Hamilton when he served as Attorney General in Pennsylvania. He received a not much greater amount as Speaker. That egregious individual Queen Marsh had suborned the two false witnesses in Van Dam's case merely by standing them drinks in a tavern. The fact that a substantial amount of money would induce no one in New York to betray the writers of the libellous pieces was a remarkable demonstration of the solidarity of freeholders and even the indigent of New York City, in James Alexander's faction.

Cosby waited ten days for his proclamations to bring forth a witness. After that, he could wait no longer. He did the only thing left for him to do: an extraordinary warrant issued, from Governor, Council, and Chief Justice all three; the Sheriff took Zenger on Sunday morning, November 17, and clapt him in the common jail of the city on the charge of "printing and publishing several seditious libels, dispersed through his journals or newspapers . . . tending to raise factions and tumults, among the people of this province, inflaming their minds with contempt of His Majesty's Government, and greatly disturbing the peace thereof . . ."

This was the turgid record Mr. Hamilton was obliged swiftly to make his way through, this stew of passions boiling in sour political stock. The end of it all was that the Governor had the wrong man in jail, the printer not the author, the hired-help, not the master. And Mr. Hamilton must enlarge him out of jail, without permitting the least hint of disclosure of the real author of the libels. Plainly, those names were what the Governor wanted. And he was in a fair way to find them out, for in libel trials the jury decided only on the single guilty fact of printing or publishing. It was the court alone who decided if the thing published were libellous, or seditious. To prove Zenger guilty of the act of printing, Mr. Bradley for the crown would summon witnesses—journeymen, apprentice printers, errand boys from the shop, nervous inexperienced youngsters. Mr. Attorney could legally ask them to tell whom they saw in Zenger's house, who the people were who brought in material to be set up in type, who conferred regularly with Zenger. Names could slip out, a record could be built; from proof of the fact of printing undoubted evidence of authorship could be garnered. . . . He must prepare against that.

Yet knowing Jaimie Alexander, Mr. Hamilton certainly must prepare to contrive Zenger's release, for Alexander was no man to let a single victim long endure punishment for them all. It was remarkable, the loyalty to Alexander these clients had exhibited. Mynheer Van Dam had come near losing all he possessed, for his lawyer's determined opposition to Cosby's measures. And Zenger was in jail, because he would not name the writers of what he had printed. If anyone should be in jail it was Alexander himself, and Morris and Smith and Van Dam, all the leaders of the opposition faction. Certainly Cosby would have preferred it.

Zenger's imprisonment, the record showed, was made uncommonly hard. Did Cosby hope by this to persuade him to give evidence of the authors' names? Or so to chagrin and disturb those authors at the sight of the prisoner's suffering that they would come forward? On Wednesday after his arrest, Chief Justice DeLancey sat on *habeas corpus*. He set bail at £400, and demanded another £400 surety, an astonishing amount. No one offered it, Zenger remained in his miserable cell. The next day, the Public Hangman was ordered by Council and Assembly to burn the *Election Songs;* the next week Council and Assembly sent "Humble Addresses" to the Governor urging prosecution of Zenger. Did these events mean Alexander had momentarily lost the Assembly? Mr. Hamilton could not tell. But he could see what happened next: the January grand jury met. DeLancey was not temperate this time. If the gentlemen of the grand jury did not find a true bill against Zenger now, they would be guilty of perjuring themselves, he said. He said it in his opening charge, "in the fullest court we had ever seen in that place," Alexander remarked; and he said it before any evidence had been offered. Mr. Attorney then presented his bill of particulars against Zenger. The gentlemen of the grand jury were still unimpressed with Mr. Attorney's facts, still entirely unawed by the young Chief Justice's imposing language. This was exactly what they had expected back in October when they had bade the Governor find out his libellers for himself. And they did what they had prepared then to do. They refused to indict.

In Mr. Hamilton's Proprietary Pennsylvania, that would have ended the matter. Zenger would have gone free. But New York was a royal colony. Here he confronted the prerogative, that mystery of vice-regal governments, the ill-defined share a governor held of the processes available to the crown. On January 28, the ninth week of Zenger's imprisonment, Richard Bradley as King's Attorney General signed and filed with the clerk of the Supreme Court an affidavit of Information, charging Zenger with being "a seditious person and a frequent printer of false news and seditious libels," and giving the court "here to understand and be informed" that the said Zenger had "wickedly and maliciously devised to traduce, scandalize and villify his excellency the governor . . . to falsely, seditiously and scandalously print and publish and cause to be printed and published a certain false, malicious, seditious scandalous libel . . ." He selected two numbers of the *Journal* (they were numbers 13 and 23) which had not been previously acted against or burnt, and alleged Zenger "did falsely, seditiously and scandalously print and publish" these certain "false, malicious, seditious and scandalous" papers, which were libellous.

Now prosecutions on Information were familiar enough to Mr. Hamilton. They were necessary in any system of law, particularly in cases of hot pursuit such as he himself had indulged in this past winter apprehending the Irish counterfeiters. But such prosecutions belonged to cases of urgency and public danger, when a grand jury could not be convened, or might delay justice—cases in which no rights were infringed or threatened. They certainly were not to be used after a grand jury had freely and regularly considered a bill, and returned an *ignoramus*. To do so, was to destroy the grand jury itself, overrule it by assertion of power without authority, eliminate a right as ancient as the oldest records of the common law. Jurisprudence in Pennsylvania was not so primitive as that. Mr. Hamilton's sense of justice was offended, his conviction was quickened that government in his Pennsylvania was superior to any other.

Evidently he would not be allowed to plead against the process. The record showed that Alexander and Smith, certainly the ablest of lawyers, nowhere protested Bradley's prosecuting on an Information filed after his bill had been refused by the grand jury. But the Philadelphia Lawyer would not conceal his surprise, nor his profound objection to the method. He would prepare something on this head, prepare a statement the jurymen could not doubt: it belonged to the substance of liberty, to *"quench the flame of prosecutions upon Informations, set on foot by the Government to deprive a people of the right of remonstrating and complaining of the arbitrary attempts of men in power. Men who injure and oppress the people under their administration provoke them to cry out and complain; and then make that very complaint the foundation for new oppressions and prosecutions. I wish I could say there were no instances of this kind. . . ."*

Bradley had drawn his Information in standard form. But as Mr. Hamilton studied its lines, the word "false" seemed to leap from the page. He did *falsely print,* did *falsely publish*—this was the language of the law: out of wickedness and malice, out of his false heart, the libeller had spread his scandals. But Mr. Attorney had used the word too often, used it beyond the language of the law. He charged the news Zenger falseheartedly printed was *false* news, the seditious libels *false* in substance. He seemed to insist on falsity. It was no technical error; Bradley was too knowledgable for that. But it was unnecessary to his case, it was more than needed to be charged. Libels were libels, false or true. Could Mr. Hamilton make a point of that? Lawyers would say the Information was ordinary in form, but why could not one lawyer for once use language in its ordinary meaning, apart from form? Zenger was specifically charged with printing *false* libels . . .

James Alexander and William Smith had made no point of it, just as they had never protested the prosecution on Information. But this was not a question of the peculiarity of law in the royal colony of New York, this was a common-law point. Had Alexander shied away from proving the libels were not *false*, because he feared the authors might be exposed? or only from regard to the common-law rule, that truth was never a defense in such actions? Truth would not have been a defnse, ordinarily; but here Bradley had plainly written *false* news, *false* libels . . .

Alexander and Smith had not done several things that would occur to defense attorneys. What they had done was the one thing they should never have tried. It seemed a curious aberration in judgment; it was unexpected in this record. Apparently Lewis Morris had sent word from England that royal approval had not yet been given for his removal as Chief Justice, or DeLancey's appointment. It meant very little, Mr. Hamilton realized. Approval might still be forthcoming. But James Alexander had seized upon it as vital news. And he stiffened himself to try an impossible stroke, a stroke with no hope of success, that only desperation would prompt. On April 15, he and Smith appeared before De Lancey with their client, for trial. Alexander objected to the court itself: it was illegally constituted, he said. It was without jurisdiction, because the Chief Justice and Justice Philipse held their commissions at the "will and pleasure" of the Governor, instead of for "good behaviour." The most he could have hoped for was an appeal point if his case went against him. Or Cosby and the Council could merely have issued new (and proper) commissions. Had he seriously wished to try the validity of the commissions, he should have done so on *quo warranto* proceedings long before this, for those commissions were now nearly two years old, and the Court had heard numerous cases under their mandates.

DeLancey seemed to sense the despair of Alexander and Smith. He bluntly refused to hear arguments on the plea, or receive it. He addressed William Smith in terms that could take Mr. Hamilton's breath away as he read them, and that certainly took away the two lawyers' licenses: "You thought," said the Chief Justice, "to have gained a great deal of applause and popularity by opposing this Court, as you did the Court of Exchequer, but you have brought it to that point that either we must go from the Bench or you from the Bar: Therefore, we exclude you and Mr. Alexander from the Bar."

Mr. Justice Philipse, from his place on DeLancey's left, also spoke out. He concurred in the order of the Chief Justice, Frederick Philipse said, and he would have it known the intention of the order was to exclude the two counsel from legal practice entirely, in the province of New York.

The suddenness of the order, the complete finality of the moment, made clear how serious a mistake Smith and Alexander had committed. They were defense counsel; they had owed more at this moment to their client Zenger than to their hot partisan cause. Through this hopeless, ill-advised plea, they had removed themselves from his side in his greatest need. Just as old Mr. Bradley had brought an unexpectedly heavy legal gun to bear when he produced a commission of rebellion against Van Dam, so now the youthful DeLancey surprised the attorneys by abruptly using the very fullest extent of his legitimate power. On neither occasion had Alexander seen it coming.

He and Smith were both barristers-at-law, welcome in His Majesty's courts anywhere—but as DeLancey well understood, welcome as officers of the court. And technically, he was right. Proceeding against the commissions of the judges was not a response in defense. To impeach those commissions required other types of action. Alexander had underestimated his opponents, and their skill at law.

For years, he had striven to separate courts from the Governor's power, to establish independency in the judges. Now, he was prepared to argue that the Governor had named judges to serve at his will and pleasure, dependent upon him, and had proceeded against an unindicted subject on an Information to be tried before that dependent court. In such circumstances, the power of the Governor would be unlimited by law, even while the forms of law were preserved. Perhaps such an argument would stand up in England before the Privy Council or the High Courts at Westminster, but he had chosen to urge it as a plea in defense instead of in a proper action before a proper tribunal, or in Assembly. He had no chance to make his points. As far as Mr. Hamilton's record showed, James Alexander had never thought of disbarment.

Disbarment was a proper power of the court, though it had not been used before as so baldly political a weapon. Disbarment had been a punishment for personal misconduct. Only one case in New York was held in memory, that for hilarity rather than high seriousness: a certain Paroclus Parmyter, barrister, had actually been disbarred five times in ten years, 1699–1708, for various sprightly performances. Once, he had hurled ink pots and candlesticks at the Collector of Customs with whom he had been drinking in a tavern, and chivvied him impishly about the room on his sword point. Another time, he had written saucily in a complaint to the Governor that "the way to justice ought to be like the way to hell, smooth and broad and open to all." Such merriness was a far cry, as grounds for disbarment, from a sober plea to a lack of jurisdiction. "We ever thought it lawful for any of our clients to bring the commissions of the judges to the touchstone of the law," Alexander said plaintively: "But we never thought it so necessary as in this case . . ." He was entirely defeated. And his whole cause was in grave jeopardy now, for he had no position left from which to direct his supporters, or even hold their loyalties.

DeLancey could have named himself or Associate Justice Philipse as counsel for the defendant. Supreme Courts did that, sometimes; they were still doing it in New York fifty years later. But DeLancey proved to be a scrupulous judge. He appointed a young lawyer his own age, John Chambers, to represent Zenger. Chambers was known for a thorough Whig. He would be as interested as DeLancey in the names of the real authors of those libellous pieces. Probably, he would seek discovery of the names as the strongest

defense he could contrive for his client, and surely the best hope for
leniency. Certainly he would stoutly and ably defend, for he was an honest,
conscientious man, a keen student of the law, student of other things too—
poetry, art, languages. Thirty years from now his nephew John Jay would
inherit half the riches of his large library. He had been in practice ten
years; in 1729 he had signed the "Agreement Made Among Lawyers" which
organized the bar of New York; in 1731 he had been called *per favor* to be
barrister-at-law by the Middle Temple.

Now Chambers has frequently been described by historians as a governor's
man. He was not that, not in the worst sense. One could be a convinced
Whig, thoroughly against Alexander's opposition faction, and still be repelled by Governor Cosby's venal schemes and evident rapacity. Chambers
was a man of probity, honor, and intelligence. Three undoubted facts prove
him to have accepted his defense assignment in good faith, and with professional responsibility. First, he pled Zenger "not guilty" and prepared for
trial August 4. Second, he consented to the association of Mr. Hamilton with
him in the case. (He must have: had he not cheerfully agreed to Mr. Hamilton's appearance he would have withdrawn.) And third, he prevented a
rigging of the jury panel.

For once more, a subordinate in administration tried to smooth Governor
Cosby's way easy, probably again without the Governor's knowledge. This
time it was the Clerk of the Supreme Court. The last week in July, the panel
of forty-eight veniremen was to be drawn, from whom juries would be
selected for trials in the ensuing August term of court. The Clerk called a
panel of specially picked men, men he knew to be favorable to the Governor.
John Chambers vociferously objected. He insisted the panel be drawn in
the customary way, by calling every third name out of the book of freeholders. A sharp exchange followed; the Chief Justice was sent for. DeLancey,
too, was evidently innocent of his Clerk's scheme. Without hesitation he
ordered the Clerk to produce the book of freeholders, and proceed in the
usual manner. DeLancey would permit no tampering with the integrity of
his court. Even had he wished to (there is no evidence he did) he would
scarcely have dared, for an appeal would lie at once to England. Chambers's
alertness ensured that his client the printer Zenger would have a fair hearing, before twelve men who could "well and truly try, and true deliverance
make, betwixt our Sovereign Lord the King, and the prisoner at the bar,
according to the evidence . . ."

If John Chambers could further arrange that the twelve men should hear
sworn evidence as to the real libellers, they could well and truly judge those
writers the actual offenders. Process against the authors could begin, and
the jury could deliver Zenger "not guilty."

This was the juncture at which James Alexander sent for Mr. Hamilton—

not for fear Chambers would defend Zenger ineptly, too weakly, would fail to get him off; but rather for fear he would defend him too ably, too strongly, with entire success produce his freedom by showing up Alexander himself and all the leaders of the opposition, expose them as seditious, discredit them in England, destroy them in New York. Then Alexander's reforms in government would never come about; then the trade and commerce of this amphibious city New York, this city of docks and brigs, would succumb entirely to the personal dominion of the Whig Governor and his favored few, his licensees, grantees, monopolists; while at Whitehall the Whiggish spirit of sacrificing colonial interest to the fortunes of English corn and the corruptions of Newcastle's *b'hoys* would proceed still further in throttling the ship-rovers of this restless port.

The Philadelphia Lawyer had plenty to turn over in his mind, on his way northward. His carriage creaked and lurched through Jersey meadows, midsummer heat baked the land and the rutted road, mists and marsh haze steamed up from dank bogs, clouds of dust and formidable Jersey insects sifted through the windows. Mr. Hamilton was ill. Others remarked his "great indisposition of body." August punished even a well man; joints swollen with summer agues could tell every turn of the wheel, sharp in the bones like the turn of a screw. New York was a far journey, and his situation was as odd as ever a Scotsman might conceive. Ostensibly he would be pleading for Zenger, but his real client would be Alexander, his cause the secrecy of those authors' names, those names which the government sought. And which presumably Chambers sought, too. The dangers he confronted from Mr. Attorney Bradley and the partisan bench were no greater than the dangers he confronted from his Whig co-counsel for defense.

Oddest of all in his situation was the unlikely fact that a lawyer from Philadelphia's tiny, new, amateurish bar should be sent for, to try a case in New York. Philadelphia was the larger city, to be sure, and busier; yet the circumstance was entirely incongruous. Law practice in New York was so far ahead of Philadelphia's; law there was an old and respected profession, a lucrative calling. New York lawyers made a goodly company, three dozen men and more, learned, skilled, well-equipped. One dozen at least were barristers of the Inns. Some of the leading men took clerks and apprentices in their offices, teaching lawyers of the future. Mr. Hamilton's friend Alexander was one of several who maintained two homes, practiced law in New Jersey and New York equally. He kept his large library of law books in Perth Amboy, from that town sold and loaned books to lawyers in far places. Through Alexander, Mr. Hamilton had often had news of the New York bar's remarkable progress in late years. He had even met one or two others of the East Jersey group. But except for James Alexander, they would not know him, these New York professionals, so concentrated on their own affairs. He would not be the formidable "Mr. Speaker" here. To be Speaker in Pennsylvania meant nothing to New Yorkers.* He would go among them as a stranger, from courts of a Province whose records were not available here and would have been of no interest if they had been. Mr. Hamilton had complained of Pennsylvania court records, how poorly they were kept. New York records were much fuller. The two governors for ten years before Colonel Cosby, William Burnet, M.A. and John Montgomerie, had been excellent lawyers themselves as well as excellent men, had encouraged the learning and scholarship of the bar, striven for improvement of courts and tried hard to install uniformity of practice throughout the several counties of the province. Their personal libraries had been large, and open to all. In New York, Mr. Hamilton well knew, were now the finest law libraries in America. He knew, because he himself had borrowed books from James Alexander. So had John Kinsey of Philadelphia. Alexander's Perth Amboy office was the only place on this side of the Atlantic where some reports and texts could be had. Indeed, Alexander's remarkable library, and John Chambers' and James DeLancey's and William Smith's and Lewis Morris' up at Morrisania in the Bronx—by will it had to stay at Morrisania—and Joseph Murray's and other barristers' collections had been powerful tools in the hands of this generation of pleaders, as they firmly established English law to be the basis of jurisprudence in New York. Courts in the Old Country had no more esoteric forms of pleading, the bar of Westminster was not more scrupulous or more learned than the imposing professional company Mr. Hamilton was thrusting himself amidst.

What could any barrister from such simple practice as Philadelphia's hope to contribute to this knowledgable bar of learned men? In the thirteen years since practice had been legal in Pennsylvania, Mr. Hamilton had seen great strides forward; but Pennsylvania would never catch up with New York, not in his time. Nor had the law of England been the firm base on which the jurisprudence of the Quaker colonies had risen. From the beginning, differences from England had been as notable as conformities. And Mr. Hamilton had preferred it that way. He was a scholar in his own law, of four colonial establishments; he was no youthful enthusiast for English practice. There was more to law than precedent, rule, conformity. An old Lower Counties Council appeals case, fifty years and more ago, had a place in his armory of pleadings: "neither hath it ever been practized in these pts.

---

* So far as I can discover, Mr. Hamilton had never pled in New York or East Jersey before the Zenger case. Paul M. Hamlin (*Legal Education in Colonial New York*, 32, 150) says "he appeared upon a number of occasions in the courts of New York," but the only other occasion I can be sure of, the case of *Palmer* v. *Van Courtlandt*, came the year *after* the Zenger trial.

though in Engld it may, where the Restraint of prisonrs is much more strict . . ." *Not in these parts, though in England it may*—Hamilton had observed it many times. Why should law in England be law for us? Laws were made by men, to serve their particular needs, their own problems. Why should truth be no defense against libel in New York, because courts would not have it so in England? Why should juries be estopped from judging a thing libellous or not, because judges in English courts estopped English juries? In Proprietary Pennsylvania, he could plead such doctrines, could carry courts and Assemblies with him. In royal New York, these learned English barristers, proudly cleaving to their English rules, would never listen.

There was one case, one English rule he might use, a case of Holt's— hard old Chief Justice Holt, revered by every Whig, and certainly leading authority on seditious libel. That would be a neat point, to cite Holt himself against Whigs like DeLancey and Bradley; even Cosby might have heard of him. Holt had once held that a man who wrote things had the burden of proving them true. It came near saying truth could be a defense. The very words were powerful in their rhythms, they turned over and over like the coach wheels: *"He who will take upon him to write things, it lies upon him to prove them at his peril . . ."*

It was not much. Holt had been high and hard on seditious libel. Even a general statement that the government was corrupt, he had punished. And these very words, these powerful rolling words, he had used in finding a libeller guilty, not innocent. The court would never miss that. Still, an ingenious mind could twist them backside-to: *if at his peril, a man succeeds in proving what he writes to be true* . . .

He would have only two chances in defense. The first, to persuade the court the things printed were no libels because they were true, was a slim chance, a forlorn hope. DeLancey would be too steeped in common law doctrine, common law doctrine too steeped in its axioms, its rules. At law, they were lost. But Zenger's case was more than a cause at law. It was a political cause. This jury like the grand juries would be men of New York who knew the truth, Alexander's men, men of passion, belief, men to feel outrage. There was the second chance, the political chance: persuade the jury to say "not guilty," because the libels were true. Not guilty—of printing *false* libels. Not guilty, in spite of the law, the facts, the instructions, because you are free men, your own masters, who will say truth must have its hearing . . .

And Mr. Hamilton considered Bushel's case. He was bound to: William Penn had been his study, that life, those Charters, the civil freedoms he had given, the uncivil abuses he had suffered. Bushel's case was something he could take from Pennsylvania to New York, something that made his going appropriate, the spirit of Penn himself, the spirit of his laws. It might even make his going significant. In such brief preparation time, it was his best thought, the thought most natural to him. He would stand before them for what he was, plead what for twenty years he had pled—his celebration of The Founder, and his works. *Bushel's case:* it would be inspiration, as always it had been.

Sixty-five years ago, the year 1670, William Penn was not yet fat but athletic, youthful, and strong, in his twenty-sixth year, tall, his dark eyes burning. He was on trial, before the Lord Mayor and Recorder of London, charged with a grave offense, a matter of state. Firmly, young Penn insisted on his rights. The Recorder grew angry, his voice rose, soon he was railing at Penn; he called him "a sawcy fellow," said he was troublesome. Penn answered in manly spirit; the Recorder shouted at him. So did the Lord Mayor. "Take him to the bail dock!" the Lord Mayor cried. Bailiffs seized Penn rudely, clapt him in the cylinder of tall bars in the corner. The trial went on. Wrathfully, the Recorder charged the jury, ordered them to find the culprit guilty. Penn clambered up the bars of the bail dock, poked his nose out, called in a loud voice, "you of the jury take notice, I have not been heard, neither can you legally depart the court, before I have been fully heard!" "Pull that fellow down!" the Recorder shouted. "Take him away into the hole!" And Penn was dragged off to a dungeon, while the jury, watching, was told to ballot.

The astonishing scene, judges bellowing from the bench, attorneys hollering, the defendant manhandled, had been too much for Edward Bushel, foreman, and the jury. In defiance of the court, they found "not guilty." Surprised, the Recorder and Lord Mayor turned their wrath on the twelve men, began to rail at Bushel, vilified him and his fellows. Bushel stood silent. The Lord Mayor ordered the jury locked up, "without meat, drink, fire and tobacco," in a room below stairs. "We will have a verdict by the help of God," the Recorder shouted, "or you shall starve for it." Penn, back in court, objected. "Stop his mouth," cried the Lord Mayor. "Bring fetters, and stake him to the ground!"

The jury was held two nights in durance, with no comforts. Bushel inspirited them, kept them firm, they persisted in their verdict, the Recorder roared and threatened, stolidly they returned their same answer. The Lord Mayor in exasperation laid a fine on the twelve men, forty marks apiece. They refused to pay; he sent them off to Newgate Prison. For months, the "phenatique jurymen" remained in jail; Bushel for his courage endured indignities the law had never visited even upon Penn himself. At last attorneys took up his case. It was "a business of great consequence to His Majesty's Government," they said. After many hearings, numerous arguments, Bushel stood before Lord Chief Justice Vaughan of Common Pleas, on a writ of *habeas corpus*. Sir John Vaughan was brand new on the high court; in his time he had been a paltering trimmer and false friend. But in the Great Civil Wars he had known the insides of jails himself, and his studies of the law, it was reported, had "disposed him to the least reverence to the crown, and most to popular authority . . ." Mr. Hamilton cherished Vaughan's sunburst decision in Bushel's case: *a jury may not be punished for its verdict.* And he knew Vaughan's language in opinion, printed long ago in curious pamphlets, coming fresh as yesterday down the decades of years:

> the verdict of a jury and the evidence of a witness, are very different things in the truth and falsehood of them. A witness swears but to what he hath heard or seen, generally or more largely to what hath fallen under his senses: but a juryman swears to what he can infer and conclude from the testimony of such witnesses, by the act and force of his understanding, to the fact inquired after; which differs nothing in the reason, though much in the punishment, from what a judge out of various cases considered by him infers to be law in the question before him. . . . A man cannot see by another's eyes, nor hear by another's ear; no more can a man conclude or infer the thing to be resolved by another's understanding or reasoning . . .

Those words might have been written for Zenger's case, for this jury: *see with your own eyes, hear with your own ears, infer with your own understanding . . .*

The ferry rolled with the winds on Upper Bay, the long hard trip was over. Mr. Hamilton made his way to the Black Horse tavern; Alexander would meet him there. He could rest in seclusion over Sunday, they would have time for conference, a last day of preparation, perhaps even time for a good Scottish visit over good Scottish fare, if his strength held out.

James Alexander bore a famous Scottish name, the name of his grandfather's father, that Alexander of James Sixth and First's court, Viscount Canada, Earl of Stirling, long "Secretar" of Scotland, the gloomy genius who was "born for a poet and aimed to be king." His descendant was far from gloomy, this large hearty man, much out-of-doors. The artist who painted his portrait recorded his pleasant half-smile in alert repose, the look of a scholar to whom all of life is engaging. He was forty-four. Mr. Hamilton appears to have known him from childhood; when he sent him letters he commenced them *"Dear Jim"*—this, in an age that never used first names in correspondence, when even husband and wife addressed each other in stiff formal language.

As a boy in Scotland he enrolled to study law, but something diverted his course. He trained for the army instead, a commission was procured for him, he was lieutenant of engineers twenty-four years old when the rising of 1715 occurred. In behalf of the Stewart Pretender, Lieutenant James

Alexander became a rebel. "The Fifteen," ill-starred adventure ever after held in wistful memory, the tragic lost cause, scattered defeated Scottish Jacobites to the remotest corners of the German King's British Empire which was never to be theirs. James Alexander went to Perth Amboy—not in furtive case as a rebel should, but through the friendly intervention of the Whig general (the Duke of Argyll) he went as a royal officeholder, Surveyor General of New Jersey. Whigs could forgive treason and rebellion in young men of parts. Promptly Alexander became one of the two-colony men of New York Bay, officeholder in New York as well as Jersey, salaried in both governments, Surveyor General of both, Commissioner to run the boundary line of both; in 1718 he was named to a minor judicial post, Recorder of Perth Amboy, in 1719 he was Deputy Secretary of New York, in 1721 Governor Burnet appointed him to the highest office a governor could give, member of the Council of New York.

By 1721 this erstwhile rebel and Jacobite rouser was practicing law in New York, already busy on his extraordinary improvements in the bar of that city, already a man of great wealth and high place. He had taken the same road to riches Mr. Hamilton had trod, surely the best road for a Scotsman in rustication: he had married a rich widow. David Provoost, "Ready Money" Provoost, had amassed a fortune by sending his ships to ports where laws forbade them to go, bringing in cargoes laws forbide them to carry. The smuggling trade was no rarity in New York, but making such a good thing of it was. When Provoost died, his widow sold his ships, his shares, his slaves on Jamaica Plain; she collected the moneys he had out on loan; she withdrew entirely from adventures on the sea and went into business for herself, as a strikingly successful provision merchant on the New York docks. Laws worked hard on the *femme sôle* trader then; doubtless it was a genuine advantage to the widow Provoost to secure the lawful protection of a spouse. Certainly it was no disadvantage to Councillor James Alexander to be vested as husband in lawful control of Mevrouw Provoost's lucrative mercantile establishment, and all the wealth behind it. The Provoost interest made him a factor in the strong political group of merchant shippers descended from the old Anti-Leislerian faction. His wife went on operating her business, he went on practicing law, to all seeming the marriage was a complete success. Their children came in the 1720's.

And in the 1720's, James Alexander became a very important person indeed. He was a new sort to appear in the Council of New York. Councillors had been Leislerian or Anti-Leislerian; governor succeeding to governor had patronized each faction alternately. And Councillors had been men of significant place in the colony—fur traders, patroons of vast estate, owners of fleets of ships in the city. Alexander, like Mr. Hamilton in Philadelphia, was an outsider. He had no other place than such place as he made for himself.

He made it with the tools of the law. In 1723, he took his first law clerk in New York City, the first of a good number who would learn the common law of England under his tutelage. He was among the first who organized the bar of the City; with Governor Burnet's encouragement and Scottish John Montgomerie's he deepened its scholarship, set it higher standards. He helped revise and publish the laws; his work in New York had parallels with Mr. Hamilton's work in Pennsylvania.

And during the same years, he did much the same thing in New Jersey. Perth Amboy remained his principal residence (and would, till a year after the Zenger trial), he kept most of his famous library there, in 1721 he listed 130 titles in the law, ten years later his legal holdings had many times increased, and he bought 150 additional volumes of acts, reports, and institutes at the sale of Governor Montgomerie's effects, the largest book sale New York had ever seen. His holdings of law books in both his homes added up to so many he himself did not know them all. On his list of who borrowed what, he would find himself writing titles he had never inventoried.

Governor Burnet's concern to develop law courts and law practice extended to his other province, New Jersey, and James Alexander was ready to his hand. Though he had served as Recorder, he had never been admitted to practice as a lawyer in Jersey courts. Burnet had a brisk way with such matters. On one single day in 1723, Alexander (now eight years after The Fifteen) found himself abruptly admitted to the New Jersey bar, appointed a member of the Jersey Provincial Council, and named Attorney General of the Province. The next year (without even appearing in London) he joined Gray's Inn and was admitted *per favor* a barrister, ten years after Mr. Hamilton's call at the same Inn.

And as Mr. Hamilton had invigorated law and courts in his Proprietary provinces, so James Alexander brought a new spirit and jurisprudence to the royal colony of New Jersey, in his four years as Attorney General. Suits had been twenty to thirty months delayed in being heard when he took office. Practice was primitive, slovenly in form; special pleadings never heard of elsewhere were allowed, special verdicts delivered; such lawyers as practiced seemed skilled only in demurrers, rehearings, and postponements. Court fees, a principal source of revenue for the Governor and his appointees, were irregular, capriciously fixed, often monstrous. Alexander made administrative reforms, and he wrote legislation for the Council: *An Ordinance for regulating the times of sitting of the Courts . . . for regulating and establishing fees to be hereafter taken by the Officers of the Court of Chancery . . . for regulating Courts of Judicature in the Province.* As in Mr. Hamilton's Pennsylvania, so in Alexander's New Jersey, session laws began to be printed more completely, with proper formal titles (once even by a New Jersey printer, instead of Bradford in New York). And Alexander put a stop entirely to the quaint old practice of the crown's attorney taking a fee from defendants, if in spite of his prosecution they were acquitted.

His four years as Attorney General in Jersey did not interrupt his law practice in New York courts, nor his place in the New York government and his lively part in the factious politics of the larger province. Perth Amboy and Manhattan: James Alexander spent many of the days of his life sailing Upper and Lower Bay in his twenty years' tale of two cities. When Cosby arrived in August, 1732, he found the erstwhile Jacobite rebel a member of his Council of New York, of his Council of New Jersey too, and the most significant attorney in both colonies. Enmity between the two men was immediate. For his first pleading in Van Dam's case, Cosby dismissed him from the New York Council. This was before 1732 had passed. Subsequently in letters to Lord Newcastle he described Alexander as his most troublesome opponent in both provinces. Now in 1735, he had dismissed him from New Jersey's Council as well. Alexander had no public place left, and DeLancey had dismissed him from the bar.

This was the situation Mr. Hamilton found his friend in, the first weekend of August. If there truly was a special Fortune who looked after Scotsmen, they had both better invoke Her now. Zenger's trial would have to be James Alexander's vindication.

Early Monday morning, August 4, Alexander called for his guest. Mr. Hamilton walked shakily from the Black Horse to City Hall, at the corner of Nassau Street and The Wall. The little courtroom was already warm, the crowd in the chamber immense. He met John Chambers, his co-counsel for defense; he met Zenger himself, pale and wasted from ten months in prison. He greeted Richard Bradley, the venerable Attorney General. This day two old men of laws, one English, one Scottish, would contend with each other for the political future of New York, a future which neither of them, full of years, would live to see.

Everyone stood up as the court made its entrance—young DeLancey in his red robes of state and curled woollen wig, Frederick Philipse, second justice, beside him. The case was called; the panel of talesmen appeared for jury selection. John Chambers had done his work well: these forty-eight free-holders were not Governor's men; they were artisans and tradesmen of the city, Dutch and a few English, people who knew James Alexander and Zenger too, and knew the truth about Cosby. Like the gentlemen of the grand jury who had three times refused to indict, they were drawn from the crowded wards and docksides where Alexander had his greatest strength. When the Sheriff tried to read certain names out of order, Chambers objected. DeLancey upheld him. Twelve men were selected; they were sworn. Mr. Bradley made his opening.

"The defendant Zenger has attacked the Governor, has falsely published false, scandalous, seditious libel . . ." Bradley read his bill of Information. And carefully he explained the law: the jury would weigh the evidence and determine but one single question, did the defendant actually publish the statements, as charged? This was their sole duty, to say if Zenger committed the act of publishing. The judges alone would determine if what he published had been libellous. His witnesses were ready.

John Chambers responded. Zenger was not guilty, he said. And he offered a strong defense, the standard defense available to counsel in libel actions. To prove, not printing but *publication* of a libel, Mr. Attorney would have to prove what the law called the "colloquium," that is, prove such actual circumstances of utterance as would show the statements allegedly made by Zenger were directed against the Governor specifically, and no one else; that even innuendos and special meanings in the statements were arrows aimed at William Cosby. But the pieces complained of nowhere mentioned the Governor by name, Chambers explained. So how would he ever be able to prove it was beyond all doubt the Governor himself who was attacked? (He was quite right; the two numbers of the *Journal* cited in Bradley's Information had not mentioned Cosby. The *Election Songs*, which had, would not be allowed in evidence here today, for they were not mentioned in the Information.) Moreover, publication was not an easy thing to prove. This was Chambers' second defense: mere printing of matter in a paper was not in itself publication of a libel. The printer was no more than the agency through which things written were spread about. Might as well charge the man who set the type, or the apprentice who turned the press screw, as charge the proprietor of the printing house. *Publication* of a libel was an act committed by the defamer himself, the one who in malice repeated tales, or in false heart wrote contemptuous matter. The author was the man guilty of publication of a libel, not the printer. Mr. Attorney would have to prove Zenger was the actual author to prove him the publisher of the libels he printed. The defense would deny it, said Chambers. Let Mr. Attorney examine his witnesses.

The young lawyer finished quickly. He had placed the difficult burden of proof (of colloquium) on the crown, and shown exactly what Mr. Attorney would have to get from his witnesses to prove publication. Most important of all, he had shown how everything Bradley might get from those witnesses relating to the real authors would undoubtedly exonerate Zenger. Chambers, in short, had placed Bradley in the curious position of losing his case on his own direct examination, for he would uncover the actual colloquium among the real publishers of libel behind the printer—the real authors, in whose hearts the express malice flourished, and to whom Zenger was no more than an instrument.

Chambers knew who those witnesses were to be: Zenger's journeymen, and his two young sons who worked as apprentices. They were here in the courtroom, to testify to the printing. Whatever Mr. Attorney opened up with them, Chambers could explore: Who were the authors? Who brought manuscripts into the shop? Who said what to whom about the Governor? About what Zenger should print in his next issue?

Had John Chambers been alone as counsel for defense, there is no doubt John Peter Zenger would have been acquitted. It is imaginable DeLancey and Bradley had planned it that way with Chambers, for neither is there any doubt that acquittal bringing with it clear testimony as to the real authors, the opposition leaders, would have been a mighty victory for Cosby and the Whigs.

"Let Mr. Attorney examine his witnesses"—before the first witness could be called, Mr. Hamilton at the defense table rose, to make his first move. Politely, he introduced himself to the court, politely he contradicted Chambers. They would not deny publication, he announced. The papers Zenger had printed were complaints against government, "which I think is the right of every free-born Subject to make when the matters so published can be supported with truth." Complaints were no crime. They would confess publication. Mr. Attorney could dismiss his witnesses.

Everyone was startled, none more so than Mr. Bradley. He had prepared specifically to prove publication, to present such evidence to the jury as would exhibit the colloquium and the malice, destroy the standard defense on the terms Chambers had indicated, oblige the jury to pronounce Zenger guilty. And certainly he was prepared for Chambers's disclosure of the names of the writers. Now he was nonplussed. There was no other evidence to present. What was left for him to do? Particularly, what way was left open for him to enquire of those other names? The venerable Bradley stood silent, at a loss. He stood so long the court finally had to prompt him.

"Well, Mr. Attorney," the Chief Justice said, "will you proceed?"

"Indeed, Sir," Bradley answered, "as Mr. Hamilton has confessed the printing and publishing of these libels, I think the jury must find a verdict for the King; for supposing they were true, the law says that they are not the less libellous for that; nay indeed, the law says their being true is an aggravation of the crime."

"Not so neither, Mr. Attorney, there are two words to that bargain," Hamilton responded. "I hope it is not our bare printing and publishing a paper that will make it a libel. You will have something more to do, before you make my client a libeller. For the words themselves must be libellous, that is, *false, scandalous, and seditious,* or else we are not guilty."

And Bradley found himself looking into a trap. By confessing publication, Hamilton had abruptly altered the rôle of the jury in this trial, and the rôle of Mr. Attorney, too. No jury would say a man "guilty" of doing an act he freely confessed doing, unless that act were plainly a crime. With no evidence to present, Bradley could get his "guilty" verdict only by persuading the jury that Zenger, who confessed publication, had thereby confessed also the false heart, the malice which made the things published a libel, and seditious. Would a man freely, readily, openly confess evil, malice, and falsity of heart? The jury would never believe it. Mr. Bradley could scarcely hope to persuade them to say "guilty" unless he could prove the utter falsity of the facts printed and published. Yet he dared not go to a proof that Zenger's charges were false, for that would permit Hamilton to bring witnesses to prove they were true. And truth was the pitfall Bradley must avoid.

The trap, of course, was fashioned of bad law. Confessing publication left the jury no determination to make, no moot question. And it destroyed Chambers' standard defense. But it was fully as dangerous a trap as if it had been good law, for it left the court waiting on the jury. The judges could rule a publication libellous and seditious only after the jury had given a guilty-of-publishing verdict. Confession of innocent publication would never induce them to do so. And most distressing of all to Mr. Attorney, Hamilton by his sudden stroke of eliminating testimony of witnesses had eliminated everyone but Zenger from the case. However Bradley had planned to expose the men behind the printer, he was now forestalled. He must claim Zenger's alone was the malice, the false heart, the evil motive.

Still, a verdict against Zenger alone without revealing the real authors would have some uses. He could prove the printer's papers malicious, scandalous, seditious; this would be libel. And it might smoke out his backers somehow. Richard Bradley had been fifty years at the bar. He had one other preparation ready, his summation for the jury. With quick changes, it would serve. He must get his verdict. He gathered his notes, drew himself up; he made an impressive figure, virtuous, substantial, a pillar of stability and order.

He read his address, read it with the authority of age and vast learning. Government was a thing sacred, instituted of God, a thing to be reverenced, held in honor. Government protected life, religion, property, protected the citizen in his person and estate. By law, by decency, by divine command, governors must be treated with respect, must be free from censure of private men. To defame a governor, to scandalize him, put him to scorn, undermined regard for the law, respect for government iself. He read from old cases, quoted the great justices of England—Coke, Fitzherbert, Brooke, all the riches of British jurisprudence. Any malicious defamation was libel, his cases held, anything said in malice, true or false, be the person injured of good fame, or bad. Zenger had maliciously asserted the Governor was a tyrant, charged him with reducing people to slavery, removing judges, erecting new courts. Zenger had defamed, scandalized, scorned. Everything he had printed was libellous, for it aimed against the Governor; it was seditious, for it spread discontent and mistrust of government; it was malicious, for that mistrust was his design. Every bit of it disturbed His Majesty's peace. It was libel in the meaning of the law. Therefore he was guilty of the act of publishing, as he confessed, and the things published made the act a crime.

Nor was the crime of publishing libel a small thing: it was against the state. To the bar of this court the Governor himself and the Council had directed the prisoner be summoned. The very guardians of the state who were libelled were now directing this prosecution, to preserve the state. It was also a crime against the laws of God. Solemnly, Mr. Bradley repeated the words of St. Paul, Acts xxiii, 5: *"Thou shalt not speak evil of the ruler of the people."*

With that, he finished. The old gentleman had served his office well. Even in the shortened version of his speech, printed by his opponents with no help from him, it is clear he made a telling effect. He had been reasonable, and fair. He had not been vindictive. People could believe him. Cosby was low, venal, corrupt; but Cosby was the Governor, the King's representative; Cosby was the symbol of order and the law.

John Chambers found little to say in answer. Just as much as Bradley, he had been caught unawares. With no witnesses to cross-examine, no plotters or conspirators to expose, no others whose malice could be shown to be greater, whose hearts more false and intentions more grave—the real rebels—he was helpless. Truth was no defense in libel. The only defense was denying publication, and denying malice, shifting the onus of the acts onto others. Mr. Hamilton by his move had deprived them of this chance. Chambers could not impair what Mr. Attorney had achieved.

Bright August sunlight streamed through the windows; the stifling air was still. So many people had crowded in this day, so many who had never seen a courtroom before, people of all conditions, trades, and stations, people who knew no law, but knew Cosby and his works . . . Mr. Hamilton's rôle was also different. He had reduced the case from disclosure of the whole political faction to defense of Zenger only. He had but one client, now. The danger of exposing others receded into the background. But his client had confessed the act of publishing. This alone might impress the jury; they might in effect say, we find you have done what you confess, and must say so, leaving the quality of your innocence to the court. Who could tell what a jury would do?

"May it please your Honours," Mr. Hamilton began, "I agree with Mr. Attorney that Government is a sacred thing . . ."

He did not read, as Bradley had. He spoke in easy conversational tones, his words firm and sure; he took his start from Bradley's speech: ". . . but

I differ widely from him when he would insinuate that the just complaints of a number of men who suffer under a bad Administration is libelling that Administration. . . ." Such was not the law. And from Bradley's words he took a startling offensive: if the Governor and Council were indeed directing this prosecution, he said, if all this great crowd of people had come here apprehensive to see, surely administration had some deeper design, the people a good deal more at stake, than appeared.

Mr. Attorney had produced cases—Star Chamber cases, from "that terrible court where those dreadful judgments were given"—to exhibit the law that protected the sovereign in his good name and respect, in his sacred person. But the Governor of New York was no sovereign. He was but subject, like everyone else in New York. "Is it not surprising to see a Subject, upon his receiving a commission from the King to be a Governor of a Colony in America, immediately imagining himself to be vested with all the prerogatives belonging to the sacred person of his Prince? And yet in all the cases which Mr. Attorney has cited to show the duty and obedience we owe to the Supreme Magistrate, it is the King that is there meant and understood, though Mr. Attorney is pleased to urge them to prove the heinousness of Mr. Zenger's offense against the Governor of New York."

He must make it clear to the jury, the Governor was no part of royalty. They would commit no treason, no offense against the crown, if they found for Zenger. The law threw no shield around the person of a Governor. He talked of the law of treason, showed how it changed from age to age, how treason lay against the crown and king, not against the administration of government, how law could differ in New York from law in England, indeed had often been different (*"not in these pts. though in Engld it may . . ."*).

"What strange doctrine is it, to press everything for law, which is so in England?"

Mr. Bradley interrupted. All this was not to the point, he said. The point was that Zenger had libelled the Governor. "Mr. Hamilton has confessed the printing and publishing and I think nothing is plainer than that the words in the Information are scandalous and tend to sedition and to disquiet the minds of the people of this Province."

You do not say *false,* Mr. Hamilton observed. You say scandalous, seditious, and tend to disquiet the people. But you omit the word false. Do you not charge they are also false?

"I think I did not omit the word false," Mr. Attorney answered. "But it has been said already, that it may be libel notwithstanding it may be true."

"In this," said Mr. Hamilton, "I must still differ with Mr. Attorney." And he explained to the jury: "we are charged with printing and publishing a certain false, malicious, seditious and scandalous libel. This word 'false' must have some meaning, or else how came it there? I hope Mr. Attorney will not say he put it there by chance, and I am of the opinion his Information would not be good without it. No, the falsehood makes the scandal and both make the libel."

The jury would see the point: Mr. Attorney would never charge Zenger with publishing "certain *true* libels." It was he who had claimed them false, in his Information. The jury might not know law, but they would know the true and false of Cosby. And they would know Bradley could never admit truth, never say to them, "the Governor truly has done these evil things, yet Zenger is guilty of libel for saying so." Mr. Hamilton had laid the groundwork; now he was ready for his second move:

"And to show the Court that I am in good earnest, and to save the Court's time and Mr. Attorney's trouble, I will agree, that if he can prove the facts charged upon us to be *false,* I'll own them to be *scandalous, seditious,* and *a libel.*" He added smoothly, "So the work seems now to be pretty much shortened, and Mr. Attorney has only to prove the words *false,* in order to make us guilty."

Bradley recognized the trick, saw how the jury would think this bold indeed, far bolder than it actually was. He was suddenly angry with the urbane Scotsman from Philadelphia, this stranger who blandly pled against settled law and precedent, who presented novelties to the jury, dangerous innovations, as if they were ruling doctrine—truth is the test of motives; falsehood makes the scandal, the libel. His anger surprised him into giving the obvious answer. "We have nothing to prove," he snapped. "You have confessed to the printing and publishing; but if it was necessary, and I insist it is not, how can we prove a negative?"

He had said it like an actor, on cue. Mr. Hamilton was ready. "I did expect to hear that a negative cannot be proved," he said. "But we will save Mr. Attorney the trouble of proving a negative and take upon ourselves to prove those very papers that are called libels to be true."

Chief Justice DeLancey saw old Bradley was in trouble. And for the oddest of reasons: this insistent stranger from another government, unused to New York's learned law and skilled pleadings in the English forms, was refusing to accept the boundaries within which this action must proceed. Whether he was ignorant of the common law and the cases, or knew them full well and was desperate for his cause, he was trying to turn the trial into a public forum, to debate with Mr. Attorney. He had surprised Bradley with his trick of rhetoric, by his syllogism forced him to open the door to a proof of the truth of the libels. Bradley had opened that door anyway, by his too-frequent use of the word false in his Information. He needed help. A trial at law was no place for Assembly debates. The youthful Chief Justice leaned forward. "You cannot be admitted, Mr. Hamilton, to give the truth of a libel in evidence," he said. "A libel is not to be justified, for it is nevertheless a libel that it is true."

"I am sorry the Court has so soon resolved upon that piece of law," Hamilton answered. "I expected first to have been heard on that point."

"The law is clear that you cannot justify a libel," the Chief Justice said. (If they didn't know it in Pennsylvania, they would in New York.)

Hamilton persisted. It was a critical moment. He had no hope of persuading the court, obviously; but perhaps he could make it seem a major defeat, and make the defeat work for him, make the court appear unjust, arbitrary, unfair, win sympathy from the jury. Already they had seen Bradley angered against him, the Chief Justice instructing him. . . . He made an eloquent effort. He argued to the judges, cited cases to prove falsehood made the scandal, that truth was never libel. Old causes sprang to life as he told of prosecutions and judgments, of kings in danger, subjects vindicated. Sentences from great writers glittered in his talk. He recited ancient and modern instances as readily as if he himself had pled in the courts of Elizabeth, or sat with Bacon in judgment. He appealed to ordinary reason. And he appealed merrily with wit: "Is it not against common sense that a man should be punished in the same degree for a true libel, if any such thing could be, as for a false one? I know it is said that truth makes a libel the more provoking, and therefore the offense is the greater and consequently the judgment should be the heavier. Well, suppose it were so," he twinkled, "and let us agree for once that truth is a greater sin than falsehood. Yet as the offences are not equal, is it not absolutely necessary that the Judges should know whether the libel is true or false, that they may by that means be able to proportion the punishment? For would it not be a sad case if the Judges, for want of information, should chance to give as severe a judgment against a man for writing and publishing a lie, as for writing and publishing a truth?"

It was outrageous of him, of course. To let the jury hear such sporting with the law, such ridiculing of its doctrines, offended all the learning, the ideals, the enthusiasm with which these New York barristers had introduced English pleadings in their practice. His sly twistings of meanings, his irony, would make the jury think the law itself foolish, an unreal realm in which truth was more sinful than a lie. He was placing the court in a position where they must rule against him, hopefully with anger, hopefully in the very terms of unreasonable doctrine he had cheerfully announced.

He picked up a book from his table, read those words of Chief Justice Holt on libel: "Can you make it appear that the words are true? *He who will take upon him to write things, it lies upon him to prove them at his peril.*"

"Now, Sir," he said ingenuously, "we have acknowledged the printing and publishing of those papers, and with the leave of the court, we are ready to prove them to be true, at our peril."

Chief Justice DeLancey was plainly startled. Nothing is more annoying to a skilled professional than to have to endure amateur bungling in his own field, and that annoyance is compounded when the professional discovers the amateur actually possessed of a point. Sir John Holt was formidable Whiggish authority DeLancey could not dismiss; every lawyer knew his severe doctrines of seditious libel. Had Holt really uttered the rule Mr. Hamilton quoted?

"Let us see the book," DeLancey demanded. For a long time he read, the stiff white curls of his wig bowed over the words of the law. The crowd in the courtroom waited. At length DeLancey looked up. He had not missed the significant substance: Holt had found that defendant guilty. His words could not be twisted about. "Mr. Hamilton, the Court is of opinion, according to the words of the book, that you ought not to be permitted to prove the facts . . ." DeLancey seemed almost angry. "Truth cannot justify a libel . . ."

Hamilton started to speak: that was a rule from Star Chamber Court, he said, a rule he hoped had died with that court—

"Mr Hamilton!" DeLancey exclaimed, "the Court have delivered their opinion and we expect you will use us with good manners! You are not to be permitted to argue against the opinion of the Court!"

"With submission," Hamilton replied, "I have seen the practice in very great courts, and have never heard it deemed unmannerly to . . ."

DeLancey would tolerate no more. "After the Court have delivered their opinion, it is not good manners to insist upon a point in which you are overruled!"

Hamilton bowed. "I thank your Honour," he said—the impeccable insult, the delicious whisper of victory. For the spectacle of the Chief Justice angrily rebuking him was more than he could have hoped for. Just so had the Recorder and Lord Mayor cried out wrathfully at Penn, and the jury had heard.

Any trial is a moment in history, unique as an episode in its own terms, a bit of the human record. In any trial lies the possibility of forging a new piece of law, a sudden departure, a new dimension for the record. Hamilton turned from addressing the bench.

"Then, Gentlemen of the Jury," he said, "it is to you that we must now appeal for witnesses to the truth of the facts we have offered and are denied the liberty to prove. And let it not seem strange that I apply myself to you in this manner . . ." The law, he told the twelve men, summoned them out of the neighborhood where an offense was alleged to be committed, because they were supposed to have the best knowledge of the facts to be tried. "And were you to find a verdict against my client, you must take upon you to say the papers referred to in the Information, and which we acknowledge we printed and published, are false, scandalous and seditious.

"But of this I can have no apprehension. You are citizens of New York; you are really what the law supposes you to be, honest and lawful men; and according to my brief, the facts which we offer to prove were not committed in a corner. They are notoriously known to be true; and therefore in your justice lies our safety."

He made the most of DeLancey's ruling against him: "And as we are denied the liberty of giving evidence to prove the truth of what we have published, I will beg leave to lay it down as a standing rule in such cases that the suppressing of evidence ought always to be taken for the strongest evidence, and I hope it will have weight with you."

He turned suddenly to Bradley, asked a question: is something written ironically, a libel? Mr. Attorney answered at once, as a learned New York lawyer would answer. A citation sprang to his mind, not from an old book but a recent one, the 1716 folio of Hawkins' *Pleas of the Crown.* Like a magician plucking forth a rabbit, Bradley gave it chapter and verse: "It is said in I Hawkins, page 193, that such scandal as is expressed in a scoffing and ironical manner makes a writing as properly a libel as that which is expressed in direct terms."

"I agree," said Mr. Hamilton. "The words are scandalous, scoffing and ironical as they are *understood* to be so." The Chief Justice leaned forward once more, as if he could not bear to be left out of the colloquy, could not miss a chance to instruct this innocent from Pennsylvania. "Mr. Hamilton, do you think it so hard to know when words are ironical or spoke in a scoffing manner? All words are libellous or not as they are understood."

"I think your Honour," said Hamilton for the second time, a frail man full of years taking brusque instruction from a young, vigorous tutor. "I am glad to find the Court of this Opinion. Then it follows that those twelve men must understand the words in the Information to be scandalous, that is to say false; and when they understand the words to be so, they will say we are guilty of publishing a false libel, and not otherwise."

"No, Mr. Hamilton," said the Chief Justice, "the jury may find that Zenger printed and published those papers, and leave it to the Court to judge whether they are libellous."

"I know, may it please your Honour, the jury *may* do so," Hamilton answered; "but I likewise know they may do otherwise. I know they have the right, beyond all dispute, to determine both the law and the fact, and where they do not doubt of the law, they ought to do so. This of leaving it to judgment of the Court whether the words are libellous or not in effect renders juries useless, to say no worse, in many cases."

And he turned to the jury directly. "It is true that in times past it was a crime to speak truth, and in that terrible Court of Star Chamber many worthy and brave men suffered for so doing . . ." But this was New York, in 1735, a free government of free men. "When a ruler of a people brings his personal failings, but much more his vices, into his administration, all the high things that are said in favor of rulers, and of dignities, and upon the side of power, will not be able to stop people's mouths when they are oppressed!"

Even in that Court of Star Chamber, in those bad times, "a great and good man durst say, what I hope will not be taken amiss of me to say in this place, to wit *The practice of Informations for libel is a sword in the hands of a wicked king and an arrant coward, to cut down and destroy the innocent.*'"

Old Mr. Bradley leapt up. "Pray, Mr. Hamilton, have a care what you say! Don't go too far neither! I don't like those liberties!"

"Sure, Mr. Attorney, you won't make any applications," Hamilton answered serenely. "All men agree that we are governed by the best of Kings . . . My well known principles, and the sense I have of the blessings we enjoy under his present Majesty, makes it impossible for me to err, and I hope, even to be suspected, in that point of duty to my King." And he turned back to the jury. Had they observed how a man, loyal and dutiful, still could speak strong words of liberty, having no fear?

Governors were but men, he continued. And notwithstanding the duty and reverence claimed by Mr. Attorney for men in authority, they were given power for good, not for evil. They were not exempt from observing the rules of common justice in public or in private. "It is natural, it is a privilege, I will go further—it is a *right,* which all free men claim, that they are entitled to complain when they are hurt; they have a right publicly to remonstrate the abuses of power . . . to put their neighbors on guard against the craft or open violence of men in authority. . . ." The Philadelphia Lawyer seemed not to know what fear was: "and to assert with courage the sense they have of the blessings of liberty, the value they put upon it, and their resolution, at all hazards, to preserve it, as one of the greatest blessings heaven can bestow!"

It was not a plea in law, nor a plea a New York barrister would acknowledge, it was not an appeal to the decisions and precedents of Westminster. Yet neither Bradley nor DeLancey interrupted. They also knew juries; they could see the effect on the jury of Hamilton's heaven-born liberty, his right in nature to complain. An interruption would advantage him, would alienate the jury. When an advocate urged natural rights, the place to cut him down was in rebuttal. "And the only restraint upon this natural right is the law,"

Mr. Hamilton was saying, "and . . . those restraints can only extend to what is false."

Calmly, without heat, he launched into an indictment of Cosby, an indictment of all governors in history who misused their power. Place-holders,, pensioners might support such a governor, he remarked—looking everywhere save at the Chief Justice and Mr. Attorney—but never free men who cared for the liberties of the people, never true subjects who would rather lose body and estate than see freedom destroyed.

When power raged as an evil let loose, complaints of injured free men were innocent, and true. Yet even truth was in danger. He related histories of men who had written truth, only to be seized by the law. "Power may justly be compared to a great river. While kept within its due bounds, it is both beautiful and useful; but when it overflows its banks, it is then too impetuous to be stemmed . . ." When government itself was evil, who should be punished for the truth?

With cases from the long past he wooed the twelve men, showed them juries who had been bold before, had judged both law and fact to protect the right to complain. He tied this day's cause to the cause of freedom everywhere. And he told them of Bushel's case, how Bushel had been foreman of a jury just as Thomas Hart sat foreman here today, how he had done his duty against threats and mistreatments, the angers of the Lord Mayor the storming Recorder, how from that day to this no jury could be punished for its verdict—how Bushel's case separated the jury considering evidence from the judge considering law, how no jury could reach its decision through a judge's understanding, a judge's reasoning. "A proper confidence in a court is commendable," he observed politely, "but as the verdict will be yours, you ought to refer no part of your discretion to other persons." And Vaughan's words from Bushel's case rolled down the years into this crowded courtroom: *"Juries are to see with their own eyes, hear with their own ears, and to make use of their own consciences and understandings, in judging of the lives, liberties, or estates of their fellow-subjects."*

The sun had worn round to the west, much of the room was in shadow. Hamilton had been on his feet two hours, talking, disputing, exhorting. Suddenly he relaxed. He told a story. Once before, an Information had charged an American with libelling a governor, he chuckled. Right here in New York it was, back in Governor Nicholson's time. (Hamilton had known Francis Nicholson, had attended him in person when he was governor of Virginia. Years before that, he had been Governor of New York, and here in this city he was still a legend, his great hot angers, high spirits, his firmness and vigor, his skill as an army man, a soldier. Cosby was an army man . . .) Governor Nicholson had stood one day on the Bridge, in the hot sun, a'tremble with fury, monstrously berating a poor parson for some obstinacy, threatening to cut off his ears, slit his nose, shoot him dead. A crowd watched, the parson endured it patiently in the heat, till he fell of a sunstroke and was borne to a house. He recovered enough to write a note for a doctor. "I think the Governor must be mad," he added at the bottom of his message. Governor Nicholson learned of those words, he burst forth again, preferred an Information of libel against the preacher, averring—slyly Hamilton quoted it, so like the Information against Zenger—averring the words of the parson to the doctor had been "false, scandalous, and wicked, and wrote with intent to move sedition among the people, and bring his excellency into contempt."

Hamilton turned his anecdote to a serious point: most any writing might be libel to a jealous mind. He amused the jury with examples, read words from the Bible to show how a governor like Cosby could call them libel. He was relieving the tension. Suddenly he changed. Who was safe, when a governor could bring Informations against printers? "How must a man speak or write, or what must he hear, read, or sing, or when must he laugh, so as to be secure from being taken up as a libeller?"

He challenged the twelve men. "If you should be of the opinion that there is no falsehood in Mr. Zenger's papers, you will, nay you ought, to say so, because you don't know whether others (I mean the Court) may be of that opinion. It is your right to do so, and there is much depending upon your resolution, as well as upon your integrity." He told them of heroes of Rome, of Hampden and patriots of England, of men who had died for freedom. This day, this jury was part of this history: "let us at least do our duty and like wise men who value freedom use the utmost care to support liberty, the only bulwark against lawless power."

Hamilton's strength was spent. It was time to close. Juries, he knew, must be left with high words, a ringing call. "The question before the Court, and you Gentlemen of the Jury, is not of small or private concern, it is not the cause of a poor printer, nor of New York alone, which you are now trying. No! it may, in its consequence, affect every freeman that lives under a British government on the main of America. It is the best cause: it is the cause of liberty!"

And slowly he formed his sentence: "Every man who prefers freedom to a life of slavery will bless and honor you, as men who have baffled the attempt of tyranny, and by an impartial and uncorrupt verdict, have laid a noble foundation for securing to ourselves, our posterity, and our neighbours that to which nature and the laws of our country have given us a right: the liberty—both of exposing and opposing arbitrary power, in these parts of the world at least, by speaking and writing truth."

The thrill of his speech hung in the courtroom, even through Mr. Bradley's summation, even through DeLancey's terse charge from the bench. You will declare only on the fact of the printing, DeLancey directed them. The Court will rule on the libel. The jury filed out of the room.

In a moment they were back. "Not Guilty," the foreman Thomas Hart pronounced. The courtroom burst into cheers. And the whole city, and all in the province who had hated Cosby's Whiggish works.

Mr. Hamilton's performance had exhausted him. His "weakness and infirmities" were genuine now, after his utmost exertions. He rested in seclusion all the remainder of the week. Next Monday, Zenger's *Journal* printed its report of the trial, and his speech. Then followed days of James Alexander's victory celebrations: city dinners honoring The Philadelphia Lawyer, happy public meetings of all the opposition faction, speeches of thanks, toasts, and resolutions. The aldermen—anti-Cosby to a man—convened City Council in a reception for the visitor, resolves were passed, Mayor Paul Richards presented a parchment scroll conferring upon Mr. Hamilton the quaint archaic grant of the Freedom of the City: "These are therefore to certify and declare that the said Andrew Hamilton, Esquire, is hereby admitted, received, and allowed a free man and citizen of the said city: to have, hold, enjoy and partake of all the benefits, liberties, privileges, freedoms and immunities . . ." A local silversmith executed a handsome Freedom Box, City Council's official gift. It was skillfully made, chased (though City Council had no right to use it) with the seal of the Province of New York, surmounted by the crown of England, and engraved with mottoes in Latin: *"Submerged laws, affrighted Liberty, will yet be rescued in time . . ."*

Finally, as his ferry stood out from Leisler's half-moon at the Battery to make its way down Upper Bay, Andrew Hamilton heard the guns boom a massive farewell salute.

Governor Cosby must have heard the guns, too, from his mansion in The Fort—this extraordinary salute to a private person as if he were royalty itself. But Colonel William Cosby was closeted in his chamber, gravely ill. In a few weeks the whole city would learn he was beyond help. He lasted over winter; on March 10, he died. As soon as he was gone, Zenger published a volume of forty-two pages, *A Brief Narrative of the Case and Tryal of John Peter Zenger, Printer of the New York Weekly Journal* (New York, 1736). A London reprint appeared; it went through four printings in three months, though there is no record how large the editions were. Two years later in 1738 a Boston printer republished it. That was all, in Mr. Hamilton's lifetime. The Zenger case was over, his friend Alexander rescued; the issues of the trial died with Governor Cosby.

But in 1755, twenty years afterwards, Zenger's *Narrative* appeared in Pennsylvania, from Dunlap's new print shop in Lancaster. And in 1770 (thirty-five years afterwards) in the midst of more troubles in New York, when newspapers were charging "infamous bribery and corruption" in elections, "the most brutal debauchery and riot," the printer John Holt, now himself proprietor of the *New York Journal,* brought out a new edition. Through these late issues of the defendant's own account of his trial, Hamilton's pleading became famous, became a challenge and an issue to Englishmen everywhere. Courts in Britain for half a century stoutly resisted the doctrine that juries might judge of law as well as of fact. Zenger's report of his case was reprinted in Howell's *State Trials,* but the learned editor noted laconically the result was "not allowed in England to be law." A century later Sir James Stephen would say of Hamilton's pleading, it was "singularly able, bold and powerful, though full of doubtful, not to say bad law."

That accusation Hamilton would have acknowledged, readily enough. It was not for learning in the law that he had been called to New York. But Sir James Stephen might in justice have added, that however poor Hamilton's legal knowledge, history had proved to be on the side of his result. Fifty years after the trial, Lord Chief Justice Camden would rule in the Court of Common Pleas that juries could decide for themselves whether a publication had been libellous, rather than leave it up to the court. It was a culmination of a long struggle Camden had waged to curb the power of prosecutions for seditious libel. Five years more, and his doctrines reproducing Hamilton's plea in Zenger's trial were written into law by Charles James Fox, the famous Libel Act of 1792. Thus before the Georgian century was over, the practice of prosecutions on Information charging seditious libel was ended in British justice as a device by which government could restrain the citizen's right to complain.

In New York, victory for Hamilton's doctrine came more slowly. Another, a more famous Hamilton, Alexander Hamilton, pled the Zenger trial as a precedent proving juries could judge law as well as fact, in Coswell's libel suit, 1802. In 1805, the state legislature passed the New Libel Act, which adopted the doctrine.

John Peter Zenger, meanwhile, went from his vindication to the preferment any printer hoped for: with James Alexander's patronage, he secured appointment in place of Bradford as Public Printer to New York, which gave him a lucrative licensed monopoly of the public printing business, so long as he refrained from offending authority. He refrained.

And Mr. Hamilton made his long journey back home to Philadelphia. His State House was finished, after a fashion, on time. His Assembly came together in their new quarters in September, though the walls were not plastered and windows were innocent of glass. He kept his place as Speaker, and his place as Recorder, and judge, and all his other offices; he still gave himself to his "best cause, the cause of liberty." At least once more he travelled again to New York to plead a case. But his years were running out. A day came—another August day, actually the fourth anniversary of Zenger's trial in New York—when he stood before his Assembly in the State House he had built to announce his resignation from public life. It is the only other speech we have from him; we have it *verbatim,* a clerk's transcription. The rhythms and cadences of the trial speech are there: the serene confidence, the conversational manner, the unmistakable touch of greatness.

He said his farewells to the people, those who loved him, those who hated him, as simply as he always said things that mattered. He mentioned "the frequent Indispositions of Body I have so long labored under, "alluded to "my Age and Infirmities which daily increase." He spoke of his years in public life, observed it was up to others not himself to say if he had done well or ill. But, he added firmly, "I know my own Intentions, and that I have ever had at Heart the Preservation of Liberty, the Love of which, as it first drew me too, so it constantly prevailed upon me to reside in this Province . . ."

Once more he paid his tribute to the genius of William Penn. The great progress Pennsylvania had made, he said, "a Progress which much more antient Settlements on the Main of America cannot at present boast of," came not from the fertility of her soil, the commodiousness of her rivers, nor the increase of her people from nearly every country of Europe. "No, it is principally and almost wholly owing to the Excellency of our Constitution, under which we enjoy a greater Share both of civil and religious Liberty than any of our Neighbours. . . . This is our Constitution; and this Constitution was framed by the Wisdom of Mr. *Penn* . . . whose Charter of Privileges to the Inhabitants of Pennsylvania, will ever remain a Monument to his Benevolence to Mankind . . ."

They were the last public words he spoke. Retired to private life, Mr. Hamilton finally did what any Scotsman should do who has founded a family: he built a Great House, a seat, where his son and his daughters and all his Hamilton and Allen grandchildren could have the center of their interests and their fortunes, and their solid inheritance. On that 153 acres on the edge of the city the Penns had given him, he erected a fine mansion. "Bush Hill," he called it—a second imposing building of his own design that would play a significant part in Philadelphia's history.

But not in his own. Mr. Hamilton had barely moved in when he came to the end of his course. The day of his death, by improbable coincidence, was the sixth anniversary of the Zenger trial: August 4, 1741. He was buried, as he wished, under the new saplings he had planted in his garden park at Bush Hill. But the great mansion proved inconvenient for the next generation—too far out of town, too costly to care for. By and by the family—more conventional than he and far more anxious to court public favor, removed his body to (of all places) Christ Church yard. Mr. Hamilton would have regretted that.

He would have regretted much that happened in the years after. His son became Governor, his son-in-law Chief Justice; but on their heels came a new rising of peoples. Citizens in angers thronged to his State House, ousted his grandchildren, seized their estates, drove them into exile. Men in the name of his "best cause, the cause of liberty" met in the Assembly Chamber he had designed, abandoned Penn's Charter he had championed, adopted their Declaration of Independence with no provision for ordered government under law, and no care for preserving those freedoms that had made Pennsylvania, for him, the first and finest of all governments on the American main. Andrew Hamilton had been a Scot, in Jacobite years. He had seen revolutions; he had seen liberty set minds free to wander, discover, explore new dimensions in freedom itself. Perhaps he had glimpsed in history the expansive restlessness that made doctrines of the fathers the chains of their sons.

The events which transformed his State House into Independence Hall belonged to a new age. When the Grand Federal Convention met there in 1787 to draft a new constitution for the rising American Empire, only one man of the new age could remember Mr. Speaker, and his years. Back in 1730, he had been a young printer hired by Mr. Hamilton to publish his Assembly proceedings, and heartily grateful for the business. Now, forty-seven years after, he was President of Pennsylvania, and famous the world over as sage and seer—the incomparable Benjamin Franklin. Everyone else had forgotten the formidable old Scotsman, his conceit, his vigor, his elegance, his blunt direct ways, his deistical talk. But they had not forgotten his "best cause," nor his words in Zenger's trial.

Those words, Gouverneur Morris of Morrisania would say, still shone as "the morning star of that liberty which subsequently revolutionized America."

2

Treason in Profile

or, The Hard Way to Wealth,
Being a Brief Relation of the Life and Successes of
Thomas Pichon, late of St. Helier

In France, in the region of Normandy, in a far corner of the Calvados plain, lies the ancient town called Vire. It is a small place, never more than three thousand people, it is not at all situated for defense. Yet it is a river crossing—the river is called Vire, too—and a pair of major high roads intersect here, so the village has from time to time been momentarily mentioned in chronicles, histories, and annals, when armies have swept through its venerable, well-traveled environs on their way to more significant prizes.

Its two products have been pork sausages, locally esteemed as very fine indeed, and a building-stone of blue granite quarried in the nearby hills. Otherwise, Vire's only claim to fame is the curious one that it gave us our word *vaudeville,* originally the description of public entertainments held out of doors here a hundred years and more ago, for the amusement of Calvados farmers: *vau de Vire,* or *vau de ville.*

Vaudeville is dead now, and so is the old-time life of Vire; but both have left wistful memories, and quaint souvenirs, and the faint regrettable fragrance of cheerful vulgarity. In this little Norman town are preserved the

71

principal records, and the only portrait, of Vire's most conspicuous son, a certain Thomas Pichon, who played a part—an appalling part—in American history.

Many French villages have their town *bibliothèques,* of which they are vaguely proud. In every one flourishes the antiquary, a species of scholar (by no means confined to France) who makes boredom a vocation, who can ruin a sunny day's dream of glories past with his spate of tedious information. At Vire, it is doubtful if much pride was ever lavished on Thomas Pichon. For though he bequeathed to the town of his birth his collection of three thousand books,* his portrait by Concourt, and his letters and manuscripts when he died in the year 1781, and though the town accepted his bequest, still it was no secret in Vire that Pichon, brilliant and learned, was also an unprincipled rogue, a rascal, a liar, a vicious predator of women. And certainly he was a traitor. Vire might better have forgotten him.

America never can. For Thomas Pichon's treason to France gave us Acadia in 1755, and prepared the way for our conquest of French Canada. He ranks with Benedict Arnold as one of the two classical traitors in our history. The fact that he was in our pay, on our side, scarcely makes his story more appealing. What does attract us, even endear him to us, is the extraordinarily intimate documentation of his life—the revelation, more precise, more detailed than almost any other record of the eighteenth century, of the course of his personal depravity, his viciousness, his sin.

The history of Thomas Pichon comes to us straight from hell. It is no somber tragedy of great issues greatly befouled; treason is never this. For how do you betray a nation? Not by traffic in ideas or hopes, not by calling to hearts from a mountain top, but by furtive dealings in little things, in plots and plans and gossip, by venal *rendezvous* in chimney corners where details are paid for in cash: details so small few can see their value, cash never enough to slake the appetite of the man who would whisper away his loyalty.

Treason is a literary impossibility. The struggle of Empire against Empire is too vast an epic to be reduced to the betrayal of a forest fort, held by a tiny garrison. Treason is a trivial personal story, an episode in a single man's will and nature, a man small enough in soul, small enough in vision, to set a price on his faith, sell informations for a pittance. Only in fantasy, only in the most jejune romance, can the traitor have dimensions of a hero gone wrong.

It was a ridiculous aberration in Mr. Kenneth Roberts to devote a major part of his literary career to a vain attempt to find merit and moral stature in Benedict Arnold. There was no stature there, not in his treason. Pichon was

---

* A surprisingly large collection. At the same time Mme. de Pompadour's celebrated library at Versailles contained 3,500 volumes.

even worse. He was cast in the very pattern of traitors, a man molded with no goodness, no values except the values of the *franc,* the *centime,* the *sou.* He was excessively able, keen, shrewd; he was filled with self-justifications; but never can we find him bent on any save an evil purpose.

Pichon fabricated many different stories of his life. There is an old tag which says a liar must have a good memory; this unfortunately Pichon did not. He contradicted himself time and time again, and he made the error of saving all his documents, so we can see every one of his lies for what it was—a bland and deliberate falsehood. He was as careless of posterity as he was careless of his contemporaries, perfectly willing to impose upon both.

Thomas Pichon was born at Vire in March, 1700, the son of a small shopkeeper of the town. Now the records are perfectly clear that his mother was of a local Norman family named Esnault, but Pichon later concocted the tale that his grandparents had been English folk who had settled in Normandy, named Tyrell. This, he declared, was why his sympathies were British, why he betrayed Beauséjour, why he called himself Thomas Tyrell. It was a blatant lie. There was no drop of English blood in this Norman impostor. Most of the time he could not even remember how he spelled Tyrell: he used no less than five different versions of his assumed name.

Till he was fourteen, he went to school. Afterwards, he said at various times, he went on to study for the priesthood, or the law, or medicine. These tales too were false. He studied for no profession at all, but became a clerk in the town Procurator's office. Later he earned money as a tutor of the children in a local nobleman's family, then served eight years as secretary to a judicial officer. During daylight hours he read widely and deeply, he became, for his tiny village, learned. During nights as a young man about Vire, he became a thoroughly unsavory character. He "made a profession," one alarmed townsman wrote, "of suborning young girls." Easily, frequently, he promised marriage to the trusting peasant lasses. He was a small chap, but well made, with large dark eyes and a straight nose. He grew accustomed to casual successes. "All means of deceiving a young gentlewoman appear excellent to him," the same worrying townsman recorded, and he explained the way to confute him: demand his intentions in writing. He would surely back down, stand convicted in the eyes of any lady. Pichon's notoriety extended for miles round about. "He will ruin the chances of your daughter," another neighbor wrote of the enterprising young clerk's attentions.

But French villages have a certain elasticity. Pichon lived forty-one years at Vire without being murdered, or whipped, or married. Certainly he added spice to life on the Calvados plain. Then he went to war. It was 1741; he joined the hospital services of the French Army in Bohemia and Bavaria. Why he went is not clear: perhaps to escape the understandable tensions of his busy life, or the angers of neighbors; perhaps to seek new and strange conquests, new challenges to his avocations; perhaps for money. Telling his story later, he exaggerated his war services. No one could check him; his stories expanded with time. He invented a duel, a conspiracy against him, an heroic endeavor. The true facts were much less vivid. He dealt in supplies and procurement, he found forage; he may indeed have done one thing he claimed for himself, organized a military hospital in the Lower Rhine. It was entirely within his capacities to do so.

Four years in the army hurled him into a world far larger than Vire, vastly more delightful with excitements. And those four years brought him new acquaintances. It was a man's world he was made for. Plainly even in his forties he still had a good deal of physical magnetism, in addition to his quick, well-furnished mind. It was a curious thing about Pichon that men of probity and parts liked him. This was true of Benedict Arnold, also. Men can be ruled by a kind of evil not at once apparent on the surface, an evil that by no means eliminates charm.

A certain Jean-Louis, Comte de Raymond, Seigneur of Oyes in Marne, had spent his whole career in the Army, risen (in the way one rose in King Louis' army, by purchasing, courting favor, having relatives high-placed) to the significant rank of Lieutenant Colonel, and the profitable duty of King's Lieutenant in Angoulême. Pichon came to know him, this wealthy officer with no female interests in his life, past-master of the processes of preferment. "We were intimate friends in the Army," Pichon wrote, but what that word "intimate" meant, if it meant anything, there is no sure way of telling. Certainly Comte Raymond was a hardworking, energetic officer, loyal, sharply impatient with pettifogging or mendacity—in others. But equally certain is it that he was vain, pompous, arrogant, ambitious, self-seeking, and these were exactly the weaknesses an attractive schemer could prey on.

Come Raymond was related to the remarkable René Louis de Voyer, Marquis d'Argenson, minister of foreign affairs and principal statesman of France, until for his enlightened liberal opinions and proposals of reform he fell under la Pompadour's displeasure (1747) and found himself dismissed. This was no help to the aspiring Colonel. But that enlightened Marquis had a younger brother, Marc Pierre Comte d'Argenson, a man entirely unencumbered with liberal opinions. This younger d'Argenson held the post of *directeur de la librarie,* which amounted to being chief censor of all published writings. He it was who imprisoned Diderot, freeing him only after the philosopher repudiated his religious opinions, and after it was represented to the *directeur* that the *Encyclopédie* could not proceed without his victim. When in June, 1751, the first volume of the *Encyclopédie* did appear, Diderot had the wry wisdom to dedicate it to that very same Marc Pierre Comte d'Argenson, who had by now become *ministre et secrétaire d'état et de guerre.* The rise of the unprincipled d'Argenson more than compensated for the fall of the principled, in Comte Raymond's prospects, particularly when his valuable connection at court became his own superior as minister of war. And Comte d'Argenson, of course, was alert to build a personal following in all key positions of the vast bureaucracy that centered at Versailles. He looked about for available relatives who would be properly grateful; that is why, in 1751, Comte Raymond suddenly found himself honored by a fine colonial appointment: Governor of Isle Royale, which today we call Cape Breton Island. This was all that was left to France of her former province of Acadie, the rest of which since the Treaty of Utrecht thirty-seven years before had been under English rule. The English changed the French name Acadie to the pseudo-Latin, "Nova Scotia." To be Governor of Isle Royale was a high post for the ambitious Colonel, a grave responsibility should war come.

What sort of hold over Comte Raymond it was that Pichon the Norman mountebank had achieved we can only conjecture; evidently it was irresistible, for when the new Governor sailed he took Pichon with him in his party, as official secretary. Pichon says that Comte Raymond refused to go to America without him, that he used the most elaborate inducements to persuade him to go. This is unlikely. They had not been many months at Louisbourg, the fortress capital of Isle Royale, before they were quarreling violently with one another. The Comte made no record of the issues, and Pichon's accusations are not to be relied on; but plainly if Pichon hoped to govern this strong-willed nobleman in his own interest, he failed. During their three years together at Louisbourg, Comte Raymond did write for Pichon a generous letter of fulsome recommendation to the minister of marine back in Paris—colonial establishments were the responsibility of the Marine—but he was evidently mistrustful of his secretary, and his mistrust gnawed when it became all too obvious that Governor Lawrence of Nova Scotia, Governor Shirley of Massachusetts, and New England ship captains generally, were being supplied with secret military information from someone high-up about the French post at Louisbourg and French garrison throughout Acadie. Comte Raymond began to rummage through Pichon's wastebasket. It was a ludicrous thing for a governor to do, but threatened with espionage even *noblesse d'épée* will stoop to housemaid's devices. One day he found an incriminating paper there, among all the sad letters from distressed females the wastebasket usually yielded.

Pichon tried to explain the evidence away. He wrote a bland letter: Would not a person really guilty have destroyed any proof? he asked. "Furthermore, has anyone noted in me the desire for gain, which is the making of rascals and prevaricators?" Many had, and Comte Raymond brooded about that wastebasket with its letters from deceived ladies. Abruptly, he transferred Pichon. He demoted him from official secretary, he put him in the commissary department; and to remove him entirely from the sensitive precincts of the Governor's office he named him to the post of chief clerk of stores at Fort Beauséjour, on the Chignecto isthmus, clear out at the westernmost reach of Nova Scotia, as far away from Louisbourg as his French authority or the islands themselves extended. Beauséjour was a frontier fort, built amidst the diked and reclaimed Tantramar marshes, hard by enemy installations. Pichon was outraged. Comte Raymond was "possibly the stupidest of all two-footed animals," he wrote.

And indeed, he was not far wrong, for Beauséjour was just across the Missaguash from the British Fort Lawrence. Comte Raymond had placed Pichon at the very throat of the French colony, the narrow entrance of the Chignecto corridor which British troops would have to use if they intended to storm Nova Scotia and Isle Royale from the continental mainland.

Of course, they would never do so: in French thinking, Louisbourg, the sea defense out on the eastern tip of Isle Royale, was the Bourbon bastion in the New World, commanding the Gulf of St. Lawrence and the whole North Atlantic. In French thinking, a land attack from behind, from the St. John River or Massachusetts, was no longer a possibility. Sea defense against the sea power of Britain was the indispensable necessity, an operation mounted by land unthinkable.

Unthinkable, that is, except to Pichon, who was now stationed at the westward margin of protection—precisely where treason could deliver the whole French province to the enemy, and render completely useless the formidable walls of Louisbourg.

Fort Beauséjour was new, and strongly built. Across the Missaguash, Fort Lawrence was steadily improving. Soon it would match the French in strength. And behind their frowning forts both French and English leaders were pursuing policies and plans bound soon to rupture the uneasy peace between two empires. The English policy was new: after thirty years and more of complete neglect in Nova Scotia, events had at last made it clear that Massachusetts, Rhode Island, and Connecticut could not survive a war if the enemy controlled the sea lanes by the imposing power of their fort at Louisbourg, and commanded the Bay of Fundy from Chignecto Isthmus. Nova Scotia, though nominally governed by the English, was still peopled by the original *habitants,* the French-speaking, Roman Catholic Acadians, loyal in their hearts to France. For many years, the easy hand of British colonial administration had touched but lightly on the Acadians; they were called "neutrals," they called themselves neutrals, administration assumed they would steadily remain non-combatant neutrals. A French priest, Abbé Jean Louis Le Loutre, missionary to the Micmac Indians since 1740, was allowed to move with no hindrance among Acadians and Micmacs alike, ministering to their spiritual needs.

The abbé for his part proved no neutral at all. Under the very noses of British administrators he preached to his illiterate Acadians, his wondering Micmacs, of their Protestant rulers with their foreign tongue, he warned of eternal damnation awaiting any who collaborated, with threats of excommunication he stiffened their French and Algonquian souls to resistance. He even fashioned a clandestine army of sorts. One winter night eight years ago (1746) he had fallen with his mixed force on Grand Pré, where 500 Massachusetts militiamen were bivouacked. The attack was a grim slaughter, surviving New Englandmen withdrew to Annapolis Royal, easy English toleration of Acadians in their French culture and religion was over. From now on, they would have to swear loyalty to Britain. Even then they were constantly watched. Abbé Le Loutre fled to France for a term, and the British, root and branch, altered their policy of governance in Nova Scotia.

First, they brought Protestant settlers in great numbers from England, Germany, Holland; they erected an entire new city in the best harbor, Halifax, on the east coast, to counteract Louisbourg. Next, they strengthened their land and sea forces at Annapolis Royal, St. Johns, and Fort Lawrence. Finally, Governor Charles Lawrence reached a serious decision, a complete reversal of thirty years' easy ways: the Acadian *habitants* would have to go. No longer could Britain, no more could New England, afford the risk of a disaffected people ready to rise against them, indulged and protected in their own colony that lay strategically athwart the Atlantic sea passage. Nova Scotia must be truly conquered, the Acadian natives gathered up and settled elsewhere; to do this, French garrisons and posts must be destroyed. It was late summer of 1754 when Charles Lawrence commenced his plans for military operations. It was, that is, the exact moment when Pichon arrived at Beauséjour.

French policy, by contrast, was not new at all. It was plainly to preserve and strengthen things as they were: to invest the Chignecto Isthmus commanding the head of the Bay of Fundy; to continue to populate the Tantramar dikes; secretly to arm Micmacs and Acadians, stir them continually to harrass the British everywhere they could; always to rely on Fort Louisbourg, mighty Gibraltar of the North Atlantic from which British shipping and New England fishing could be destroyed, the lifeline to Canada protected.

This was the policy Comte Raymond was charged with; these were the measures he pursued with vigor. Abbé Le Loutre returned from France as Raymond took his post. The good abbé was now Vicar-General, an imposing dignity equivalent to bishop. With Raymond's support he resumed his activities among Indians and Acadians in the French interest. Troops assigned to Beauséjour, *marine* and *armee,* were ordered strictly to maintain, meticulously to observe all the niceties of formal peace. They did. They held easy daily intercourse with the English garrison across the Missaguash marshes. They even sympathized with their English brethren every time a Micmac raid descended on Fort Lawrence, burned supplies, destroyed British forage; all the while they pretended ignorance of the abbé's busy machinations.

It was not Beauséjour which was weak. Beauséjour was a conspicuous success, a French fort boldly built on the English frontier, which the English could not reduce short of a major war, a hindrance to British operations out of their own capital on the Bay of Fundy, a deterrent to a thrust across the corridor. The weakness lay elsewhere: in the French at Louisbourg blandly ignoring the English buildup much nearer by, at Halifax, and even more in Raymond's, in every Frenchman's, extraordinary faith in Louisbourg—that fort which had fallen once to Massachusetts men, but which the French still regarded as impregnable, a castle far out in the sea, invulnerable from land.

Louisbourg had been rebuilt, regarrisoned, rearmed. Behind its walls nestled a town now of 4,000, the largest French city in America, as the fortress was the strongest anywhere in the New World. So confident was Comte Raymond in his citadel that one of his first measures—he pursued it with his undoubted energy and efficiency—was to build a fine military road from Louisbourg's shore gate all the way down south to St. Peter's, opposite the Gut of Canso—a distance of fifty miles. It was a dubious achievement. One of Louisbourg's greatest strengths had always been its inaccessibility from the shore, its long land-distance from anywhere British, clear out the stretching length of Isle Royale. So convinced were the French that no land attack would be mounted, particularly after Beauséjour was built, that Raymond actually opened this easy route for any land army to use. After Beauséjour fell, his road became a danger, not a joy. Then, he was angrily criticized at Paris, recalled, blamed for furnishing the British a perfect means of reaching Louisbourg. But at the time no one objected, or advised against it. Attack, if it came, would come by sea. (In justice to Comte Raymond, who needs every doubt we can give him, let it be said that when Wolfe and Amherst finally did reduce Louisbourg four years later, they came by sea. They found no use for his fine new military road from St. Peter's.)

Pichon went to his new post at Beauséjour with extravagant recommendations, warm letters from Comte Raymond and numerous others. The French commandant (a venal, cheating, peculating man, almost illiterate, an entirely congenial type for Pichon) welcomed him enthusiastically. So did the Vicar General, Abbé Le Loutre, who found in the new clerk of stores an efficient supplier of secret arms and materiel for his people. Curiously, the busy abbé had no notion that Pichon was preparing from the moment of his arrival to betray France to the English.

Now treason is an overt act, and the overt act is the melodrama of a treason story: secret meetings, bizarre disguises, concealed documents, the treason that fails is unmasked in a thrilling scene of denunciation and retribution. But Pichon did not fail. He succeeded. And so there is no climax to his story, no romance. Figures slinking to murky assignations in the forest primæval, the murmuring pines and the hemlocks, become not breathless actors in a suspenseful scene, but sordid agents of commercial transactions. Melodrama pales; the actual drama is private, the depravity of characters buying and selling high trusts, their countries, themselves. The plot of any treason lies in this: what manner of man is it who betrays his commitments?

Pichon was fifty-three years old at Beauséjour. He was inclined to stoutness now; his chin hung in folds over his stock. Penniless, with no prospects, he found in his Chignecto exile no young women to fulfill him. He found corruption all about: corruption cloaked in righteousness by the abbé, corruption naked and exposed in the commandant. The clerk of stores did not hesitate to make his own contributions to the game. The British captain, George Scott, seized so promptly on Pichon as a spy that it is impossible not to conclude the Norman secretary had made British connections before he left Louisbourg, and had served them well. That incriminating paper in his wastebasket so disturbing to Comte Raymond plainly had been far from the innocent missive Pichon pretended.

Captain Scott promised him hard money now, and a pension later. Soon Pichon was sending him, by Acadian carters, secret couriers, by various contrivances the most detailed reports on the French garrisons: Beauséjour; Baye Verte; the outpost on the St. John river; and news of flints and powder and balls, of rations and boots, all the miniscule informations a storekeeper has which add up to the strength and movements of an army. Every effort of Abbé Le Loutre among the Micmacs, every sortie they attempted against the English, Pichon frustrated by information in advance (yet he managed to remain in close friendship with the abbé, even long after his treason was accomplished). And he furnished Scott with an excellent plan, the very plan the British enemy would follow, of how to reduce the French forts and conquer all Acadia.

"I was of English origin," Pichon told Scott, in the pitiful attempt of a spy to seem a patriot.

"The French have treated you with base ingratitude," Scott murmured, as he handed over livres and pounds sterling. Scott was replaced by Hussey, Pichon continued to relay news of the forest province.

Nearly fifty documents that Pichon sent to British commanders have survived. On the basis of the information they contained, the British planned their campaign. Rarely was an attack so thoroughly prepared, rarely so quickly successful. Governor Lawrence proceeded with the cold efficiency of an honorable man obliged to deal with scoundrels. Under his direction a large force came up from Massachusetts, Shirley's colonial levies plus 250 British regulars. General Monckton commanded, Robert Monckton, only twenty-eight, now about to engage in the most distasteful assignment of his long, honorable career. The army assembled at Fort Lawrence. On its appearance, the French commandant at Beauséjour summoned all Acadians and Micmacs from miles about to support his small garrison. On a June morning, 1755, Monckton led his force through the marshes, crossed the Missaguash at low tide. The Acadians before him promptly deserted, the Indians melted away, Monckton fired the village, and the church. The fort offered him brief resistance, no more than a token. Soon he was inside. Pichon had delivered Beauséjour; now he delivered himself to the English, prepared to collect his payment for services rendered. He arranged a plausible charade of his "capture." Acadians, quite like Abbé Le Loutre, never knew of his part in their fall.

With swift strokes, Monckton seized the remaining French forts in Nova Scotia, in a few days the whole province was British in fact as well as name. Then the young general began his dismal task of pursuing Acadians in their villages and farms and woods, gathering them up, herding then in ships for transportation to faraway lands. Pichon, for his part, began in leisure and remarkable complacency his comfortable life as pensioner of the British crown.

Of course he had to leave Nova Scotia. As Thomas Tyrell, he settled in London at the age of fifty-six. The British government fixed his pension at £200 a year, a substantial sum; and the military actually employed his talents once again. This was in 1757. He travelled through Pennsylvania among Acadian exiles there, disguised as a captured French officer; he informed Lord Loudoun, British comander in North America, of Acadian leaders who were stirring the lost peoples to dissatisfactions with their British captors, their Protestant neighbors. The exiles were hard used in Pennsylvania. They declared they would flee to the back country and join the French beyond Fort Duquesne, unles their children were freed from forced labor. When Pichon delivered the names of their five principal leaders, they were arrested and sent to serve on a ship of war as convict laborers.

It was easy, congenial service, quickly over. Soon Pichon was back in his cushioned life in London. And in London, the traitor of Beauséjour finally met with a genuine humiliation. It was no matter of state or warcraft which brought him down; it was not even money. It was a woman. Pichon at last met a female who was, to put no edge upon it, too much for him.

This adventure, also, left a full and shocking record of its course. Pichon (Tyrell) spoke no English; his circle of acquaintances in London was limited to the small colony of French expatriates in the city, and the few

French-speaking Londoners who could tolerate him. Among the last was an egregious individual, John Cleland, onetime British consul at Smyrna, then an East Indian civil servent, then a wanderer about the world and lately (1750) become notorious through the publication of a book so lewd and priapic, so entirely pornographic, that it is still in ill fame everywhere—and still in print: *Fanny Hill, or, The Memoirs of a Woman of Pleasure.* Not a few high courts of law in England and America have been obliged—some are still being obliged—to consider the merits of this work. The very first trial was of its author, and its results are instructive. For the publication of *Fanny Hill,* Cleland was hailed before the Privy Council. There the author made no protestations of literary merit, or the freedom of the artist in por-traying the human condition, or the freedom of the press. He blandly admitted the work was erotic and obscene; he had meant it to be. He was in extreme poverty; he needed the money he knew such a work would bring; his desperate need he pleaded as his excuse for writing it. The Privy Council, seized on this occasion with one of those inane impulses busy men and courts sometimes suffer, committed the incredible obliquity of conferring upon Cleland a pension of £100 a year, in order that he might employ his talents more worthily. This novel solution of the problem of an obscene novel, surprisingly enough, worked. Cleland deserted pornography, in litearture at least; he published serious essays in the press, wrote several presentable plays, and then embarked on a major work of scholarship, a study of the Celtic language, the employment in which he was engaged when Pichon swam into his ken.

Pichon swam in, accompanied by a handsome and formidable female, Marie-Barbé Leprince de Beaumont, a woman whose history is even now disturbing, after two hundred years. Madame de Beaumont was of gentle birth, from a distinguished family of Rouen. As a young lady, she entered a convent, but after two years abruptly left to marry a man much older than herself. This union was not satisfactory. Her first infatuation soon left her, and so did her husband, who was revealed to have an incapacitating disease—a "loathsome one," so Madame averred. She procured a declaration of nullity of the sacrament of this marriage, through the complex processes prescribed by the Canon Law. She wrote a novel. It was called—the title falls with serene impudence in the midst of the story of Thomas Pichon—*The Triumph of Truth.* And when she moved to London, where she gave lessons in French, and wrote more than seventy books—books for children, in education, geography, history, including the successful *Nouveau Magazin Français, ou Bibliothéque Instructive,* full of the highest sorts of morality and the most improving precepts; and including also the noteworthy, one-time famous *Magazin des Enfants.* This last has been called, by those who study the history of juvenile literature, epochmaking—and indeed Mme. de Beaumont must be credited, if that is the right word, with revolutionizing writing for children. She banished the elves and fairies and goblins, the animals who talked and the ogres who sharpened knives to feed on lost childen in the wood. Perrault's *Tales of Mother Goose* was sixty years old now;* generations of children in many lands had grown up on the delicious terrors, the unforgettable delights of Little Red Riding Hood, Hop o' My Thumb, Cinderella, Sister Anne, Puss-in-Boots. Madame de Beaumont would have none of such nonsense. Children should be taught, through their reading, not merely entertained. Entertainment was trivial, a waste of time; life is earnest, no chance must be lost to give even the youngest tot right principles, right morality, correct knowledge. Madame commenced a new vogue. The epoch she made was the epoch of those grim books of puerile instruction, pallidly sugarcoated, by which children were too soon transformed into tiresomely knowledgable little dullards, after which even the monstrosities perpetuated by New England Puritans as children's reading could be wistfully remembered with longing.

She called herself the "Wise Governess." The title of her famous work translates: *The Children's Magazine, or Conversations of a Wise Governess with her most distinguished pupils . . .* It was a repelling production, this revolt of Enlightenment against imagination, against art, a book far different from *Fanny Hill.* But who would be bold enough to say its influence was not infinitely worse?

Yet The Wise Governess was no slouch. She wrote with unmistakable talent, she knew people, and poetry, and the sadness of life; she could be called, in her own reasonable way, an artist—if only Reason's way had left some bit of room for art. And she wrote one glowing tale that will never die: "Beauty and the Beast." Beauty found Beast lying forlorn in the forest, despairing; he would surely die for want of love, yet who could look upon his repulsive shape, his ugly countenance with aught but loathing? Beauty could: "No, my dear Beast, you shall not die! You shall live to become my husband. At this moment I give you my hand. I swear I shall be only yours, forever. Hélas! I thought I felt only friendship for you, but the pain in my breast tells me I cannot live without you!" At her words, fireworks burst in the heavens, celestial music swelled, and there on the ground before her lay Beast transformed, a Prince more handsome than Love itself, who blessed her for breaking the magic spell . . .

The Wise Governess had her moments.

One day, visiting a French refugee in King's Bench Prison, Madame de Beaumont met Thomas Pichon. Beauty recognized her Beast, fireworks burst,

---

* *Contes de ma mère l'Oie* was the inscription on Perrault's frontispiece; the actual title of his book, published by Barbin in 1697, was *Histoire ou Contes du temps passé, avec des moralités.*

music swelled, in a trice the full-fashioned Wise Governess of forty-six felt the divine pains of love for the stout little rougue of fifty-six, her fellow Norman who would surely transform into a Prince. For his part, Pichon did not fail to contrive a certain affection for Madame—at least for her success, her fortune, her fame and position, her hearty if virginal good looks. Wisdom quite deserted Wise Governess; that busy and learned lady pursued her new friend with the most abandoned determination, spewing forth letters which now decorate the archives of three countries. Pichon played a canny game, subtle and irresistible. He led her on, he drew back, he re-appeared; finally he had the lady on the terms he wished, and she made a great preparation for giving herself to him. Pichon could not resist a minor peculation, even when major profits were in view. He murmured something about his landlord, Madame laid a hundred guineas on the altar of love. The union was consummated.

But unhappily, Pichon's capitulation awakened in Marie-Barbé de Beau-mont needs, and enthusiasms, which in her previous celibate life she had not experienced, needs which Pichon at fifty-six was by no means equipped to satisfy. Beauty was voracious. She was insatiable. Her passion flourished, it exfloriated, it consumed her. It nearly consumed Beast. Pichon's passion cooled instantly. Letters amazing and adroit flew back and forth; finally Pichon moved into her apartments in Woodstock Street. Promptly, he began to maneuver her out.

Madame, needing more money for her reluctant and aging Prince, opened, of all things, a ladies' seminary. It did not proposer, nor did Madame find her situation entirely fulfilling. It occurred to her a warmer climate would assist Pichon in his flagging endeavors; they made plans to remove to France. Madame would go first, Pichon would join her later. Madame did go, in 1760, whereupon of course Pichon relaxed, comfortable and released, in her Woodstock Street apartments. He sought to restore his depleted vigor; apparently he concealed from Madame the treason which made forever im-possible his return to his native land; certainly he discovered no intention of joining his quenchless inamorata.

For the remaining twenty-one years of his life, he saw Madame de Beau-mont no more. He kept her ardor constant and alive, and her money flowing in, by letters—and he neatly forestalled her return by abundant promises in answer to her pleadings. He took an easier mistress, moved her into Madame's home, a French lady who had been Madame's best friend. He failed to send over to France the Beaumont furniture; he even kept the silver plate Madame had expected and stood sorely in need of. In her lonely Continental dwelling she had not even a spoon to stir her coffee, Madame complained. Pichon, in his now reposeful situation, could not have cared less. He collected his large fine library; soon he began to beguile his idle time writing a book of his own, a description of Cape Breton. It was an excellent performance, the best, most authoritative book done on Isle Royale. It made him a name. Poor Madame fumed and railed by packetboat mail, but she would quickly follow her angry outbursts with tender, longing, remembering letters, letters full of pathetic desire. She was faithful to Pichon, hideously faithful ("I shall be only yours forever," Beauty had sworn). Pichon on his part went from woman to woman, rebuking Cleland the *Fanny Hill* author at one point for trying to steal the favors of his current comfort. As Thomas Tyrell, Pichon the pensioned traitor of Beauséjour spent fourteen years in Madame's apartments, on Madame's bounty, in the pensioned pornographer's circle.

Yet slowly stole now upon Pichon the only defeat he could not avert: old age. His life of deceit had made him rich, but riches could not deceive the decay of the flesh. Age made him morbid, cranky, suspicious, and very tired. As his seventieth birthday drew near, he roused himself, put fleshly things aside; he left his dubious companions. He even left London, removing to the village of St. Helier on the island of Jersey, in the midst of Acadian refugees there. Again he dissembled: he pretended to be one of their number. Here at the end of his life he was still informing the British government of the plight and plans of the transplanted *habitants*.

And here he was still writing letters, brilliant letters, brilliant even when decay became his theme, self-pity his single passion. From lugubrious pages springs a hymn to old age—the kind of hymn a Pichon, or a Faustus, would write:

> What a horrible thing is old age! I am barely the shadow of the man I was! The springs of my origin are worn by time, and, possibly, by debauch, the result, as the saying is, of having lived too much. My infirmities are constantly increasing, and my days are spent in insupportable torment. My legs, once an adornment which aroused admiration at balls and assemblies, are extended, immobile, and œdematous, on a chair or footstool. My cheeks, once glowing and plump, are parched and shrivelled with wrinkles; my lips are merely covered with tense and livid skin. I have lost, not only the power to enjoy pleasure, but even the desire for enjoyment. I am avoided as a pitiful and disgusting object, and, far from complaining of the solitude in which I am left, I should like, if it were possible, to escape from myself.

Pichon, whose life had been physical, was afraid of physical death. And rising to the last resort of scoundrels, in the trembling fear of his seventies he finally succeeded in deceiving himself. Looking back over all his years, he decided he had lived decently, had been honorable and just. Blandly, his traitor's pen shaped astonishing words: "The moral probity which I made my idol . . ." Through it all, he had committed one mistake. He had neglected the worship of God. His moral probity wanted only piety to perfect it. His reason, his learning, had hidden God from him. Now he must turn to that True Light. "I protest that I am a Christian," he said in his will. He convinced himself. Alone, apprehensive, fearful, in his late-arrived piety he composed the epitaph for his tomb. It was his final insult to the truth:

The great age I reached I neither wished to have, nor blamed when I had it. The troubles of life I calmly endured, just as its joys did not move me to disproportionate happiness. Death I neither scorned nor feared. Dear God, who regardest this world and the anxieties of men, take pity on my soul.

The name of God has fallen from strange lips since men began to think on what is just; from none stranger to its beauties than the lips of Thomas Pichon.

3

"A Certain Great Fortune and Piddling Genius"

Philadelphia's summer heat poured through the windows, Philadelphia's summer smells hung hot in the air. Monday afternoon, a July afternoon, still and close: July was cruel in the toll it took of tempers and energies. John Adams sat all day in the sweltering Congress Chamber, the big high Assembly Room in old Andrew Hamilton's State House. Sunlight reflected from the treeless graveled yard, picked out patterns on the ceiling, poured over the portrait of the King above the mantel.

Adams seethed with impatience. All around him, Congressmen bustled despite the heat, speaker followed speaker, delegates clamored for recognition. Governor Ward of Rhode Island was in the chair. The delegate from Massachusetts scarcely bothered to listen. It was a tedious debate, over "a Continental Treasury . . . a Paymaster . . . and a Committee of Correspondence or Safety, or Accounts, or something, I know not what, that has confounded Us all Day . . ." Adams was testy, irritated, annoyed. Finally the session ended, nothing accomplished. He stamped the three blocks to his rooms in high dudgeon; he sat down in the heat to write letters.

As he wrote, his choler rose. For months, he had argued for a simple, straightforward program, stated exactly what ought to be done, plainly, clearly.

86

There could be no doubt of it, at least no doubt in Adams's mind. John Adams's mind was a firm, orderly, neatly arranged instrument. He reached conclusions with anguish and doubt, but once he reached them his doubt was gone, and he anguished only that others would not see the exact truth as he exactly saw it.

New England men did; and Southerners were generally "sound in their principles," which was to say, they generally agreed with Adams. Not South Carolinians, of course; they stood apart. And it must not be thought any Southerners were reliable. They weren't. They were likely to be shifty, easy-going; they were bound to boggle over matters such as slaves and tobacco and indigo and rice. But Southerners were "ready" men. They agreed on strong measures.

The trouble was, these mid-colony people. New York, New Jersey, Pennsylvania, Maryland, Delaware—here was the very heart of the American seaboard, the best harbors, the most trade, fully half the people of British America, these "shamefully interested Proprietary people," Richard Henry Lee called them. They had seen all that Massachusetts had suffered; they had suffered themselves. But the middle-colony men held back, delayed, stood cautious in the moment for action, delayed even though Bunker Hill and the bloody battle was a month old in history. John Adams had talked, debated, cajoled, persuaded; he had been virtuous, and patient—at least *he* thought he was patient—but still the mid-colony men refused to join him on one great issue. On that, they paltered and trimmed and palavered, all because one man, one famous, cautious man—one man of wealth and power and great reputation—would not accept the facts, and the truth, and the rightness of John Adams's proposals.

At his desk, Adams's patience ran out, the last vestige of self-possession deserted him. He suddenly added a postscript to his wife: "I wish I had given you a complete history, from the beginning to the end of the journey, of the behaviour of my compatriots. No mortal tale can equal it. I will tell you in future, but you shall keep it secret. The fidgets, the whims, the caprice, the vanity, the superstition, the inability of some of us is enough to ——" He could not finish. He drew a long eloquent line, and closed his page.

He took another sheet, began a letter to his friend James Warren. "Philadelphia, July 24, 1775," he wrote. "Dear Sir, In Confidence. I am determined to write freely to you this time. A certain great Fortune and piddling Genius, whose Fame has been trumpeted so loudly, has given a silly Cast to our whole Doings. We are between Hawk and Buzzard . . ." His pen raced, he poured out his frustration, and his anger: "We ought to have had in our Hands a month ago the whole Legislative, executive, and judicial of the whole Continent, and have completely modeled a Constitution; to have raised a naval Power, and opened all our Ports wide; to have arrested every Friend to Government on the Continent and held them as Hostages for the poor Victims in Boston, and then opened the Door as wide as possible for the Peace and Reconciliation. After this they might have petitioned, and negotiated, and addressed etc, if they would. Is all this extravagant? Is it wild? Is it not the soundest Policy?"

He folded his sheets, addressed them; and he omitted to add his Congressman's frank, because for these particular charges of explosive matter he had a personal messenger. Benjamin Hichborn, the courier, was riding back to Boston. Adams gave young Hichborn his very personal letters, to be delivered by hand to Mrs. Adams, and to Mr. Warren.

Now John Adams took the Rule of Secrecy—under which the delegates to Congress were bound—very lightly indeed. He violated it constantly, to the subsequent delight of historical enquirers. He was not one to imagine rules were meant to apply to him. But on this occasion, certainly, he had no idea his letters would be seen by anyone except his wife, his friend James Warren, and perhaps those intimate companions who made up the Adams circle. ("You must not communicate without great Discretion what I write about our Proceedings, for all that I hint to you is not yet public," he had recently told James Warren.) He could never have anticipated what happened. As Benjamin Hichborn crossed the Hudson river, boats from a British man-of-war halted his ferry, British officers took the young courier prisoner; of course they searched his saddlebags, of course they found Adams's personal letters. They dispatched them at once to General Gage in Boston, and of course that busy gentleman, Governor and Commander-in-Chief under the Crown, was delighted with the find, and all it meant. To him, it meant serious divisions among the rebel leaders.

General Gage caused the letters to be published in Draper's *Massachusetts Gazette,* on August 17—published in their full crackle of angry indiscretion, for the world to read. Most regrettable of all, for John Dickinson to read: *A certain great Fortune and piddling Genius . . .*

Apart from the issues, apart from all the disagreements, the language was so surprising, so petulant and petty, so unlike the apparently manly, able Yankee. Once, Adams had liked Dickinson, insofar as he could ever like a rich man. When he first came to Philadelphia ten months before (September, '74) he had met the famous "Farmer" with pleasure. "Mr. Dickinson is very modest, delicate, and timid," he wrote in his dairy. After further meetings he added, "Mr. Dickinson is a very modest man, and very ingenious as well as agreeable; he has an excellent heart . . ." Dickinson stretched far above him in height; Adams had to stand back on his heels to look at him. He usually had to look up to people. "Mr. Dickinson has been subject to hectic complaints. He is a shadow; tall, but slender as a reed, pale as ashes;

one would think at first sight that he could not live a month; yet, upon a more attentive inspection he looks as if the springs of life were strong enough to last many years . . ."

He was right, on that more attentive inspection. The springs of life in the shadow-thin, elegant Pennsylvania Farmer were taut and resilient, in spite of agues, fluxes, fevers, in spite of marsh and river miasma; the springs of dissent, too, and disagreement, and an assertive separateness of thought, the springs of originality. May, June, July this summer of '75 Adams had known the power of that inventive, complicated mind as Dickinson prevailed in Congress again and again, brought before the delegates such measures as they all could unite in, leaving no opinion behind, steering the middle course between both extremes, the course that would keep every colony a part of things, every delegate unoffended, in line. Stocky round little Adams had frequently admired that analytical mind which refused to see things in simplicities, which would never cease qualifying, deliberating, considering, seeking adjustment among all points of view. The Yankee's impatience was a long season ripening. He was ready for action—had been, long months ago. So was Dickinson. But there were some actions Dickinson rejected outright, some on which he held back for others to come along, some points on which he waited for the middle land. Dickinson had reasons: cogent, impressive, plain, logical, convincing—but not to New England men. They could never think seriously of his reasons as impediments. Dickinson had his own plan, his own "soundest policy" for united American resistance to parliamentary measures. He was never less than polite, he was always good-tempered and pleasant, but he was as firm as the bricks of the State House itself. When he and Adams clashed, the amiable "Farmer" yielded not an inch. Adams lost his fight.

He blamed it on Dickinson alone. Dr. Franklin he respected, sometimes he even approached admiring him; but he was disappointed now in Franklin. The old man *seemed* resolute and bold, ready for the highest actions; but he would never move. "He has not assumed any thing, nor affected to take the lead; but has seemed to choose that the Congress should pursue their own principles and sentiments, and adopt their own plans." Such tolerance, such permissiveness, John Adams could never understand. One younger man in Pennsylvania, a certain James Wilson, he entirely esteemed. Wilson had been Dickinson's law student, but, said Adams, his "fortitude, rectitude, and abilities too, greatly outshine his master's." (Looking backward on that observation today, past the scene of Mr. Justice Wilson abjectly begging leniency from his creditors, fleeing their judgments, dying a bankrupt fugitive in a Carolina swamp, ruined by his avarice and wild speculations, carrying others down with him in ruin, we may well wonder at Adams preferring him in rectitude to John Dickinson, whose integrity no one else at any time in his whole long life ever thought to question.) On that July day, Wilson was ineffectual; and as for the others, Adams noted regretfully that Biddle was ill, Mifflin gone off to war, Speaker John Morton sick in bed too. Only Dickinson and Willing of the Pennsylvania delegation were in their seats beside Franklin and Wilson. Adams considered the two men. They both possessed immense wealth, everyone knew that. Wealth was ever a sensitive point to Adams. He had written his wife about Dickinson and Willing just yesterday (in a letter which happily Dickinson was never obliged to read in the public prints): "this province has suffered by the timidity of two overgrown fortunes. The dread of confiscation or caprice, I know not what, has influenced them too much; yet they were for taking arms, and pretended to be very valiant."

Shocking, stabbing words: *the dread of confiscation . . . pretended to be valiant!* Adams quickly added a line: "This letter must be secret, my dear; at least, communicated with great discretion."

In these July days of '75, particularly with the incident of the ugly letters intercepted, all possibility of fellowship between John Farmer and John Yankee came to an end. These two scholar-patriots, Pennsylvania's Dickinson and Massachusetts's Adams, so equal to each other in intellect, so apt for yoking in harness, so full of the same passions and the same learning, so keen for news of virtue and news of nations past and present, could never meet again with ease. The words had been too pointed, too crude and contemptuous: *A certain great Fortune and piddling Genius . . .*

Congress adjourned August 2; the delegates went home. On August 17, Adams's letters appeared in the Boston newspaper, subsequently in other papers elsewhere. On September 12, Congress reconvened in Philadelphia. It was still "Mr. Dickinson's Congress," his firm constitutional policy was succeeding, step by step, taking all the delegates along with it in unanimity; his program was still America's sober, lawful policy, even while the British made war. But now John Dickinson would have to meet John Adams again, face him, look upon him, sit in the same room with him. He would have to deal, somehow, with those appalling, detestable words—those surprising words, for Adams had voted *with* Dickinson on every great measure in June, in July; he had willingly signed the Second Petition to the King; Adams had agreed with everything, except one minor question, on which Dickinson had prevailed. ". . . *a silly Cast to our whole Doings. . . .*"

Four weeks now Philadelphians had talked of the Adams letters, thrown them up to Dickinson, chuckled behind his back, guessed at their meaning, their dreadful effect. Dickinson was humiliated by the words. He said nothing, he endured all the jibes, the discomfort. But now he must face Congress, all his moderate men, face Adams in person.

Saturday morning, September 16, walking down Chestnut Street toward the State House for the meeting of Congress, The Farmer looked up. Adams was right there in front of him, heading his way. They could not avoid meeting, as they neared the steps of the State House. He had to decide . . . They came close together, even next to each other. Adams doffed his hat, made a bow. Dickinson stared coldly above him, walked by him, held his hands rigidly in place, his head averted. It was his answer, his only answer, to Adams. Did the Yankee think to apologize, like a child say "I'm sorry," and so make it right? ". . . *whose fame has been trumpeted so loudly . . ."*

John Adams never forgot the moment, the snub in Chestnut Street. He described it in detail: "We met, and passed near enough to touch elbows. He passed without moving his hat or head or hand. I bowed, and pulled off my hat. He passed haughtily by. . . . I shall, for the future, pass him in the same manner; but I was determined to make my bow, that I might know his temper. We are not to be upon speaking terms nor bowing terms for the time to come . . ."

But they were to be colleagues in Congress, daily in each other's presence. Long afterward, Adams wrote this: "We continued to debate, in Congress, upon all questions publicly, with all our usual candor and good humor . . ." It was a grudging tribute. Any man other than John Adams might have said the same thing another way, might have written: *Mr. Dickinson preserved his good humor even after my attack upon him was discovered and made public.* Not Adams: "the friendship and acquaintance was lost forever."

During the next twelve months, Adams pounced gleefully on any news or opinion unfavorable to Dickinson. September 24, Dr. Benjamin Rush paid a Sunday call on the brace of Adamses. John Yankee wrote these words at the beginning of his famous forty years' friendship with the lively Philadelphia physician:

> Dr. Rush came in. He is an elegant, ingenious body, a sprightly, pretty fellow . . . He complains of D[ickinson], says the Committee of Safety are not the representatives of the people, and therefore not their legislators; yet they have been making laws, a whole code, for a navy. This committee was chosen by the House, but half of them are not members, and therefore not the choice of the people. All this is just. He mentions many particular instances in which Dickinson has blundered; he thinks him warped by the Quaker interest and the church interest too; thinks his reputation past the meridian, and that avarice is growing on him. Says that Henry and Mifflin both complained to him very much about him. But Rush, I think, is too much of a talker to be a deep thinker; elegant, not great.

And throughout the rest of his life, Adams attacked Dickinson every time he could, recorded every piece of news or opinion unfriendly to The

Farmer, every defeat, every crumb of gossip, made light of every victory. The thought of those unfortunate words, that boorish letter, published, celebrated, hawked about, never ceased to rankle in Adams' breast. Years later, an old man remembering, he invented historical episodes, fabricated stories, made up details that never happened, could not have happened. He launched against Dickinson an amazing series of inventions; they grew more plausible as the years passed, and no one said him nay. Even he himself came to believe them, these delusions of his guilt. Adams was safe in his fictions. He could not contain his resentments. Once, he even contrived to blame on John Dickinson the loss of Charleston, the defeat of Bunker Hill, the failure at Quebec, the death of Montgomery.

He wrote so freely of the intercepted letters, wrote of them so often, so openly, almost gaily, showed no regret for his crude wounding words, his egregious insults, that one concludes his embarrassment was deep and hard to live with, over the whole episode.

John Dickinson, for his part, never mentioned it. He went into Congress that Saturday, faced the smirks, the whispers, said nothing of his feelings. He issued no challenge, demanded no retraction. He stood just as tall, smiled just as pleasantly, not by one whit did he diminish the vigor of his opposition to the hot violent men of New England. But he made no personal allusions in debate, wrote no single word of personal attack in private letters. "The cause of liberty"—he had published the words long before—"is a cause of too much dignity to be sullied by turbulence and tumult. It ought to be maintained in a manner suitable to her nature. Those who engage in it, should breathe a sedate, yet fervent spirit, animating them to actions of prudence, justice, modesty, bravery, humanity, and magnanimity." The Farmer kept his hurt to himself. In silence.

And all his hurts, always. It was his way: his lawyer's way, his patrician way, his middle way—not from weakness, from strength; not from humility, from pride, the proud way of a proud man.

Now Adams had the gift of words. So did John Dickinson. Both wrote a vigorous prose, which we cherish today as classic in the literature of liberty. But there is a peculiar characteristic of the American Revolution, which is this: that in the critical twenty-two months from the meeting of the First Continental Congress in September, 1774, to the adoption of Independence in July, 1776, the debates and deliberations of the American colonials in rebellion took place in Philadelphia. That geographical fact means for us, so much later, that Massachusetts men, New Englanders, and Southerners, were far from home. They wrote letters back to their families and friends, letters which constitute the largest part of the record of what transpired in debate and discussion. During this period, the Pennsylvania delegates—

Dickinson, Franklin, Wilson, Mifflin, Morton, Willing, Allen, Biddle, Morris, Rhoads, Galloway, Humphreys, Ross—were living in their own homes, with their families about them, and their friends within easy reach of the conversational voice. They wrote no such letters as Adams or Jefferson wrote; they sat in their parlors and talked. Conversations around the hearthstone, alas, leave the historian no records to study, nothing to consider.

Moreover, it is a peculiarity of this period that save for William Livingston, Caesar Rodney, and Samuel Chase—and theirs were local rôles—the whole leadership of the middle-colony men fell upon these Pennsylvania delegates, who were actually Philadelphia residents—except for Speaker Morton who lived out near Chester, and George Ross who came from Lancaster. New York delegates were not leading figures, even in their own colony; New Jersey and Maryland delegates, even those personally able and passionately partisan, wrote very little that helps us understand the mid-American point of view. Perhaps it was because their distance from home was a short one; they knew they would have a week-end visit, or a quick trip at any time. Long absences, of the far delegates, produced detailed letters; and the far delegates, New England and Southern, were united frequently in one certain and particular mind. The Pennsylvania delegates, who were at home among their intimates, were, in particular details, of another mind; but this great area of dissent, this mid-colony attitude of combining conciliation and negotiation with programs of resistance, did not express itself in anywhere near as full an epistolary record as the hot violent men of New England left.

Suppose, when the First Continental Congress adjourned, it had by resolution called for the Second to meet in Charles Town, South Carolina, or in Williamsburg, or Hartford in Connecticut. Then, perhaps, we would have had explicit presentations of the middle-colony point of view. But Philadelphia once chosen proved convenient, so the men who thought otherwise were, during the critical months, domiciled in their own homes.

Another curiosity of the Revolutionary period is, of course, those narratives which Adams and Jefferson, years after the events, kept writing in one form or another. They were recollecting in tranquility all the high emotions of the period, recollecting them with uneven accuracy and puzzling mistakes. Some scholars judge these mistakes to be innocent, and indeed some of them were. When Jefferson, speaking of one debate, wrote that "the two Rutledges" participated, and it is evident from contemporary sources that only one of the Rutledge brothers was present, nothing serious is at stake. In no sense can it be imagined Jefferson was purposefully falsifying the record. Still, that absent Rutledge had *been* absent from Congress for fully seven months at the time Jefferson was talking about, and this tiny fact ought to give historians some pause as they evaluate the rest of Jefferson's document in terms of its accuracy. But other mistakes, of Jefferson as well as Adams, were by no means the innocent memory telescoping events in time. Both men were far from phlegmatic; both wrote with a sense of drama, and a dramatic sense of self. History seemed to have been on their side. They lived so long, they saw their nation great and powerful and strong beyond any dream they had ever had; thus it appeared to them that what they themselves had advocated had been right and those who opposed them wrong in anything they might have advocated at any given moment.

Historians have fashioned their accounts and opinions of the Revolution from the writings of far-from-home men, their letters in the years 1774–76, and their later recollections. It takes a certain amount of discrimination on the part of historians to realize the partisanship of youth is not always justified by mere survival to a great age; to realize also there was a whole different point of view toward the issues of 1775 which the written sources do not adequately develop. Adams was so abundant in his letters, Dickinson so spare in his; and for the hardest problems in the hottest months of controversy Adams wrote most, Dickinson the least. What historian can fashion his history out of records which are not there?

Even when the historian knows very well that Adams and Jefferson ended up political opponents, Jefferson and Dickinson ended up in political and philosophical agreement? All of our writers have relied on the spirit of Adam's partisan letters in the months before Independence, and his *Autobiography* written so long afterwards. From these, they have condemned Dickinson as over-conservative, slow to move, unaccountably and unwisely delaying. Our writers should have cast forward, to the scenes of the 1780's and 90's, when Dickinson among mid-Americans was the very epitome of humanitarian and egalitarian ideals, while Adams—he who accused The Farmer of avarice in '75 and the interest of great fortune—became in the '90's the political monolith of stability and property. When did wealth and high place have ever a more explicit political expression than both received from John Adams's wing of the Federal Party?

Now perhaps Adams was inconsistent. Was Dickinson also? Let us consider the issues of that July day in 1775, and see just what were the "whole doings" to which that "great Fortune and piddling Genius" had given "a silly Cast," and how silly that cast was. The American common reader of our times, used to having his history served up to him by writers bent on justifying today's social or political or intellectual attitudes of one sort or another, and to whom history itself is often no more than a placebo to reconcile him to the justice and rightness of what happened, is scarcely prepared for the genuine tenseness of events in the past. Our heroes, like our agreed-upon myths, have become national possessions. Readers will resist their being presented in controversial lights, or stood up for defense. But the historical investigator finds richness in his sources; they are quick with excitements; and sometimes a student with imagination and a carefree turn of mind can glimpse for an illuminated moment that the truth of history may lie, not in what was, but in what might have been. He may see, that had the mid-colony men prevailed, had the thrust toward independence been resisted until quarrels among the colonies were settled, arms secured, foreign alliances contracted, an army firmly established, the public opinion of middle America led into consonance with advanced views elsewhere—those advanced views of New England and the South led into spheres of agreement on union—then nationhood might have been achieved on a firmer basis, with a firmer constitutional league, at far less than the appalling cost of a seven years' civil war, countless lives, and unnamable human hardships.

In dealing with John Dickinson we are, after all, dealing with a man who did not oppose independence, but thought it a subsidiary issue, not the real question at stake. He did not oppose it on principle, he opposed it as policy, opposed it *when* it was done, as unwise and premature; and though Adams sneered at him as one who *pretended to be valiant,* Dickinson did actually go off to war once the resolution of independence passed over his opposition, and afterwards labored effectively in Congress and in the states to strengthen the governments, federal and state, which he helped to set up. He would not have written the Articles of Confederation, had he not approved of confederating; all he disapproved of were foolhardy and ill-advised measures, and perhaps—*perhaps,* if we look carefully at the record both men had before them in 1775 and '76—we may come to believe independence at the moment of its passage was actually that: foolhardy, ill-advised, and a costly delay of American liberty established under law.

John Dickinson was no piddling genius, and Adams knew it. He had won his great reputation single-handed, by the productions of his own pen; he had succeeded in building in Pennsylvania a party uniting many factions, that held the middle ground between Galloway, William Allen, and the loyalists on one side, and the excesses of leaders of the city's mechanics and the counties of the west on the other. For Dickinson, for all leaders of established governments in the middle colonies, the relationship between the actions of the Continental Congress and the continued control of provincial politics by moderate, stable, experienced groups in each colony, was of the utmost importance. It meant nothing less than the persistence of civil liberties, civil order, constitutional processes. The over-throw of one government should not, must not, result in the over-throw of all governments. Steps continental and local should be taken in such concord, that the erection of state governments and constitutions would be effected by the same parties of men who had led the thirteen movements of protest from the beginning. The alternative possibilities were frightening: no government at all, or governments set up by the inexperienced, unenfranchised, the unpropertied, those bent on government by passion rather than principle. Adams had seen it happen in Massachusetts, this end of councils, assemblies, executive, and courts. Chase and Paca in Maryland, Livingston in New Jersey, Dickinson in Pennsylvania, were determined to prevent it in the middle land. New York was a special case: there, dominant opinion was specifically timid. There, the provincial congress was actually drafting a plan of conciliatory measures, far more hesitant than the Pennsylvania leaders would have accepted. New York was the middle colonies' problem. An American confederation without New York had no chance of military success or of permanence, but plainly the immediate enactment of Adams' violent program would lose New York to the cause of resistance. Dickinson, closer to Duane of New York than Adams was during these summer months of '75, perceived the necessity of going no faster than a pace which would take New York along.

And South Carolina. That colony, so peculiarly special in its rice and indigo staples, so entirely different in its social structure and social attitudes from all the others, was firm in its support of Dickinson's steady program, but by now entirely at odds with the gentlemen of New England. Even Mr. Thomas Lynch, the most amiable of men, had nothing but distrust for Yankee leaders. He would warn Washington particularly of John Adams, when Adams went home for vacation: "One of our members of Congress sets out today for New-England. Whether his intents be wicked or not. I doubt much; he should be watched." Mr. Lynch had been watching Yankees, ever since the Stamp Act Congress of '65. There he had known Dickinson, too, and McKean: middle-colony men he had confidence in.

Cool, deliberate measures were necessary to bring South Carolina into harmony with all the rest. Later, after John Rutledge went home to form his state's government, Mr. Lynch would be the leading delegate of the Charles Town planters left in Philadelphia. He bent every effort to support Washington, and all commanders in the field; every time, he stumbled over the erratic behavior of New England men. When the short-term enlistments began going home, leaving Washington's camp in droves, Mr. Lynch hoped officers from other colonies, outside New England, could persuade them to re-enlist, since their own Yankee officers could not. "it woud be a Capital Point to convince the World that it is not necessary to have bad Officers of that Country in order to raise men there," he wrote Washington. "I can scarce bear their Tyranny." No Yankee could doubt Mr. Lynch's firm sentiments in the American cause. After the King hired mercenaries from Europe, sent into America the largest armed force ever sent against a subject peoples in all history, Mr. Lynch's resolution stiffened. He was among the highest, the most tireless, for resistance. But to Mr. Lynch, Boston and Massachusetts were never the foci on which resistance should fasten. Yankees heard him move, again and again, for supplies for Montgomery in Canada, even though they defeated his motion every time. With Montgomery's needs, Mr. Lynch wrote, "I as constantly attended Congress as ever Nurse did her Patient with a Bolus," till it was all too late. Yet repeated defeats of his hopes for the Canada campaign did not discourage this uncommonly determined, remarkably gracious gentleman. No Yankee would ever understand Mr. Lynch: how such easy charm, such merriness, such a façade of vast wealth, could cloak a persistence, a doggedness, a purpose entirely, absolutely inflexible. Mr. Lynch was so oddly cheerful. He assured Washington, "the destruction of the Parliamentary Army in America will certainly produce Peace . . . the seizing of Quebec will produce the same Effect. I have no doubt America stands now indebted to her General for the One and will before the Return of Spring for the other. . . . Do not bate them an Ace, my Dear General, but depend on every Support of your Friends here. . . ." Mr. Lynch's revolution was a genuine one, but it was not John Adams' revolution.

Adams had no quarrel with Dickinson by the end of the First Congress, October, 1774. During that subsequent winter of 74–75 events moved so rapidly that the Continental Association, the rudimentary league which the First Congress established, was already by May not only inadequate to the necessities of the spring but actually a hindrance, for with the war in actual prosecution after Lexington and Concord the need for importations of supplies, banned by the Association, was imperative; and in July the Association had to be relaxed. At once on its first assembling in May, 1775, the Second Continental Congress began taking the place of the Association, and going far beyond it began to do some of those things which a *government* does— run a military force, acquire and arm ships, raise money, correspond with foreign governments, administer a post office, do all manner of things which a people at war must have done for them by a governing authority of some kind.

In these activities, no delegate was more vigorous, nor more effective, than John Dickinson. He served on as many committees as Adams, he debated as often, he worked with as constant attention to the demands of the summer.

And Dickinson, receiving personal letters from numerous foreign correspondents, was continually alert to the possibilities of a change in British policy, to the friendship of British Whigs and mercantile groups, to the chance of an adjustment of the difficulties within the empire. Adams was already far advanced toward independence in his thinking. Dickinson was by no means startled by the word or thought of independence, but he was exploring for other solutions, anticipating every difficulty ahead, searching particularly for the solutions of peace, not of war. What after all was the purpose of the war? Was it not to defend the colonists against the military establishments barracked amongst them, against the exactions of the ministry and the penal measures levied against Massachusetts and Boston, against the claim of parliamentary supremacy; ultimately to secure a restoration of the harmonious relations that had so long and so fruitfully existed under orderly constitutional government?

Independence was no new idea. It was as old certainly as 1765 in discussion. "The word REBELLION hath frozen them up like Fish in a pond"—these words from Shakespeare Dickinson had placed on the title page of a pamphlet as long ago as the spring of 1766, his vigorous *Address to Barbados*. Then and since he had warned that British policies might drive the Americans out of the empire. But neither was independence a particularly appealing idea, if it meant a nationhood without commercial or political identity, and without a constitutional structure of law-limited power, guaranteeing liberty.

As we follow Adams's letters about Dickinson during the summer of '75, and his recollections in his *Autobiography* written so much later, we find the picture he gives of Dickinson the picture of a man of impossible obtuseness and political innocence. Such is not the truth about John Dickinson, and Adams in his less partisan moods certainly knew that, too. But Adams in his less partisan moods rarely wrote letters. Dickinson was partisan also. The Pennsylvania Farmer, long a sophisticate in political assemblies and legislatures, had many more weapons in debate than amiable courtliness. He made undoubted enemies. Eliphalet Dyer of Connecticut, exercised about Connecticut's Wyoming Valley land claims in Pennsylvania, at the same time Adams was calling Dickinson a piddling genius, declared "Mr. Dickinson the Pennsylvania farmer as he is Called in his Writings is lately most bitter against us and Indeavours to make every ill Impression upon the Congress against us but I may say he is not very highly Esteemed in Congress. He has taken a part very different from what I believe was expected from the Country in general or from his Constituents." He was, though Dyer did not know it, driven almost to the wall by the uncertainty of his success in the Pennsylvania Assembly and provincial developments at the moment, and would have been overthrown completely, had he lost in Congress to the New Englanders in the last of July. Adams cared as little about Pennsylvania's politics as he cared passionately about Massachusetts's. He was perfectly willing that the party equivalent to his own in Massachusetts should lose in Pennsylvania, if he could win in the Congress.

Now a careful reading of Adams's writings during this summer of '75 will reveal his frequent use of such words as Peace, Negotiation, and Reconciliation. Similarly, a careful reading of Dickinson's writings provides us with plenty of strong phrases of resistance, unyielding opposition, and relentless defense against ministerial measures. What then was the real differences between the two leaders?

The difference, indeed, existed. But it was not the difference between strength and weakness, rashness and timidity, boldness and caution. The record is plain: there is no more talk of reconciliation in Dickinson's writings that summer, than in Adams's or Jefferson's. There is as much talk of sturdy resistance in his, as in theirs. But Dickinson had the delicate problem of a massive, articulate urban public opinion in Philadelphia to sway behind him, he had a care for the New York situation, and he was entirely committed to those policies which would bring about a union of the colonies— all the colonies. It may be just to say that Adams, in the summer of 1775, profoundly affected by warfare and bloodshed in his own Boston, by the sufferings of Massachusetts—that "bitter cup" which the middle colonies had not yet tasted—came to Philadelphia predisposed against anyone not equally involved, anyone who would not address the issues of that urgent day in his own particular vocabulary, and share his own impulses toward the strongest measures; while Dickinson, affected deeply by the collapse of constitutional government and the threat of anarchy in the middle colonies, was prepared to resist any measures which would alienate the effective majority of expressive opinion in the trading centers of the Hudson and the Delaware, which would exclude South Carolina, and which would overthrow orderly local government.

But what measures could these have been, on which John Yankee and John Farmer disagreed, and so sharply? The episode which sparked Adams to anger in his bitter intercepted letters was certainly not, as historians now invariably say it was, the Second Petition to the King. Even Adams did not say it was—until many, many years later, when he had forgotten the details of what happened, and was enmeshed in the web of his own inventions. The angry "great Fortune and piddling Genius" letter was written on July 24. The Second Petition to the King had been adopted fully twenty days earlier, July 5, and signed by all the delegates July 8; by Monday, July 24, it had long since ceased to be an issue before Congress.

As nearly as can be told from the imperfect records of journals and private letters that summer, the debate that actually caused Adams's excessive wrath to erupt against Dickinson may probably have been on the question of opening American ports to the trade of all nations. It was an important issue, a much more immediately significant one than the Petition to the King; it involved the matter of securing foreign aid and loans, as well as arms and supplies; and curiously, it was an issue on which Philadelphia merchants and Boston merchants might well have been in complete agreement. They were not.

The issue had been debated hotly for a whole month. It was the most controversial of all issues that summer; it involved the success or failure of merchant houses; it affected all the disagreements over appointments to the

army, over procurements, over missions to the Indians; it even related to
the Connecticut settlers being sent with arms to populate the frontiers of
Pennsylvania on supposed Connecticut land grants. Delegates on every issue
this month were in bad temper. "The Congress have now sat, without a
day's respite, since the 10th of May, and consequently are much fatigued,"
Silas Deane wrote, on July 21. On Sunday the 23rd Benjamin Harrison of
Virginia told Washington (in a letter which was also intercepted and published by General Gage) that he expected the breakup of Congress in a
week: "indeed I think it is high time there was an End of it. we have been
too long together." Talk of adjournment was constant; delegates were speculating on where they should reassemble in September, perhaps Hartford,
closer to the theatre of war. It was a poor time to debate any serious point,
let alone one so vital as opening the ports to the trade of France and Spain
and Holland.

Dickinson was decidedly against the move to open trade now. He won,
on July 22. "We have had in Contemplation a Resolution," John Adams
wrote snappishly on July 23, "to invite all Nations to bring their Com-
modities to market here, and like Fools have lost it for the present." Just
how foolish the decision was, no one now can say. Relaxing the Association
had already helped the well-established merchant houses; opening the ports
would have been a boon to such New England merchants as had been accustomed to trading outside the British code of regulations, but would have
hurt Philadelphia merchants in regular and legal trade by providing opportunities for innumerable speculators and ship captains to compete with
them, in an open market. Prices were already going up, war-inflation had
commenced, merchants who had been hurt by the Association were beginning to recover some losses. Dickinson knew he could not win them, in
New York and Philadelphia and Maryland, to the program of supporting
armed resistance and seeking negotiation from a strong position, unless he
consulted their economic well-being. Opening the ports would probably
destroy them, at least some of them. Adams evidently approached the debate
enthusiastically, but unprepared. He acknowledged the whole three months'
Congress had been difficult: "It is a vast and complicated System of Business
which We have gone through, and We were all of us inexperienced in it.
Many Things may be wrong, but no small Proportion of these are to be
attributed to the Want of Concert and Union among the Mass. Delegates."
On opening the ports, he wrote his friend Warren innocently, "This is a
great Idea. What shall we do? Shall we invite all Nations to come with
their Luxuries, as well as Conveniences and Necessaries? or shall We think
of confining our Trade with them to our own Bottoms, which alone can lay
a Foundation for great Wealth and naval Power? Pray think of it."

Dickinson evidently had thought of it, and approached it with firmness.
That firmness was enough for Adams.

Now so far as the records tell, this was the only point on which John Adams was actually defeated that whole summer, and it was not a defeat which he made much of, at the time. His only other *contemporary* remark was the (for him) mild one, "like fools we have lost it." Even his angry intercepted letter represented opening the ports as but one link in a chain of the most radical measures, many of which he himself would not seriously have advocated in Congress; yet in his subsequent writings he would elevate the single setback in what he did advocate to the level of a major disaster, as if he had suffered defeat in everything.

On the Second Petition to the King, the Olive Branch Petition, Adams had actually not felt nearly so strongly as our writers have represented him to feel—and indeed as our writers themselves seem to feel. In his intercepted letter, he did not speak bitterly of the Petition, he only said it should have followed his chain of advanced measures—that chain which was more the heated passion of the moment than a serious proposal of policy. Of course, he could have marshalled reasons for opposing this Olive Branch Petition: he could have argued that such a petition by Congress, at the very time the delegates had appointed a Continental General, formed a Continental Army, and were seeking to animate the soldiers already in the field, would be regarded as evidence of Congressional weakness, timidity, and insincerity. How could men fight for a Congress which would urge them against an enemy with one voice, and with another at the same time petition the King, that enemy, to receive them back in amity? Adams *could* have said these things—but he did not. There is no *contemporary* record that he opposed the Petition at all.

Dickinson, of course, had equally good reasons for insisting on the Petition for Redress of Grievances—it was in point of fact that, rather than a petition to receive the colonies back in amity. Most important of all, the King was not the enemy; Parliament and ministry were the enemies. This was the whole point of the Congress program Dickinson (with Adams's entire support) had developed—the significant assertion of established constitutional rights under the Crown, which Parliament had violated. Further, Dickinson knew that leading men of influence and probity in Pennsylvania, Maryland, and New York, men who had been taking over each government and must lead in the vacancy of public affairs which would follow the end of the Assemblies, would support the Congress in measures of resistance, only if they saw spread before them a desirable end, an end consistent with their beliefs, their convictions, and their determination to right the ills which were wrong. Both men, Adams and Dickinson alike, certainly wished to keep the door open for negotiation, though Adams dreaded that negotiation and thought Americans would lose in it; both men certainly wished to prosecute armed resistance to the fullest limit of American strength. The Petition passed, and Adams, while he had no enthusiasm for it, was not by any contemporary evidence exercised against it when he signed his name—not so exercised as he became later.

For in his *Autobiography* many years afterwards, Adams gave an utterly different account of the Olive Branch Petition, and his feeling about it. "This measure of imbecility," he called it. His narrative is strange, too strange for us charitably to attribute it to the fuzzy memory of an old man in retirement. His own diary was before him; and his memory in other respects was excellent. Adams in his *Autobiography* launched into an attack, embittered, specific, and curious, on John Dickinson. He invented, he imagined, he created with a novelist's zeal; and what he created was a romance. He wrote that Pennsylvania's leaders on first seeing independence approaching suddenly started back, and retreated—which was not true, as the progress of Dickinson and Thomson in Pennsylvania plainly showed. And then Adams described what he remembered as his effect on the delegates in the Congress of '75: "In some of my public harrangues, in which I had freely and explicitly laid open my thoughts," he said, "on looking round the assembly I have seen horror, terror, and detestation, strongly marked on the countenances of some of the members, whose names I could readily recollect; but as some of them have been good citizens since, and others went over afterwards to the English, I think it unnecessary to record them here." Such a description of the faces of the hard-working, patient men of the Second Continental Congress may have appealed to Adams long years later as what he would *like* to have seen, but there is actually no possibility of finding in the records of that body either a debate, or any occasion for a debate, at which the well-known views of the busy and vocal Yankee could have occasioned in any delegate either horror, or terror, or detestation. Nor were the forty-eight or forty-nine men then daily attending Congress in the habit of bothering themselves with such melodramatic registration of the manly and unmanly emotions. It was ridiculous of Adams to say so. Just as ridiculous was his implication that no one who disagreed with him could have been a good citizen, but that subsequent good citizenship in later life excused such a contrary person from censure for his earlier behavior.

His next sentence is even more surprising. "There is one gentleman, however," he wrote, "whom I must mention, in self defence: I mean John Dickinson, then of Philadelphia, now of Delaware." Now Dickinson had never attacked Adams; on the contrary, it was Adams who had attacked Dickinson, was attacking him now, would continue to attack him long after "The Farmer's" death. And why, "in self defence" it was necessary for him to single out Dickinson, among all those others whose names he "could readily recollect" but did not, is a question which can be answered only by speculating on the undoubtedly bitter memories Adams carried with him always, of his boorishness in the summer of '75.

He then proceeded to aver that Dickinson at first had agreed with him that the balance of opinion in Congress lay with the delegates of South Carolina (*though it never had*), and those delegates were thereupon wooed by all hands, particularly by Pennsylvania Quakers and proprietaries (*which they were not. If anything, the wooing was on the other side*). He conjured up an alliance (*which never existed*) between Dickinson and the Rutledges (*the elder of whom Dickinson true enough knew well and quite liked*) and Arthur Middleton (*who was not even a delegate in Congress till eleven months later*). He said that this alliance made no attempt to enlist Christopher Gadsden because they despaired of winning him (*which was nonsense; for all his high talk and shifting views, Mr. Gadsden was certainly going to follow Lynch's and John Rutledge's lead. If he didn't, the other Carolinians wouldn't care. They had little patience with Gadsden's fustian, and his trimming. Mr. Lynch was entirely open about that. One day he would write, to a New Yorker, "Business now goes on Swimmingly, for Why? my Colleague Gadsden is gone home, to Command our Troops, God save them"*). This Dickinson–Rutledge–Middleton alliance, Adams went on, began "to waver and clamor about independence." And he concocted a pretty drama: "I became the dread and terror and abhorrence of the party. But all this I held in great contempt." Arthur Middleton (*that delegate who was yet to be elected and would not attend for many months*) was the villain of his drama, "the hero of Quaker and proprietary politics in Congress." The absent Middleton, he declared, repeatedly attacked him in debate: "I made it a rule to return him a Roland for every Oliver, so that he never got, and I never lost, any thing from these rencounters."

Now all this was fiction, but still it was not enough for Adams. He stated, and he said Charles Thomson told him it was so, "that the Quakers had intimidated Mr. Dickinson's mother and his wife, who were continually distressing him with their remonstrances." In a peculiarly ugly sentence, ugly even amid the vitriol of Adams' *Autobiography,* he described the two Dickinson ladies as bewailing the fate awaiting them and their families if Dickinson persisted in revolutionary measures. Adams wrote:

> His mother said to him, "Johnny, you will be hanged; your estate will be forfeited and confiscated; you will leave your excellent wife a widow, and your charming children orphans, beggars, and infamous." From my soul I pitied Mr. Dickinson. I made his case my own. If my mother and my wife had expressed such sentiments to me, I was certain that if they did not wholly unman me and make me an apostate, They would make me the most miserable man alive . . . I was happy . . . I always enjoyed perfect peace at home.

Now only the slightest acquaintance with the histories and characters of Mary Cadwalader Dickinson, John Dickinson's mother, and Mary Norris Dickinson, his wife, is necessary to perceive this picture is entirely untrue— as untrue as it was churlish and malicious.

In the first place the two Marys, mother and daughter-in-law, never at any time lived in the same household; and while friendly enough, they were not on such intimate terms with each other as Adams's words suggest. The two ladies were of different Meetings; they moved in entirely different social circles of Friends; both their circles were tight little groups of intimates that did not open up to include newcomers. Mrs. Dickinson (now past seventy-five) had never had much enthusiasm for John's marriage five years ago (at thirty-eight) into the Norris-Logan clan. In the second place, though Mrs. Dickinson paid occasional visits to Philadelphia, she was actually making her home these days at "Belleville," near Trenton, in New Jersey, with her younger son Philemon and his wife. That wife was another Mary, Mrs. Dickinson's own favorite niece. And that son Philemon, charming but perennially unsuccessful, was far hotter in radical political sentiments than John Dickinson, and far more removed from the Friendly persuasion. He was already among the most advanced people of New Jersey's resistance; he was second-ranking officer of the new-formed militia, firmly determined upon a military career. If Mrs. Dickinson had actually been distressed at John's high opinions, she would have been appalled at Colonel (soon to be General) Philemon Dickinson's martial aspect. She was neither.

Long ago—this is the third point—Mrs. Dickinson had ceased trying to bring her sons to Meeting, or Meeting to them. Their father, her late husband Judge Dickinson, had quit the Friends thirty-four years ago, from pain and disgust at their treatment of him down in Maryland. He had never gone back into fellowship, even though he was not disowned, and even though Mrs. Dickinson (his second wife) remained always a devout and pious Friend. The two sons, from childhood, followed their father in separation. In that family, a truce had many years ago been struck, regarding Mother's place among Friends. Mrs. Dickinson would never have bothered to try to influence John with the Meeting's opinion; if she had, John would scarcely have listened.

In the fourth place, what Quakers could it have been who so "intimidated" John Dickinson's mother and wife? Mrs. Dickinson's Cadwalader and Meredith relatives in the Arch Street Meeting were heartily supporting the American cause, short of war; her nephew Lambert Cadwalader went even further—he was actually a colonel of militia, just as John and Philemon Dickinson were. Many Quakers of Philadelphia, Jersey, and Delaware too were high in resistance measures. Mrs. Dickinson was not part of Friend Israel Pemberton's "principled" group of pacifists in Philadelphia, any more than she was involved with Samuel Wetherill's schismatic group, willing to fight, that was forming. Trenton and Burlington Friends were similarly divided amongst themselves, but Mrs. Dickinson, full of years and full of a sensible lady's weariness of the strifes forever agitating Meeting, merely looked on. Every Quaker who might have spoken to her opposing vigorous measures, was matched by another who would have embraced them entirely, in manner as energetic as John's, as high as Philemon's, as gallant and prideful as Lambert's.

Adams, of course, never really understood the Quakers' place in Philadelphia political life, nor bothered to try. He might have, had his motives been less mixed. He knew Thomas Mifflin, and his attitudes; he knew the egregious Timothy Matlack; he knew old Governor Hopkins of Rhode Island, a Quaker; he knew Joseph Hewes, the pious former Friend from North Carolina. But since his first week in Philadelphia, when Friend Pemberton had scolded him for Massachusetts' religious intolerance, Adams had detested Quakers, and damned everything of which he disapproved in Pennsylvania policies with the adjectives "Quaker" and "Proprietary." (One almost wonders if he was actually unaware that John, Thomas, and Richard Penn were Church of England. But then the Church of England was pretty much a mystery to Adams, too.)

One thing he did certainly know, and it casts the hardest light on his offensive words to realize he knew it, was that the senior Mrs. Dickinson was living at Trenton, not with John here in town. He would know it next spring, too, when Mrs. Dickinson died quietly at Belleville, March 22, 1776, in her seventy-seventh year, an event which took "The Farmer" briefly from Congress.

What of the junior Mary, John Dickinson's wife? Well, in the fifth place, this Mary was closeted in illness and mourning during the months Adams was writing about. She was frail always, especially so following childbirth. On May 5, 1775, her baby daughter died, after a precarious twelve months of life. Mary took to her bed; John clad himself in black. They had only one other child, a girl Sally, aged three and a half. This is the juncture of the family history at which Adams would have us believe Mrs. Dickinson wailed, "Johnny, you will leave your excellent wife a widow, and your charming children orphans . . . "

Sixth, what Quakers could have intimidated Mary Norris Dickinson? All her Logan uncles were gone; her only sister had died before her marriage; her cousin Charles Norris was active in resistance, his mother her "Aunt Norris" was a spirited lady of Dickinson's own vigorous opinions. At Fairhill Meeting her cousins and connections heartily supported her "dear johnny Dickinson" in politics; indeed he held his seat in the Pennsylvania Assembly as their representative, from the Northern Liberties. Throughout her life, no one ever dared try to intimidate Mary Norris of Fairhill. She was the leader in her circle, not a follower; she spoke French and read Latin; she loved art and music and conversation, cared little for politics, loved piety and poetry and sweet intellectual fun. She detested Dr. Franklin, which was fashionable to do in her circle of the great Welsh families. And she had all the vast Norris wealth. Friends at Fairhill listened to Mary Dickinson, accepted her guidance, they did not tell her what to think. And certainly she did not tell her "dear johnny."

Finally, in the seventh place, it is unimaginable that Charles Thomson told Adams this fantasy. Thomson was not the sort of man who made things up; he was the sort of man who translated the Bible out of Greek. He was one of Dickinson's oldest and closest friends, his entire supporter up to May of '76. Right now in '75 he was Dickinson's political lieutenant. He had no fortune of his own. His first wife had died; he was an eligible, well-respected man, not so old and not so plain and quite prepared to marry again, when he began frequently to visit the Dickinsons at Fairhill. For there he had met Mary Norris Dickinson's cousin and cherished intimate, Hannah Harrison, who possessed a Norris estate of moderate size which Dickinson was administering. (That estate seemed princely to the wondering Adams: Hannah Harrison, he said, was "a relation of Mr. Dickinson's, with five thousand pounds sterling.") Last year, 1774, Thomson had married Hannah; they set up housekeeping as tenants at "Somerville," one of Mary Dickinson's several entailed Norris plantations in the Northern Liberties. Charles had married her on Thursday; the next Monday he rode into town to pay bridegroomly respects to his wife's Aunt Norris in her great mansion across Fifth Street from the State House. He was just tying up his horse when a man ran up to him, bade him come at once to The Carpenters' Hall where he was wanted on urgent business. Thomson went, to discover he had been elected secretary of the newly assembled Continental Congress—the position he would hold for the next fourteen and a half years. He would hold it with honor, and efficiency, and remarkable fidelity. Through all those years he would never be known to commit an indiscretion, reveal a single secret, nor lose so much as a scrap of paper. Only once did he take a vacation.

All the rest of his long life, Charles Thomson would live in Norris-Logan great homes, usually with Dickinson his landlord, administrator of his wife Hannah's moneys, and his devoted friend. After Dickinson died, Thomson would fall into a sad penury, receive gifts from Hannah's fond connections.

Thomson knew well both the Mary Dickinsons. And from the purity of his nature, his integrity, his affectionate character, it is impossible to believe that he spoke in this fashion of John, or Mary, or Mrs. Dickinson. Thomson knew, better than anyone else, that The Farmer was the one who "always enjoyed perfect peace at home."

When Adams wrote that egregious passage, he was either imperfectly recollecting vulgar gossip, or he was improvising. Both were unworthy of him.

And so was it unworthy, when he proceeded to unite the Quakers (with whom Dickinson was not in fellowship) with the Proprietary and the South Carolina delegates as a faction behind The Farmer, bent on vilifying him (Adams) and discrediting him in Congress. Solemnly, he wrote: "The party made me as unpopular as they could, among all their connections, but I regarded none of those things. I knew and lamented that many of these gentlemen, of great property, high in office and of good accomplishments, were laying the foundation, not of any injury to me, but of their own ruin; and it was not in my power to prevent it."

The entire passage is regrettable. John Adams does himself less than justice in the character of a self-righteous, condescending prig; and it is sad to see him fabricating legends. Nor was he actually defending himself against any attack, by anybody. He was simply attacking Dickinson, in a piece of private writing to which Dickinson would never have an opportunity to reply.

He proceeded in his *Autobiography* to give his highly imaginary version of the introduction of the Second Petition to the King: how Dickinson procured it, arranged to have long speeches given in its support, how Adams spoke opposing it, and was followed by John Sullivan of New Hampshire in opposition also.

Now Sullivan may indeed have spoken against the Second Petition, when it was first proposed and a committee was appointed to draft it. He was in Congress that day, June 3. But he could not possibly have spoken when the committee reported, and the final draft of the Second Petition was passed and signed, because on June 22 he was chosen to be Brigadier General. The last day could have been in Congress was the session day of Monday, June 26, for on Tuesday June 27 he left to follow Washington up to Cambridge— a week before the Second Petition was considered and adopted, a whole month before the intercepted letters.

Adams described Sullivan as speaking "in a strain of wit, reasoning, and fluency, which, although he was always fluent, exceeded everything I had heard from him before." It was the only time John Sullivan was ever described so, for as a speaker he was more notable for heat than reasoning, for Irish anger than Irish wit. But Adams declared, "I was much delighted, and Mr. Dickinson, very much terrified at what he said, began to tremble for his cause. At this moment I was called out to the State House yard, very much to my regret, to some one who had business with me. Mr. Dickinson observed me, and darted out after me. He broke out upon me in a most abrupt and extraordinary manner; in as violent a passion as he was capable of feeling, and with an air, countenance, and gestures, as rough and haughty, as if I had been a school-boy and he the master. He vociferated, 'What is the reason, Mr. Adams, that you New-Englandmen oppose our measures of reconciliation? There now is Sullivan, in a long harrangue, following you in a determined opposition to our petition to the King. Look ye! If you don't concur with us in our pacific system, I and a number of us will break off from you in New England, and we will carry on the opposition by ourselves in our own way.' I own I was shocked with this magisterial salutation. I knew of no pretentions Mr. Dickinson had to dictate to me, more than I had to catechize him. I was, however, as it happened, at that moment, in a very happy temper, and I answered him very coolly. 'Mr. Dickinson, there are many things that I can very cheerfully sacrifice to harmony, and even to unanimity; but I am not to be threatened into an express adoption or approbation of measures which my judgment reprobates. Congress must judge, and if they pronounce against me, I must submit, as, if they determine against you, you ought to acquiesce.' These were the last words which ever passed between Mr. Dickinson and me in private . . ."

Such is Adams's narrative of the Second Petition in his *Autobiography*. Admittedly a reconstruction from memory some thirty years after the event, careful historians sometimes acknowledge that it is not to be taken too seriously. But they then proceed to take it seriously, quote it, adopt its tone and general spirit. Even the two latest serious studies of Adams have followed it, as if it were reliable. Yet in the light of other sources, his narrative cannot be accepted, in any of its terms, as true in any of its aspects. "The more I reflected on Mr. Dickinson's rude lecture in the State House Yard, the more I was vexed with it," Adams wrote late in life; "and the determination of Congress in favor of the petition did not allay the irritation."

And then, he states, he wrote the letters which Benjamin Hichborn carried. "Irritated with the impoliteness of Mr. Dickinson, and mortified with his success in Congress," he scratched off in haste his "great Fortune and piddling Genius" words.

Now let us look at the record. That angry conversation in the Yard had to occur before July 5, when the Petition was adopted. If Sullivan were truly speaking, it had to occur June 3 or before, when the Petition was first proposed. If we believe Adams, we must believe he sustained his irritation during daily debates on other subjects, and daily intercourse with Dickinson, at the least for twenty days—from July 5 to July 24; at the most, for fifty-four days—from June 3 to July 24. Either is an impossible assumption. And three other considerations vitiate his narrative: first, Adams wrote as if he had suffered defeat over the issue of the Second Petition, whereas as a matter of fact he did not. The Petition to the King did actually carry, and actually Adams was not, by any evidence, distressed that it did. It seems hard to believe he would have, and certainly Sullivan could not have, spoken opposing the Petition *after* it was written and reported from committee; at most he would have been debating a detail, which would scarcely have caused Dickinson to tremble in terror.

And about that terror: in a debate early in June, Sullivan might perhaps have moved Dickinson to vigorous opposition, even anger, for the Irish

Sullivan was frequently "warm," and The Farmer frequently impatient. But what could have "terrified" him? Dickinson was no trembler. And certainly anyone as used as he to Assembly and Congress debates would never be intimidated by an expected speech, in expected opposition, from an unprepossessing delegate, of a not-too-significant colony. Indeed, there is only Adams's word for it that Sullivan *was* in opposition. Two letters from Sullivan and Langdon exist before Sullivan's departure June 27; both mention the necessity of secrecy; one says "all the Colonies are firmly united and are preparing for the worst"; the other (June 20, *after* whatever speech Sullivan would have given against the Petition) says: "It is impossible to conceive of a greater unanimity in the Colonies, than that which at present subsists, one and all being Determined to defend our Rights to the last." Sullivan and Langdon, it is sometimes pointed out, were political foes in New Hampshire, but this was not until several years later; all that separated them in sentiment now was the difference in their stations, for the wealthy Langdon and the struggling Sullivan came from the opposite extremes of New Hampshire's social structure. Yet in the Second Congress they seem to have acted in concert, and the attractive Mr. Langdon, in one of his thoughtful, modest letters, regretted the necessity of Sullivan's departure.

Second, many parts of Adams's narrative are uncharacteristic: Sullivan's wit as a speaker, which I regret to say about so estimable a personage as General Sullivan was unfortunately not one of his admittedly abundant gifts; Dickinson's peremptory manner, which certainly does not square with every other contemporary account of The Pennsylvania Farmer. Dickinson's "violent passion," rough, haughty speech and gestures, are no more believable than his "trembling" in terror for his cause—for Dickinson certainly knew when debate began how many of the twelve Congressional votes would be cast for the Petition.

Third, while it is altogether possible that some conversation of some kind of adversary content did actually take place at some time between the two men in the State House Yard, regarding the Second Petition, I cannot believe it took place when Adams said it did, at the time of the intercepted letters, nor can I believe it was the conversation Adams records. I cannot believe it, because this is what Adams wrote, to his most intimate male correspondent, on July 6, 1775, the day following the adoption of the Second Petition to the King, under the heading "SECRET AND CONFIDENTIAL, AS THE SAYING IS." You will notice, if you attend to it carefully, that he speaks regretfully, but not in anger, of the ideas of the middle-colony men; and ruefully but in *favor* of the Olive Branch Petition:

Secret and Confidential, as the Saying is.
    The Congress is not yet so much alarmed as it ought to be. There are still hopes, that Ministry and Parliament, will immediately receed as soon as they hear of the Battle of Lexington, the Spirit of New York and

Phyladelphia, the Permanency of the Union of the Colonies etc.: I think they are much deceived and that we shall have nothing but Deceit and Hostility, Fire, Famine, Pestilence and Sword from Administration and Parliament. Yet the Colonies like all Bodies of Men must and will have their Way and their Humour, and even their Whims.

These opinions of Some Colonies which are founded I think in their Wishes and passions, their Hopes and Fears, rather than in Reason and Evidence will give a whimsical Cast to the Proceedings of this Congress. You will see a strange oscillation between love and hatred, between War and Peace—Preparations for War and Negociations for Peace. We must have a Petition to the King and a delicate Proposal of Negociation, etc. This Negociation I dread like Death: But it must be proposed. We cant avoid it. Discord and total Disunion would be the certain Effect of a resolute Refusal to petition and negociate. My Hopes are that Ministry will be afraid of Negociation as well as We and therefore refuse it. If they agree to it, We shall have Occasion for all our Wit Vigilance and Virtue to avoid being deceived, wheedled threatened or bribed out of our Freedom. If we Strenuously insist upon our Liberties, as I hope and am pretty sure We shall however, a Negotiation, if agreed to, will terminate Nothing, it will effect nothing. We may possibly gain Time and Powder and Arms.

You will see an Address to the People of G. Britain, another to those of Ireland, and another to Jamaica.

You will also see a Spirited Manifesto. We ought immediately to dissolve all Ministerial Tyrannies, and Custom houses, set up Governments of our own, like that of Connecticutt in all the Colonies, confederate together like an indissoluble Band for mutual defence, and open our Ports to all Nations immediately. This is the system that your Friend has arrived at promoting from first to last: But the Colonies are not yet ripe for it—a Bill of Attainder, etc., may soon ripen them.

This was Adams's "secret and confidential" opinion, at the time of its adoption—of that often maligned, scorned, scoffed-at Olive Branch Petition, which both Jefferson and Adams in their old age declared to be a testimony of Dickinson's conservatism and timidity. *"We cant avoid it. Discord and a total Disunion would be the certain Effect of a resolute Refusal to petition and negociate."** Now it is not to be thought that Dickinson, whose British correspondence was extensive and whose opportunities for knowing the opinions of government and anti-ministerial men in Parliament were more

---

* And Abigail Adams, at the time of the Petition to the King, recorded no opposition nor objection to it. She wrote to John on July 25, "Your address meets with general approbation here, your petitioning the King again pleases (forgive me if I say the timid and weak) those persons who were esteemed the Luke Warm, and who think that no Works of Supereragation can be performed to Great Brittain—whilst others say you heap coals of fire upon the Heads of your Enemies. You know you are considered here as the most perfect body—if one Member is by any means rendered incapable of acting tis supposed the difficency will be made up. . . ." (Butterfield, L. H., ed., *Adams Family Correspondence*, I, 263)

abundant than most Americans, can have had any illusions about the possibilities of restoration, negotiation, and harmony. At the age of forty-three,
after twelve years' vigorous and effective public life in opposition to ministerial measures, he was certainly not more näive than the younger statesman
Adams, at thirty-nine, the much younger new delegate Jefferson, at thirty-
two. Dickinson was worldly, realistic, well-informed; he was used to public
affairs. He did things on purpose.

He had written the Second Petition to the King. He composed it carefully,
and while most people who talk or write of it fail to read it, it is actually
true that he used in this Olive Branch Petition stronger language, more precise terms of attack on the cabinet ministers, than had hitherto been employed in Congressional papers. He spoke plainly to the King of his cabinet
ministers as "those artful and cruel enemies, who abuse your royal confidence
and authority, for the purpose of effecting our destruction." He did not
hesitate to address the sovereign in words accusing and bitter:

> We shall decline the ungrateful task of describing the irksome variety
> of artifices, practised by many of your majesty's ministers, the delusive
> pretences, fruitless terrors, and unavailing severities that have from time
> to time been dealt out by them, in their attempt to execute this impolitic
> plan, or of tracing thro' a series of years past, the progress of the unhappy
> differences between *Great Britain* and these colonies, that have flowed from
> this fatal source. . . .

That "candid mind" of whom the eighteenth-century writer was so fond of
talking might well consider that if this was an Olive Branch, it sprouted
several thorns.

Of course, as every one on both sides of the Atlantic fully understood, the
Second Petition, though addressed to the King in form, was less an actual
petition than a propaganda address to British and American people. Its
function was to stress for British and Americans both, that it was Parliament
the Americans were opposing, not the Crown. Its fate, as a legal process of
approach to the throne, was of less significance than its usefulness in
strengthening the hands of Whigs in England and its effect in encouraging
union among Whigs in the colonies. And far from being a weak document
of mild councils, it was—when lawyers and merchants and thoughtful mid-
colony men in New York, Albany, Trenton, Elizabeth Town, Philadelphia,
New Castle, Wilmington, Baltimore, Annapolis perused it, when opposition
leaders in London still striving for reconciliation studied it, when the
brothers Howe preparing for their peace conference examined it—a vocif-
erating protest, well calculated to assure the public opinion of the world
that America was firmly determined to resist parliamentary usurpations.

John Dickinson knew England, and English politics. He certainly knew that a petition couched in such language as this could never be accepted by the ministry it attacked, and he surely knew the King was not about to change his ministers. His Second Petition was not addressed to these phantom possibilities. Rather, it was addressed to the mind of middle-America, in words designed to persuade the governing classes that their situation, dominated by the punitive measures of the present ministry, admitted of no other policy than the system articulated by Congress, of armed resistance coupled with specific proposals of reconciliation.

Nor did Dickinson ever regard his Olive Branch Petition as a weak or conciliatory measure. Such strong language was aggressive, threatening, froward, not pacific. He regarded the Petition as a constitutional measure, and a sound measure of political persuasion. He staked something on it, but not much—certainly not the passion and trembling apprehension Adams fancifully described. It was part of a program, but by no means a whole program. Actually, he regarded it almost precisely as did Adams.

For on the second day following its passage he, too, wrote a letter—not to an intimate correspondent, but to a frequent correspondent he had learned to handle with care, for the best effect of the letters he sent him. Arthur Lee was in some ways an unreliable man; Dickinson knew that. He was one of those strange people who could never seem to settle down. He earned a perfectly good medical degree, from Edinborough, but he deserted medicine, went to the Inns of Court, studied law, became a London barrister. Now he was aiding and abetting his brother William, as that particular Lee of Virginia got himself elected first a sheriff of London, then an alderman. But Arthur Lee for all his restlessness was useful, and busy with the Whig friends of America at Whitehall. To him, Dickinson wrote in terms so precisely like Adams's that we may well be surprised that the two men, who would be in the posture of embittered opponents July 24, could be so exactly similar in view July 7:

Dear Sir,
Before this comes to hand, you will have received, I presume, the Petition to the King. You will perhaps at first be surpriz'd, that we make no *Claim,* and mention no *Right.* But I hope, [on] considering all Circumstances, you will be [of] opinion, that this Humility in an address [to] the Throne is at present proper.

Our Rights [have] been already stated—our Claims made—W[ar] is actually begun, and we are carrying it on Vigorously. This conduct and our other Publications will shew, [that our] spirits are not lowered. If Administration [be] desirous of stopping the Effusion of British [blood], the Opportunity is now offered to them [by an] unexceptionable Petition, praying for accommodation. If they reject this appl[ication] with Contempt, the more humble it is, [the more] such Treatment will confirm the Minds of [our] Countrymen, to endure all the Misfortunes [that] may attend the Contest.

It is always said that Adams and Jefferson signed the Olive Branch Petition reluctantly. They said so themselves, many years afterwards. And probably it is true, that they signed it with no expectation that the King would ever receive it, or treat it with anything other than the contempt with which he had treated the First Congress' petition. Plainly, Dickinson deceived himself with no more sanguine expectations than Adams and Jefferson. At the time of its passage, Adams described the Second Petition as *necessary* ("We can't avoid it"). Dickinson described it as *advisable:* it offered the ministry an opportunity, and if rejected, would show Americans the contempt in which they were held by their government.

So much has been made of Dickinson's Olive Branch Petition, and of his subsequent opposition a year later to the Lee Resolution of Independence when it was proposed, that from these two episodes in his busy political life, he has been made to serve our writers as the symbol of timidity and conservatism. This opinion is an unfortunate distortion of events, and of his principles and his views, and leads us into misunderstanding the work of the Second Continental Congress. It comes, not from the sources of '75, but from the later narratives of Adams and Jefferson when they were in the easy position of justifying their successes. By now, in our traditional history, the myth is firmly embedded that Adams's "great Fortune and piddling Genius" letter was occasioned by the Petition to the King. We shall probably never be able to persuade the historian who writes as he runs that it had nothing to do with that issue of June and the first days of July, but rather was prompted by a sour disagreement on some other issue, three weeks later, probably an issue of commercial importance and of military and diplomatic significance, but not a constitutional matter, the issue of opening the ports.

Both Adams and Dickinson throughout this summer's session proposed a similar program, at a pace that would preserve and improve colonial union: on the one hand strengthened resistance; propaganda addresses to Americans, British, Canadians, and colonials in the West India islands; on the other hand steadily renewed proposals of negotiation and reconciliation. In pamphlet propaganda, no one in the Congress was so experienced a hand as Dickinson. From 1764, his great fame had rested on his eloquent and popular statements of the rights of citizens in the constitutional structure of the empire, and the rights of men. Jefferson's reputation was yet to come, in the activities of propaganda. Adams' reputation was a local New England fame; even his recent *Novanglus* papers as yet had appeared nowhere save in a Boston newspaper. But every literate American knew the writings of the celebrated Pennsylvania Farmer. And no one, in or out of Congress in June and July of '75 regarded him as a symbol of timidity, conservatism, or slowness.

What then exactly were the "whole doings" to which the "great Fortune and piddling Genius" gave what Adams said was "a silly cast"? The answer, I am sorry to say, is that no one now can be sure, for there are no records left of those long, spirited debates on opening the ports. Clear it is, that the mid-colony men succeeded in defeating the measure on Saturday, July 22; that the New England men succeeded in reopening the question for debate on July 31, only to lose it again. This may have been the issue at stake on Monday the 24, when Adams wrote. It is also possible that on the 24 the fires of Wyoming Valley and Connecticut's arming their settlers in the heartland of Pennsylvania flamed up; at least, the Connecticut delegates were high against the Pennsylvanians by adjournment August 2. Whatever the "whole doings" were, they were not doings that involved Adams and Dickinson in disagreement over the major policies Congress should pursue in fashioning the Continental Army, appointing Washington to be General and Major Generals and Brigadiers to serve under him, dealing with General Gage, and with Great Britain. They were not doings that went to the roots of principles or the canons of constitutional liberty. Yet Adams's harsh, picturesque words have been enlarged into an image of political conflict in '75, an image unfortunately entirely false, even though it is the image projected, from various motives, in the late writings of the longest-lived patriots.

Of all the transactions of the Second Continental Congress, none was more important, nor more attended to, than that document which Adams referred to in his "Secret and Confidential" letter of July 6, as a "Spirited Manifesto." On that very day, the next day after the Petition to the King was adopted, Congress heard, approved, adopted, and ordered printed, *A Declaration of the Causes and Necessity of Taking Up Arms*. This *Declaration* of July 6, 1775, containing so much of eloquence and feeling in it, so well calculated to dignify, to the soldier in his trench and the militiaman on his training ground, the cause for which he was in arms, containing too so many of the phrases and ideas used a year later by Jefferson in his Declaration of Independence—this *Declaration,* which remains for us today one of the major statements of the American purpose and collective will at the birth-time of our nation, in company with the Declaration of Independence and the Articles of Confederation—this *Declaration* of 1775 was written, in its most vivid parts, by John Dickinson. The very man who wrote the Olive Branch Petition of July 5, wrote the high words of the Spirited Manifesto of July 6. Both were bold, aggresive, confident statements.

Mr. Julian Boyd has studied the drafts of *A Declaration of the Causes and Necessity of Taking Up Arms*. With a finality that admits of no doubt, he has proved two significant things about it: he has separated out carefully from the various drafts exactly what Dickinson, exactly what Jefferson, wrote; and he has destroyed the myth that Dickinson softened or weakened Jefferson's draft. Quite to the contrary, Dickinson strengthened it. Always, historians have said the opposite. They have said so, because Jefferson in *his* autobiography, written sometime after the year 1821, said so. Jefferson wrote,

> I prepared a Draught of the Declaration committed to us. It was too strong for Mr. Dickinson. He still retained the hope of reconciliation with the mother country, and was unwilling it should be lessened by offensive statements. He was so honest a man, and so able a one that he was greatly indulged even by those who could not feel his scruples. We therefore requested him to take the paper and put it into a form he could approve. He did so, preparing an entire new statement, and preserving of the former one only the last 4 paragraphs, and half of the preceding one. We approved and reported it to Congress who accepted it.

Now Jefferson's statement was written in his old age, thirteen years and more after Dickinson's death; only Adams was left alive, and Adams would never spring to Dickinson's defense. Mr. Boyd has demonstrated that nearly every word Jefferson wrote is inaccurate. So far from softening Jefferson's passages, Dickinson, at every point he made a change or retained any of Jefferson's draft, stiffened the language, gave it higher and hotter tone. So far from retaining those last four eloquent paragraphs from Jefferson's draft, he wrote them himself, with no model to go on. Mr. Boyd concludes that the differences between them, "instead of revolving around polarities of radicalism and conservatism, are reduced to issues of style and method of presentation between two of the great penmen of the Revolution." But because of Jefferson's inaccurate statements, once again, Dickinson has been the victim of late-recorded opinions of those who were not friendly to him, and historians have accepted their unjustified portrayals of The Farmer as the symbol of timidity. A true and just picture would present him, in 1775, as every bit as much a symbol of advanced and vigorous American opposition as John Adams or Thomas Jefferson, though more careful that summer to preserve unanimity of opinion among the colonies, which alone could lead to union.

Where Jefferson's draft had admitted the colonies might previously have acquiesced in Parliamentary power over them, Dickinson struck out the admission. Where Jefferson had spoken mildly of Parliament's "new legislation," Dickinson used harsh, accusing words: "the pernicious Project." He referred to British troops quartered in Boston as "Murderers of the Colonists." He spoke of the contempt with which the First Petition to the King had been treated. He described Lord North's proposal "to extort from us, at the point of the Bayonet, the unknown sums that should be sufficient to gratify, if possible to gratify, ministerial Rapacity." Where Jefferson had made a veiled allusion to the possibility of independence, Dickinson was blunt and breathlessly frank: "We have not raised Armies with ambitious Designs of separating from Great Britain, and of establishing Independent States." Where Jefferson had stepped off from his veiled allusion—"That necessity must be hard indeed which may force upon us this desperate measure"—Dickinson plunged into it with boldness: "Necessity has not YET driven us into that desperate measure."

And of Gage's proceedings after Lexington and Concord, Dickinson had this to say for distressed Massachusetts: "By this perfidy, Wives are separated from their Husbands, Children from their Parents, the aged & sick from their Relatives & Friends who wish to attend & take care of them; and those who have been used to live in Plenty & even in Elegance, are reduced to deplorable Distress." It was far more than Jefferson had thought to say in behalf of John Adams's cause.

In short, Dickinson, in the most important affirmative statement of Congress in 1775, added toughness and inflammatory language to a document which men, whom historians generally say were advanced beyond him in their thinking, had originally couched in milder terms—terms he knew, from his sensitive ear and long experience with his gift of the word, would be entirely inadequate to animate the amateur citizen-soldier fighting and dying at Bunker Hill during those very days when the *Declaration* was being drafted.

History, in the long run, is what historians write. And what historians write becomes the traditions and folkways of a people. But sometimes one comes across, in the literature of history, errors and easy judgments, which make the past unreal, conceal the human aspects of the human story historians are called upon to tell. The real issue of the problem of '75, is not whether we today think well or ill of Adams, or Dickinson, as statesmen, persons, or patriots. Rather, the issue is understanding the subtle intensities of the independence movement as a movement led by, inspirited by, directed by, men in search of a political structure that would respond to the actual needs and political impulses of all the colonial American peoples, no longer apt for containment in the novel system of tutelage which an imaginative but insensitive ministry sought to impose upon them.

Jefferson, Adams, others too, writing when full of years in the lengthening shadows of their memories, give us a picture of unbelievable simplicities. If *historians* reduce things men have thought, and done, and said, and felt in the past to simplicities, then they give us a history in blacks and whites, a history in rights and wrongs, they leave no room for the individual man reacting, thinking, contending; nor any for the better world which, with better men, might indeed have been. They leave room only for the misfortunes that were, and they give us a history which is no more than a celebration of that which took place. Surely, history must be more than this.

Dickinson's vigorous opposition to Independence, so steadily conducted, so comprehensively argued by him in the next summer of 1776, will be understood as the reasonable view of a reasonable man, entirely consistent with love of country and dedication to those principles of a law-limited government which he had done so much to enunciate for his generation, only if such words as *timidity, conservatism, slowness, hesitation, avarice, dread,* and *caprice,* words used by Adams and Jefferson three, four, and five decades afterwards, are eliminated from our description of the policy and program he urged. Dickinson was, after all, from the opening of the ministerial contest to the day of independence itself, one of the most notable and respected of American advocates.

On a single question, probably that of opening the ports, Adams called him a "great Fortune and piddling Genius," said he had given a "silly cast to our whole Doings." But Adams, and all Americans, received with justifiable pride the stirring words written by that same Fortune and Genius, in the *Declaration of Causes,* his "Spirited Manifesto."

The *Declaration,* overshadowed by its successor of the next year, has dropped out of popular memory now. But those words of John Dickinson rang like a bugle call when Washington ordered them proclaimed aloud in his camp above Boston, when soldiers heard them around drumheads in every colony in the days following Bunker Hill:

". . . a Reverence for our great Creator, Principles of Humanity, and the Dictates of Common Sense, must convince all those who reflect upon the Subject, that Government was instituted to promote the Welfare of Mankind, and ought to be administered for the Attainment of that End.

"The Legislature of Great Britain, however, stimulated by an inordinate Passion for a Power not only unjustifiable, but which they know to be peculiarly reprobated by the very Constitution of that Kingdom, and desperate of Success in any Mode of Contest, where Regard should be had to Truth, Law, or Right, have at Length, deserting those, attempted to effect their cruel and impolitic Purpose of enslaving these Colonies by Violence, and have thereby rendered it necessary for us to close with their last Appeal from Reason to Arms. . . .

"We are reduced to the alternative of chusing an unconditional Submission to the tyranny of irritated Ministers, or resistance by Force. The latter is our choice. We have counted the cost of this contest, and find nothing so dreadful as voluntary Slavery. . . .

"Our cause is just. Our union is perfect. Our internal Resources are great, and, if necessary, foreign Assistance is undoubtedly attainable . . . With hearts fortified with these animating Reflections, we most solemnly, before God and the World, declare, that, exerting the utmost Energy of those Powers, which our beneficent Creator hath graciously bestowed upon us, the Arms we have been compelled by our Enemies to assume, we will, in defiance of every Hazard, with unabaiting Firmness and Perseverance employ for the preservation of our Liberties; being with one Mind resolved to die Freemen rather than to live Slaves."

July 1, 1776

4

The Day of American Independence

Monday, July first, 1776. A little before nine o'clock in the morning, Delegates to the Continental Congress began to make their way toward the State House.

This morning there were forty-three of them. Most had been up since first light, had taken breakfast wherever they had their bed and board in rented quarters all over the city; they had already spent busy hours with Monday's tasks. Servants had scurried out to hair-dressers with wigs for combing, to the Post Office to pick up mail, to the Coffee House for latest advices, news of a ship arrival, perhaps an express come in. Light summer coats were sponged and brushed (horsehairs stiffening the linings would soon be daggers pricking at armpits in this weather, clean stock freshly starched in an hour would wilt). And letters: before time for committees to meet, Delegates could snatch moments for the most urgent letters, scratch them out with Saturday's quills on such paper as could be had nowadays (poor stuff it was, and dear, too), sprinkle their lines with sand, melt sealing wax in the flame of a breakfast candle, press hand-seal or signet ring neatly in the gleaming ceraceous blob that wafered the folds of their sheet.

Then the quick endless work: committees, conferences, boards—with in-

119

terviews, testimony, petitions, reports received, reports drafted, accounts to pay, bills to audit—every morning at dawn a host of tasks clamoring to be done, more work than any man could get through. "I find there is a great deal of difference," a new Delegate would soon confess, "between sporting a sentiment in a letter or over a glass of wine upon politics, and discharging properly the duties of a senator." These earliest daily duties were the toughest gristle: only forty-three men, to manage the whole business of a continental war, for thirteen governments. Nine o'clock was mid-morning.

The day was already hot. A tiny breeze moved sulkily up from mosquito swamps below the city; sultry humid air gave some hope of a shower. Three steps in Philadelphia's summer dankness and a man was sticky with sweat.

Streets thronged with Monday's people, Monday's noises, thronged with drays and carts and quick two-wheelers, here and there a gentleman's chair, thronged with pigs, lambs, calves, oxen on hoof for the market, citizens and country folk. Every breath was heavy with horse smells, stable smells, human smells, earth smells. Monday, a man walked carefully in Philadelphia, this city too large, too full of people, rooms too small, streets too narrow, airless and dirty.

Citizens paid scant attention to the Delegates. A year ago they had paid attention, when first blood spilled, when news came of Lexington and Concord, Bunker Hill, Boston invested. Philadelphians had welcomed Congress then, celebrated the New England Delegates, fêted them as heroes. But soon the visitors disappeared behind closed doors in Congress; they sat in secret session, no one knew what went on in those day-long meetings. By and by, few bothered to ask. The war was a daily fact now; citizens were busy here and there.

Today, only the ringing of the State House bell reminded that Congress was about to sit. Even that went scarcely noticed, for the bell rang every hour anyway. It was the city's clock-bell, mounted on the roof in a little bell-hut, faintly heard above the noise of Chestnut Street. It was not old Isaac Norris's great Liberty Bell, hung on its cherry log twenty-three years ago, high in the steeple atop the tower. Around the bead lines of that bell had been wrought an inscription, from which the bell took its name. The words were God's words to Moses on Mount Sinai: PROCLAIM LIBERTY THROUGH ALL THE LAND TO ALL THE INHABITANTS THEREOF. The old Liberty Bell had not rung for years. Nor would it. Nor would people want it to. Speaker Norris, that canny Quaker, had been swindled. He had ordered the Liberty Bell ("a good Bell of about two thousand pounds weight") to mark the fiftieth year of the Province of Pennsylvania—"*And ye shall hallow the fiftieth year,*" God had said to Moses, "*and proclaim liberty through all the land unto all the inhabitants thereof: it shall be a jubilee unto you.*" The jubilee bell had been shoddily cast in England; it looked fine, but it cracked wide open when first tested. Two youngsters here in Philadelphia had made bold to melt it down and re-cast it. One was an immigrant lad from the island of Malta, the other the son of the State House doorkeeper. They had never cast a bell before; they botched the job. The Liberty Bell gave out a horrid sour noise when it sounded; everyone was glad to have it silenced. It had to be silenced, because no one dared pull the bell-ropes lest the great ton of metal come crashing down. The timbers in the high steeple had rotted; the steeple itself was entirely unsafe. Pennsylvania's Assembly had been meaning to rebuild for several years now, even order a new bell. Every session they talked of it; somehow they never quite got around to the job.

Not only the bell tower: everything else about the State House this morning was shabby, ill-kept, dulled with use. Andrew Hamilton's fine red-brick structure was an old place in 1776—forty years old, full of history, full of words, old-fashioned, inconvenient, entirely inadequate to the great city, the growing commonwealth. People wanted to change it. Who loves a building forty years old?

The great Yard behind, intended for a park, was a treeless, dusty expanse. Ground was still brown where huge mass meetings had trampled these past weeks. An elevated wooden platform twenty feet high gave the only shade, a "temporary" platform thrown up seven years ago for astronomers to observe the Transit of Venus. The "Observatory," Philadelphians called this ugly bare structure. To John Adams of Massachusetts it was "that awful stage in the State House Yard." The public privy ("the necessary house") down in one Walnut Street corner was unattended, a noisome place. And other odors hung all about: on each side of the red brick State House stood wooden sheds, opening to the Yard, built for Indians to camp in when they came here for treaties. The sheds were dirty from the Indians, high-smelling and damp; on a hot day like this the foul aroma of the sheds would waft through every room of the public buildings.

Around the whole Yard was the Wall, solid brick, seven feet high. A towering gate in Walnut Street looked over to the prison, that "monster of a large, strong Prison" across the way. The Wall shut off every breath of air, every freshness.

Congress Delegates were accustomed to the crowd gathered daily in Chestnut Street in front of the State House. It was not that Philadelphians were more civic-minded than citizens elsewhere, and flocked to official doings to have a part in things; rather it was because a public pump had been sunk at the very doors of the public buildings, for people to water their horses, and themselves. Past this indifferent cluster at the watering trough, Delegates moved up the few shallow front steps, under the Royal Arms of King

George mounted over the high double doors, and into the building. Here, inside the wide, straight-through hall, the doorkeeper waited, to admit them and only them to their meeting.

He was Congress's own doorkeeper, hired and paid by Congress; he was the only visible sign of their presence here. No official seal, no coat-of-arms, no uniformed guards or troops-of-state were anywhere about—none of the trappings of a court or government. For Congress was not a government— not yet. These Delegates were met to consult together, report back to their thirteen separate sovereignties. Congress owned nothing. The room they met in was borrowed: it was the Province of Pennsylvania's Assembly Chamber, nobly proportioned in old Andrew Hamilton's plan, high-ceilinged, handsomely panelled; tall windows formed the north and south walls. By noon this July day the sun would be pouring hotly through those vast south windows. Everything in the room was Pennsylvania's: delegates sat in Pennsylvania Assemblymen's chairs, Secretary Thomson used the Assembly secretary's desk, Clerk Matlack the Province clerk's table; President Hancock on the low dais between the two fireplaces at the far end was enthroned in the Speaker of Assembly's seat of state; he dipped his quill in Isaac Norris' old silver inkstand from that jubilee year long ago.

Congress was a guest here. Congress would always be a guest, here and elsewhere, all the years of its existence.

"PHILADELPHIA, 1 July, 1776," wrote John Adams. *"This morning is assigned for the greatest debate of all"*—the debate on Lee's resolution, the debate on American Independence, "the greatest question which ever was debated in America . . . a greater, perhaps, never was nor will be decided among men."

For three weeks Lee's resolution had laid before Congress in its stark simplicity: "RESOLVED, *that these United Colonies are, and of right ought to be, free and independent states: that they are absolved from all allegiance to the British Crown; and that all political connection between them and the State of Great Britain is, and ought to be, totally dissolved."*

Three weeks ago the motion had been read, and hotly debated. A majority was against it—"the sensible part of the House," said young Edward Rutledge of South Carolina. Finally, that first sharp debate of June 8–11 had ended in a compromise. *Union* was the crucial issue; union of all the colonies in war. The "United Colonies" must be united in fact, not merely in name. No resolution could do it. Three new committees were appointed with no opposition: one to draft a Declaration stating the reasons for independence; a second to draw up Articles of Confederation uniting the colonies; a third to prepare a plan of foreign alliances. On these strong measures of resistance, everyone agreed. But on dissolving allegiance, dissolving all government by declaring independence now, *before* new governments were operating in each colony, *before* union in a confederation, *before* alliances with France, Spain, and Holland, members were by no means agreed.

Indeed, they were vociferous in opposition. And the central question, independence itself, was postponed till July 1, "in order," wrote little Mr. Gerry of Massachusetts, "to give the Assemblies of the Middle Colonies an opportunity to take off their restrictions and let their Delegates unite in the measure." Mr. Gerry, his sharp mercantile eyes peering ever through a Yankee's clouded lenses, should have looked more closely about him. It was not only the middle colonies: Yankee New Hampshire had so far failed to send new instructions, despite repeated and urgent pleas of her delegates, Dr. Bartlett and Captain Whipple. And South Carolina was by no means ready. Adams had thought so, but Adams was wrong. Only five colonies had voted for independence on June 11. All the others had carried postponement.

And now July 1 had come—the day of decision, the day when (John Adams hoped) "the last finishing strokes will be given to the politics of this revolution." All these three weeks, Congress had gone on with the hard early-morning tasks of war, with long daily sessions for debate, with committees sitting late in the evening; the three new special committees had labored over their special assignments, Delegates had written home for instruction.

Their letters moved at a breathless pace. The new fast mail coach, the *Flying Machine,* leaving on Saturday, took only two swift days for the journey from Philadelphia to New York. Delegates could hire an express rider to set out after dark, follow the mail coach, catch it at the halfway house where it spent Saturday night before it left in the morning. (*"This letter will reach you by yesterday's mail . . ."*) In such fashion the time could be cut in half, a letter written Saturday evening would reach the New York post office late Sunday and could be picked up Monday morning, or sent on to Boston. To Baltimore the roads were excellent; it was the ferries that slowed expresses up. To the south, Philadelphia riders could sometimes reach Williamsburg in four days.

Independence men, "the hot violent men," waged a hot violent campaign these three weeks by post every day, by the *Flying Machine,* by stage, by express rider, by private persons: *"The Bearer waits. Adieu." ". . . Our hurry must apologise for this Scrawl . . ." "This goes by express early tomorrow morning . . ." "We shall be in full expectation of an answer by the return of the post . . ."* They struggled to convert five colonies into nine—the nine votes needed in Congress to carry independence.

At most, they could count only seven, as July 1 neared. New Hampsire finally acted: news came June 18. But this was no eighth colony, it was only one of the first five, making certain, a vote already counted. Adams could rely on Massachusetts, Rhode Island, Connecticut, now New Hampshire; and on Virginia, North Carolina, Georgia. Seven votes. Always the enthusiast, always wonderfully convinced by his own high opinions, Adams all these three weeks greeted every slight alteration, every minor change, indiscriminately as a victory. *Delaware:* "McKean has returned from the lower counties with full powers"—Adams failed to note that those full powers were powers to do what seemed best, that though Thomas McKean was strong for independence, George Read was equally strong against it, Speaker Rodney had not returned. With Rodney absent, Delaware's two remaining Delegates would be divided—no vote. *Pennsylvania:* the Assembly upstairs had indeed drafted new instructions before they adjourned June 14. But Adams failed to note the new instructions merely authorized the Delegates to use their own judgments, which was far from commanding Pennsylvania's vote be given for independence. And the Delegates were the same old Delegates, chosen last November 4. John Dickinson had written those new instructions. Dickinson was chief of the delegation. And John Dickinson's judgment would certainly never coincide with John Adams's. *New Jersey:* the royal governor (he was Benjamin Franklin's illegitimate son William Franklin) was "dethroned" June 15; the Assembly elected new Delegates, "high charged them for independence." A friend in Jersey assured Adams the new men would "vote plump!" But Adams had to acknowledge that as of this Monday morning, the new members from Jersey had not yet arrived. One of them, a tiny bustling little person, Francis Hopkinson, had been here: he had made his first appearance in Congress on Friday, officially become a member. But apparently he had returned home. At any rate, he had not played the organ in Christ Church on Sunday, as he often did when he was in town. "One of your pretty, little, curious, ingenious men," Adams described Mr. Hopkinson, to his wife. Perhaps he had gone home to hurry the others down at once. It was too bad; by Jersey's new instructions, one Delegate alone could cast the vote of the whole state.

New York was hopeless, her Provincial Congress refused to act. Maryland was still deliberating, her Convention passing odd resolves of a sort no other colony bothered with. Yet Adams could be jubilant, confident, as Monday dawned. Let South Carolina go; he had his seven votes, Delaware was ready, eight; New Jersey committed, nine; perhaps Maryland would act, ten——

Or perhaps only seven. No one knew better than John Adams the traps his enthusiasms laid for him, the disappointments he could suffer. If only Mr. Bulloch of Georgia were still here, in his American homespun suit; if only Mr. Wythe and Richard Henry Lee had not left for Virginia's Convention—Adams had lost his closest acquaintances from the south, his principal allies. The men remaining from Virginia he scarcely knew, nor the Georgians. So often he was wrong, as he had been about South Carolina. Young Edward Rutledge had been vehement against independence that long first day, June 8. Who would have expected such depth from him, such uncommon passion? particularly since his own colony had already set up a new government, under his own brother John as president? It was as long ago as last April when William Henry Drayton, chief justice in South Carolina's new government, addressing the first grand jury ever assembled without royal writs in Charles Town, had charged them that George III had abdicated the government of South Carolina, that Americans were entirely absolved from all allegiance to the King. His powerful words flew up and down the whole continent, they had struck every independence man in America like electric sparks striking Dr. Franklin's lightning rods: *"The Almigthy created America to be independent of Britain . . ."* Apparently Edward Rutledge was a non-conductor.

For once, Fortune favored John Adams. In the earliest hours this Monday morning, as he sat in his lodgings writing letters, waiting for seven o'clock to come round when the Board of War and Ordnance would meet, a post rider pounded into Philadelphia. He bore a hurried note for Mr. Adams, in confidence, from Samuel Chase in Annapolis. It was dated "Fryday Evening 9 o'Clock." The Maryland Convention had finally resolved for independence, Chase's note said, "an Unan: Vote. . . . I am this Moment from the House to procure an Express to follow the Post . . ." He was sending the new instructions, sending them by special messenger as soon as they could be signed and sealed.

John Adams was transported. "May Heaven prosper the new-born republic," he wrote, just before he set out to meet the Board of War, "and make it more glorious than any former republics have been!" For Maryland meant an eighth colony, if Chase's express arrived in time—meant victory, if the New Jersey Delegates came in, or if Rodney of Delaware should arrive. . . .

It was John Adams who had encouraged little Mr. Chase (that "pernicious elf," a Tory called him) to go down into Maryland as soon as he returned from Canada June 11; it was Adams who had urged him to canvass the province in person, county by county, use his considerable influence for speedy action to be sure new instructions would reach Philadelphia before the voting. Two weeks ago he had sped him on his journey: *"Mr. Adams ever was and ever will be glad to see Mr. Chase; but Mr. Chase never was nor will be more welcome than if he should come next Monday or Tuesday fortnight, with the voice of Maryland in favor of independence . . ."* It was Adams who talked with, wrote back and forth with, men in every colony, every city; it was he who fostered in correspondence and in person every developing independence sentiment, recorded every news that would hold fast the Delegates in Congress. Major Walton had come in just this past Saturday afternoon, to take his place in the delegation from far-off Georgia, and Major Walton had brought letters for Adams with him in his elegant coach. Certainly it was Adams who was the master of this day's affair, "author of all the mischief," he called himself. John Adams was the architect of American independence.

Other Delegates had supported independence in Congress; but they had not shared Adams's organizing efforts, nor participated with him in the politics of thirteen capitals, nor informed themselves so well of the colonies' opinions. And so they knew less how close the issue was, how divided the people, how uncertain the chance of two more votes coming in. Hewes and Penn of North Carolina, for instance: their instructions had been drafted months ago, perfectly clear for independence; they both spent the weekend calmly enough, aware that Monday would begin "an era of great importance" but unaware of serious opposition. Mr. John Penn, quite ready for independence himself, thought "all the Provinces but Maryland are for it" and Maryland was coming round. Quakerish Joseph Hewes was by no means ready. "We do not want to be independent; we want no revolution," he wrote. "But every American is determined to die or be free." He felt bound by his instructions; he expected independence to carry "by a great majority." He wondered only what name the new country would bear. Both were, of course, ill-informed. Joseph Hewes particularly should have been more alert to the Delegates around him. He supported independence *now,* with genuine reluctance. He was convinced confederation and foreign alliances should come first. Had he known how many shared his view, he might have leant his voice to the moderate couse. Instead, he thought that cause already lost.

Adams, over-sanguine in his enthusiasms, over-confident, quick to miscalculate as he studied all his informations, was at least prepared for opposition. Elbridge Gerry was not. In his innocence, he thought Pennsylvanians had pretty well swung about, and "now more confide in the politicks of the New England Colonies." Young Mr. Gerry's talent for being wrong was never more evident than that. Whipple of New Hampshire was convinced the "central provinces" were "getting in a good way." Over the weekend he wrote, "Next Monday being the 1st of July, the grand question is to be debated, and I believe determined unanimously. May God unite our hearts in all things that tend to the well-being of the rising empire." Whipple entirely ignored the news from New York, entirely misread the words of Pennsylvanians.

It is not unnatural for Congressmen to be in error about other colonies. These are ambassadors, these forty-three delegates making for the State House this morning. They are not legislators; their duty is to announce the official policies of the colonial governments which have sent them, not to make policies for those governments, not to make laws to govern citizens. There are no citizens—except of thirteen separate commonwealths. There is as yet no American body-politic. Congress makes no laws. Congress makes only resolutions, recommendations; sitting as a guest in Pennsylvania's State House, Congress sends no more than requests to every colony—requests for militia, funds, supplies, for barrels of flour and leather for shoes, for all sorts of thirteen separate legislative actions.

Requests—or reports; for managing a war means managing affairs, buying, selling, bargaining, appointing factors and agents, commissioners, dealers, issuing paper money. The journals every day show an administrative structure at work: those early-morning and late-evening committees result in actions on the floor. Bills are paid, sums appropriated, claims allowed, the continental Post Office is well organized, Dr. Franklin at its head, Indian commissioners are this very moment entertaining sachems at Pittsburgh, holding treaties "at the expense of the United Colonies."

John Adams is chairman of the Board of War and Ordnance; it sits every morning. He is on a committee to fix a salary for Secretary Charles Thomson, and on a committee to consider Americans who are spying for the British army or giving aid and comfort to the "enemy" (Britain is the enemy now; loyalism is becoming treason). He is appointed June 11 to the committee to draft the proposed Declaration of Independence, June 12 to the committee for a form of treaties.

John Dickinson is on the mysterious Committee of Secret Correspondence, clandestinely conducting foreign affairs every day; he is on a committee to raise a battalion among the Germans, the committee for a form of treaties; he is chairman of the June 12 committee to draw up Articles of Confederation. Most members have as many assignments: Colonel Harrison of Virginia is on every military committee, and almost every special-problem or temporary committee; John Alsop of New York and Robert Morris of Pennsylvania find themselves together whenever finances are involved. "There are so many irons in the fire, I fear some of them will burn," Whipple of New Hampshire writes. Poor Captain Whipple: he is Colonel now. Things had been easier with him in the old days, when he strode his own quarterdeck at sea.

It is all governmental work, but for thirteen governments, not for one. And those thirteen governments are jealous of their powers. They will take no direction from Congress, no orders; they will take only requests, and reports. They brook no interference with their internal concerns—nor does Congress intend any. The idea that a Delegate from Virginia should vote in Congress on a policy for Connecticut, a Rhode Island member consider

Delaware's problems, is repugnant. Three separate times, Congress has rejected such proposals. "You have no right," one member tells the Delegates, on interfering with a colony's internal concerns, "you have no right—any more than Parliament has." Union among the colonies, if it comes at all, will come from each colony's Assembly, Convention, or Committee; it cannot be forged here, in this Hall, by ambassadors. Here, union can be no more than reflected, as in a glass—if union ever grows strong enough to cast its image. Most of these forty-three Delegates have only vague impressions of political struggles within colonies not their own, and they feel no involvement in results.

This was the nature of Congress this summer of '76: forty-three instructed envoys, to cast thirteen votes. Adams had no need to count noses; he needed only to count colonies. Had it been otherwise, had these forty-three individual Delegates voted by head, his problem would have been vastly more difficult, the outcome impossible to predict. Eighteen of the forty-three men were undoubtedly against independence now—before union, before confederation and alliances. Three more were uncertain; so far they had steadily leaned toward waiting, toward putting first things first—and Union was the first thing. These twenty-one men, the opposition, amounted to dangerously near half. On the other side, Adams's side, were twenty-one undoubted independence men; and Adams hoped two more: the new Delegates, Hopkinson from Jersey and Georgia's Walton. But no one could be sure. Debate could change minds; news from war camps could change minds; every one of the forty-three Delegates would put Union above everything else, and if independence threatened Union, that threat could change minds.

Eight of the forty-three had not been in Congress to hear the three-day debate June 8–11: Nelson of Virginia had reached town June 9, had taken his seat when Wythe and Richard Henry Lee left June 13; George Clinton of New York and Mr. Penn of North Carolina had both come June 24; little Mr. Hopkinson and Major Walton would be new this very day. Thomas Lynch Junior had been home taking care of his father; Mr. Paca down in Maryland at his colony's Convention. And Dr. Franklin had been all month laid low with gout. These eight had not observed the opponents' prodigious efforts, heard their aguments, nor seen their victory that first debate when only five colonies voted for independence. These eight might be swayed.

Everyone might be swayed, because of the curious sectional imbalance among the forty-three men in Congress. This imbalance was painfully evident to John Adams. New Englanders had formerly held the prestige of battle here: Massachusetts invaded, her neighbors threatened. But now Virginia had seen battle too, and New York, and Georgia, and North Carolina; General Howe with his great army borne in a great fleet was this moment

ANDREW HAMILTON. *Judging by the wig and costume and the bright, proud, young face, Hamilton's portrait must have been made long before he came to Philadelphia in 1714 at the age of thirty-eight and began his late course toward fame. This copy was painted after "Mr. Speaker's" death; the original has entirely disappeared.*

(Reproduced by permission of The Historical Society of Pennsylvania.)

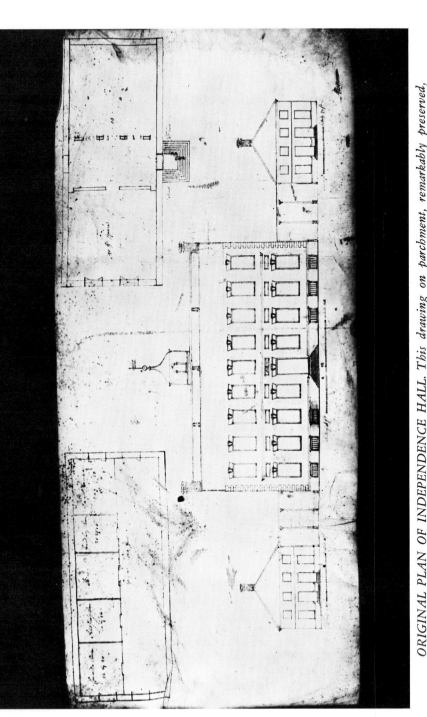

ORIGINAL PLAN OF INDEPENDENCE HALL. This drawing on parchment, remarkably preserved, is the actual "Draught of the State House, containing the Plan and Elevation of that Building," which Andrew Hamilton presented to his Pennsylvania Assembly at the end of several days' debate, on August 11, 1732.

(Reproduced by permission of The Historical Society of Pennsylvania.)

WILLIAM PENN'S CHARTER OF LIBERTIES, 1701. *The original charter
"of Liberties Franchises and Priviledges" on vellum bearing Penn's signature
and seal. In a sentence admittedly obscure and surprisingly casual in its word-
ing it conferred upon the Assembly the power "to prepare Bills in order to
pass into Laws," but then added "and all other Powers and Privileges of an
Assembly . . . as is usual in any of the King's Plantations in America."*

(*Reproduced by permission of The American Philosophical Society
Held at Philadelphia, for Promoting Useful Knowledge.*)

JOHN DICKINSON. *By Charles Willson Peale. Peale was twenty-nine when he painted this striking portrait, nearly lifesize, of the celebrated 'Pennsylvania Farmer." It was March–April, 1770, only a few weeks before Dickinson's marriage.*

(Reproduced by permission of The Historical Society of Pennsylvania.)

MRS. JOHN DICKINSON AND HER DAUGHTER. By Charles Willson Peale. As is evident from the age of the baby Sally, Peale painted this portrait of Mary Norris Dickinson more than two years after his picture of The Farmer, but he contrived to make it a companion-piece in spirit as well as size.

(Reproduced by permission of The Historical Society of Pennsylvania.)

8

JOHN ALSOP OF NEW YORK. *After the Revolution the New York legislature passed its Act to Remove Doubts Concerning the Chamber of Commerce, and John Alsop, one of the original founders back in 1768, became
president of the reconstituted body—first president of the first Chamber of
Commerce in the new republic.*

(*Photograph by Pach Brothers. Reproduced by permission of
The Chamber of Commerce of New York.*)

INDEPENDENCE HALL IN 1776. This engraving after a painting by Charles Willson Peale shows The State House pretty much as it looked during the debate on American independence. The main building, tower, arcades, and east and west "offices" envisioned in Hamilton's "Draught, Plan, and Elevation" of 1732 are now all completed.

(Reproduced by permission of The Historical Society of Pennsylvania.)

WASHINGTON'S MULE SHED AT MOUNT VERNON. When he first returned home after the Revolutionary War, Washington built a new stable barn on sloping ground at Mount Vernon. The upper level provided a center section for coaches and carriages, and stables with box stalls and mangers at each end. The lower (south) level he extended to make an open "lean-to" or protective shed beneath the barn, where mules were tethered at a long manger without stall separations.

(Photograph reproduced by permission of The Mount Vernon Ladies Association of the Union.)

INTERIOR OF THE MULE SHED, AS RESTORED. *The arrangement of fences enabled handlers to lead mules to the manger, or into a small fenced corral, or turn them from the shed into the close beside the barn.*

(Photograph reproduced by permission of The Mount Vernon Ladies Association of the Union.)

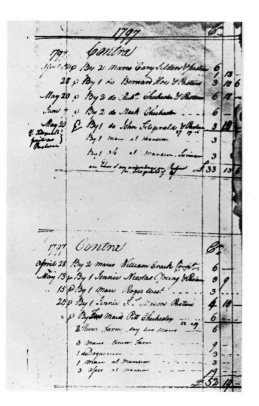

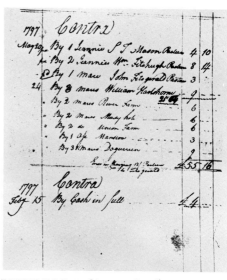

WASHINGTON'S FARM LEDGER: MULE BREEDING. In his own hand, Washington records the mares and "Jeannies" sent by various planters to his Mount Vernon farms.

(Photograph of the original in the National Park Service collection,
Morristown, New Jersey. Reproduced through the courtesy of
The Mount Vernon Ladies Association of the Union.)

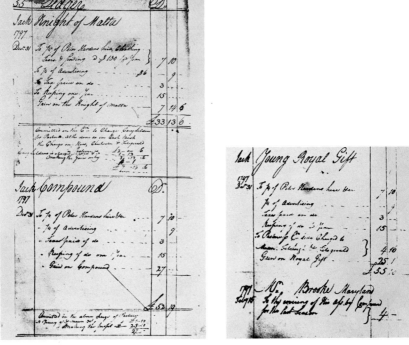

PROFIT FROM THREE FAMOUS JACKS. The General carefully enters charges and expenses, including pasturage, hire of groom, advertising and even tax on advertising against each of his jacks.

(Photograph of the original in the National Park Service collection, Morristown, N.J. Reproduced through the courtesy of The Mount Vernon Ladies Association of the Union.)

FRANCIS HOPKINSON. By Robert Edge Pine. Hopkinson was judge, scholar, writer, musician, poet, and painter; he would probably have chuckled at this thoroughly romantic portrait.

(Reproduced by permission of The Historical Society of Pennsylvania.)

Seven Songs for the HARPSICHORD OR Forte Piano. THE WORDS AND MUSIC Composed by Francis Hopkinson. Philadelphia Publish'd & Sold by T. Dobson

LAITKEN Sculp.

THE FIRST AMERICAN SONG BOOK. Hopkinson was proud of being "the first Native of the United States who has produced a Musical Composition." He said so, in the dedication of this book to General Washington. John Aitken's crudely engraved title page was canceled after a few copies were published, and an eighth song was added.

(Reproduced by permission of The Free Library of Philadelphia.)

PAT LYON AT THE FORGE. By John Neagle. When Neagle's portrait was first exhibited, it was immediately purchased from Pat by the Boston Athenaeum. So Pat had Neagle do this second, somewhat larger and more detailed version. The elements of the masquerade are carefully retained: the white shirt, the bright shoe buckles, the cupola of Walnut Street Prison in the background.

(Reproduced by permission of The Pennsylvania Academy of The Fine Arts.)

THE WALNUT STREET PRISON. The great prison lay just across Walnut Street from the State House Yard. A lofty gate in the wall around the State House block faced directly the bleak entrance to the prison. West of the prison across Sixth Street was another public square; the Debtors' Prison was a separate building in back of this main gaol, and faced on Prune Street. It is impossible to tell for sure which barred window was the 12' x 4' store-room where Pat Lyon was incarcerated. This view is an engraving by William Birch.

A SPURIOUS "PORTRAIT" OF PAT LYON IN JAIL. Used as a frontispiece in some copies of Lloyd's trial report, "Robbery of the Bank" (1808), this fanciful picture is also occasionally found bound or tipped in copies of Pat's own "Narrative."

PATRICK LYON'S MASTERPIECE, THE DILIGENT ENGINE. *In the days of the rival Fire Com-panies, this handsome pumping engine was famous everywhere. When it was sixteen years old (Pat was seven years dead by then) the Diligent was reconditioned by an engineer named John Agnew. When it was thirty-two years old it still won every competition, throwing four ½-inch streams simultaneously a dis-tance of 134 feet, or a single 1-inch stream nearly 200 feet.*

To Mess.rs Daniel Brown, Hezekiah Mason, Jonathan Richardson, John Waterman and John Wells jun.r a committee of the town of Cheshire in Massachusets.

Gentlemen

I concur with you in the sentiments expressed in your kind address on behalf of the inhabitants of the town of Cheshire, that the constitution of the United States is a charter of authorities and duties, not a charter of rights to it's officers; and that among it's most precious provisions are the right of suffrage, the prohibition of religious tests, and it's means of peaceable amendment. nothing ensures the duration of this fair fabric of government so effectually as the due sense entertained, by the body of our citizens, of the value of these principles, & their care to preserve them.

I recieve with particular pleasure, the testimony of good will with which your citizens have been pleased to charge you. it presents an extraordinary proof of the skill with which those domestic arts which contribute so much to our daily comfort, are practised by them, and particularly by that portion of them most interesting to the affections, the cares & the happiness of man.

To myself this mark of esteem from freeborn farmers, employed personally in the useful labors of life, is peculiarly grateful. having no wish but to preserve to them the fruits of their labour, their sense of this truth will be my highest reward.

I pray you, gentlemen, to make my thanks for their favor acceptable to them & to be assured yourselves of my high respect and esteem.

Th Jefferson

PRESIDENT JEFFERSON RECEIVES THE MAMMOTH CHEESE. "With this Address we send you a Chees by the hands of Messrs John Leland and Darius Brown," the committee of Cheshire town informed Mr. Jefferson. "We wish to prove the love we bear to our President not by words alone, but in deed and in truth." The committee was Daniel Brown, Hezekiah Mason, Jonathan Richardson, John Waterman, and John Wells Jr., husbands of the ladies who had accomplished the work.

(Reproduced by permission of The Chapin Library,
Williams College, Williamstown, Massachusetts.)

LANDING OF GENERAL LAFAYETTE IN NEW YORK. The scene on Monday, August 17, 1824, when LaFayette was transported from Vice President Tompkins's home on Staten Island across to Castle Garden at the tip of Manhattan. Anthony Imbert was the artist, Samuel Maverick engraved the plate.

(Reproduced by permission of the Prints Division, The New York Public Library, Astor, Lennox and Tilden Foundations.)

M. DE LAFAYETTE. By Samuel F. B. Morse. New York's City Council commissioned this, the first of many portraits LaFayette would sit for during his year as The National Guest. It still hangs in City Hall. The painter Morse was thirty-three in 1824, nine years back from his English study, highly esteemed in the city for his portraits. Quite obviously, only the head in this large canvas is painted from life.

(Reproduced by permission of The Art Commission
of The City of New York.)

A SOUVENIR OF THE NATIONAL GUEST. American ingenuity produced souvenirs of bewildering variety as The National Guest moved from place to place. Someone engraved this plate, and the Germantown Print-Works printed it on linen, an oversize handkerchief to wave at LaFayette during his Philadelphia visit.

(Reproduced by permission of The Historical Society of Pennsylvania.)

NEW ORLEANS' CELEBRATION. Triumphal Arches in successive cities contrived to vary surprisingly, at least in detail. In New Orleans the "monument dedicated by a grateful republic to LaFayette" exhibited four shields representing the original Thirteen States; in the spandrils figures of Trumpeting Fame lay the laurels of Washington and LaFayette before the symbol of the Republic united, the Constitution is the keystone of the arch, Pallas Athena gazes thoughtfully on Dr. Franklin atop the structure, Justice sits at the gates, and the two basements memorialize the Signers of the Declaration of Independence, by name.

(Reproduced by permission of The American Antiquarian Society.)

CHENERY HOUSE, SPRINGFIELD. Every capital town has its political hotel. Springfield's was the Chenery House, where lounges, lobbies and parlors thronged with leaders of the new Republican Party from many states and cities after the surprising victory in November, 1860.

Photo print by permission of The Illinois State Historical Library, Springfield.)

THE GREAT WESTERN RAILWAY STATION, SPRINGFIELD. "All the strange, chequered past seems to crowd upon my mind . . ." At this little station, from the back platform of his tiny special train, Lincoln said his farewells to Springfield folk. "To you dear friends, I owe all that I have, all that I am. . . ." The depot building is still standing. For a long while it was used for freight handling; now it is a museum. This photograph from Lincoln's time shows something of what he saw as his final sight of his home town.

(Reproduced by permission of The Illinois State Historical Library, Springfield.)

PRESIDENT-ELECT AND FORMER PRESIDENT, 1861. Millard Fillmore standing at Lincoln's side (on the balcony of Buffalo's American Hotel) was a disturbing sight to many Republicans. In his 970 days as President, 1850–53, Fillmore had represented the old politics of compromise, of preserving the Union by ignoring slavery and abolitionism both, and making concessions to the slave-holding states. He also represented the failure of this policy.

(Reproduced by permission of The Buffalo and Erie County Historical Society.)

standing into New York harbor, he had made his first landing yesterday on Staten Island; Philadelphians had witnessed an action of their city gunboats against a British man-of-war in the Delaware River. And from South Carolina, news was that Charles Town, attacked from both land and sea, would probably fall this week. "Suffering Massachusetts" was old hat to Congress now. And too, New Englanders had a stigma to live down. They were far from popular with other Delegates, these Yankees so quick to give everyone the word. The very name "New England" had become a byword for arrogance, selfish demands, rash inconsiderate actions, a byword particularly among men of the Middle Colonies. Pennsylvania and New York were sending more men, arms, and money to the war nowadays than all New England. Delaware in proportion to her size and resources was sending most of all. Leaders of this middle land regarded their proprietary governments with their free constitutions as in every way superior to the governments east of the Hudson. Yankee strength this morning, and Yankee leadership, would be thin. Of the forty-three Delegates, only eleven were New Englanders, while eighteen were Middle Colony men. The rest were fourteen Southerners divided—the four youthful South Carolinians opposed to independence *now*, the ten Virginians, North Carolinians, and Georgians in favor. By sectional alignment, independence would lose—twenty-two against twenty-one.

Each member, by the rules, could speak but once on an issue. The rule might work hard on Adams's cause. Seven, maybe eight of Pennsylvania's nine-man delegation would be here; six of New York's ten. These were the largest delegations. Virginia would have five of her seven, but not her leaders: Wythe and Richard Henry Lee had gone off to Virginia's Convention. This left Benjamin Harrison the senior Delegate in charge; and to Adams Harrison was no help. He was not even liked by his own colleagues. Only Thomas Nelson had a mild word for him. Francis Lightfoot Lee was his enemy in Virginia, Braxton and Jefferson were rarely seen in his company. Adams's own Massachusetts delegation numbered five men. One of them. Mr. Gerry, stuttered when he spoke, though his affliction did not deter him from speaking often and at length. Another, Mr. Hancock, never spoke at all, though everyone knew him, for he sat in the chair as president. (Strange to say, Mr. Hancock was sharing a private residence with Middleton of South Carolina, a man whose person and views Adams found entirely unacceptable. Hancock was also seeing a lot of Dickinson lately, and that huge pouter pigeon Colonel Harrison of Virginia. He was irritable, peevish, sour-tempered in his conversation, from his exquisitely painful gout. In every way, Hancock was disturbing to John Adams.) Of South Carolina's five Delegates, only three young men were usually present, for their chief member, senior both in age and service, the much-admired Thomas Lynch, was gravely ill, and his frail son Thomas Junior, also a Delegate, most days stayed home at his bedside. This morning, Lynch Junior would certainly attend. That would make four of these elegant tidewater youths, only a few years returned from their British schools and the Inns of Court and European travels. They were a glittering gaggle of worldly, talented freshness: Edward Rutledge aged twenty-six, Thomas Lynch Junior twenty-six, Thomas Heyward Junior thirty, Arthur Middleton thirty-four. Maryland would have three of her seven Delegates, since Mr. Alexander had withdrawn entirely; Johnson and Tilghman were down at Convention in Annapolis where Chase had gone to call at them from the wings. Mr. Paca would be in charge—the beloved Paca, a man universally esteemed, contentious in nothing. Connecticut would have only two of her five, for Hosmer and Williams had never shown up at all, and curiously Oliver Wolcott had chosen to leave for home last Friday, June 28, in spite of the critical debate coming up this Monday. The two Connecticut judges, Huntington and Sherman, would cast the vote today, Huntington silent as usual, Judge Sherman, "that republican machine" someone called him, probably anything but silent. Georgia would have three, with Major Walton coming in. Of Delaware's three only two would be present. New Hampshire, Rhode Island, North Carolina never had more than two men in Philadelphia.

Adams could count himself lucky he had not won his voting-by-head measure back in '74. Two thin voices from Connecticut would make a small noise compared with eight from Pennsylvania, six from New York.

Thomas Jefferson occupied the early hours Monday morning listening to a merchant from Montreal tell of the war in Canada. It was part of a committee assignment Jefferson had drawn. Then at nine o'clock he noted down the temperature on his new thermometer—82½ degrees—and proceeded to walk out to the State House. The Declaration he had labored over was finished, it had already been reported. It would not be discussed on the floor till tomorrow at the earliest. It would not be discussed at all, if independence failed to carry today. Jefferson had taken no part in Adams's preparations. He set himself for another day of silent hours of listening, note-taking, voting when called on with his four colleagues from Virginia.

John Alsop was known to be a'courting. The wealthy widower was certainly a catch, with his own merchant house in New York City, his vast landholdings up-river in Connecticut, his family estates on Long Island. He was formidable as a financier, he was learned and bookish; certainly he was socially acceptable even among Philadelphia's great folk, for Alsops were an old people. They had settled Flatbush a whole generation before ever Penn had founded Pennsylvania. Alsops had been Quakers in that long-ago time;

not all the quietness of Friends had disappeared from this gentle, steady man—this "soft sweet man" John Adams called him, this unmistakable gentleman, of virtue and serene good sense. Persons of great wealth liked John Alsop—Lynch of Carolina, Morris of Pennsylvania, Langdon of New Hampshire, Paca of Maryland. It was odd of him to board with an uncertain straddler like Thomas Wharton when he came here for Congress, but gossips knew why: there was a lady of Mr. Wharton's family, high-born, well dowered . . .

By everyone, John Alsop was respected, even by those who were diffident of his wealth. He had sat in Congress from the beginning; his first election had been fully two years ago, July, 1774. In May, 1775, when the Second Congress met, he and seven other Delegates had established a table at the City Tavern, where they took dinner together after sessions every day in the week except Saturday—on Saturday all the Congressmen generally dined in company together. His seven dinner companions were a various group: four Virginians, Peyton Randolph, Richard Henry Lee, George Washington, Benjamin Harrison; two Delawareans, Caesar Rodney and George Read; and Samuel Chase of Maryland. Now the group had broken up: President Randolph was dead, Washington was commanding the Army, Lee and Rodney and Chase had gone to their colonies' Conventions. Mr. Alsop was dining these days with the Whartons, *en famille*.

He had firmness and judgment; he was none of your thin-dipped men like Duane; he supported every strong measure of resistance; he even initiated a few. He had not hesitated to join in the Association, and in the non-import, non-export agreements; he had willingly entered the clandestine scheme to nullify the imperial laws of trade. Indeed, his experience as an overseas merchant had been invaluable in Congress: he had served as agent for the Secret Committee, had planned with Morris the mercantile part of Silas Deane's secret mission to France, had himself drawn the contracts for Deane's illegal sale of American produce in France, illegal purchase of French goods for America—gunpowder, arms, saltpeter. He had chosen which French merchant houses to deal with, helped choose the ship captains and drawn their secret commercial instructions. Civil war in no respect terrified Mr. Alsop, so long as it was war in the just cause of resisting unlawful parliamentary measures, defending the rights of citizens. For the Supply Committee he purchased flour, and trade goods to win Indians; he arranged an embargo on salt pork and beef so the Continental Army might be fed. He went though a good deal of work speedily, efficiently, with a merchant's clarity, and a businessman's way of "getting on with it." And Mr. Alsop would not be imposed upon. When General Charles Lee, that egregious character, presumed to impose a loyalty oath on all inhabitants of New York,

Mr. Alsop proclaimed it a momentous point, an arrogant assumption of political authority by a military figure: "There can be no Liberty where the military is not subordinate to the civil power."

This morning, John Alsop was troubled. The home about him was quiet; Thomas Wharton had gone to his country seat, "Twickenham," to escape the heat. The ladies had gone with him. Mr. Alsop's mind was free to dwell on today's debate. He and his colleagues could take no part in it; that was clear. The New York Provincial Congress had refused instructions; they were not authorized, they said, nor capable, of giving the sense of the inhabitants on so great a question. Instead, a Convention was being called, an election being held, a new government would be formed; then the Delegates would be instructed. The election, Mr. Alsop knew, had gone badly. New York was falling into the wrong hands: the irresponsibles, the Lambs, McDougalls, "King" Sears—mean cunning men were winning everything. Independence now, would be their victory, their achievement, would deliver the province to such men entirely. Independence now, would be the end of good government.

Would independence any time be wise? Mr. Alsop was by no means certain. It was one thing to contend virtuously against Parliament for liberty and rights. Rights and liberties were worth a civil war. But these were British rights, British liberties, guaranteed by the British constitution. What would guarantee them when that constitution was abandoned? The British empire was an umbrella over every citizen. Without the Crown, without an institution on the American Continent to take its place, how could courts hold, what law would they administer? How could American merchants trade overseas, from no nation, flying no flag? In what currency would they trade, and what credits? He and his brother were financing Connecticut River settlements; how could his bills be discounted? His London bills, his West India bills, his Dublin bills?

Here was Mr. Button Gwinnett, formerly a failure in his trading ventures out of Bristol and Liverpool, now removed to America and a Delegate in Congress from Georgia. Gwinnett was a merchant trader still hopelessly swamped in debt. Even in New York, by Alsop, by all the merchants, it was known Gwinnett could meet no payments due, no settlement dates. If Georgia were entirely independent, how could any New York merchant, how could anyone anywhere outside Georgia get a confession of judgment against him, this hard-pressed, none-too-scrupulous nondescript? Gwinnett was trading now with the notorious L'Hermite, at Cap François. What navies would protect his ships, what factors accept his notes, what courts guard creditors' interests against his conversions, against L'Hermite as well?

For ten years, American resistance to ministerial measures had been a lawful cause, conducted by law-respecting men. Mr. Alsop had been one of them, bold for liberty as Americans in the empire understood liberty, determined in plans to overcome the ministerial armies, resolved to bring Whitehall to the conference table, restore the ancient constitution. Were they to end up today, only rebels? Were they to give everything up, let such men as "King" Sears with his rabble try to lead the fight against British arms? Sears would fail; New York would fall.

And what of Union? New York Delegates had no power to act. Instructions from the new Convention could not come for days yet. Independence this July 1 would have to leave New York out, isolated, the continental union split in two, just as the British invasion of the Hudson was beginning. These hot violent men of New England, even his Virginia friends, apparently had no intention of waiting for New York. Were they willing to surrender the province to Howe's armies, permit a British wedge to be thrust in the soft middle of the American confederacy?

John Alsop walked his short way to the State House, a patriot sure of sorrow. His decision was already forming: with New York in the hands of the radicals, soon in British hands, he had no place left in that city, his city. He would marry his lady, leave public life forever, go up to Middletown on the Connecticut. His brother Richard's sons were growing up; they both loved to read, one was already writing clever verse. His own vast collection of books, combined with Richard's, would give the boys one of the largest libraries in America, of many languages, all knowledge; he and Richard together could build the Connecticut valley. . . .

The first step was, resign from Congress. Soon "soft, sweet" John Alsop would shape his hard, bitter letter to his "countrymen" of New York: "As long as the door was left open for a reconciliation with Great Britain upon honourable and just terms, I was willing and ready to render my country all the service in my power . . ."

Poor Mr. Lynch was up and about some, nowadays. Soon, not this morning, but one day soon, he would even venture out of the house—with his son's help, of course. If only his son would get well enough to help him. In the fifteen weeks since his paralytic stroke last February, Mr. Lynch had made steady progress. He could hold a pen now, even sign his name. Sometimes he could see friends—Mr. Paca, Robert Morris. The doctors gave him hope: he was not so old, only forty-nine. (People were always wrong about that. When they met him they thought he was sixty.) His plain simple life, temperate habits, his serene mind certainly favored his case. So did being one of the richest men in the whole empire, though the doctors never mentioned that. His wife and daughters with their company of servants had tended him lovingly where he lay all this while at Mrs. McKenzie's. And his son: it had been so decent of South Carolina to send his son. When

John Rutledge resigned, the Assembly could have sent an older man to Congress—Laurens, one of the Draytons, General Pinckney, even the noisy Gadsden who would have been delighted. Instead, they had called Captain Thomas Lynch Junior from the field and elected him Delegate, for no other reason than so he could care for his father. Not that the young man was unworthy; far from it. He was Eton and Cambridge and Middle Temple, with superior records at each; he was barrister and planter, and had been in public life before he took the field. But he was so young—only a couple of months older than Ned Rutledge. They were all so young. Mr. Lynch was needed back in Congress. . . .

Thomas Junior took a month to wind up his affairs in Carolina before he made the long ride to Philadelphia. His wife and body slaves went along; they rode with the Heywards, which made the journey as pleasant as any journey could be. Heyward's poetic gifts were always a joy. The two young men could leave the managing of the trip to their coachmen, and the bedding and feeding of four gentlefolk and a dozen slaves, while they reminisced for hours of their years together at the Temple, and in Europe. They rode through Spring in the land; they reached Philadelphia April 24. Congress welcomed the new Delegates, and at once resolved "on account of the alarming ill state of health of his father" that young Lynch be granted formal leave of absence.

With his only son by him, Mr. Lynch mended slowly through May and June. Thomas Junior was able to leave his side now and then to attend sessions, give his father news of them afterwards. Attendance was never easy; young Captain Lynch for all his youth and striking good looks was racked with a cough, he spat blood, he was subject to sudden nausea, ugly vomiting attacks. Service with his company in the field had almost destroyed him entirely, so had the long journey northward. But this morning Ned Rutledge insisted he be present, and of course Thomas Junior would go. There was much of his father in him; these Lynches were never known to shirk a duty. One day they might even sit as delegatss at the State House together, father and son. It would be the first such spectacle: Henry Middleton had left Congress before his son Arthur came in to replace him. Delegates were used to pairs of brothers sitting among them: the Rutledges, the Lees, the two Livingstons from two different colonies. John and Sam'l Adams were cousins, Ned Rutledge and Arthur Middleton were brothers-in-law. But if he could bring in his poor father some day with him, young Captain Lynch could treat Congress to a unique, a warming moment . . . If only Death would be patient a while, wait a few weeks longer for them both. . . .

Edward Rutledge, by Saturday's post-haste, sent another urgent message to John Jay in New York. Mr. Jay *must* come back to Congress, come at once, come tomorrow, to be in attendance Monday next. "I know full well that your Presence must be highly useful at New York, but I am sincerely convinced that it will be absolutely necessary in this City during the whole of the ensuing Week." The rule of secrecy did not stay Rutledge's hand; Jay, after all, had been a Delegate from the very first; and these New Yorkers were elected permanently, not for a year, or a term, or nine months like the Georgia men. He could write freely. He explained what was afoot: independence, a confederacy, a plan of treaties. "Whether we shall be able effectually to oppose the first and infuse Wisdom into the others will depend in a great measure upon the exertions of the honest and sensible part of the Members." Alas, the honest and sensible members willing to make any exertions seemed mighty few, as Rutledge counted his support. Take Jay's colleagues from New York: Floyd, Wisner, Lewis, Alsop—good men all, but never willing to speak, they "never quit their chairs." And the new man, George Clinton, when he did bring himself to say something, was scarcely listened to. Jay *must* come. Edward Rutledge liked nothing of what was going on. He needed allies; too much was descending on his shoulders.

Indeed, with Mr. Lynch out of things, Tom Junior rarely here; with his radiant brother-in-law Arthur Middleton (that romantic aesthete) busier with artists and craftsmen and scholars in the city than affairs of state, forever worrying his Greek texts or translating Horace; with Tom Heyward amiably silent as always, in his portfolio no committee work at all but only whatever poetic effusion he was currently shaping and reshaping, the whole duty of South Carolina fell on Ned Rutledge, the youngest man in Congress. And on South Carolina right now seemed to be falling the whole duty of preserving American Union.

Youngest member though he was, Rutledge stood next senior to Mr. Lynch. He had come here for the first day of the First Congress, two years ago (September 5, 1774), and had not missed a session since. The others were new: Heyward and Lynch Junior had been here only nine weeks, Middleton only five. Sometimes Arthur Middleton would speak, reveal his astonishing gifts, his shocking sarcasm, wry cutting wit, the rich furnishment of his mind. But he was not yet in Congress's way of doing business, not yet effective. Rutledge had to find his help elsewhere. Jay was another young man, but Jay was steady and respected, he was listened to. If only Jay would come back . . . In the miasmas of Philadelphia's summer heat, young Edward Rutledge, his long large-boned frame already too heavy with flesh, was decidedly uncomfortable.

John Adams instinctively disliked these young Carolina dandies. He disliked their wealth, their clothes, their merriness, their British education, their European travel; he resented their striking abilities. On his very first meeting with Edward Rutledge he had found him unattractive. ("Young

Rutledge told me he studied three years at the Temple. He thinks this a great distinction ... This Rutledge is young, sprightly, but not deep; he has the most indistinct, inarticulate way of speaking; speaks through his nose; a wretched speaker in conversation. . . . He seems good natured, though conceited.") After a month, he thought him "a little unsteady and injudicious ... very unnatural and affected as a speaker." Another two weeks, he held him in contempt: "Young Ned Rutledge is a perfect Bob-o-Lincoln—a swallow, a sparrow, a peacock; excessively vain, excessively weak, and excessively variable and unsteady; jejune, inane, and puerile." Strange words these, for the heavy slow-moving youth, who was working so faithfully in America's cause. By Carolina standards he was not vain, not variable. By Yankee Siles Deane's standards he was "a tolerable speaker," ingenious, impetuous, in the cause, zealous. By Philadelphia Dr. Rush's standards he was "a sensible young lawyer, of great volubility in speaking, and very useful in the business of Congress." But by John Adams's standards it was too bad America had to include in it at all such people as these Carolina brilliants, so mannered and rich, so tolerant, so Anglican, yet so high in the spirit of resistance.

Edward Rutledge never stretched himself up to speak, but John Adams's bile fermented and out poured his liquorish detestation. After a year together in Congress, he pronounced the young man remarkably wanting in judgment, tedious on frivolous points, warm and boisterous on matters of no consequence (no consequence, one imagines, to Adams). Even his appearance in speaking, Adams condemned. Rutledge was already celebrated in Charles Town as an orator, and as a mimic of oratorical styles. But Adams called him "a very uncouth and ungraceful speaker; he shrugs his shoulders, distorts his body, nods and wriggles with his head, and looks about with his eyes from side to side, and speaks through his nose, as Yankees sing." Language spouted out from him "in a rough and rapid torment, but without much force or effect. . . ."

It was not in John Adams to like, or understand, these Rutledges of Charles Town.

Edward Rutledge gave not a fig for what John Adams or any Yankee thought of him. He had abundant assurance, this direct young man. And that is a matter of no little surprise, considering his brief history. For hulking Ned Rutledge was the youngest of seven children. He never knew his father, who died the year he was born. That shadowy, somewhat questionable person had been an Irishman, with a couple of terms at Trinity College Dublin behind him. He sailed as an East India ship's surgeon; by and by he came to Charles Town, where he practiced medicine—or what passed with him for medicine. When twenty-five, he married the vastly rich orphaned heiress Sarah Hext, a girl only fourteen years old. Promptly he gave up medical practice, invented a new drink he called "Officers' Punch," devoted himself to the pleasures of the Coffee House and tavern, died of a surfeit at thirty-seven. He left Sarah a widow of twenty-six with her house full of children. The young widow turned out to be quite a person. She was notably pious; happily she now possessed a portion of her fortune in her own right, and somewhere in the short course of her life she had come to admire learning. She gave all her children remarkable educations; when Edward was twelve, his oldest brother John at twenty-two came back from the Middle Temple an "utter barrister," set up in law. Edward read in his office during his teens; at twenty-one he himself went to the Temple, returned after three years in 1773, married Henry Middleton's daughter, commenced his law practice. A year later with his brother John he went to Congress. Nowhere was he ever known to express any diffidence of youth, toward his brother or anyone else, as he moved among his elders.

Nor was Edward Rutledge easily dislodged from any position, whatever Adams might say to the contrary. He was one of those who had defied the whole Congress in 1774, persisted until South Carolina's rice and indigo were excepted from the Continental Association, and the peculiar situation of the "unique staples" acknowledged even by the Massachusetts Delegates. As he scratched out a place for himself in his family and his city, the youngest Rutledge had developed an uncommon toughness of mind. "I must do what is right in my own Eyes, and Consequences must take Care of themselves," he declared. Though freshest from London of all the Delegates except Dr. Franklin, he had been among the strongest in resistance to ministerial measures. He was entirely committed to the American program. That program by now was fourfold: continue to state the rights of man and constitutional liberties which Parliament was abusing; unite the mainland colonies of British America in a single political federation and a single military effort to repel British armies wherever they invaded; secure foreign aid by secret negotiation, and by opening American ports to foreign trade as well as carrying American produce to foreign ports; finally, to do all these things in the attitude of loyal subjects courageously resisting ministerial tyranny, so that Britain would be always in the wrong, Americans in the right. Thus Americans, insisting only on established constitutional principles, would be no rebels against monarchical theories, nor threats to other colonial powers. No European nation need hesitate to aid them. It was imperative to keep clear every path to reconciliation with Britain, on just terms—keep those paths clear even now that reconciliation had become impossible, for only thus could Americans prove they were no innovators, no levellers, no rioting mobs overthrowing thrones.

Liberty, union, armed resistance, foreign aid, firmness: this program had not been of Rutledge's conceiving; John Dickinson, another Middle Temple barrister, had been its guiding genius, its principal statesman. But young Rutledge had been a strong right bower in Dickinson's game more than a year now, and he had no intention of changing.

It would be so weak, to change. The independence men, just because things were going badly, wanted to abandon the American cause, repudiate what Americans had fought for. It was running away in the face of the enemy. True enough, the King's proclamation of rebellion, his sending armies and hiring alien troops, had effectually dissolved allegiance; but that was *his* doing, not ours. Equally true, he was just now sending peace commissioners; we must certainly hold back independence until they discharged their mission, lest we be accused of a surly refusal to negotiate. If the peace commissioners brought every concession, offered everything Americans demanded, then we would have won total victory, without further war. It was unlikely, such complete capitulation by the King. But it was not impossible. It was a legitimate hope; it would be a glorious vindication of liberty, yet still within the freest constitution in the world. Independence now, would vitiate that hope. If the peace commissioners, on the other hand, brought nothing worth considering, then it would be Britain at fault for offering nothing. Americans would still stand as defenders of liberty, our position the stronger for one more proof of Britain's oppressive designs.

Rutledge was satisfied with his own part in the first great weekend debate June 8-11. "I wish you had been here," he wrote Jay. Only four Delegates had taken upon themselves the burden of speaking out fully and extensively against Lee's resolution: John Dickinson and James Wilson of Pennsylvania, young Robert Livingston of New York, and himself. Yet these four had prevailed against "the Power of all N. England, Virginia and Georgia." Wythe and Richard Henry Lee were formidable antagonists, so was the clever Dr. Hall of Georgia, that transplanted Yankee; so was the determined radical Button Gwinnett, that transplanted Englishman; so were the Adamses and Gerry and Sherman and old Mr. Hopkins and all the New England men. It had been Rutledge who moved postponement for three weeks, till Monday July 1—moved it for grave and substantive reasons; he would rather have postponed it three months. Only after his victory in that first great debate did the independence men, smarting in defeat, begin to circulate the tale that postponement had been "to let the middle colonies get ready," the assemblies alter their instructions. They circulated the tale, too, that the inhabitants were ready; that the American people were clamoring for independence, that only their representatives held back. Rutledge heard no such clamor, certainly not from South Carolina; the independence men could not pretend to have some special way of knowing, better than anyone else, what the people thought and felt.

All the four moderate debaters of June 8–11 acknowledged that reconciliation as a practical matter would probably never come; that the colonies
were now bound to remain separated from the Crown. They were not opposing independence as a realistic fact; they were opposing its *declaration*
at this time, as a political act. Independence declared now would put the
Americans in the wrong: it would nullify in advance any talks with the
peace commissioners; it would serve no useful purpose among the legislatures or the soldiers in the field; it would impede the struggle for union; it
would commit us to war rather than negotiation as the instrument of policy.
Dickinson, Livingston, Wilson, Rutledge "had no objection to forming a
Scheme of a Treaty," Rutledge told Jay, nor "uniting this Continent by a
Confederacy"; but to declare independence at this moment would be "giving
our Enemy Notice of our Intentions before we had taken any steps to execute them." It would be attempting to bring foreign powers "into an Union
with us before we had united with each other."

"And a man must have the Impudence of a New Englander," young
Rutledge of Charles Town added, "to propose in our present disjointed state
any Treaty (honorable to us) to a Nation now at peace." Independence
before Confederacy, *before* foreign aid, could do immense harm; it could not
possibly do any good. "No reason could be assigned for pressing into this
Measure, but the reason of every Madman, a shew of spirit."

Winning postponement on June 11 was the last satisfaction Fortune permitted Edward Rutledge. Every mail rider the rest of June, every coaster,
brought alarming news from home, news always seven days and more old:
it seemed possible, then likely, finally it was certain, Sir Henry Clinton's
army and Lord Cornwallis's fresh troops were moving against Charles Town.
Admiral Sir Peter Parker's warships were expected, then sighted, finally reported massing in the harbor. Attack would come any moment. In Philadelphia the young Carolinians agonized in speculations: their city was no
fortress; their families would be seized; Mr. Lynch's square miles of rice
fields would be flooded; all their plantations fired; their town houses would
be burned as Norfolk had been burned; the militia would be powerless. By
Sunday, the last day of June, word was that the far-off battle had commenced.

All these three weeks of June, weeks of apprehension and tormenting
worry, Rutledge had held firm his steady way, determined still in his conviction: independence must wait upon Union, on alliances. But every day in
committee these three weeks, Edward Rutledge was learning a very hard
lesson. Not his courage, not his confidence, not his intellectual integrity—it
was his youthfulness melting away.

On June 11 independence was postponed. On June 12 two committees
were appointed: one of five members to draft a Declaration stating the

reasons for independence; the other a "Grand Committee," directed "to prepare and digest the form of a Confederation to be entered into between these
Colonies." It was called a Grand Committee because it consisted of one member from each colony. The Confederation Committee met at once, in the
library room of the State House (back of the fireplaces of the Assembly
Chamber, in the little east wing). A bust of Thomas Penn Lord Proprietor
of Pennsylvania looked sternly over their deliberations. The eleven members—there was no member from New Jersey, unrepresented just now; and
McKean of Delaware had been named while briefly absent—entrusted the
drafting of Articles of Confederation to John Dickinson, member for Pennsylvania.

None of the twelve—McKean soon came back from Delaware—started
out more eager for Union than Edward Rutledge. "For daily experience
evinces that the Inhabitants of every Colony consider themselves at liberty
to do as they please upon almost every occasion," he had written Jay June 8.
And certainly none could have been more pleased with the choice of Dickinson. The famous Pennsylvania Farmer had led the three-day debate against
independence; he and Rutledge were allies. Another ally, young Livingston
("my friend Bob," Ned Rutledge called him) was a member too, for New
York. Their victory of June 8–11 would be consolidated now; things would
go smoothly . . .

Edward Rutledge was in for a swift maturing. In sessions of the Grand
Committee he abruptly learned, as a young man must, how the easiest words
of public life are charged with specific meanings—meanings real, in the real
world, where words are mere breathings. It was one thing to speak high
for "Union" as a general notion, it was quite another to erect the actual
government that could create Union, to endow it with actual powers, to
take away powers from South Carolina while merging her with the whole.
Writing a constitution is a job of imaginative statecraft; imagination was
one gift the Graces had failed to bestow on Edward Rutledge. His devotion
to principles of constitutional liberty was undoubtedly intense, and sincere;
but his principles of liberty did not include freedom for slaves and bonds-
men. His determination to support the armed resistance to ministerial
armies was unquestionably sturdy and tough, but that determination did
not involve diminishing the governmental authority of South Carolina, nor
inhibiting her free traffic in her unique staples, indigo and rice. Never before had he faced up to the reality that "Union" would mean surrender by
his colony, every colony, of pieces of sovereignty. Never had he imagined
South Carolina would sail into a "Union" flying anything less than the full
rigging of self-government she had just this spring suited out for her new
ship of state. Galloway's plan of union in '74 had proposed no invasion of
sovereignties; the Continental Association had left every colony full and

whole in its government. These, Rutledge (after winning exception for rice and indigo) had willingly considered.

But now the Grand Committee was contemplating a nation, a single state among states of the world; and a nation is an entity which wields actual powers. A nation does "Acts and Things" (as Jefferson was writing just now for the Declaration committee), does them of right; it would do "Acts and Things" to South Carolina. Rutledge could not imagine it.

Constitution-making is also a job for experienced hands. On this Grand Committee Ned Rutledge was outclassed. So was his friend "Bob" Livingston, inexperienced at thirty. So was Button Gwinnett, the merest amateur, new to public life. So was Thomas Hope Stone of Maryland, an earnest country lawyer, friend to "universal liberty," enemy to slavery; but unequal to the task of translating general principles of liberty into the distributed powers of a federated government. So was Colonel Nelson of Virginia, just now back in Congress from a four-month absence. ("A fat man . . . He is a speaker, and alert and lively for his weight," John Adams said. Certainly Colonel Nelson had the dimensions of a hero: in the five years ahead he would sacrifice his health and his entire fortune, a large one, in the American cause, end up finally in abject poverty. For generations people would tell how as Governor of Virginia commanding militia at Yorktown he directed the bombardment of his own fine mansion house, which Cornwallis was using as headquarters. But for all his undoubted patriotic fervor, no one ever imagined Thomas Nelson a man of thought, or a statesman.) And Joseph Hewes, the troubled former Quaker of North Carolina—he too was outclassed: "I think it probable that we may split on these great points, if so our mighty Colossus falls to pieces . . ."

Outclassed, they made difficulties, these six—objected to everything, protested every grant of power that would make "Union" real, waved all the bright parochial plumes they could never bring themselves to doff. The Grand Committee in three weeks failed to do its job. Its failure was unexpected: Congress had supposed Confederation would be the significant work of June, the Declaration merely a justification *ad hoc* of Lee's resolution. The event proved otherwise; that smaller committee of five—Jefferson, Franklin, Adams, Sherman, Livingston—accomplished their Declaration in such fashion that the world has never forgot them. Jefferson's words became the very words of America's cause, and of liberty's cause everywhere, ever since. But the Grand Committee of twelve for "the Articles of Confederation, or a Continental Constitution," shattered on the obstructions of its six inexperienced men—half its membership, taken by surprise.

Some crises in public life allow no time for reflection. At such moments the prepared mind, the experienced statesman, is ready. At this moment, on this Grand Committee, six experienced statesmen, the other half, were boldly ready to make significant sacrifices of the sovereignties, even the interests if need be, of their own colonies (their "countries," they called them) for the sake of creating a single continental government where thirteen now existed. They were men long in public life; the realities and necessities of Union would never take them by surprise. They were also high in disagreement. They reflected interests in conflict. But the conflicts were familiar to them, susceptible of adjustment; they were ready to discover areas of agreement. These six were: Dr. Josiah Bartlett, a New Hampshire physician, notably original in medical practice, in public life brisk, incisive, for twelve years a leader in his colony's revolution, and constitution-making; Sam'l Adams, organizer of Massachusetts' early resistance, now prepared for any republican endeavor that would further diminish the "establishment"; Roger Sherman of Connecticut, deliberate, sensible, remarkably pious, already twenty years in public services, seventeen years a judge; Thomas McKean of Delaware, bencher of the Middle Temple, perennial legislator and office-holder in his own colony and Pennsylvania as well; and two of the most unusual men in British America: Stephen Hopkins of Rhode Island and John Dickinson of Pennsylvania.

Chief Justice Hopkins—you could address him by many other titles, he had been governor fully twenty years ago, a judge on some bench contin-uously for the past forty years, often in assembly, a founder and chancellor of Rhode Island's college, indeed you might justly address Stephen Hopkins simply as "Mr. Rhode Island," though if you were a scientist you would call him "Doctor," to celebrate his achievements in mathematical scholarship, astronomy, legal gloss, and history too—Stephen Hopkins had been advocat-ing a strong Union of the colonies all his long life. He seemed old beyond measuring; actually he was a whole year younger than Dr. Franklin. His next birthday would be only his seventieth. But everything about him seemed an-cient: he had a frightful palsy; he could not so much as sign his name with-out grasping his right hand with his left; he trembled even when he sat still. And he was a strict-professing Quaker of such conservative persuasion that he never permitted himself the vanity of having his hair cut. It cascaded down over his frail shoulders in long, straight, white streams. In the way of old-fashioned Friends he always wore his hat indoors, even while sitting in Congress or committee or any public meeting. But for all his apparent frailty this quaking old Quaker was formidable in debate, never slow to state his position, never uncertain in expression. He had a gift for unforgettable sentences: "I have never known a modest man that was not brave." "The liberties of America would be a cheap purchase with the loss of but 100,000 lives." And on generals who wrote long letters back to Congress: "I never knew a General Quillman good for anything."

Back in '54, when he was forty-seven (Ned Rutledge was not yet five),

Mr. Hopkins had been with Franklin a delegate to the Albany Congress. He supported the Plan of Union of that Congress, wrote a book to advocate and explain it. Twenty years and a myriad of activities later, he was one of the members of the First Continental Congress to argue in favor of Galloway's Plan of Union. The realistic problems of uniting the colonies—unequal representation, voting by head or by unit, regulation of commerce, surrender of western lands, the power to tax—were no novelties to him.

Nor were they to John Dickinson. The Pennsylvania Farmer had entered public life debating the Constitution of the Empire; he had written books on the federal theory, on sovereignty divided, the distribution of powers between parts and the whole—books, and tracts, and newspaper pieces, and state papers for Pennsylvania's Assembly, and resolves of the Stamp Act Congress a dozen years ago (his lifelong friend McKean had sat in that Congress with him). No one this month of June, '76, was better prepared on Union than he.

For this Grand Committee, Dickinson did his work swiftly, almost over night. There was no difficulty about it; he has only to digest previous plans and put them in some order. There was the old Albany Plan of Franklin and Hutchinson, and Galloway's Plan; and last year Dr. Franklin had drafted some additional general proposals which had been circulating among the delegates for many months; most members had taken copies of the draft for study. And there were all the recent instructions of the colonies on forming a Union, sternly reserving their own internal police powers to themselves. They were all entirely too general, of course. Dickinson, as he "digested" twenty years' thinking on the problems of Union, turned general principles into specific provisions—into the actualities of Union. To Edward Rutledge, these specific actualities sounded like the funeral knell of his country, South Carolina.

The very words of Dickinson's draft were disturbing: *The United States shall have the sole and exclusive right and power to . . . The United States shall have authority for . . . Every colony shall abide by the determination of the United States . . . No Colony or Colonies shall engage in . . . enter in . . . No Colony or Colonies without the consent of the United States . . . no colony . . . no colony . . .* Throughout, Dickinson seemed to be erecting a strong over-state, the very sort of over-state that crown, parliament, and empire had been. Was nothing to be left of self-government? Yes: *Each colony shall retain and enjoy as much of its present laws, rights, and customs, as it may think fit, and reserves to itself the sole and exclusive regulation and government of its internal police*—but then those destroying words: *in all matters that shall not interfere with the Articles of this Confederation.*

Sacrifice of statehood horrified Rutledge, horrified all the six members inexperienced in Union. For the other six, who were ready, who had dealt abundantly with these matters before, there was not enough time. Between appointment of the Grand Committee June 12, and the last report-day of the three weeks' postponement, June 28, only fifteen session days intervened. Even had the committee met on every one of these days, Hopkins, Dickinson, Sherman, Sam'l Adams, Bartlett, and McKean could never in that brief time have accustomed the remaining six to the issues of continental government, nor persuaded them to take back to their "countries" and advocate the adoption of a charter of surrender of those countries' sovereign powers. And all the disagreements among the strong-government men deceived the objectors: they thought them irreconcilable disputes. Fisheries, slavery, western lands, ocean trade, colonial rivalries and claims, local tariffs, a national tax, the fostering of religion—every question split independence men among themselves, split Yankees from one another, split Union men asunder. Small wonder Rutledge thought the splits could never mend.

By Monday June 17, "some difficulties have arisen," Dr. Bartlett confessed: "I fear it will take some time . . . The affair of voting, whether by Colonies as at present, or otherwise, is not decided, and causes some warm disputes . . . ." Every provision caused warm disputes. Finally, Dickinson had to acknowledge the Articles of Confederation were not ready. June 28 came and went; the Grand Committee could make no report. Independence would be debated on Monday, with no Union of the colonies in sight.

For portly young Ned Rutledge, the committee all these three weeks had been grim disillusionment. Now he had no one left to side with, no one on whom he could depend. John Dickinson, three weeks ago his firm ally and Cicerone in opposing independence, had revealed himself an enemy to be feared, for the powers he would vest in a strong central government. The "honest and sensible part of the members" must have none of John Adams's independence, if it included John Dickinson's Union. For this reason, most of all, Jay must come back. By Saturday's post, Rutledge sent his loneliness galloping northward:

"I have been much engaged lately upon a plan of a Confederation which Dickenson has drawn; it has the Vice of all his Productions to a considerable Degree; I mean the Vice of Refining too much. Unless it's greatly curtailed it never can pass, as it is to be submitted to Men in the respective Provinces who will not be led or rather driven into Measures which may lay the Foundation of their Ruin. If the Plan now proposed should be adopted nothing less than Ruin to some Colonies will be the Consequence of it. The Idea of destroying all Provincial Distinctions and making every thing of the most minute kind bend to what they call the good of the whole, is in other Terms to say that these Colonies must be subject to the Government of the Eastern Provinces."

The Eastern Provinces—Rutledge, who had entered the Grand Committee inveighing against "the Impudence of a New Englander," emerged at the end of three weeks convinced Yankees were thoroughly detestable. He suspected their motives, mistrusted their words, doubted their professions, found their manners abominable. Everything that odd, awkward Judge Sherman, slovenly Sam'l Adams, sharp Dr. Bartlett had said, everything squeaked out by old Chief Justice Hopkins from under his quivering, Quakering hat, had been pistols presented one by one to the breast of South Carolina. These New Englanders were dangerous, not for their power, but their persuasiveness:

> The Force of their Arms I hold exceeding Cheap, but I confess I dread their overruling Influence in Council. I dread their low Cunning, and those levelling Principles which Men without Character and without Fortune in general possess, which are so captivating to the lower classes of Mankind, and which will occasion such a fluctuation of Property as to introduce the greatest disorder.

The conventional Episcopal piety Sarah Hext had instilled in her big Rutledge sons had nothing in common with, could not even recognize, the Dissenting piety of a Sherman, the Inner Light of a Quaker. Friend Stephen Hopkins had been called many names in his long busy walk through life, and he had made enemies. But never till now had anyone deemed him a man without character or fortune, a man of low cunning. Some gulfs between Provinces on the American Main were deeper, wider, than the vast Atlantic itself. "I am resolved," Rutledge told Jay, "to vest the Congress with no more Power than is absolutely necessary, and to use a familiar Expression, to keep the Staff in our own Hands; for I am confident if surrendered into the Hands of others a most pernicious use will be made of it. If you can't come let me hear from you by Return of the Post . . . ."

So firm for Union June 8, so firm against Union June 28—at least, against *this* Union—Edward Rutledge on his way to the State House Monday morning was far less concerned with South Carolina's independence from Westminster than he was with South Carolina's independence from Philadelphia.

John Dickinson spent the weekend at his country seat, "Fairhill," north of the city, on the Germantown Road. He sent off no letters, marshalled no support, talked with no colleagues. Instead, he wrote a speech.

On long folio sheets of lawyer's foolscap, fine rag paper left over from happier days, he set down exactly the reasons why he must oppose independence at this juncture of affairs, how he felt about Lee's resolution, why he regarded it as a piece of folly, approaching almost to madness. He composed carefully at first, balanced his sentences, rounded phrases, reworked, rewrote, interlined, expanded, developed. But time was short—time was always so short, whenever he set himself to writing. Every book he had ever produced, every piece he ever wrote for Bradford's paper or Claypoole's, every one of his little books, every resolve of Assembly or Congress state document, was something he had been obliged to turn out in the hard pressures of the nighttime, or a Sunday's pause. It was always too quick, so much in every issue to consider, so many points, so many shadings. . . . Now as his thoughts touched all the subjects involved in Monday's question, he wrote hastily, swift abbreviated notes, snatches of phrases, key-words to guide his mind, channel his tongue: *Our Intt. to keep GB in Op th We mean Reconon . . . What Advt to be expected from a Declon? 1 Animatg our Troops . . answ unness . . . . As to Aid from for Pow   our Declon can pcure Us none this Campaign . . .*

It was so excessively difficult: the most important decision ever called for in America, yet everything had been said before, nothing was new, or changed, he could add no argument these Delegates had not heard before— heard, and until now, always followed.

So particularly difficult, here at Fairhill. These cool lofty rooms, these long tree-shaded vistas, yellow wheat blowing heavily in the breeze, these polished surfaces of fruitwood and mahogany, Turkey carpets where servants silent, invisible, glided about—these rooms were no place for a thoughtful man's work. It was a serene home, Fairhill, lovely in its restrained elegance, and famous, this handsome old mansion built in imitation of a Welsh noble manor, with its terraced gardens, avenues of elms, fields stretching out of sight in three directions, its separate library building filled with books. Delegates who dined here in state with The Pennsylvania Farmer assumed of course this was the celebrated "farm" of which he had written. Actually, it was not. Fairhill was the great-house of the Norris family. Speaker Isaac Norris II had inherited it from his father, forty years back. When the Speaker died ten years ago, John Dickinson, leader of the Philadelphia bar, was executor of his estate. He managed all things for the two Norris daughters; but he managed them, as he did everything, from his law office and bachelor's home in the city. It was in the busy midst of the city, too, that he had written his most famous book, with its pleasant though entirely imaginary conceit, "*I am a Farmer* . . . " Then six years ago, at the height of his fame, The Farmer had married lovely Polly Norris. Her family had frowned, in their Friendly way, his own mother had not liked it much; but John Dickinson thought himself blessed indeed in his gracious lady who adored him, blessed in their little daughter, and certainly not un-blessed to find himself now, by title of courtesy initiate, possessed of most of Speaker Norris's wealth. It was a wealth even greater than his own.

His own was in Kent County, Delaware, in Talbot County, Maryland, in western Pennsylvania lands and Jersey farms, in Philadelphia city lots, and legal fees and mercantile investments, in London bills and credits. His own books and furniture, his curious stand-up writing desk made to his own design in London years ago, all his records, notes, and papers, were in his Philadelphia city home where he and Polly received the year 'round. Fairhill was their summer retreat, and Polly's home; but Fairhill was never home to John Dickinson. Portraits on the walls were Norris portraits, Logan portraits, the handsome English furniture was Norris furniture, books in the library building were three generations of Norris books, Logan books, and young Charles Norris' medical library. Madeira in the lock-cellar was his own, claret, and the fine *rosé*; the gout he suffered was certainly Dickinson gout. But when he drove back and forth to town in his coach-and-four, it was Isaac Norris's coach he rode in, Norris gray livery his slave coachmen wore, Norris-of-Dolobran arms the door-panels bore in faint, fading colors. Even after six years, Fairhill was still more Speaker Norris's seat than his.

Dickinson refused to go on First-Day to the little Fairhill Meeting House the Norrises had built a few rods from the mansion, a sort of private summer Meeting for family and connections. Polly always attended, with their daughter; the usual weekend company of in-laws filled the benches. John Dickinson was a birthright Friend—Polly would never have accepted him had he not been at least that. But long, long ago, thirty-five years ago, in Talbot down in Maryland, Third Haven Friends had tried to discipline his father, when his half-sister Betsy married out of Meeting. "*Consenting to a disorderly marriage,*" the Friendly offense had been recorded. John had been the merest child then; poor Betsy was dead now nearly thirty years. But that wound had never healed: his great-grandfather Powell had founded Tred Avon Meeting, had received George Fox in his home when he first landed on American soil to commence his missionary journey. His grandmother had been a famous preaching Friend; his father had been Overseer of Choptank Meeting, had paid its debts, even built the new Meeting House school. But when his wealth grew, when he doubled his holdings, and doubled them again, and then again and again, kept on adding plantation to plantation, with a fleet of coasters in the bay trade, a chasm opened between him and Meeting folk. . . .

Dickinsons were a proud people. They could forgive, but forgetting was another matter. Smarting, indignant, his father had removed from Maryland to Kent County on Delaware, had never again passed among Friends. The Farmer was his father's own son, a Dickinson of Talbot, of Kent, he had never become a Cadwalader of Philadelphia, for his mother, he would never become a Norris of Fairhill, not even for Polly . . . .

In this alien air, at Speaker Norris's stretcher table, away from his own desk, his own books, his office noisy with youthful clerks, on paper from Speaker Norris's stock, he must write alien words—words alien to every con-

viction the saintly Norris had held so stoutly, to the Friendly way he had
exemplified in such perfection. They must be words of war, which the
pacific Norris had abhorred. They must be words of union with other colonies, colonies where Friends had been viciously persecuted, at which he
had seen Friend Isaac Norris weep. They must be words of independence, of
a new sovereignty, abandoning Penn's Great Charter and Frame, that purest
and freest of constitutions, which had been Speaker Norris's ideal of inspired
organization of public polity, and private liberty, among men.

They would be words alien to Congress, too, for he must say independence, *but not yet*; do not abandon your own agents abroad, Deane, and
Arthur Lee; do not interrupt the negotiations which may bring us aid, by
violating the commitments you have made; alliances *first*, and supplies,
arms, military victory; peace among ourselves and an end to all our controversies *first*; do not abandon citizens to the savageries and unchecked riot
of no government over them at all, for a mere slogan; a firm confederation
with established governments *first*, western lands given up to the united confederated government, *first*, to finance the war. . . .

And Congress would have none of this. Monday's decision was already
taken, it would go against him, nothing he could do now would change it.
He must write words alien to his own nature—words of defeat, of the end
to all he had worked for.

John Dickinson in the plain splendors of Fairhill was tired beyond uttering. All his efforts, every resource of his keenly honed lawyer's mind and
his vast political skill had led at long last only to this weekend's hopeless
waiting, this girding for sure defeat.

That it was sure defeat, Dickinson had no doubt. On Friday, the last
session day of the three week's postponement, the small committee of five
on the Declaration had come in with its work completed. (*"Congress was
impatient,"* John Adams said. *"I consented to report it . . ."*) This was the
last masterstroke of strategy, the fullest development by the hot violent men
of their case. The Declaration Jefferson had drafted was read aloud to
Congress, its first reading. Adams introduced it with a speech. He spoke
"in a high and violent manner." With a curious sense of shock, Dickinson
heard him say that "there were people in this house who had held independence in view for more than twelvemonth." He had known it, of course;
he himself had spoken of independence for ten years—but never as an end,
only as a means (if all else failed) to free government. Adams had supported
all the measures of Congress policy. Now he was saying, in effect, he had
supported them insincerely, cynically, from the first.

Members heard the Declaration without comment, listened silently to
its bill of particulars against the King: *he has dissolved Representative houses
. . . he has suffered the administration of justice totally to cease . . . he has*

kept among us in times of peace standing armies & ships of war ... he has
plundered our seas, ravaged our coasts, burnt our towns & destroyed the
lives of our people ... he has waged cruel war against human nature itself ...

The time for discussion was not yet; the Declaration was ordered that
Friday to lie on the table. But no one remained unmoved by Jefferson's high
sentences, nor by the pledge he proposed they mutually make to each other,
of "our lives, our fortunes, & our sacred honour." Congress, as Friday ended,
had already heard the best arguments the hasty men had to offer, their
warmest persuasions to independence. It was with Jefferson's phrases ringing
in his mind that Dickinson had ridden out to Fairhill to write his speech.

And with tragedy in his mind, too. Just as he started, a final piece of
news came in: the defeat and surrender of the largest part of the army in
Canada, General Thompson's command—Pennsylvanians, Thompson, and
all of them. General Gates would find little but death, disease, and disaster
when he reached Canada to supersede Sullivan—the "Post of Honour" to
which Congress had recently named him.

It was a sad, spent scarecrow of a man who greeted his frail wife and
little daughter at Fairhill this last Saturday in June. They were his whole
family now, since his mother's death last March. They would suffer, even as
he, when the hot-tempered mob leaders seized the Pennsylvania government—as surely they were bound to, after Monday. Those leaders, the
newcomer Thomas Paine, the egregious Timothy Matlack, foolish James
Cannon, Christopher Marshall who should have known better, had raised a
great anger against him in last May's election, made him the special object
of their vilest personal abuse, their ranting attacks. They had waxed even
viler since his remarkable victory in that election. They would not spare
Polly, with her Norris heritage. They would spare no one who belonged
to him.

Dickinson would never forget those acid sour days before election, never
forget how those closest to him dropped away: George Bryan, magistrate
and friend before whom he and Polly had stood up to be married; Charles
Thomson on whom he had counted; George Clymer, usually so steady; even
Thomas McKean; even Caesar Rodney, his next neighbor on Jones Neck
down in Kent.

"When Int'rest calls off all her sneaking train,
    When all the oblig'd desert, and all the vain ..."

Yet despite everything his enemies could do, despite desertion of his friends,
that election had proved it was he who spoke for the most of Pennsylvanians.
It had been the largest, freest election ever held in Pennsylvania; and Dickinson had won, with nearly all his candidates. The Assembly had met—the

new Assembly, chosen on his new plan, with seventeen new members, new representation finally given to the western counties, and the city itself. (It was a reform he had striven for, through many years.) He would never forget the resentment of those leaders, fairly defeated, who refused to accept the people's mandate. Free elections were the very heart of free government, but these disgruntled hotheads cared nothing for the orderly processes of free government under a free constitution. They cared for power. Indoors and out, by the most astonishing, the most ruthless campaign, they had sought to discredit the elected Assembly, impede it, reject it, ignore it. They succeeded. It was an end to government itself, when minorities could conspire to overset elections. The Farmer knew, everyone knew, that Cannon and Matlack and Marshall had frequently met with Sam'l Adams, frequently conferred with his cousin John. The brace of Adamses, "those Cunning Men of the East," had undoubtedly had a busy hand in the lawless overthrow of lawful government in Pennsylvania. That end to courts and law, those "absurd democratical notions," that "spirit of levelling, as well as that of innovation" which John Adams deplored in Massachusetts and set himself to oppose, he was perfectly willing to encourage in Pennsylvania; chaos and collapse would defeat John Dickinson, drive him from Congress, ensure Pennsylvania's vote for independence. That it would also throw a great province into chaos, and into the hands of "The Mobility," what Adams himself called "the violent wrongheaded people of the inferior Class," Adams cared not a whit. Pennsylvania was not his country.

Pennsylvania was in a fair way to be nobody's country, at this moment. Strange to say, there was actually no government at all in the Province of Pennsylvania, no government to defend settlers in the western mountains against Virginia's armed invasion, to oust Connecticut land-grabbers from the Wyoming valley; no government to raise troops, furnish money, supplies; no governor, no council, no legislature, no court. General Howe had only to march his army tomorrow swiftly across the soft middle of New Jersey, present himself at the Delaware River, and Philadelphia would be his. It was a terrifying thought. The Assembly had adjourned June 14. They had no choice; its violent members—a minority, less even than a third—rendered it helpless by staying away and thus preventing a quorum. They hid, when the sergeant-at-arms went after them. June 14 was the end of the old Constitution, of Penn's Great Charter and Frame, the freest government anywhere in the world. The new Constitution had not yet commenced. The Conference of Committees of Inspection from all the counties met for a noisy week, June 18–25, in Philosophical Hall (as Christ Church School house was now called). It was a rowdy bunch, a hundred and more men new to public business—rough, unlettered, unused to city ways. One country member (Elisha Price, from Chester; "all the most curious characters among us in

Pennsylvania are Chester county men," a city judge observed) "got beside himself so farr that he run in the yard, jump'd over the fence so into the Street where he was pursued took to his Lodgings & Continued so, as not to be Capable to attend again. . . ."

The Conference called for an election, which would not be held till July 8, to choose members of a Constitutional Convention, which would not meet till July 15—two weeks after the fatal Monday, July 1. The Conference then passed a strange resolution, which was read aloud in Congress on June 25: all members "unanimously declare our willingness to concur in a vote of the congress, declaring the united colonies free and independent states"— though their concurrence could be only as individuals; they had no authority, represented no electors, spoke for no one but themselves, an hundred men. Then the Conference adjourned. After Tuesday June 25 there was nothing left of government at all.

Even the New Englanders in Congress were finally disturbed, as they contemplated this result of all their doings. Pennsylvania's arms and supplies were needed; someone must be able to vote money, call up troops. At the moment of Howe's landing with his mighty force, there must be *someone* in power in Pennsylvania for Congress to write to. Early Sunday morning, June 23, Cannon and Marshall had sought out Sam'l Adams, conferred with him for "some time." Afterwards, they appeared in Conference (this inno-cent body sat even on Sunday) and they passed through two hasty resolutions: the first was an instruction to the Constitutional Convention to appoint in July new Pennsylvania Delegates to Congress; the second was the statement that in the empty interim from June 25 to July 15, "the whole of the executive powers of government" in Pennsylvania, "so far as relates to the military defense and safety of the province" would be exercised by—the Committee of Safety!

To anyone, even to Sam'l Adams whose influence seems to have occasiontd it, even to Thomas McKean who (strangely) was presiding over this inept Conference, even to the schemers Cannon and Marshall themselves, this statement must have seemed palpably inane. The Conference had no man-date, nor any power nor even enough public influence, to delegate any authority of any kind to anybody. These were the very men who had dis-credited the Assembly, and with it discredited the Committee of Safety; they had destroyed public confidence in the old government—yet when they faced up to the disastrous result of what they had done, they blandly threw everything back on the Committee of Safety of that very Assembly and Charter Government they had effectively eliminated.

John Dickinson was by no means the only one appalled at these events. Overthrow of a firm and free government, so recently elected by such a large canvass, was more urgent than a matter of principle alone; it was a

daily disaster, a catastrophic reality. Congress had just asked Pennsylvania
for 6,000 Militia, to stand in North Jersey against Howe, keep him hemmed
in on Staten Island. Robert Morris rose grimly in Congress to tell the Delegates the facts of life. The Assembly was no more. If Congress wished to
procure these 6,000 men, they must now present their request to the Committee of Safety; and they had better do so very publicly, in exact, specific
terms, for, said Morris, himself a member of the Committee of Safety,
"under the present circumstances of the Province, he very much doubted if
they would be obeyed . . ." Congress debated most of a day about making
such a request. They needed those troops; yet once more the New England
men were drawn by the Adamses, in yoke: if Congress should address the
Committee of Safety, that would be recognition of the Committee's authority,
an acknowledgment of Assembly, of Mr. Dickinson's government, which the
violent men in Congress were determined to destroy. Robert Morris was
just as determined to smoke them out. He forced a vote; the independence
men won, the request failed. Congress would rather have no army in Jersey
than acknowledge the old government of Pennsylvania.

Morris was a careful, meticulous man. In defiance of the Rule of Secrecy,
he wrote out a terse memorandum of that day's debate, and the loss of the
motion in Congress. He had it attested by others: "The above is a true state
of facts," he wrote, and three Delegates signed for him as witnesses: Edward
Rutledge, Stone of Maryland, Joseph Hewes of North Carolina, "I have made
this memorandum on the spot," Morris wrote, "to appear when it may be
necessary, and to prevent blame being cast where it is not merited."

It was like Robert Morris, this self-serving declaration: there must be
someone to blame, and evidence to prove it: someone to bear the odium of
the end of civil government in Pennsylvania, of the failure to conclude a
Confederation in Congress, of defeat in Canada, of the collapse now of
military plans in North Jersey—these, at a moment when armies were
landing, warships standing off, peace commissioners offering an olive branch
on the points of Hessian bayonets; the very moment when a Congress without funds, without allies, without arms, helpless in Charles Town and hurled
back in Canada, had decided to declare the independence of thirteen jealous,
quarreling, disorganized colonies, putting to the last hazard their union, their
safety, their continued existence.

Blame was not an issue to John Dickinson—not now. Men like the
wanderer Tom Paine with his flaming, irresponsible *Common Sense,* his
uninvolvement in affairs, his delight in conflicts not his own, were bound to
appear when public leaders concerted on immoderate measures, roused up
the people to intemperate acts. Always Dickinson had warned that the
moderate way, the calm judicious way, was liberty's only way. Desert that,
and you invite the turbulence of mobs, the overthrow of law. Voltaire had

written, "History is filled with the sound of silken slippers going downstairs, and wooden shoes coming up." Heated tempers, angry proposals, violent rushing programs of the incautious men for a year past had made inevitable the rising of the city poor, the rural landless, the dissatisfied, the unready; and inevitable the emergence of uncounselled leaders among them, plausible men like, of all people, Timothy Matlack—low, uninformed, unprincipled, persuasive perhaps to the uneducated, but a Quaker disowned by Monthly Meeting, a gambler, bull baiter, cock-fighter, a failure in all he had tried, now eking out a miserable living by selling beer in bottles. Compassionate Friends had paid his way out of debtors' prison; but why had Charles Thomson thought to confer on Matlack the post of his Clerk in Congress? And why had Matlack been named Colonel of a Battalion?

Revolution was bound to be filled with the stench and noise of humanity. Blame fell on every leader, for these ten years past, who had rejected moderation, and the program of reason—that program which would have brought a united America, supported by foreign alliances, into independence with firm, effective governments of laws. At any moment, John Dickinson could have joined with the violent men, taken the easy way, the way a timid man would take, the way Thomson, McKean, so many others, those "Cleons of politics, courting popular favor," had taken. He could have done so with an easy grace; there had been plenty of chances this past year: when the King refused to accept the Olive Branch Petition, when he issued his Proclamation of Rebellion, when he hired foreign troops to send against his own subjects. On news of the Hessian mercenary contracts, in January, Dickinson was heard to say, "I see no alternative, but independence or slavery." He could have abandoned his program, saved his personal position in a dramatic moment of public leadership. Or he could have been, like old Franklin, unavoidably absent. His gout was as severe, he could have made it as convenient. ("Dids't thee ever know Dr. Franklin to be in a minority?" a Quaker asked pointedly, publicly.) Dickinson would do neither. He persisted in his steady program: independence was a step to be prepared for, to be planned; national sovereignty meant national responsibilities accepted in advance, national credit established, the liberties of the citizens ensured . . .

Dickinson was abundantly grateful to Robert Morris. He was one who did *not* desert; he was the one more than any other who saw exactly what The Farmer's program was, with what deliberate steps he was making the shift, from opposing ministry and Parliament, to opposing the King himself. He was moving deliberately, in order that every new measure the King took would come as a measure unprovoked, an act of punishment, unconstitutional, unjust. "What topics of reconciliation are now left?" Dickinson had asked, ten months ago. He had asked it of Arthur Lee, whose place in London was to preserve every public attitude of reconciliation, preserve among English friends to America the impression that reconciliation was desired. And he had continued to furnish Lee with topics, arguments, anti-ministerial ammunition to strengthen the Whig opposition in Parliament, and in London. It was not without effect: the latest votes in Parliament against the ministry's American policy were perceptibly greater than the votes had been last fall and winter; London merchants had sent in still another petition in behalf of America; prominent officers had abruptly resigned their commissions in famous regiments rather than serve against the American colonists. The policy of reconciliation was worth preserving, particularly now as we moved into the policy of independence, for it weakened the British government. Independence now, would strengthen that govern-ment in its war measures, would lose the support of English Whigs in Parliament, in the city, in the country.

Morris had been privy to Silas Deane's mission. He knew, certainly—for he drew part of the commercial instructions—the embarrassment our first envoy would suffer if, as soon as he opened negotiations at Versailles, news of independence should arrive, discrediting his mission. He knew also the text of Dickinson's diplomatic instructions last spring, bluntly announcing the intention of independence to France, Spain, and Holland while concealing it from Britain, soliciting foreign alliances in advance of the event. . . . Morris had never been popular in the city; by now the Independents had succeeded in making him thoroughly hated. But Morris stood firm.

Defeat was a step to be planned for, too. Let Morris gather evidences, store up his defenses; was there nothing more to be done? The Farmer's plans were made. He had met defeat before; he could meet it now. He would persist to the last in urging his moderate way; the people needed that. Afterwards, he would say it all again, and again. Life would go on, politics would go on, liberty and law and justice would go on as a thoughtful man's cause. And war would go on. Those 6,000 men must still be placed in Jersey, and swiftly, regardless by what authority. If there was no authority at all, he must do it himself: after Monday's defeat, he would move at once to march his Battalion, take some position of some kind opposite Staten Island. His men would follow him; so would Cadwalader's. Whether Matlack's would, or McKean's, no one knew. John Dickinson was First Colonel, first ranking officer of Associators, Commander of the First Battalion, he had been a first founder of the Militia. The Independents dared not throw him out, not now. An express had just brought exact word: Howe's fleet sighted off Sandy Hook was 52 large war vessels, 27 armed sloops and cutters, 400 transports. . . .

And he would miss no slightest chance to stress the wisdom, the success, the firmness that had been in his moderate program, the purity of Assembly leaders. Even the wildest of the unprincipled Independents realized that his

Assembly government had moved fully staffed, fully effective and strong, right into the final crisis. Every measure—Confederation, alliances, repeal of test oaths, a constitutional convention—every measure except independence itself had been voted by the Assembly, and independence had not been voted down, only deferred. The Independents had determined that none of these, their favorite measures, should come from the Assembly. This Monday, when Congress would decide for Lee's Resolution over his opposition, the formal vote would have to show unanimity among the colonies. Losing in debate, Pennsylvania would have to bow, accept the loss, vote with the majority. The cause of American Union demanded it. Who would cast the vote? Franklin, of course; once the majority was clear, the old man would take his stand. To join with him, Dickinson would send not himself, nor Willing or Morris or Humphreys; he would send to cast Pennsylvania's vote for independence the two men Pennsylvania Independents resented most, but whom they had been able to hurt least: James Wilson—they detested him for his agreeing with their ends while opposing their methods—and blunt tough John Morton, Speaker of the hated Assembly, the most out-spoken, most implacable of all foes of the Conference men. It was a tiny thing; but at least the Delegates of Pennsylvania voting for independence would be old government men, men loyal to the Great Charter and Frame, men the people had honored and esteemed, men who honored the people.

Meanwhile, a man facing defeat did not give up in advance. Even in defeat, perhaps especially in defeat, a thoughtful man must maintain the rightness of his opinion, must—he had said this to Marylanders last winter—"breathe that Spirit which ought to govern all publick Bodies, Firmness tempered with Moderation." It was the hardest position to take. Moderation had no magic to win men's minds; moderation did not call to high places. It called to reason, but never to the heart. Moderation had only pale words to offer, words of good sense and sound judgment, but colorless words of caution, wan dim words of prudence. He must find the words.

Three weeks ago, he had found them, Saturday June 8, an incredible day—the tall pale Farmer was everywhere at once, taut, controlled, drawing deep on his frail reserves, spending all his mind, all his skills. Upstairs in the State House, the Assembly was waiting his draft of new instructions; down-stairs Congress in Committee of the Whole had begun debating Lee's reso-lution; in the city all the officers of militia battalions were gathered in angry conclave demanding his attendance. Still coughing from his last month's trip to Kent, his lungs filled with marsh damp and ague, Dickinson went briskly through early-morning committee work. At nine, he climbed the great stair-case to the Assembly, presented the new instructions he had written for himself and the other Pennsylvania Delegates in Congress. He spoke care-fully, exactly; he must not give out Congress's secrets. He spoke urgently of Union, of the hope of support from abroad. Overnight he had reshaped his instructions to meet Lee's resolution. They were bold, froward: Delegates were to vote in Congress for a Confederation uniting the colonies, for treaties with foreign powers; of independence he said nothing explicit, only this: Delegates were "to concur on such other Measures as, upon a View of all circumstances, shall be judged necessary for promoting the Liberty, Safety and Interests of *America.*" (Assembly was used now to the new formula; the interests of America, not of Pennsylvania, should guide them all.) Independents orated, protested; but the instructions passed, finally. The vote was 31 to 12.

He was downstairs the moment the votes were counted. Congress was high in temper; Dickinson joined with Wilson, Livingston, and Ned Rutledge; he was one of the four who sustained the whole argument for "the sensible part of the house," urging postponement. Independence would not be achieved by a mere declaration; independence meant a government, recognition, allies; we had taken none of these steps to be genuinely independent, not yet. . . .

Congress was interminable that day. Debate ran on all afternoon, long past the dinner hour; finally it ended at seven in the evening, with confederation and treaties in principle approved, independence still undecided.

Others might dine then, or caucus by delegations, plan Monday's steps. But Dickinson must hurry off to the meeting of officers—Colonel Dickinson of the First Battalion. He expected to be attacked; he was. Independents were roused to fury at the proposal that the Assembly appoint a Brigadier General over all Pennsylvania's Militia. The Assembly was the duly constituted government, of course, properly elected; but the Assembly would appoint someone other than the new-risen leaders. Probably, the Assembly would appoint the Colonel of the First Battalion. As soon as Dickinson entered, one of the officers launched into a violent diatribe, charging the Assembly with every offense in the radicals' book: the Assembly must have nothing to say about a Brigadier General; the Assembly must come to an end—the Assembly had chosen Delegates to Congress who were enemies of the people, had dared to make innovations in the government without a vote of the people, had refused to give its Delegates new instructions to vote independence; "the authors and abettors of those instructions would find they had lost the Confidence & affection of the people!"

For the third time that long day of ordeals, Dickinson had found the words. Assembly, Congress, Militia—to each he had spoken of moderation, firmness, an orderly plan; spoken of liberties under law, and the rights only governments could maintain. The intemperate battalion captain he answered with grim sharpness. At the end, he fell into the loose rhetoric of fatigue.

Almost, his control deserted him. From sheer exhaustion, the elegant Farmer became for once nearly common clay:

"We are blamed for appointing men who had not the confidence of the people & we are also blamed because we gave not those suspected men unlimited powers: You say the Assembly has no right to alter the constitution without the consent of the people, & you condemn the Assembly because they gave not their delegates powers to alter it.

"The loss of life, or what is dearer than life itself, the Affection of my countrymen shall not deter me from acting as an honest man. These threats then that we just now heard might have been spared. I defy them. I regard them not. I stand as unmoved by them, as the rock among the waves that dash against it. I can defy the *world,* Sir! But—I defy not heaven. Nor will I ever barter my conscience for the esteem of mankind. So let my Country treat me as she pleases still I will act as my conscience directs."

A youngster among the officers, a convinced Independent at that, heard the famous First Colonel (his father's friend and patron) with awe and wonderment. His words, he declared, "appeared to be the unpremeditated effusions of the heart. His graceful actions, the emotions of his countenance & a plaintive yet manly voice strongly imposed upon my judgment. He was clearly wrong yet I believed him right. Such were the effects of oratory."

More experienced men than Billy Bradford had made the same mistake— had failed to learn that nothing The Farmer ever said, or did, was unpremeditated.

That weekend, in Speaker Norris' library building at Fairhill, he prepared his final appeal to the reasonableness of Americans. Saturday passed, and Sunday. Monday July 1 dawned in the full heavy heat of a Philadelphia summer.

The forty-three Delegates passed into the lofty East Room; the doorkeeper closed out the world behind them. President John Hancock moved painfully to the chair, Charles Thomson took his place as secretary, Timothy Matlack sat at the clerk's table.

Promptly, the session began—began not with the debate all were primed for, but with the day's agenda of administrative business. Congress was running a war. Debates, even "the greatest debate of all," must wait on the public business.

Dr. Lyman Hall and Mr. Button Gwinnett rose, advanced to the President's dais, a younger man, richly dressed, between them. With some formality they presented the Hon. George Walton, new Delegate from Georgia. (They must have done so with meagre satisfaction; Walton was among their bitterest opponents back home. Next spring, just before Button

Gwinnett was killed, Walton would call him "a rotten hearted designing enemy.") The new arrival handed his credentials to Secretary Thomson, who read them aloud to the room. It took some minutes; credentials were never short. Members talked busily with each other, paying scant attention to the secretary's familiar tones in a routine procedure. President Hancock welcomed Major Walton with a brief nod and a word; the Georgians took their seats.

Then began the legislative day. A letter from New Jersey's Provincial Congress was read, and one from New Hampshire's. President Hancock read these in person, for they were communications from sovereign authorities, official business. Funds were needed; Delegates heard Robert Morris's terse report, they voted six thousand dollars for the Deputy Paymaster-General of the Southern Department (no debate on that, no discussion even of where Congress would find the money). And all the late-arrived reports from military commanders were opened: three from General Washington, filled with problems, dangers, shortages; letters from the northern generals, Schuyler, Arnold, Sullivan; and from colonels in the field.

They brought dismal news, these military letters—words of fear and shuddering, words of defeat that rang like the slow peal of grief when read aloud. Yankee John Sullivan was known to all New England Delegates, known to the other senior members, too, for he had sat here in Congress last year. Sullivan was no alarmist, this sober aggressive Irishman of sturdy fortitude, good sense, still commanding general in Canada. His news was black from his camp at Sorel, his words had the cadence of an Old Testament dirge: ". . . Our Enemies multiply upon our hands and we have few to oppose them. I now think only of a glorious death or a victory obtained against superior numbers. . . ."

We have lost Canada, Colonel Antill writes bluntly. We must retreat, or the enemy will be in Crown Point before us. Antill had been at Montgomery's side last New Year's Eve when he fell; Congress had listened to him for two hours describing that action. Edward Antill was no coward. General Benedict Arnold tells of "the greatest confusion . . . three thousand sick." Small pox is raging through his tents. He has ruthlessly put the sick on half-rations to save the well—a shocking though to Congressmen silent in their chairs. Arnold, too, the bold, impetuous Arnold, urges retreat: give up Canada, secure our own land before it is too late, Congress must act, Congress must let us if possible save *some* remnant of our army. "I am content to be the last man who quits this country, and fall so that my country rise—but let us not fall all together."

Arnold's words bring Canada close to the State House, the sick and the starving soldiers just over the Wall. Congress must act, must decide. . . .

Desertions, fatigue, retreat, plunder, corruption, deceit of Canadians, the great force of the enemy—this is Colonel Moses Hazen's letter, picturing Sullivan's "Distressed Dissatified & undisciplined army." "For God's sake, Secure your retreat," he begs Congress, "there is no time to lose."

Appalling, ominous words; strange words to hear on the day of independence. Secretary Thomson's tones were a litany of disaster, a lamentation. *"Our Enemies multiply upon our hands and we have few to oppose them...."* The morning hours slipped by, the day's heats rose. Each letter had to be considered, answered, or referred.

At last there were no more. Routines were over, the fearful realities of war for another day done with. Congress could now become a senate. The order of the day was read, members resolved themselves into Committee of the Whole, President Hancock stepped gingerly down, his gout severe, took his place among the Massachusetts delegation—Gerry, Robert Treat Paine, the brace of disapproving Adamses.

As had been his wont ever since March 15 when Governor Ward of Rhode Island had sickened and died, Hancock called to the chair to preside in Committee of the Whole the untidy, elephantine figure of Colonel Benjamin Harrison of Virginia. The other Virginians found this arrangement entirely agreeable; it removed Harrison from debate. John Adams found it abominable. The rough, hearty Harrison, apparently so much fonder of his horses, of low talk and good food than of serious business anywhere of any kind, was an offense to Adams: "another Sir John Falstaff . . . his conversation disgusting to every man of delicacy of decorum . . . I took no notice of his vices or follies . . ." It was ever a mystery to Adams that Washington and Harrison should be such friends. To him, the enormous bluff colonel was entirely unacceptable: "This was an indolent, luxurious, heavy gentleman, of no use in Congress or committee, but a great embarrassment to both. . . ." Adams never bothered to notice how much actual work flowed smoothly over the easy-going Harrison's desk, how swiftly his committees moved, nor how many times by a pungent remark he effectively put an end to criticisms of Washington, or votes unfavorable to the army. "My soft way," Harrison called it. Hearty men, merry men, men of steady good humor who cared nothing for dignity and laughed at his earnestness, his heats, Adams could never abide. Harrison was more generous toward human kind. "Your fatigue and various kinds of trouble I dare say are great," he comforted Washington, "but they are not more than I expected, knowing the people you have to deal with by the Sample we have here .... indeed, my friend, I do not know what to think of some of these men, they seem exceeding hearty in the Cause, but still wish to keep everything among themselves." The men Benjamin Harrison loved were not those John Adams could like. He loved

Hancock: "Our President is quite of a different Cast, Noble, Disinterested and Generous to a very great Degree . . ." There were those who said the same of Colonel Harrison.

The big Virginian lumbered cheerfully to the chair. Then, as the members settled down for debate, the door behind them opened.

The doorkeeper brought in an express rider, dusty and reeking of horse-heat. He had pounded up from Annapolis, in his hand was the resolution of the Maryland Convention Chase had promised Adams he would send as soon as it passed and was properly signed. Maryland had used strong words, sent positive orders to vote for independence, "to concur in all points with Congress." Her words gave out ringing sounds, not of a knell, but of bells of jubilation. They cheered the members, helped them put out of mind those horrid letters from the generals in the north. Maryland was a grateful antidote to Canadian miseries.

Colonel Harrison rapped for order; in a mood entirely different, the Delegates settled again. Lee's resolution was read aloud. Someone—no record tells us who, no record even hints—formally moved its adoption; and someone seconded, to open debate. We can only guess who these opening speakers were. By custom, Virginia would have moved, for hers was the original resolution June 8; Massachusetts would have seconded, for she had originally seconded three weeks ago. Richard Henry Lee, the original pro-poser, was no longer present here in Congress; of the remaining Virginians, Colonel Harrison, senior Delegate, was in the chair, so he could make no motion; Nelson was but newly returned; Jefferson was almost always silent, and in his abundant jottings gives no indication that he spoke this day. Two Delegates were left: Francis Lightfoot Lee and Carter Braxton. Lee was four months senior to Braxton in service. Perhaps it was he who moved the adoption of his brother's "resolve for independency." If Massachusetts seconded, it could not have been John Adams, for he would speak later. Sam'l Adams rarely said anything these days, from an obscure kind of tactfulness; Robert Treat Paine was another who "seldom quit his chair" unless to object to something. He was described by one colleague as "the Objection maker." Perhaps it was Mr. Gerry who stammered out the seconding.

Debate then began with an entirely unexpected twist. From the New York delegation, Mr. George Clinton, latest arrived, was recognized. Everyone knew New York's Convention had not acted; would Clinton demand post-ponement? Or point out the danger of leaving one critical colony outside the general whole? Independence must be unanimous, or Union would be forever impossible. Clinton surprised them. He had contrived a formula for today's proceeding; he proposed something Congress had not done before. He begged consideration for the peculiar situation he and his colleagues found themselves in: their instructions, now a year old, still forbade them from taking any action in Congress likely to impede reconciliation with Britain. They had sent an express home, asking new instructions; the reply was in his hand. And Mr. Clinton read it—the letter of June 11 from the New York Provincial Congress, stating there was at present no body existing which could give the sense of the Province of New York on the momentous question of independence. Her Delegates in Congress certainly must not presume to do so. But measures were already under way to ascertain the sentiments of the inhabitants—the election, the new Convention—and at the earliest opportunity the Delegates would receive their new instructions.

There was no side to Clinton; he spoke plainly, briskly, he seemed a very ordinary man. He seemed ordinary, when he explained the "earliest opportunity" would not be for days yet, certainly not this week. In his matter-of-fact manner, he stated that he and his colleagues had decided they were not justified in voting either way on today's question. He seemed ordinary, matter-of-fact, as if he had no special point to make about it, when he went on to say the New York Delegates here present were in favor of independence themselves, and they were assured their constituents were for it. To Mr. Alsop sitting beside him, "soft, sweet" Alsop, the words were far from ordinary, and this was certainly a point. He was by no means in favor, nor had any such assurance been given to any of them, by anybody. Indeed, there was no one who could have given it. As far as Mr. Alsop was concerned, Clinton was deceiving the members. In fact, George Clinton, holding a wetted finger to the wind, was choosing sides. He would not choose for John Alsop. Only New Yorkers realized Clinton's personal stake, as he twisted that June 11 letter into an expression of implied consent. Bound as they were, Clinton smoothly concluded, New York asked formal leave of Congress to withdraw from the question.

The surprised Congress granted leave; the chair ruled as he asked. Harrison, experienced parliamentarian, surely saw what was afoot: that formal leave was entirely unnecessary. New Yorkers could simply have refrained from voting, or they could have stepped beyond the bar of the house when the roll was called and been recorded "absent." But that would have allowed New Yorkers to join in debate; members could have recorded their opposition. By securing this formal permission of the whole house to withdraw from the question, Clinton had not only forestalled a "no" vote, he had also forstalled his colleagues from speaking out on the issue. And by his bland assurance they were all in favor—Harrison, most everyone present, knew better—he had removed any reluctance other colonies might feel to voting "yes" because of New York's long-standing opposition.

Clinton sat down. What John Alsop had witnessed was one of those small, subtle strokes in George Clinton's twisting, turning dance through public life, at the outset of his forty years of artful straddling, which would lead him to permanent domination of New York's rambunctious mobs in demo-cratical revolution. This same George Clinton would one day, for his numerous remarkable achievements, be called "father of New York." Late in life, widely celebrated, he would serve as Vice President under two different Presidents of the United States. This morning he had revealed, in his or-dinary way, how well he already knew the secret of eating his cake and having it, too.

What Edward Rutledge had witnessed was the collapse of another hope. Even had John Jay yielded to his pleadings and come down, he could have said nothing, done nothing, to help. What John Adams had seen was that this made no difference at all. He still waited for Jersey to come in, or Rodney of Delaware, his ninth state. . . .

From Pennsylvania, John Dickinson was on his feet. He held a manuscript in his hands, long sheets, several of them. He began to read—deliberately, carefully; there was nothing ordinary about this man, or these words:

"Sir:

"The consequences involved in the motion now lying before you are of such magnitude, that I tremble under the oppressive honor of sharing in its determination. I feel myself unequal to the burden assigned me. I believe— I had almost said, I rejoice—that the time is approaching when I shall be relieved from its weight. While the trust remains with me, I must discharge the duties of it, as well as I can—and I hope I shall be the more favorably heard, as I am convinced, that I shall hold such language, as will sacrifice my private emolument to general interests. My conduct, this day, I expect will give the finishing blow to my once too great, and, my integrity con-sidered, now too diminished popularity. It will be my lot to know, that I had rather vote away the enjoyment of that dazzling display, that pleasing posses-sion, than the blood and happiness of my countrymen—too fortunate, amidst their calamities, if I prove a truth known in heaven, that I had rather they should hate me, than that I should hurt them. . . ."

Dickinson's words were formidable. Here in this closed chamber, among men who knew him well, it must have been only his grace of manner, his unmistakable earnestness, which saved what he was saying from being a little embarrassing. The Delegates found him strange. They had expected a speech from him today, but nothing so formal, so pretentious as this. It was not Congress's way. Debate here was never recorded: everything was secret, speeches were always *ex tempore,* no one ever before had written out his words in advance, a prepared speech, orated like a member of Parliament for the country, for posterity. The Farmer was addressing them as if he had never seen them before, as if they were considering this question for the very first time:

"I might, indeed, practise an artful, an advantageous reserve upon this occasion. But thinking as I do on the subject of debate, silence would be guilt. I despise its arts, I detest its advantages. I must speak, though I should lose my life, though I should lose the affections of my country. Happy at present, however, I shall esteem myself, if I can so far rise to the height of this great argument as to offer to this honorable assembly in a full and clear manner, those reasons, that have so invariably fixed my own opinion.

"It was a custom in a wise and virtuous state, to preface propositions in council, with a prayer, that they might redound to the public benefit." (They were all classicists. Education was knowing Thucydides, Tacitus, Livy; they would all recognize his allusion. Scholars among them, old Hopkins, Sherman, Middleton, Wilson, Adams, would be touched to alertness.) "I beg leave to imitate the laudable example—and I do most humbly implore Almighty God, with whom dwells wisdom itself, so to enlighten the members of this house, that their decision may be such as will best promote the liberty, safety and prosperity of these colonies, and for myself, that His divine goodness may be graciously pleased to enable me, to speak the precepts of sound policy on the important question that now engages our attention."

John Adams was taken unawares. Years later, he would recall how Mr. Dickinson "had prepared himself apparently with great labor and ardent zeal, and in a speech of great length, and with all his eloquence, he combined together all that had before been written in pamphlets and newspapers, and all that had from time to time been said in Congress by himself and others. He conducted the debate not only with great ingenuity and eloquence, but with equal politeness and candor, and was answered in the same spirit." Labor, zeal, ingenuity, ardor, eloquence—John Adams always kept in the first place of all, at the head of that long, long list of persons he thoroughly detested, the name of John Dickinson. Yet he could use these words, remembering this speech in the suffocating heat of the Assembly Chamber Monday, July first, 1776. He failed only to remember his own apprehensive uneasiness, for his ninth state had not come in; and he found no need to record the effect his opponent was making.

"Sir," Mr. Dickinson was saying, "gentlemen of very distinguished abilities and knowledge differ widely in their sentiments upon the point now agitated. They all agree, that the utmost prudence is required in forming our decision, but immediately disagree in their notion of that prudence. Some cautiously insist, that we ought to obtain that previous information which we are likely quickly to obtain, and to make those previous establishments that are acknowledged to be necessary. Others strenuously assert, that though regularly such information and establishment ought to precede the measure proposed, yet, confiding in our Fortune more boldly than Caesar himself, we ought to brave the storm in a skiff made of paper!"

A skiff made of paper: this was the Declaration they had heard read last Friday—a paper ship of state, launched without plan, without Union, without allies, without rudder or helmsman, in the midst of a war. With this phrase, Dickinson became The Farmer again, incisive, acid, ruthless in clarity, in logic. On every sentence The Farmer's hallmark was stamped: his sure swift way of cutting to the very heart of the matter, his disarming candor, his striking dignity of thought and expression, his marshalling of more information than others had or would use, in support of positive programs of deliberate, unified action.

"In all such cases, where every argument is adorned with an eloquence that may please yet mislead, it seems to me the proper method of discovering the right path, to enquire, which of the parties is, probably, the most warmed by passion? Other circumstances being equal or nearly equal, that consideration would have influence with me. I fear the *virtue* of Americans. Resentment of the injuries offered to their country, may irritate them to counsels and to actions that may be detrimental to the cause, they would die to advance."

The clock bell high on the roof had long since chimed noon; the sun was streaming in through the tall south windows. The Farmer had plunged to the core of his argument: What advantages can be claimed, from declaring independence now? Gentlemen say, it will animate the people. Certainly for that it is unnecessary; the general spirit of America is already aroused. Life, liberty, and property have proved motives enough to animate the people. Or, they say, independence will convince foreign powers of our strength and unanimity, and they will in consequence thereof send us aid. But who has had any news that our declaration will be agreeable to France? Foreign powers will not rely on words. Our strength and unanimity will be proved, not by words, but by the outcome of this summer's campaign. This is but the first campaign; its event will determine if we shall fight on, or go down to defeat. A declaration now, will not strengthen us by one man, nor by the least supply. What must France think of us, if we begin our empire in so high a style, with no foreign support, when on the point of being invaded by the whole power of Great Britain? of if we commit our country upon an alternative, where to recede will be infamy, to persist may be destruction?

And these foreign powers, why should they help us? France and Spain must perceive the immediate danger of our revolution, to their colonies lying on our doorsteps. Their seat of empire is in another world: suppose Spain proves more interested in recapturing Portugal, as Prince Masserano is urging, than in recapturing East and West Florida? Why then should she help America?

It would be more respectful to act in conformity to the views of France. Let us take advantage of French pride, give the French reason to believe that we confide in them, that we desire to act in conjunction with their policies and interests. Let us know how they would regard this stranger among the states of the world. People are fond of what they have assisted in producing. They regard it as a child. A cement of affection exists between them. Let us allow France and Spain the glory of appearing the vindicators of liberty. It will please them.

It is treating them with contempt to act otherwise, especially after the application we have already made to France, which by this time has reached them.* (Everyone knew Dickinson's place on the Committee of Secret Correspondence, that very special small committee whose transactions were not open to the rest of the members, not even to the members of that other Secret Committee, for trade. In front of him was Colonel Benjamin Harrison, at his side Dr. Franklin and Robert Morris of that arcane Committee of Secret Correspondence. Only Jay was missing. Harrison, Franklin, and Morris knew, though Adams did not, nor any of the independence men, nor any in the room save these four, the folio of secret diplomatic instructions Silas Deane had taken with him when he sailed on the *Rachell* last March, a clandestine agent in elaborate commercial "cover," sent to try France's disposition, seek arms, money, supplies, offer France our whole trade in exchange. Dickinson drafted those instructions; Franklin, Robert Morris, Colonel Harrison worked them over, added points; they all signed them. They could have told the house The Farmer's bold words for Vergennes in those March 3 instructions: ". . . *if we should, as there is a great appearance we shall, come to a total separation from Great Britain, France would be looked upon as the power whose friendship it would be fittest for us to obtain and cultivate. . . .*" Dickinson dared not reveal the deepest mysteries of foreign affairs, but at least he could tell them what the Committee of Secret Correspondence had done, how he as a member felt about it. (In this he was on the verge of the best-kept secret of Congress.) Consider the abilities of the persons to whom we have sent, the ministers at Versailles, at Madrid. What will they think, if now so quickly after applying to them, without waiting their determination, totally slighting their sentiments on such a prodigious issue, we haughtily pursue our own measures?

"May they not say to us, Gentlemen! You falsely pretended to consult us, and disrespectfully proceeded without waiting our resolution. You must abide

---

* Actually, it hadn't, though Dickinson could not have known this. Silas Deane's voyage was delayed by a series of the most improbable accidents; he did not arrive in Paris till July 7.

the consequences. We are not ready for a rupture; you should have negotiated till we were. We will not be hurried by your impetuosity. We know it is our interest to support you, but we shall be in no haste about it. Try your own strength and resources in which you have such confidence. We know you dare not look back. Reconciliation is by now impossible. Yours is the most rash and at the same time the most contemptible senate that ever existed on Earth!"

And what do we have to offer France or Spain, that will bring forth the aid gentlemen seem so certain we shall receive? Suppose, on our declaring independence, England should offer to return Canada to France, the Floridas to Spain, with an extension of their old limits: would not France and Spain accept them? "Gentlemen say, the trade of all America is more valuable to France than Canada. I grant it. But suppose she may get *both*? If she is politick, and none doubts that, I aver she has the easiest game to play for attaining both, that ever presented itself to a nation.

"When we have bound ourselves to a stern quarrel with Great Britain by a declaration of independence, France has nothing to do but to hold back and intimidate Great Britain till Canada is put into her hands, and then to intimidate us into a most disadvantageous grant of our trade. It is my firm opinion these events will take place, and arise naturally from our declaring independence."

And now a point thrown in almost casually, almost as if in afterthought, an old trick of The Farmer's—a trick of his writing, his courtroom pleadings, his Assembly debating: as to aid from foreign powers, our declaration though we should make it today, can procure us nothing for this present hard campaign. That is impossible. (So why this urgency, he wanted them to think, why this hazardous hurry? We still have to win this summer, meet the three invading armies—Canada, New York, Charles Town—and contain them. We still have to do it by ourselves.)

The sun was brightest now in the south windows, the heat at its worst. It was time to change pace, shift to a positive program. This was Congress, he had to give them something to do, not just something to oppose. This was The Farmer; he was ready.

"Now consider, if all the advantages expected from foreign powers cannot be attained in a more unexceptionable manner? Is there no other way of giving notice of a nation's resolution, than by proclaiming it to all the world? Let us in the most solemn manner inform the House of Bourbon, at least France, that we wait only for her determination to declare independence. We must not talk generally of foreign powers, but only of those we expect to favor us. Let us assure Spain that we never will give any assistance to her colonies. Let France become guarantee for us in arrangements of this kind.

"Besides, let us first establish our governments, and take the regular form of a state. These prudent measures will show deliberation, wisdom, caution, and unanimity.

"It is our interest to keep Great Britain in the opinion that we mean reconciliation, as long as possible. The opposition in parliament, which boldly supports us in our cause, is the principal disadvantage the present administration suffers. Once we declare independence, that opposition must turn against us, and join the administration in supporting the war; the wealth of London and the outport towns, now involved in our trade, will be poured into the treasury, the whole nation will be ardent against us. We shall oblige her, by our attitude, to persevere in her spirit. But if we delay, if we continue to offer reconciliation, our friends in England will continue to support us."

And he spoke of the recent petition to the throne from the city of London, justifying colonial arguments, praying for a restoration of constitutional liberties under the crown. English Whigs were convinced loss of American trade would ruin them, and ruin the Empire. Their conviction was our best opportunity to keep vigorous and alive a strong anti-ministerial opposition in Parliament.

And suppose we did succeed in ruining England: France would rise on her ruins, a nation ambitious for trade, for empire, for colonial dependencies, a nation Roman Catholic in religion. Our dangers from French dominion on the seas will be far greater than those dangers we now confront. We shall weep for our lost liberties. And we shall be overwhelmed with debt: that debt is already computed at six million pounds Pennsylvania money a year.

If we declare independence now, the war will certainly be carried on with more severity than heretofore. Burning of towns has only begun, setting loose Indians on our frontiers, we have not yet seen. So far war has not been harsh. Boston might have been fired; it was not.

As declaring independence is not necessary to animate our troops, so it is not necessary to strengthen our union. Indeed, it may weaken that union, when people find themselves engaged in a war rendered more cruel by such a declaration, with no prospect of an end to their calamities even by a successful continuation of the war, and no prospect of paying for war, or for peace. Western lands could pay for both, if colonies were willing to give up the whole western empire to the Union, thus forming a general fund for the Congress to back its moneys, support its credit, to provide for armies and for arms.

"People are changeable. In bitterness of soul they may complain against our rashness, and ask why we did not apply first to foreign powers, why we did not settle differences among ourselves, why we did not take care to secure for the people of the whole of America, unsettled and unlocated lands for easing the people's burthens, instead of leaving those burthens for posterity to bear? Why we did not wait till we were better prepared, till we had made an experiment of our strength?"

Abruptly, he changed again; he spoke of the Family Compact, that alliance which had bound France and Spain together for sixty years, since the Peace of Utrecht in 1714. Could we rely on it? France and Spain might be alarmed with one another. On diplomatic matters, and on news of nations and the great world, Delegates heard John Dickinson with respect. They knew his correspondence was extensive, both privately and for the Secret Committee. They also knew (everyone did) that the Spanish King, Charles III—an old hand, austere, pious, liberal, firm, governing his vast empire with great vigor in person—was by no means the inferior partner in his dealings with the youthful, indolent Louis XVI at Versailles. Now Dickinson spoke of dangers to be apprehended from Charles III: Portuguese in lower Brazil had seized Spanish outposts on the Rio de la Plata these past few months, Spain was probably planning revenge, perhaps an invasion of Portugal itself; France would be reluctant to support such a war, for England was Portugal's ancient ally. Supporting Spain in an attack on Portugal would involve France in war against England. Some in the Spanish court, high in council, were nevertheless willing to commence a war against Portugal and England both, without France—willing, that is, to dissolve the Family Compact. One such was the Neopolitan, Prince de Masserano. And Charles III, evidently willing to listen to warhawks of his court, had just sent Masserano as Spanish Ambassador to England. Obviously, Masserano was testing England's willingness to support Portugal if Spain should march against Lisbon. Appointment of Masserano to London, Dickinson told the Congress in Philadelphia, was a calculated insult to France. The Spanish King was moving separately, along a way France would not willingly go. The Family Compact was strained; if it should break, America would be caught in the shambles of a European system in ruins. Alliance with either empire would make an enemy of the other, and no ally could protect us from England and another warring empire as well.

Even if peace should be preserved in Europe, by an alteration of policies now under way, there was still not the least evidence as yet that France would grant us favorable terms of alliance. She would extract conditions from us; we would have to meet them. The glory of recovering Canada might well prove quite enough to satisfy France. She would take Canada, then make her own peace, and dictate terms to us.

"A partition of these colonies will take place, if Great Britain cannot conquer us. Declaring independence, we would be destroying our house before we have got another—in winter, with a small family, then asking a neighbor to take us in and finding he is unprepared."

Yet gentlemen said, the "spirit of the colonies" called for such a declaration. The answer was, the "spirit of the colonies" was not to be relied on. Not only treaties with foreign powers, but treaties among ourselves should precede this declaration. We should know on what grounds we are to stand with regard to one another. Consider the declaration of Virginia just now, about colonists in *"their Limits!"* (Mr. Carter Braxton had come to Philadelphia charged with Virginia's case against Pennsylvania. The Lady Juliana Penn had authorized sale of more Proprietary lands; just this spring Thomas Wharton had raised money and floated The Indiana Company, to sell for the Penns their family lands in the west included in the Charter of Pennsylvania —lands below Pittsburgh. Braxton demanded Pennsylvania show her "Right to that Country as the same with within the Limits of Virginia." Delegates had been struggling for a year and a half now with claims and counter claims everywhere, with open rivalries, even battles, over lands. In the disputed "Indiana" tracts below Pittsburgh, Virginians and Pennsylvanians were actually fighting. Connecticut had subsidized settlers to go armed in bands to occupy interior parts of Pennsylvania she claimed; New York viewed the Hampshire Grants (Vermont to be) as a threat; South Carolina and Georgia were in open and angry dispute. Everyone knew The Farmer was right. Mr. Braxton, a few seats away from the speaker, back in mid-April had written his uncle, "some are for Lugging us into Independence. . . . If it was to be now asserted, the Continent would be torn in pieces by Intestine Wars and Convulsions. Previous to Independence all disputes must be healed and Harmony prevail. A grand Continental league must be formed and a superintending Power also. . . ." April was not so long ago. Yet Carter Braxton would vote for independence today, despite "Intestine Wars and Convulsions," silently obey his colony's instructions, knowing the dangers, the probabilities . . .)

"The Committee on Confederation," Dickinson announced, "dispute almost every article. Some of us totally despair of any reasonable terms of confederation. . . ." *Totally despair*—yet surely Confederation should come, before we assumed our station among sovereigns. "A sovereignty, composed of several distinct bodies of men, not subject to established constitutions, and these bodies not combined together by the sanction of any confirmed articles of union, is such a sovereignty as has never appeared in the world."

It was nearly all he could do. He had been speaking, not to independent minds, but to ambassadors instructed. His only hope had been to reach those delegates whose instructions left them some discretion, some room to exercise their own judgment: not Maryland now, but his own Pennsylvania, and Delaware, New Jersey, the Carolinas. It was time to make a close. No soft close would do, no peroration either; he must be brisk, give them phrases:

"Once committed, we cannot look back. Men generally sell their goods to most advantage when they have several chapmen. We have but two to rely on: what will Britain offer, what will France offer? We exclude one by this declaration, without knowing what the other will give.

"Great Britain after one or more unsuccessful campaigns may be induced to offer us such a share of commerce as would satisfy us, consent to councillors appointed during good behaviour, withdraw her armies, agree to protect our commerce, establish our militias—in short she may offer to redress all the grievances complained of in our first petition. Let us know, if we can get terms from France that will be more beneficial than these. If we can, let us declare independence. If we cannot, let us at least withhold that declaration till we obtain terms that are tolerable.

"We have many points of the utmost moment to settle with France: there is Canada, and Acadia, and Cape Breton Island. What will content her? Trade, or territory? What conditions of trade? Will she protect our ships from the Barbary Pirates? from Spanish frigates in West India waters, Portuguese in the Doldrums, at the Azores? Will she demand an exclusive trade as compensation, or grant us protection against piratical states for a share only of our commerce?

"When our enemies are pressing us so vigorously, when we are in so wretched a state of preparation, when the sentiments and designs of our expected friends are so unknown to us, I am alarmed at this declaration being so vehemently presented." And then abruptly a comment on John Adams's words last Friday: "A worthy gentleman told us, that people in this house have had different views for more than a twelvemonth. This is amazing, after what they have so repeatedly declared in this house, and in private conversations, that they meant only reconciliation.

"But since they can conceal their views so dextrously, I should be glad to read a little more in the Doomsday Book of America—not all; that like the Book of Fate might be too dreadful!" He played with his conceit for a moment, gave his Doomsday Book a title page, described its binding. But only for a moment: "I should be glad to know whether, in twenty or thirty years, this commonwealth of colonies may not be thought too unwieldy, and Hudson's river be a proper boundary for a separate commonwealth to the northward.

"I have a strong impression on my mind that this will take place!"

As Dickinson finished speaking, thunder roared, and a rain began to fall. The south wind rose in a sharp summer storm. It cooled the air in the big East Room.

For a while, no member rose to answer him. Then John Adams, "author of all the mischief," commenced his reply. It was, said Adams, the first time in his life he had ever wished for the talents and eloquence of the ancient

orators of Greece and Rome. He mentioned Demosthenes and Cicero. They
would have begun with solemn invocations to divinity for assistance. But the
question was not difficult; he had such confidence in plain understanding, in
simple reason and common sense, that he believed he could answer to the
satisfaction of the house all the objections to independence which had been
produced, notwithstanding the abilities displayed, and the eloquence with
which they had been enforced. He spoke pleasantly enough, his manner
informal, easy, a contrast to Dickinson's. He had prepared nothing in advance; he had nothing new to offer. Yet he was at his best. Jefferson later
remembered him as "our colossus on the floor . . . not graceful nor elegant,
nor remarkably fluent, but he came out occasionally with a power of thought
and expression, that moved us from our seats."

This last, of course, Mr. Jefferson scarcely meant to be taken literally.
Delegates in the Congress were not accustomed to cheering, nor to leaping
up from their seats in enthusiasms. They were, however, given to strong
opinions, heady partisanships. Major Walton of Georgia, on his first day in
Congress, was deeply stirred. More than ten years later he would write
Adams, "I can truly assure you, that, since the 1st day of July, 1776, my
conduct, in every station in life, has corresponded with the result of that
great question which you so ably and faithfully developed on that day—a
scene which has ever been present in my mind. It has then that I felt the
strongest attachments; and they have never departed from me."

Adams finished; the debate continued some time—on details, side issues,
no one else had a major oration to give. As the rain beat down outside, each
colony expressed its views. Paca of Maryland spoke nobly, freed by his new
instructions to open his thoughtful mind. Members estimated the tally:
Pennsylvania and South Carolina against, Delaware split, New York withdrawn, New Jersey absent. If the vote came now, only eight colonies would
favor independence. It was a gain, certainly, over the five of June 8 but it was
still not enough. For the moment, John Dickinson could glimpse the postponement he hoped for, Adams the defeat he dreaded.

Then, just before the final roll of the colonies was called, the new Delegates from Jersey entered the hall. They were wet and spattered with mud;
they had ridden through the rain storm from Trenton—Abraham Clark;
President Witherspoon of the college at Princeton; Judge Richard Stockton;
cheerful little Francis Hopkinson. They were Adams' legion of victory as they
entered. They were the ninth vote.

The Jerseymen desired to hear the arguments, they said; they wished to
know the sentiments of the members. Judge Stockton seemd especially insistent. Adams demurred. The question had been so long disputed in pamphlets, newspapers, at every fireside, that they could not be uninformed, they
must have made up their minds. Yes, the Jerseymen answered, they knew

what had been passing abroad, but they had not heard the opinions of the Delegates. Finally Adams was persuaded to speak again. Years later, he wrote it was Edward Rutledge who "came to me and said, laughing, 'Nobody will speak but you upon this subject. You have all the topics so ready, that you must satisfy the gentlemen from New Jersey.' I answered him, laughing, that it had so much the air of exhibiting like an actor or gladiator, for the entertainment of the audience, that I was ashamed to repeat what I had said twenty times before, and I thought nothing new could be advanced by me. The New Jersey gentlemen, however, still insisting on hearing at least a recapitulation of the arguments, and no other gentleman being willing to speak, I summed up all the reasons, objections, and answers, in as concise a manner as I could . . ."

Perhaps something of the sort did happen, though the spectacle of young Ned Rutledge laughingly cajoling John Yankee, and Adams laughingly responding with shy modesty, is far from likely. In another account, written in 1807, Adams omitted to mention Rutledge; he said merely "Judge Stockton was most particularly importunate, till the members began to say let the Gentlemen be gratifi'd and the Eyes of the assembly were turned upon me and several others of them said come Mr. Adams you have had the subject at heart longer than any of us and you must recapitulate the arguments. I was somewhat confused at this personal application to me and would have been very glad to be excused; but as no other person arose after some time I said . . ."

What Benjamin Harrison was doing during this interruption on the floor described by Adams, no record discloses. Certainly the arrival of the Jerseymen was an event of vast importance, for it determined the vote. That formalities were suspended briefly is understandable, and reasonable to believe. But that the whole house fell to pieces, lost all semblance of an organized body, is scarcely credible, particularly under the chairmanship of the firm, experienced Harrison. Yet Harrison himself needs some explanation at this moment, for he must have made an unauthorized ruling. Apparently, from Adams's account, the new Delegates were permitted to take their places in Committee of the Whole without being formally enrolled as members of Congress, and to participate—at least to the extent of Judge Stockton's "particularly importunate" requests—in the debate: and to cast New Jersey's vote. No one, on either side of the question, left any record that clears up the mystery of this collapse of Congress's established way of doing business.

What Adams said, in this second speech he does indeed seem to have given, in spite of the rules, is also lost to us. In his writings much later, his memory telescoped his two speeches together, and he gave the content of the first speech as the remarks he made for the new members from Jersey. This we certainly cannot imagine— that Adams would repeat word for word the beginning he had used in responding to Dickinson, wishing for the eloquence of Greece and Rome, invoking divinity as Demosthenes had done. He was frank to say he had forgotten his observations. "I wish someone had remembered the speech, for it is almost the only one I ever made that I wish was literally preserved."

Apparently, Adams summed up in a concise manner all the points he had made, Dickinson's objections, his answers to them. The New Jersey Delegates pronounced themselves satisfied. Judge Stockton called Adams "the Atlas of American independence . . . He sustained the debate, and by the force of his reasonings demonstrated not only the justice but the expediency of the measure."

The sun was low in the sky when Secretary Thomson began his roll call of the vote. "New Hampshire: Mr. Bartlett? *Aye.* Mr. Whipple? *Aye.* New Hampshire, *aye,*" Thomson intoned, his quill entering responses on his paper. "Massachusetts: Mr. S. Adams? *Aye.* Mr. J. Adams? *Aye.* Mr. Gerry? Mr. Hancock? Mr. Paine? Massachusetts, *aye.*" Rhode Island: Ellery, old Hopkins, Rhode Island *aye.* Connecticut: Huntington, Sherman, Connecticut *aye.* That Yankeeland east of the Hudson did truly seem a solid confederacy. New York: withdrawn. Thomson omitted to call New York, he left a blank. New Jersey: four new Delegates, Hopkinson, Clark, Judge Stockton, Dr. Witherspoon, each casting as his very first vote in Congress a vote for American independence, New Jersey *aye.* "Pennsylvania: Mr. Dickinson? *No.* Mr. Franklin? *Aye.* Mr. Humphreys? *No.* Mr. Morris? *No.* Mr. Morton? *No.* Mr. Willing? *No.* Mr. Wilson? *No.* Pennsylvania, *no.*" The secretary's own state, Dickinson his most intimate friend, Hannah's administrator, now his defeated opponent. . . . "Delaware: Mr. McKean? *Aye.* Mr. Read? *No.* Delaware, *divided.*" Maryland, Virginia, North Carolina, all *aye,* South Carolina *no,* Georgia *aye.* Two *no* votes, one divided, one withdrawn, nine votes *aye.*

By Maryland's last-minute action, by New Jersey's tardy arrival, John Adams had won his independence.

It was now evening. The members, Thomas Jefferson wrote, were "exhausted by a debate of nine hours, during which all the powers of the soul had been distended with the magnitude of the object." The Committee of the Whole rose, Hancock resumed the chair, Colonel Harrison from his place with Virginia reported to the same tired members as a Congress that the resolution was agreed to, and recomended to pass. Edward Rutledge of South Carolina was on his feet first. He moved—a formal motion now, in formal Congress, the motion of a colony—that the vote on the Committee's report on the order of the day be deferred till morning. Everyone understood: South Carolina would change its vote overnight. Independence had carried, by the skin of its New Jersey teeth. The next vote would be official, and official votes were recorded, entered in the Journal. It ought to be unanimous. The country must never know how near the issue had been, how divided the Congress in secret.

Besides, Ned Rutledge could recognize that if South Carolina was ever to have complete self-control in the new confederation, the swiftest, surest way to that goal was not to weaken the Dickinson draft, but to accede to Adams's independence with no confederation at all. Then the Charles Town planters could stand alone in the purple splendor of their indigo and rice, free from Parliament and Congress alike. The motion passed. McKean of Delaware sent off a fast express to The Lower Counties, ordered him to search for Speaker Rodney.

In front of President Hancock, the new Delegates from Jersey stood to be formally presented. Mr. Hopkinson had already signed the Resolution of Secrecy, on Charles Thomson's desk, last Friday. Now Mr. Clark and Dr. Witherspoon added their signatures, and so did Major Walton of Georgia. All members were required to sign this Resolution of Secrecy, passed November 9, 1775; it was the official act by which a Delegate appointed to, became an actual member of, the Congress. If he violated the secrecy it enjoined, a member was liable to be "expelled this Congress & deemed an enemy to the liberties of America." Historians ever since, whether enemies or friends to those liberties, have been trying to probe behind the thick curtain of secrecy that Resolution dropped. It is never easy; we shall never know, for an instance, why Judge Richard Stockton failed to sign—that day, or ever.

Two more items of military business were disposed of, and Congress adjourned for the night. The day of independence was over.

"If you imagine," John Adams wrote that evening, in his hot damp rooms, "that I expect this declaration will ward off calamities from this country, you are much mistaken. A bloody conflict we are destined to endure. This has been my opinion from the beginning. . . . If you imagine that I flatter myself with happiness and halcyon days after a separation from Great Britain, you are mistaken again. I do not expect that our new government will be so quiet as I could wish, nor that happy harmony, confidence, and affection between the colonies, that every good American ought to study, labor, and pray for, for a long time. . . ."

"*Every good American*"—it was the first time that phrase could be used to describe the citizens of an independent sovereignty, in the world of nations. Abraham Clark, Delegate from New Jersey, was a good American. After Tuesday the second, when South Carolina changed her vote, Speaker Rodney arrived in his boots and spurs to carry Delaware, when Dickinson, Willing, Humphreys, and Morris stood behind the bar "absent" that Franklin, Wilson, and Morton might vote Pennsylvania's *aye,* when the New Yorkers stood mute so Congress could with technical correctness, if something less than candor, announce to the public that independence had carried "without a single *dissenting* vote," after the prolonged debate on the Declaration clause by clause during that Tuesday the second and Wednesday the third, Abraham Clark on the morning of the first fourth of July of an independent America wrote a letter to his friend Elias Dayton of New Jersey:

"Our Seeming bad success in Canada, I dare say gives you great uneasiness. In Times of danger, and under misfortunes true Courage and Magnanimity can only be ascertained. In the Course of Such a War we must expect some Losses. We are told a Panick Seized the Army. If so it hath not reached the Senate. At the Time our Forces in Canada were retreating before a Victorious Army, while Genl. Howe with a Large Armament is advancing towards N. York, Our Congress Resolved to Declare the United Colonies *Free and independent States. . . .*

"We are now Sir embarked on a most Tempestious Sea; Life very uncertain, Deceiving dangers, Scattered thick around us, Plots against the military and it is whispered against the Senate. Let us prepare for the worst, we can die but once. . . ."

Yet Clark did full justice to the independence men among his colleagues, the hot violent men in this company now of forty-seven Delegates, who amidst defeat and retreat and divided councils, in the very face of the enemy, whether wisely or in folly had dared act the bold part. Clark knew the thrills of freedom. "I am among a Consistory of KINGS . . ." he exulted. "I assure you Sir, Our Congress is an August Assembly, and can they Support the Declaration now on the Anvil, they will be the greatest Assembly on Earth."

5

General Washington and the Jack Ass

General Washington was through with eight and a half years of war. Independence had been won, a treaty would be signed; he said his affecting farewells to the Army, to Congress, to his staff. Finally he came to his busy life, as master of Mount Vernon.

Then at long last he found time to turn his mind to the matter of mules.

Mules were curiosities, in George Washington's day in America. During his years as farmer and general, only a few of the grotesque hybrids had come his way—"very ordinary specimens," he pronounced them. Yet he had tried what he called "little experiments" with these few, and he learned that even ordinary mules lived longer than horses, did much more work on considerably less feeding, stood better the punishing, careless handling of ignorant farm hands. These results caught the General's imagination. "As a farmer, Wheat and Flour constitute my principal concerns," he told his Philadelphia agent, but still if he could breed a superior race of mules, "a race of extraordinary goodness," he would have "the best cattle we can employ for the harness," and the high cost of horse power, one of the American farmer's sorest economic problems, would be solved.

This was the sort of enterprise George Washington loved. He dreamed

176

happily of great long-eared beasts bred of Mount Vernon blood lines, drawing ploughs and wagons in every state, correcting "the ruinous mode of farming, which we are in." Mules "this mongrel race" and their promise for national life were romance to his planter's soul. They might even replace the horse for genteel display. "Indeed, in a few years, I intend to drive no other in my carriage," he declared.

By "an excellent race of mules," of course, the General meant a larger, stronger race of jack asses to cross with mares. To produce such a race, he would have to import breeding stock from Spain, for Spanish asses were the finest, largest, strongest in all the world. But the monarchs of Spain had long since forbidden the export of blooded stock. They were proud of their huge Andalusian ass, a monopoly bestowed upon Spain by Nature, dearly cherished and jealously guard in firm Mercantilist policy. The present king, even more than his ancestors, was said to delight in nothing so much as his asses and mules. Report had it he intended to make mules the fashionable mount of Madrid. For a Virginia planter to secure a fine Spanish jack was, as a practical matter, beyond imagining.

Still, Washington imagined. Over many years he seized every opportunity to learn all he could of the exotic Spanish cattle; he longed to find some way of acquiring a high-bred stud. Even in the midst of war, asses were never very far from his thoughts. Back in 1780 an elegant acquaintance had appeared at Washington's headquarters camp near Morristown, New Jersey, on a more or less official visit. He was the Cuban factor from la Habana, Don Juan de Miralles, now serving as secret agent and "observer" of the Spanish king to the American colonies in rebellion. Don Juan talked smoothly of state loans, munitions, arms and alliances, of the issues of battles and the war, talked delicately of the critical question of Spain's tight control of Mississippi River traffic and its effects on American settlers in Western Lands. To his astonishment, he found the tall, thick-limbed, slow-speaking American General with his constant wracking cough, quizzing *him* about jack asses: how to obtain one, how mules broke to harness, was it true the Spanish King could be seen drawn by mules in his state coach? Don Juan was skilled in a stern diplomatic tradition. He promised with mannered Spanish sincerity to procure an ass for the General, a suitable beast. Washington's hopes rose. But a few hours after their talk, on the very first evening of his visit, Don Juan was seized with "a violent biliary complaint." That night he sickened alarmingly. Washington was informed; he went at once to the diplomat's tent, he watched over him in person, brought in his own surgeons. Day after day, the illness advanced. Headquarters work ground slowly to a halt while the Commander in Chief attended on his patient, even performed the most intimate offices of the sickroom with his own hands, as his lifelong experience of illness had taught him. Alas, nothing helped.

On the tenth day, Don Juan de Miralles died—before he could do anything about a jack ass.

"In his death I met a disappointment," General Washington observed.

Another Spaniard promised to see what he could do, but he made no serious exertions. Washington feared he was trifling. "I am desireous of having more strings than one to my bow," he remarked, and in 1784 from blessed retirement at Mount Vernon he wrote to his friend Colonel Hooe, whose merchant-house partner, Richard Harrison, was at that moment American consul in Cadiz. Harrison had married the daughter of Washington's close friend and physician, Dr. Craik. If anyone could get him an ass, surely it would be Harrison. Would Hooe please send him this letter? He asked for "a good Jack ass, to breed from," if Harrison could arrange it. "An ordinary Jack I do not desire. I will describe therefore such an one as I must have, if I get any. He must be at least fifteen hands high; well formed; in his prime; and one whose abilities for getting Colts can be ensured. . . ."

Washington knew from the Florida question that Spaniards were cunning; he suspected them of devious dealings in the Mississippi navigation issue. Perfidious Spanish tricks might be played on him, or on his jack ass. He warned Harrison to beware:

for I have been informed, that except those which are designed to breed from; and more especially such as are suffered to be exported; they very frequently have their generative parts so injured by squeezing, as to render them as unfit for the purpose of begetting Colts, as castration would, when from a superficial view no imperfection appears.

Of course, Don Juan de Miralles had been a model of probity, a paragon. Perhaps his suspicions of Spaniards were unjust. "But as I would have a good Jack or none, I am induced to mention the circumstance," the General concluded to Harrison.

When LaFayette made his farewell visit to Mount Vernon that fall of 1784, Washington told him his dream of mules. Now young LaFayette would cheerfully have delivered elephants, camels, or wallabies to Washington had the General discovered a mind for them. A jack ass seemed easy; he unhesitatingly engaged to send one himself when he returned home to France. No sooner had he left America, however, than Washington learned from Colonel Hooe how difficult it would be to obtain a Spanish jack because of the export laws, and the enormous sum of gold a proper specimen would cost. The price horrified the General. He wrote Harrison and LaFayette both, countermanding his commissions. Much as he wanted a jack, he had no such reserves as that to invest. For the moment, he gave up his dreams.

But one element the General (always abler in strategy than in tactics) had failed to take into account: George Washington was probably the only man of his time genuinely unaware of the importance of the name of Washington. Harrison's enquiries around Cadiz seeking a jack ass for the General reached the ears of William Carmichael, American *Chargé d'affaires* in Madrid. Carmichael, in the course of an interview on other matters, took occasion to mention the subject to the foreign minister, the Condé de Floridablanca. Promptly, Floridablanca told the King; promptly the King rose to the occasion.

His Most Catholic Majesty Lord Charles, King of Castile, of Leon, of Aragon, King of the Two Sicilies, of Jerusalem, of Navarre, of Corsica and a dozen other ancient places, of the East and West Indies, of the Islands and Terra Firma of the Ocean Sea, Archduke of Austria, Duke of Burgundy, Count of Flanders, Milan—the venerable Charles III in all his dignities issued a royal pronouncement. He himself, He the King, would present to General Washington, as a personal gift, not one but *two* of the best jack asses of his realm.

Charles III was one of those rulers called an Enlightened Despot. That his enlightenment as he neared the age of seventy extended to jack asses was the result less of his well-known pride in that interesting quadruped, than of Floridablanca's apprehensions concerning the forthcoming American treaty. In his obscure Spanish way, the foreign minister saw some connection between Washington's wish for a mule-breeding jack, and Spanish control of Pittsburgh, Ohio, and Tennessee traffic through New Orleans at the Mississippi mouth.

To serve General Washington, King Charles waived the strict embargo on blooded jacks. A fine letter full of high words was prepared for his sign-manual, "I the King"; grooms were appointed to accompany the beasts, and Carmichael furnished with the very best Spanish information on how to propagate mules.

Washington was delighted. Through Carmichael he sent the King hearty thanks "for so condescending a mark of esteem from one of the first crowned heads in Europe." Two jacks "of the first race" were unimaginable riches. "I have long endeavored to procure *one* of a good size and breed, but had little expectation of receiving *two* as a royal gift," he wrote. And he made elaborate preparations against the beasts' arrival.

Then he heard from LaFayette. The Marquis had not taken lightly his chance to serve his General. He, like the King of Spain, had secured not one, but two jacks: the first by dark and devious methods he had spirited out of Cadiz, the second he had purchased on the island of Malta. He was shipping them over.

Four jacks—mules were suddenly an elaborate project. Yet the whole summer of 1785 passed, and no jacks appeared. Washington knew it was risky to send them over the sea. Still it was for that very reason His Most

Catholic Majesty, LaFayette as well, had each procured two, had each dispatched his two in separate vessels, that all should not be lost together. The four ships had sailed months ago, from four different ports. At least one of them ought to reach Virginia, in summer, the easiest passage, a mild summer at sea. . . .

Summer wore into autumn, apples were plucked, nuts gathered, corn dried in the field and was shocked, leaves of the hardwoods turned to copper and gold. Finally, October 26, the northern mail brought a letter from the Hon. Thomas Cushing, a longtime acquaintance from the First Continental Congress days back before the war, now Lieutenant Governor of Massachusetts. A Spanish jack ass, forty-four Spanish inches high, attended by a Spanish keeper, had reached Gloucester on the *Ranger,* Job Knight master, consigned to General Washington by the Spanish King. Jack and groom had been brought to Boston and were now in Judge Cushing's care. What should he do with them?

Washington acted swiftly. He sat down at his writing desk, sharpened a quill. After months of waiting and planning, he knew exactly how to proceed. He could not go himself; he would send John Fairfax, his chief overseer, northward that very afternoon. In a few quick minutes he drafted a certificate for Fairfax to carry, addressed to the principal men of Pennsylvania, New Jersey, New York, and Connecticut. "The bearer is sent by the subscriber to Boston for a Jack Ass," the General wrote, and so urgent was his pen that grammar, diction, and syntax—never his constant companions—forsook him entirely: "But as sickness, accident, or other unavoidable delay may impede the journey and cause him to require aid to prosecute, the subscriber would esteem it as a favor done him by any who shall render it; and will thankfully repay any advance or expence which may be incurred."

Next, he briskly filled three long folio pages with careful instructions to Fairfax for his journey. The overseer was standing right there at his elbow, but still the General wrote everything down. No communication Washington ever sent to Congress, no detailed orders to his army officers, no formal exchange with enemy commanders Howe, Clinton, or Cornwallis, no public paper he would ever draft as President, exceeded this imposing document in dignity, precision, and clarity. "You will proceed in the Stage from Alexandria to Boston, without losing a day that can possibly be avoided," he directed Fairfax. The stage would be quicker for so long a journey than riding a single horse, he wrote.

Every night as soon as the coach reached its stopover, Fairfax was to engage his passage for the next day, lest he lose his place. Beyond New York he must inquire now and then along the road if the jack had already left Boston—"the circumstance of which will be very notorious if it has happened." Fairfax was to take his orders from Mr. Cushing, but in one matter he must act on his own judgment. He would have to ride back, so at Boston he must buy two open mares, which could later be bred to the jack at the next covering season. Coming home, he must take pains to travel no faster than an easy walk for the jack, and he must devote his whole care to the beast and its keeper.

As he drew his instructions, Washington suddenly realized that the Spanish groom would probably speak no English. He ordered Fairfax to find an interpreter in Boston, through whom to talk with the Spaniard, to

> communicate your sentiments to each other, to settle all necessary points for your journey: that is, your hour for setting out in the morning, which let be early; taking up in the evening, number of feeds in the day, and of what kind of food; also the kind and quantity of liquor that is to be given to the Spaniard in a day.

Having settled these matters before leaving Boston, Fairfax could easily understand the keeper by signs at least to New York, where the Spanish Minister's household would again translate for him. This would put Fairfax in command, Washington explained, and leave the Spanish groom nothing to do, "but to be attentive to the animal."

John Fairfax set off, complete with instructions. The General sat back in his chair. And for six long weeks he waited patiently the arrival of his exotic new beast. He ran his five farms of Mount Vernon and the affairs of the more than three hundred people who lived on them; he received visitors, he wrote letters— letters on canals, on rivers, on The Society of the Cincinnati, on the "truly shocking lassitude" of Congress and the need for constitutional reform, on seed wheat sent him from South Africa, on the "illiberal and contracted policy of Britain" and the "virtuous characters of Ireland" who opposed it. These were significant matters; but he kept thinking of his jack ass, plodding that long slow way down from Boston. He remembered the colds and heats of a New England autumn—the damp frosty mornings, how hard they had worked on his own frail constitution. He remembered the mouldered hay. He thought of the busy turnpikes, reckless travellers, of thieves and marauders. A good many accidents could happen to a shy foreign beast amid alien corn, on so long, so hazardous a journey. The General could scarcely visualize his prize. How high exactly was "forty-four Spanish inches"?

He studied his breeding stock. Thirty-three of his own mares could go next covering season to the jack, "if he should arrive safe," but he turned down requests from Eastern Shore Maryland planters to have their mares served too. Newspapers all up and down the coast published accounts of the ass's advent. The Maryland planters read the stories—garbled, exaggerated paragraphs which Washington resented. He would have no strangers, not yet. But he must look forward to that, eventually: he began to ask around for a she-ass, whom the jack could also cover, that the advantages to be derived from him "may not end with *his* life." From Boston came word that the King of Spain's second jack had perished in a storm at sea.

All these six weeks John Fairfax was obeying instructions, letter and spirit. Finally on Monday, December 5, 1785, he reached Mount Vernon in triumph. He was accompanied by a Spanish groom, Pedro Tellez by name, who sure enough spoke not a word of English; he led behind his two open mares the royal jack ass himself.

Never was a beast so odd. Fairfax and Pedro Tellez conducted onto the verandah of the Mansion House before the General and his "family," a huge, ill-shapen gray creature, four years old, "his body and Limbs very large in proportion to his height," his great gaunt head too big for his body, his ears enormous, too big for his head.

Washington was enchanted. He beheld on his own porch that winter day the first blooded Spanish jack ever brought into America, sire of a new race of animals. It was an occasion of moment. He thought the ass "in appearance is fine," observed how he was "very bony and stout made, of a dark color, with light belly and legs"—and, he added, with an all-too-unhappily-prophetic phrase, his sturdy frame indicated "strength and firmness almost beyond conception."

Then and there the beast was measured. He stood nearly fifteen hands high—five feet at his shoulders. The General christened him "Royal Gift."

The royal groom he treated with courtesy which must have astonished that laconic individual, who had never met a Republican before. He found himself quartered in a guest room in the mansion house, dining in company with the General and his lady at table. Three days, Washington and Pedro Tellez made signs at each other as the General inspected Royal Gift. But it was excessively difficult to learn about a jack ass through gestures and motions. How was Royal Gift to be handled? When was his covering season? What were the exertions which might be expected of him?

The General found a ship captain in Alexandria and a former army officer from New York, accomplished enough in languages that he had served as General Steuben's aide during the war. These gentlemen he invited to dinner, and through their scanty knowledge of Spanish he asked Pedro Tellez all his intimate questions, carefully committing to writing such answers as he comprehended. It was all too brief a session; soon Tellez left. "I have not been able to understand him perfectly," Washington complained. But he gave him £21, and friendly letters to help him on his way. Wistfully, he hoped he had made no serious mistakes, either in protocol or husbandry, with the King's stable groom. To Lieutenant Governor Cushing in Boston he sent his thanks for "your obliging and disinterested attention to my Jack."

Then he settled down to the esoteric enjoyments of proprietorship of Royal Gift.

In his home-farm stud stable at Mount Vernon, his slave Peter had long been groom to Magnolio, Washington's fierce Arab stallion. Magnolio was a noble creature, famous everywhere for his get. To Peter, the General entrusted his new prize after Pedro Tellez departed. He caused a mule shed to be built south of the stables; he looked in every day as he made his busy rounds. Peter had no need of the Spanish language: he and Royal Gift took an immediate shine to one another. Washington beamed contentedly, enjoying Peter's officiousness. The slave waited on Royal Gift constantly. He would do nothing, the General wrote, but "peddle about the stables, and conceives it to be a kind of degregation to bestow his attention on horses of plebean birth."

If the big Spanish jack introduced new excitements to Peter's routines, he did even more for the master of Mount Vernon. Royal Gift's spirit, his sharp glancing eyes and imperious manners, his suspicion of all creatures human, entirely charmed the General. Humor, a quality Washington had found scant use for in fifty-three years, fairly sparkled in his letters about his beast. It was rough farmer's humor, full relished, and plain. When he wrote of his jack, his pen twinkled merrily.

Royal Gift fed well over winter, and for spring covering season Washington advertised in papers as far away as Philadelphia that his Spanish jack would serve mares for £10, jennies for £15, lawful money. An immense throng of open mares turned up; for weeks the roads to Mount Vernon were dusty with brood stock and their keepers. But when covering came, Royal Gift unaccountably scorned the great harem gathered in his well-fenced yard back of the Green House. He was vigorous, fit, and ready, no Spanish deceptions had been practiced upon him, Peter pronounced him in every respect perfect. Yet he displayed stolid indifference to the abundant opportunities presented him to demonstrate his evident virility. Royal Gift, Washington wrote, was "too full of Royalty, to have anything to do with a plebean race."

To LaFayette he wryly described the celibacy of the King of Spain's jack ass: "his late royal master, th' past his grand climacteric, cannot be less moved by female allurements than he is; or when prompted, can proceed with more deliberation and majestic solemnity to the work of procreation." He liked his rueful joke so well he repeated it again and again, as Royal Gift persisted in continent behavior. "At present, tho' young, he follows what one may suppose to be the example of his late Royal Master, who cannot perform seldomer or with more majestic solemnity. . . ." It was exasperating, after all the General's dreams, after all his trouble.

Peter tried every inducement, General Washington tried patience—an attribute necessary in stock breeding quite as much as in managing wars. Royal Gift was encouraged, cajoled, solicited, tempted; he still held aloof. "I have my hopes," the General wrote, "that when he becomes a little better acquainted with republican enjoyments, he will amend his manners and fall into our custom of doing business; if the case should be otherwise, I shall have no disinclination to present his Catholic Majesty with as valuable a present as I received from him." Republican enjoyments made no appeal to Royal Gift: on April 20 he covered "a she Mule" and two mares; on June 5 a mare from a neighboring planter. That was all, as Washington kept the meagre record. He could hold his mares open no longer, nor the visiting stock gathered for Royal Gift to come to. He sent them all to his Arab stud Magnolio.

Late in June, by accident, the way of persuading Royal Gift to fulfill his biological destiny was discovered. Richard Sprigg, Esquire, of Annapolis (one of those Spriggs whose vast landholdings and slave legions made Mount Vernon seem small) sent down a jenny to be bred. The diminutive she-ass was let into the pasture with all the big, broad-rumped mares; Royal Gift caught sight of her at once. The proximity of a female of his own species "excited desires in the Jack," the General happily recorded, "to which he seemed almost a stranger." He wrote gaily to Lawyer Sprigg of his jenny: "Tho' in appearance quite unequal to the match, yet like a true female, she was not to be terrified at the disproportionate size of her paramour, and having renewed the conflict twice or thrice, it is to be hoped the issue will be favourable."

Unluckily, Magnolio had covered the whole great crowd of mares before Royal Gift commenced his work. But Washington had learned the technique. If a jenny nearby would dissipate the jack's somber humors and induce him to serve mares, he must have one. The General ordered a she-ass "of good appearance" from Surinam, to use both as exciter, and as a dam for more jacks. Surinam was a long voyage in summer; before the good-appearing female could reach Mount Vernon, LaFayette's affectionate efforts bore timely fruit. A Frenchman arrived unannounced in the fall, escorting (along with a gift of Chinese pheasants from King Louis XVI's aviary at Versailles) a jack and two jennet asses. The Marquis had secured them from Malta.

It had taken LaFayette two years, much money, and a good deal of trouble; the jack he had spirited out of Cadiz had been lost on the ocean voyage. He intended the asses as a present, but would never say so to Washington, knowing the General would refuse to accept such bounty from him. Washington in turn tried to press money on his youthful admirer, which LaFayette adroitly prevented. Finally, the General opened a ledger account in LaFayette's name, with the entry: "By one Jack Ass and two Jennetts sent to me by you from the Island of Malta." He entered no sums on the page till one time seven years later when in the turmoil of revolution and war LaFayette was captured by Austrian armies and hurled into prison at Olmütz. Then, while Washington strove to induce the Emperor to release the Marquis, he also sent two hundred guineas to the destitute Marchioness Adrienne de LaFayette, that wife of his young friend whom he had never seen, but whom he had often saluted by packet-boat mail. The money, he wrote, was a return for services her husband had done him, with no accounting.

The new jack was smaller than Royal Gift, entirely different in appearance and temperament. He was youthful, clean-limbed, and active—quite like the splendid youth who had sent him; he exhibited "the fire and ferocity of a tiger." Only Peter could handle him, "and that always at considerable personal risk." He was dark brown, with white belly and muzzle. Washington christened him "The Knight of Malta." The new jennies solved Royal Gift's emotional problems; The Knight of Malta expanded the General's horizon. Now he could breed two different strains of mules "which will stock the country" —from Royal Gift heavy slow-draught coursers and drays, from The Knight of Malta light saddle mounts, carriage pairs.

Four days after LaFayette's gifts arrived, the jennet from Surinam turned up; at the same moment the new Spanish Minister in New York sent a gracious letter, offering to find a suitable Spanish mate for Royal Gift. To this letter Washington hastily replied, begging his excellency by no means to trouble himself to effect such a purpose. There could be too much of a good thing, even of asses. With Maryland jennies, and Maltese and Virginia and Surinam, the General and Royal Gift, too, were content.

Life was otherwise cluttered just now, as Mount Vernon became a harbor for asses from all the world. Massachusetts boiled in arms, every part of the American Confederacy seethed with turbulent factions, Washington was expected in Philadelphia for the Constitutional Convention early in May, 1787—right in the middle of the covering season. He hated going. Before leaving, he advertised that Royal Gift and The Knight of Malta would cover at Mount Vernon for five guineas the season, visiting mares could have good pasturage at one-half dollar a week. (Prices had been lowered because of Royal Gift's disdain his first year.) As the General set out he had good news from Peter: proudly, he informed Mr. Sprigg at Annapolis his jenny was with foal by the Spaniard. The days were nearly fulfilled that she should be delivered; Mr. Sprigg better come fetch her.

From Philadelphia all the hot summer long the General wrote wistful inquiries of the covering. Drought in Virginia worried him; he feared for the progress of his plans. If the jacks did not perform what was expected of them, all the mares must go again to Magnolio, he directed. The Federal Convention dragged on and on, through angry exchanges, endless debates, wearisome wrangling; Washington strove to "erect a standard to which the wise and just may repair." But his heart was at the home farm, with his jack asses. Finally late in September he signed the new Constitution, his burden lifted, he was home again, to learn the good news of the spring's activities. "Royal Gift never fails," Peter and the overseers told him. Jennies and mares big with foal had been sent home to a dozen plantations. Royal Gift had become the father of a race. The Knight of Malta was still "a young hand," but he too was learning republican enjoyments. Washington was confident he would prove "equally sure."

That winter he tried mules in harness: they broke quickly, and well. But that winter also he suffered hard losses from the drought. Feed was brittle, dry, full of burrs, mares slunk their mule colts, one of the Maltese jennies cast a jack foal, "for which I would not have taken a large sum of money had he come to maturity." Still, the next covering season, 1788, filled him with schemes and hopes. He advertised as usual; early in spring he sent both big drab Royal Gift and the smart, white-nosed Knight of Malta up to the election at Marlboro in Maryland, "that they might be seen." He invited John Jay, Secretary for Foreign Affairs, to send a jenny down from New York if he wished. From his second Maltese dam he got a jack colt by Royal Gift—first crossing of lines. The cross jack he christened "Compound." He even found medical use for asses' milk, weaning the new colt and sending the Maltese dam to a neighboring planter to provide milk for his ailing wife.

Financially, Royal Gift did well this third season. Requests came to offer him at stud in other states, and the General began to consider it—but only for ready cash in advance, no credit, "no after claps to negotiate, or settle." ("Letting a jack on shares I never will; for in that case expences are trumped up, one may be told of difficulties in collecting money, and many other things, when accounts come to be settled, with a view of staving off payment. . . .") Four promising mule colts were now pasturing at Mount Vernon. Washington cut them that fall to prepare them for work. But public matters claimed him more and more. Everyone demanded he take the Presidency of the new government. The General was genuinely reluctant to do so. He was not a little alarmed at the prospect of national duties, and he knew well what would be lost at home should he accept. Mule-breeding was a long, slow process, a gamble of eleven months between covering and foaling, a year more of close tender care before the colt reached his first growth. Interruptions were disastrous. The Presidency would certainly be an interruption.

The Presidency came, nonetheless; and as Royal Gift's fourth siring season began, the General went regretfully off northward to become, in his own way, Father of his Country.

"I see nothing but clouds and darkness before me," he wrote. For the next eight years, he witnessed none of the covering. In New York, in Philadelphia, he went through somber, stately duties with patient firmness—frequently unhappy, hard-driven, fatigued, plagued always with his enervating illnesses, his old pulmonary weakness, that hacking cough, his fevers and agues and bouts of malarial chills; in New York Dr. Bard cut him for a malignant carbuncle which laid him low, for days near to death; in Philadelphia Dr. Glentworth cut him for piles. Yet through all the miseries of the Presidency, he remained immensely energetic, resolute, determined, keenly discerning. "Never did nature and fortune combine more perfectly to make a man great," Jefferson said. But he missed all the episodes of breeding; he could make few plans good at long distance. In the winter of '92 he passed his sixtieth birthday. He knew he was an old party, destined soon to leave life, destined never to see the full issue of his experiments with mules.

"Are the Jennies with foal?" the President-General asked his new overseer, in an anxious letter from the seat of government. "And how many Mule Colts is it supposed I shall have this Spring. Let there be a regular Register of all the Mares that go to the Jacks. . . ." One generation a year was so slow; he should have started as a young man. In the midst of his struggle for neutrality, as France killed King Louis and Europe erupted in war, in the midst of Mad Anthony Wayne's campaign against Indians in the west, the President worried about "the Roan, or which may perhaps distinguish her more clearly, the Mad Mare." Had she foaled a mule colt? Was it by the young jack Compound, or by The Knight of Malta? All the troubled years of his Presidency, Washington hungered for news of Royal Gift. People around him in Philadelphia feared the President's high tempers, regretted his stiff distant manners; a few learned the sure way to win his attention was to ask about his jack ass.

As the years crept on, not all days were dark. Washington had ever learned to accept what life offered, the bad with the good; he had the soldier's way of making the best of things. He made the best of the Presidency; and by and by he discovered the highest office in the land actually afforded certain unexpected advantages to a mule-breeder. Congressmen came from all states, all kinds of farm lands. Frequently, one of them would apply for the loan of Royal Gift for his constituency, the lease of his talents. The General deliberated, always with Royal Gift's welfare in mind. "It is the anxious wish of the people of this and the States northward of it to get him nearer to them," he wrote from Philadelphia. To every inquirer, the President always described Royal Gift's habits with scrupulous honesty: "It is proper you should know that this Jack, though *sure,* is *slow* in covering, and that it has been found necessary to have a Jennett or two always at hand during the season, by way of stimulus, when he is in these slothful humours."

The Hon. Jeremiah Wadsworth, Representative in Congress from Connecticut, asked the President of the United States for a jack ass for his neighbors. The President-General thought of selling Compound, offspring of Royal Gift and a Maltese jenney, for £500; briefly he considered parting with Royal Gift himself. He changed his mind on both. And nothing would induce him to sell The Knight of Malta. Congressman Wadsworth in the end received only friendly advice.

In the course of his first term, Washington toured New England, and he made an official progression of 1,887 miles in his coach through the Southern states—that the whole people might see and know their President. Everywhere, he was greeted with requests for a jack ass. Finally, when Compound was old enough to cover at Mount Vernon along with The Knight of Malta, the President did agree to send Royal Gift on a Southern tour—that the whole people might have mules. Fully guarded, attended, fully heralded, the big grey jack started off. Washington planned every mile of the journey, prescribed every movement. He wished he might go himself; he could not. Worse still, he could not even send his own reliable men. A stranger took charge of the trip, a man well-recommended, carefully selected; but alas, the power of the Presidency did not reach effectively down to stable grooms. Royal Gift stood three years at Charleston, but results were a sad disappointment. In Philadelphia, Senator Izard of South Carolina informed the President-General he had got a fine mule from the great Spaniard, but from other less political Carolina planters Washington heard alarming stories of Royal Gift's failures—all because of the way he was handled on his journey. The man Allan who fetched him had behaved abominably: "instead of moving him slowly and steadily along as he ought," the President fumed, "he was prancing (with the Jack) from one public meeting, or place to another in a gait which could not but prove injurious to the Animal, who had hardly ever been out of a walk before. . . ." From this rough handling, Royal Gift's covering was not sure in the South, as it had always been at Mount Vernon; indeed, he was never sure again. Something obscure happened to Royal Gift on his Southern journey, something (as one might say) vital. The President entertained harsh suspicions of Charleston planters. Perhaps they were not being straight with him. Perhaps their mares, whom they said Royal Gift failed with, had cast their colts prematurely, and they concealed it.

Discouragements of public office, and bad news of Royal Gift from Charleston, sank Washington's spirits. At Mount Vernon, planters would not pay their stud fees, pasturage was trampled down or eaten bare, even his own trusted overseers were unaccountably misusing mares by taking them out after dark. From his fine mansion in The High in Philadelphia, the President complained bitterly of night-riding. It cost him priceless stock. Drought made the mares poor enough, they were slinking their colts again. On top of this, "Night rides and treading Wheat will forever deprive me of foals," he lamented.

He added sadly, "I make a miserable hand at breeding Mules."

He thought for a while of renting the Mount Vernon farms, of giving up farming entirely; "from my present situation; from my advanced time of life; from a wish to live free from care. . . ." Even Peter failed him, faithful obedient Peter, by putting mule colts to the plough too young. In this year 1794, this year of the *ça ira*, of his greatest unpopularity, of Jefferson's defection, French plots, British angers, rebellion in Pennsylvania, his whole plantation seemed to be falling to pieces while he was off running the country. Unexplainable things happened, things that would not have happened had he been there in person tending to business: "I am unlucky in the loss of Mules; not less than five or Six within two, or at most three years, have died by violent means. . . ."

He had to change overseers, even bailiffs. The new men never seemed to understand. Sitting at his desk, the President of the United States explained mule culture to his hired staff: "A Mule does not come to his strength until he is eight or nine years old, nor said to be in his prime until he is 12. or 15. . . . To put them in the plough when they are rising three and work them as my Overseers have done mine, as they would have done a dray horse in his prime, is, in one word, an infallible means to prevent me from raising any to be valuable: whereas with proper usage, and due care, they would serve well for thirty odd years."

Sometimes errors were his own fault. Sometimes, he simply forgot things. "My public duties press so much upon me. . . ." Sometimes he had to leave crucial judgments to others, to managers: "If you think the Wheat in No. 2, at Muddy hole, will not be too much injured by turning the young Mules on it, I do not object to the measure . . . with respect to the young Jack, it is my earnest wish that he may be fed high, Winter and Summer, to see to what size he can be made to grow. . . ."

At last during the eighth year of his Presidency he began to see an end to office, a return home. His spirits rose: *January, 1797: "In Six weeks or thereabouts, I expect to be a resident at Mount Vernon. . . ."* Peter was to feed well the six covering jacks making ready, *"keep them in a very thriving order . . ."* Finally he was there, an old man weary with the storms of state, filled with gloomy apprehensions of his end—just as covering season began.

Mount Vernon was always healing to Washington, never as a soft easy retreat, but healing as a congenial enterprise, each day big with problems he loved to meet, profits he longed to make, big with nature and weather, crops, animals, men. Thirty-two months were left to the General, so brief a time, only three covering seasons. Some of these precious days were taken by his last public trip Northward, when his country called him again, the Lieutenant General, to raise a new army, organize the military for defense.

In eight years, Royal Gift and The Knight of Malta had wrought mightily in republican enjoyments. The General began to sell young jacks, crosses of Spanish, Maltese, Surinam, Maryland, Virginia stock; he broke mules to carriage and plough, forty-two of them on the five farms of Mount Vernon. Royal Gift at the age of seventeen was beyond his best usefulness, still suffering from his sportive adventures on the road to Charleston. But his hulking progeny carried on in his stead, and The Knight of Malta was just now in his fierce, neat prime. Washington reflected what he might have achieved with mules had he stayed home where he was needed, managed the hard day-to-day enterprise himself, instead of being off on other concerns eight years, eight long crucial years.

By now, money was tight. Every Virginia planter was pinched, war on the sea hurt trade. The General was seriously embarrassed for lack of funds. He wrote everyone he thought might be a possible purchaser, offering mules, even jacks, describing their merits, their rarity, their value. In 1798 disaster struck: a strange accident, some kind of poison in the feed. It killed two jacks, one of them the incomparable Compound, "whom money would scarcely have induc'd me to part with." Washington stood with Peter in the mule shed south of the stables, watching helplessly while Compound died "in violent agonies."

In the fall of 1798, fever was rife; the winter came on mild, a bad sign; in '99 all summer Virginia once again burned with drought. Mount Vernon made no oats at all that year, and very little corn. The General was frantic. He supported twice as many slaves in his "family" as he needed or ought to keep; they ate everything Mount Vernon could produce, yet he would not sell ("I am principled against this kind of traffic in the human species") nor hire them out ("to disperse the families I have an aversion"). Though we would wish it otherwise, the last months of George Washington's life were worrisome, vexed. He looked out on cherished meadows "as bare as the pavements." Ruefully, he acknowledged he could feed no new stock. He would even have "to reduce the Mouths that feed on the Hay."

Still, his bold experiment had succeeded—not grandly, as he had dreamed, of course; life never gave the General the full promise of his dreams. Partial successes, mere fragments of victories, were always Washington's lot. From youth, he spent his powers in public and private employments, resisting the inner defeats of harsh outer discouragements.

Yet as he and his century finished their course together, he left a nation behind him—and he left it stocked with mules. Both were bizarre, astonishing legacies of one man's substance: the nation of his strength, the mules of his imagination. Both measured his quality, the mules no less than the nation. "For the multiplication of useful animals," Washington observed, in his grave farmer's way, "is a common blessing to mankind."

6

The Grand Federal Processions

"The little Fiddle," "Little Francis," "that pretty, little, musical, poetical witling"—when people described Francis Hopkinson, they used words that smiled. When they saw him, they smiled, too. It was something delightful, something improbable and elfish, the spectacle of this quick little mite of a man sitting in court as Judge of the Admiralty. He looked like a player in some merry masquerade. His long flowing robe enveloped him entirely, his tiny head quite disappeared beneath the curls of his stiff full-bottomed wig.

Litigants didn't smile, nor the lawyers who pled before him as proctors in admiralty. Lawyers treated the busy little Judge with a special deference. Theirs was an honest respect, paid willingly to his vast learning, his skill, his patience, his devotion, his alertness. The Judge treated *them* with unfailing courtesy. (There is nothing from the bench a lawyer values more.) He listened attentively to everything they said. Consequently, they rarely said too much. Judge Hopkinson ran his court with swift efficiency. He cleared his docket every term, his decrees were brisk, crystal-clear, incisive. And strikingly original.

They were bound to be, for this court of "the Admiralty of Pennsylvania" was itself original. It was an American invention, significantly unlike the old colonial Vice-Admiralty. Congress recommended to the states that they set up admiralty courts; accordingly in 1778, Pennsylvania's revolutionary government erected such a court, in such terms and with such powers as to exhibit to everyone the independent American states were free now of British law and British systems, as well as merely free of British government. "Judge of the Admiralty," Hopkinson sat both as court of first instance, and as prize court, ruling on "things done on the seas." The "seas" included the Delaware River. He applied not the English Common Law, but the law of nations, the provisions of treaties, the Civil Law, maritime law and consular law—applied them to prizes, captures, piracies, and felonies; to insurances, ladings, hypothecations and bottomry bonds; to disputes of seamen with masters, masters with owners; to wrecks and salvage and recoveries; to wages not paid and cargoes not delivered; to all the martime concerns of those who went down to the seas in ships. Being Hopkinson, he made daring innovations. On one occasion, he decided to destroy the venerable English distinction between Prize Court and Admiralty Court. The lawyers before him were startled; their clients were three of Philadelphia's most important merchant ship-owners. They objected, they appealed. On appeal, John Dickinson upheld the little Judge. Law in England proceeded one way, the martime law of nations another. Must we then, because of England's way, reject the "universal and immemorial compact of mankind?" No, Dickinson said. He followed Hopkinson: England's rules do not bind us. *"There was a time, when we listened to the language of her Senates and her Courts, with a partiality of veneration, as to oracles. It is passed. We have assumed our station among the powers of the earth, and must attend to the voice of nations, the sentiments of the society into which we have entered."*

American independence was becoming real indeed, when appeals court could say that.

Little Hopkinson thoroughly loved his Admiralty work. His courtroom and chambers were on the upper floor of Philadelphia's Market House, at the Third Street stairs, just above the pillory where criminals were displayed in the stocks on Market days—Wednesdays and Saturdays. The noise of the city was all around him, and the smells—vegetable smells, cattle smells, offal, rotting sheeps' heads, drying blood in the Market below. He worked with remarkable concentration, made copious notes all the time, for he intended to publish his cases. He did, too: Hopkinson's volume, *Judgments in the Admiralty of Pennsylvania* (1789), marks a step in our history. It was a thing new judges in the new nation were doing, publishing reports. Case law makes tough law, settled law; reports would make an American law, distinct from Britain's. Judge Hopkinson was a lawyer's lawyer. He believed the new nation should have its own new law, make its own precedents, its own jurisprudence. Lawyers knew that about him—that, and the quickness of his insights, the freedom and firmness of his mind, his austere principles, his wit, his twinkling charm, his sudden diamond-hard high seriousness. Lawyers saw a side of him no one else knew. They were grateful for him.

Everyone saw his talents. Out of court, the little Judge moved with happy vivacity, through an amazing variety of creative employments. He played concerts on his harpsichord for friends, he directed the choir and played the organ at Christ Church; for a while he even tried giving singing lessons to Episcopal children, but pretty soon he gave that up. He composed church music, psalm tunes, anthems, and hymns, odes set to music on public occasions; sometimes they were published. He wrote gay secular tunes as well, with words to be sung to them. In November 1788 the printer Dobson issued *A Set of Eight Songs. The Words and Music Composed by the Honorable Francis Hopkinson . . . for Young Practitioners on the Harpsichord or Forte Piano.* John Aitken engraved the musical staves and notes. It was the first collection of secular music by a native-born American ever published in America. He did sober duties, too. He helped run The Library Company, even served as librarian for a couple of years; he served other institutions of the city as well. Up in Bordentown (his wife was Anne Borden), he was admired for his paintings in oil, his drawings, his quick clever portrait sketches. Philadelphians, those serious folk, spoke more of his chemical laboratory, his studies of physical properties, his mathematics, his "mechanicks," his designs and inventions.

Every artist, every craftsman in the city, was his friend. He haunted their shops. It was at Charles Willson Peale's studio one day by accident that John Adams met him. Lawyer, painter, poet—even stiff solemn Adams responded to his qualities. "I have a curiosity to penetrate a little deeper into the bosom of this curious gentleman," he wrote. "He is one of your pretty, little, curious, ingenious men. His head is not bigger than a large apple . . . I have not met with anything in natural history more amusing and interesting than his personal appearance—yet he is genteel and well bred, and is very social." Adams had to reduce things to his own level. He reduced the remarkable Hopkinson, and with him all art itself: "I wish I had leisure and tranquillity of mind to amuse myself with these elegant and ingenious arts of painting, sculpture, statuary, architecture, and music. But I have not."

Franklin never condescended; Jefferson rarely. Jefferson was a musician (of sorts) himself. "I have but few Words," he wrote Hopkinson once, "3 of them are, I love you." And Dr. Franklin loved "Little Francis" too, as he had loved his father before him. It was to that father, he said, that he was indebted for his discovery that metallic points would "throw off the electrical fire"—from which knowledge he invented his lightning rods. The Judge had opponents a'plenty, for he lived by his firm opinions, but never an enemy among people who knew him in person. There was a glow around him, a glow of pleasure, affection, of joy. "A facetious agreeable man," Dr. Rush wrote. "His domestic character was unsullied by any of the imperfections which sometimes cleave to genius. . . . He was so agreeable and kind as a neighbour that he constantly created friends . . ."

People told wondering stories about him: how he found a mouse making his home in the wainscoting of his dining room and trained him to come out when he sat at dinner, frolic about the table, take food from his hand; how pigeons flocked daily in his garden, waited his coming, settled on his shoulders as he walked, and on his head and arms, sat attentive when he sang them a song. They told how in his youth visiting England he had actually known Lord North, had taken dinner a guest at his table. It was quite true; and Lord North had appointed the diminutive young colonial to offices, given him preferments. Hopkinson accepted the offices, but he joined in rebellion nonetheless when North's ministry began repressive measures. He was in every way American, one of the brand new Americans. The word "first" clung to him: first in music, first graduate in the first class of the college at Philadelphia, first American ever to stand for examination to be admitted to the bar. (George Ross and John Dickinson had been appointed to examine him, back in April, 1761.)

Yet far more than all the affectionate stories, more than the music or the law or the admiralty actions, people knew his writings—those merry rollicking pieces that made fun of everything even in the worst days of the war, A Prophecy, "A Pretty Story" By Peter Grievous, The Character of the British Nation, an hundred others; and his poems, from the stirring Camp Ballad for soldiers in winter bivouac, to his most celebrated piece of hilarity, The Battle of the Kegs. Everything from his pen was signed with his happiness, his gaiety, his love. His tingling, jingling satires could ridicule without bitterness, pillory without pain. Never was deadly rapier wielded with more comic thrusts, never with more immediate effect. But so many of his best things were lost in newspapers, printed anonymously, or over some fanciful name; people, even his close friends, by no means realized how much of a writer he had actually been, till after he was gone. In a period of relative quiet, he decided to bring all his things together in two books— one of poetry, one of prose. He was engaged on this agreeable task when, on a May morning in 1791, a sudden stroke of apoplexy took him off. He was fifty-three years old.

His son Joseph finished the work. (He was a judge too, and a poet; he wrote "Hail Columbia," among other things.) Three thick volumes came out late in 1792: The Miscellaneous Essays and Occasional Writings of Frangis [sic] Hopkinson—a thousand pages of prose, two hundred of poetry, the latter titled Hopkinson's Poems on Several Occasions. For the first time, people could see his work whole, and they saw qualities in him they had never bothered to notice while he lived. "Little Francis" had always made them laugh; certainly there was abundant laughter here. But there were tears too, and a greater depth than they had suspected, more rugged conviction, more of an artist's eye, and there was a lovely lyricism, a singing of the heart strange to Americans in their reading, pure gold in any land. Long after the little judge had run his own merry course, youth in the American West would be singing his lyrics: *My Days Have Been So Wondrous Free, Be She So Ever Fair, My Love Has Gone to Sea.* . . .

One time in Francis Hopkinson's busy years, he was given the chance to stand before everyone as an artist—no concealment for once, no sheepish acknowledgment, the worldly men of money and big affairs needed him, demanded him. They suspended their eternal condescension toward "the trifling arts," their patronizing attitude toward music, they came to him with hats in hand. "Little Francis" leapt at the opportunity.

It was 1788, the year of the Great Controversy, the year two national political parties first formed in the land, the year of Ratification. The Federal Convention sat in secrecy all summer, 1787. Then in September the new Constitution was submitted to the people. In every one of the thirteen states, debate began. The whole nation became a forum, the public mind concentrated singly on one subject. It was a notable subject—the issue of liberty and order, of the power to govern and the freedom of the citizen, the issue of loyalty, to one state or this anomalous new entity called The *United* States. Those who favored the new Constitution, the Federals, began to organize, correspond, to form committees in towns and counties. Those who opposed, the Anti-Federals ("Antis," people called them) were slower to band together, but all the more bitter when they did. Ratification was the first national political experience of Americans.

No one doubted the vast importance of the debate. General Washington, greatest figure of all the Federals, wrote Patrick Henry, Virginia's leading Anti, that our whole political concerns were "suspended by a thread." Hamilton, Jay, Madison composed the *Federalist* papers, Dickinson in Delaware wrote *Letters of Fabius,* a battle of pamphlets commenced, soon every clerk and tavern boy was a political philosopher, as various Old Romans hurled arguments back and forth in the newspapers. Nine states must ratify to put the Constitution into effect. The struggle for the Nine States lasted nine months.

Right away, Federals won significant victories. The Antis were unprepared. Delaware ratified swiftly, unanimously, December 7. She was the First State. In Pennsylvania violence occurred, Antis were manhandled, the "cold and sour temper" of the West broke out in riots, but Federals rushed through an election, skillfully managed the convention, ratified by a two-to-one vote

December 12. New Jersey unanimously approved December 18, the Third State; Georgia unanimously January 2; Connecticut by three-to-one January 9. This was the Fifth State.

But it was all too quick, too hasty and hurried, too easy. Antis were angry. They were just getting their opposition started. Federals might rejoice that a strong, firm government would soon replace the anarchy of the Confederation, cure inflation and depression, restore public credit. But Antis found in the proposed Constitution "an awful squint—it squints toward monarchy." A "Farmer-Planter" of Maryland called it aristocracy, "government in the hands of a very few nobles or RICH MEN is therein concealed," it was "the most artful plan that ever was formed to entrap a free people." Thoughtful Federals began to wonder if their hasty action in five states had been wise. And they began to write all the more.

In Philadelphia, little Judge Hopkinson was thoroughly Federal. He chose his side at some cost; the new Constitution would put an end to his Court of the Admiralty of Pennsylvania, for by its provisions admiralty would be taken from the states and given exclusively to the federal government. In spite of this, Hopkinson told everyone the strong national government was exactly what Americans required. As in the early revolutionary crises, so now at fifty he acted from principle, not from interest. His principle differed somewhat from the usual Federal line. Some there were who advocated the new Constitution for the support it would give to their speculations in Western land companies; some expected it would help their business and commercial transactions; "little Francis" was concerned for the artisan, the craftsman, the "mechanick." These produced the goods and services by which Americans lived. Under thirteen states loosely confederated, they were caught in the vortex of inflation, squeezed by merchants, by ship-owners, by tolls. The new Constitution would set them free, one national government over commerce would give them a vast national market. For the industrious mechanick, Hopkinson wrote his essay, *The New Roof.* And, of course, he wrote a poem, too, *The New Roof: a Song for Federal Mechanicks:*

For our Roof we will raise, and our song still shall be,
Our government firm, and our citizens free.

"The New Roof" became the Federals' symbol everywhere.

Yet ever since that hasty ratification in December, Pennsylvania Anti-Federals had been gaining. Every narrow majority was encouragement to them, and in the news of Anti sentiment from Providence, New York, and North Carolina, Pennsylvania Antis even glimpsed the possibility of winning back their state. They got up a petition with five thousand names, praying the Constitution be rejected. Now they were demanding a new state convention be called. Antis everywhere discovered plenty of leaks in the New Roof. And for the Five States which had ratified by January 9, they could show five of their own still to vote. Rhode Island was all their way, so was New York; the Carolinas seemed Anti. Even Virginia despite Washington's prestige was far from Federal: Richard Henry Lee was an Anti, and old George Mason, and young James Monroe. Then the Massachusetts convention met at Boston.

Now this was none of your tiny, select assemblies. Massachusetts's ratifying convention January 9 contained no less than 355 delegates. They were evenly split: most of Boston was Federal, most of the country Anti. Massachusetts just a year ago had suffered armed rebellion. No state was more restless, no people more thoroughly aroused. Nor more divided in councils. Mr. Elbridge Gerry, though he had worked energetically all summer in the Federal Convention, had ended up bitter against the proposed Constitution, as bitter as he had been a year ago against Dan'l Shays and the western rebels, whom he now found joined with him in opposition. Little Mr. Gerry was admittedly odd, irascible, unpredictable. But Governor Hancock was the soul of stability, and he too opposed the new Constitution. So did Sam'l Adams. "I stumble at the threshold," Adams wrote of the New Roof. "I meet with a national government instead of a federal union of sovereign states." But Boston mechanicks and shipwrights gathered in caucus at the Green Dragon, a great company of them, "more than were stars in the sky." They sent Paul Revere to tell Sam'l Adams they were Federal to a man, and the doughty old republican had to give in. John Hancock was elected president when the convention met. He refused to take his seat; then Federals whispered promises that he would be vice president if the New Roof were erected, and Hancock, too, gave in. The convention debated four weeks; finally ratification carried by a slim majority of 19 votes out of the 355.

When the result was announced, Boston made jubilee. Bells sounded, cannon fired, crowds paraded in the streets. Bonfires blazed all through the night, and on the Commons people burnt a ship's boat named the *Old Constitution*. Long Lane, in front of the meeting house where the convention sat, was that day rechristened Federal Street.

Antis scoffed at the celebration. One newspaper column paraphrased an old nursery rhyme:

> And there they went up, up, up,
> And there they went down, down, downy,
> There they went backwards and forwards,
> And *poop* for Boston towny.

But Federals were pleased. There had been quick planning, hurried organization behind the various scenes of rejoicing. Everything went off well enough.

General Lincoln wrote Washington, "The Gentlemen provided at Faneul Hall some biscuit & cheese four qr Casks of wine three barrels & two hogs. of punch the moment they found that the people had drank sufficiently means were taken to overset the two hogs. punch this being done the company dispersed and the day ended most agreeably."

Massachusetts was the Sixth State. But to all Federals, that Boston convention was a warning. The narrow majority was shocking; it showed how strong the Antis had grown. And to win at all, Federals had been obliged to see gables put on their New Roof. For Massachusetts annexed to her ratification nine proposals for a bill of rights—nine limitations on the power of the new national government—and enjoined her representatives to use every legal means to secure their adoption.

To Federals, this was a second alarum. At once they realized Antis could destroy the entire scheme with amendments. They could erect a whole second roof over the New Roof, until ratification itself became a hollow victory. Wisely, Federal leaders accepted the idea of amendments, shrewdly they took over the device and made it their own, a concession on some points to win the main issue.

Still, every amendment was an implied defeat. And in February New Hampshire's convention proved so full of vigorous Anti-Federals that New Roof men were glad to adjourn till June. By this they avoided actual defeat, but they generally considered New Hampshire lost. From February till April, the count stood at Six States.

Then in April, Federals won the Seventh State with ludicrous ease, won it without even conceding amendments. Some of Maryland's principal men were Anti-Federals—Samuel Chase, William Paca, Charles Ridgely—but their leadership fell to Luther Martin, who for all his brilliance and his legal insights was an offensive person. He talked interminably, in speeches that went on not just for hours, but for days; he was not always sober when he talked, he was lamentably careless with the truth. Mr. Carroll, that distinguished gentleman, brought him up short when he grew too offensive. Ratification carried by a vote of six to one in convention at Annapolis. When the news reached Baltimore, a "procession" was held, with floats, flags, seven-gun salutes for the Seven States, and a symbolic ship was built overnight, christened *Federalist*. Rigged and manned like a real ship, she was hauled through the streets for crowds to gape at. Afterwards, the merchants of Baltimore didn't know what to do with the good ship *Federalist*. They exhibited her for a month; then they loaded her on an actual vessel and sent her down to Mount Vernon as a present for General Washington.

If Maryland in April had been an easy victory, South Carolina in May looked a near thing. Federals here were apprehensive. They wished Virginia had acted, giving them guidance; they wished North Carolina were not so thoroughly against them. Most of all, they wished Antis were less vehement. The first debate was in the legislature, in January. *Despotism!* cried James Lincoln, from way out west in Ninety Six. This new Constitution would establish aristocracy, destroy freedom. Had the people no rights? Were South Carolinians a parcel of children, to cry for a toy, liberty, and then rashly give it away? Another country man saw only mischief and woe in the new scheme—corruption, oppression, a standing army of Turkish Janissaries, enslavement of brave industrious people by the wealthy and powerful. Delegate after delegate demanded amendments. And elegant little Mr. Rawlins Lowndes, ornament of the Charleston bar, governor once, in '77, spoke passionately against ratifying. Everyone thought it strange of Mr. Lowndes. He should have been on the other side. Gossip whispered Antis must have hired him as counsel, to plead their cause. Lowndes pled earnestly. When he died, he said, he wished graven on his tomb no other words than "Here lies the man who opposed the Constitution, because it was ruinous to the liberty of America."

Yet Lowndes for all his pathos could not win the day. John Rutledge, Pierce Butler, General Pinckney and his brilliant cousin young Charles Pinckney answered all his objections. These Federals had an eloquence of their own. By a single vote, they carried the legislature. Then they went among the people, county by county, just as had John Rutledge during the war. ("Where John Rutledge's carriage is, there is the government of South Carolina.") The ensuing election was all theirs, the state convention was Federal. Antis were strong enough to pass amendments, but that was all they could do. By a two-to-one majority, 149 to 73, the convention voted South Carolina the Eighth State, Friday, May 23.

On Saturday, May 24, as soon as the vote was announced, the Federal committee of Charleston met. (It was *Charleston* now, by legislative act, no longer the old *Charles Town* of provincial days.) They raised money, planned a huge celebration, appointed stewards. The stewards worked feverishly all weekend. The procession, prepared in three days, was presented on Tuesday, May 27.

It was a notable spectacle, full of triumph, but full of conciliation too. Antis had much to look at that took the sting from defeat. No less than 2,800 persons out of Charleston's 10,000 white inhabitants took part in the show, as the rest looked on. At Roper's wharf marchers assembled, at high noon they began their procession, up Broad Street, over Meeting Street, on to the Green—"Federal Green," it was called this day. A band of music led off, a battalion of artillery followed, then "Gentlemen Planters," then "Gardeners," then inspectors of all three staples, rice, indigo, tobacco, with a hogshead of tobacco drawn over the cobbles by horses. After these came thirty-five separate groups of tradesmen, each group bearing a decorated banner with the name of its craft: butchers, bakers, brewers, shoemakers, peruke makers, hair dressers, brass founders, tallow chandlers, soap boilers, coach painters, whitesmiths, tanners-curriers-and-skinners—a bewildering succession of artisans proclaiming the variety of the port city of America's South. On a horsedrawn stage, printers mounted a whole printshop, with press, frames, and type cases; compositors and pressmen set up and imprinted handbills as they rumbled through the streets.

And here, too, the stewards built a symbolic ship of state. Preceded by marching pilots, commissioners of the pilotage, and harbor masters, came the man-of-war *Federalist,* her master, officers and crew standing stiffly erect. She was drawn by eight white horses, each with a plume on its forehead bearing the name of one of the eight ratifying states. After the ship came forty-seven more groups of crafts and professions; finally at the end of the great long line marched the government officials of state, county, and city, the parade marshal Captain Hamilton, and a company of fusiliers.

When all the immense throng congregated at Federal Green, a collation was served. The Butchers' Company provided "a fine ox roasted whole," the entire city sat down and ate together—"without distinction," it was said. "A joyful spirit of republicanism seemed to pervade every breast; the utmost order and good harmony was preserved, and the day closed with hilarity." In the evening the ships in the harbor sent up rockets, swung lanterns and torches from their mastheads and fixed flares on their spars.

The Federal committee, impresarios of Charleston's procession, described its glories in an article for the *Columbian Herald.* Soon, Federal papers all up and down the country reprinted their glowing account. It gave no hint or opposition or dissent; it celebrated only the unity of all interests and classes, of humanity itself, under the New Roof.

Now, only one more state was needed to make the necessary Nine. But which could it be? Rhode Island and North Carolina were still hopelessly Anti, New York, too. And Virginia—well, Virginia was the great question mark. General Washington's influence in Virginia was prodigious. His prestige might carry the state for the Federals; but by the same token if the Antis could defeat the new government here, they could probably defeat it in the remaining states too. Patrick Henry, George Mason, Richard Henry Lee gathered their Anti forces togehher in convention at Richmond, June 2. James Madison and Chancellor Wythe opposed them, and John Marshall and Edmund Pendleton. It was a grave and spirited debate, it went on for three weeks. Obviously, no easy sweeping victory could be won here, obviously amendments would have to be conceded; even this might not be enough. The eyes of the whole nation turned toward Virginia during June.

And while every eye turned toward Virginia, Federals won a surprising victory in a quarter no one had thought of. That New Hampshire convention, which had adjourned in February, reassembled in mid-June, and swiftly, on June 21, ratified the Constitution—with amendments, to be sure, and by a slim majority, 57–46, but ratified nonetheless. New Hampshire was the Ninth State.

Post riders galloped all over the union. But so long were the roads from New Hampshire that when expresses reached Alexandria a week later, two hours before dawn, they found that little town in the midst of nocturnal revel. For on that day, June 27, Virginia had voted ratification. The decision at Richmond had been closer even than New Hampshire's, 89–79, the amendments even more elaborate than the Ninth State's attempt to "guard against an undue Administration of the Federal Government." But still the Federals now had ten ratifications, one more than needful. The existence of the new government was assured. And the news reached everywhere in time for Fourth of July celebrations.

In Boston ten pillars were erected on the Commons, and ten guns fired. Citizens paraded by candlelight, rockets burst bright in the sky, and all the bells chimed.

At Providence bells were rung, holiday declared, and Federals erected a great open tent near the city where they invited all citizens to join them the evening of Independence Day. An ox would be roasted, they announced. But Rhode Island was the Antis' stronghold. Countrymen flocked in, a huge mob mischievously accepting the city men's invitation, led by a judge and three legislators. The mob was armed with rifles; the rifles had bayonets fixed. The judge entered the tent. Abruptly, he demanded festivities cease. Federals protested it was the Fourth of July, a holiday even in Rhode Island. They argued. Very well, the judge finally said. The celebration might proceed, so long as the word *Nine* was not mentioned. Thirteen, not nine, cannon must be fired, for the thirteen original states. And the toast to the Nine States must be omitted. The Federals, outnumbered, agreed.

In Albany Antis broke up the Federals' celebration, shot off thirteen guns where ten had been fired, publicly burned the new Constitution. Federals retaliated by nailing another copy to a pine pole, parading it through the streets. Antis met them in a narrow alley, attacked with stones, sticks, and cold iron. A sharp battle ensued. Finally, the Antis were routed.

In the wilderness West out at Pittsburgh, high on Grant's Hill, the Federals gathered. Orations were spoken, meat roasted, toasts proposed. As twilight fell, bonfires blazed and young couples danced to a fiddler's tune. A huddle of Indians, silent and puzzled, watched from a distance.

Expresses from New Hampshire galloped into Philadelphia Thursday night, June 26. In a moment, the city committee of Federals met, fixed Independence Day for a mighty celebration. Then sent to Judge Hopkinson: would he

plan and direct the fête? Judge Hopkinson would. He began at once. He
designed a pageant of the Nine States, he called artisans to him from all
crafts of the city, huge floats appeared on his drawing board. His sudden
schemes were breathtaking.

Friday, Saturday, Sunday a constant succession of citizens streamed up the
Third Street stairs of the Market House. Some were defeated Antis, surly,
ill-disposed. The cheerful little Judge treated everyone alike. In his merry
bustling way he heard their plans, gave them directions, sent them hurrying
off with tasks to do. He studied what other cities had accomplished, he
organized everything, planned work schedules, in free moments he began to
write an *Ode* for the occasion. There would be a theme—The New Roof,
edifice of the new nation. He drew a sketch, gave it to The Carpenters' Company to build. There would be symbols—the number thirteen for the thirteen
states, the eagle for the Federal Union, the Temple of Freedom. Of course
there must be music. He sent to his friend Mr. Reinagle, would he please
to compose a *Federal March*? And lose no time about it? And would he
rehearse the bands and the orchestral groups? And nine—the whole procession would be in nines, for the nine ratifying states. Nine would be the
talisman number.

By Sunday night his plans were finished; at dawn Monday morning, June
30, work began. Everything had to be ready Thursday night.

Even as he fashioned his wonders, Judge Hopkinson knew the Antis were
seething with rage. There was Mr. Oswald, in his *Independent Gazetteer*,
filling every issue with the most appalling personal attacks on leading Federals. Because Justice Rush was Dr. Benjamin Rush's brother, the *Gazetteer*
declared, no one but a Federal could expect fair treatment in the Supreme
Court. Already one libel suit had been filed against Eleazer Oswald. There
would be others. The editor blamed it all on the new Constitution, kept
saying in print that, with the new government in operation, every citizen
would be at the mercy of a tyranny harsher than ever seen in the world.

Seven long months of party angers was enough. Now, peace must come—
peace, and a chance for temperate men to shape this Federal victory into
effective government. If Antis organized, Federals must reorganize. The new
Constitution must embrace them both. Hopkinson conceived a pageant, not
of victory but of peace, a public testimony of the end of dissension, of the
joining now of merchant and artisan, farmer, mechanic, seaman, soldier, and
shipper under The New Roof. This procession would make a single party of
all Americans, of all opinions, men free in their differences, but all united
in one national enterprise of union. It would heal the wounds of the past year.

The city bustled with activity, scarcely any business was done. Hopkinson
was everywhere at once; nights he worked on his *Ode*. Then, Wednesday
evening, came the post from Virginia. There were ten states to celebrate

now, not nine. It was too late to change everything; Hopkinson spent Thursday doing what he could: another pillar here, a tenth horse there, more flags, more marchers, a tenth ship in the river. But he could not undo work already done. The procession would have two talisman numbers, both nine and ten. The artist in "Little Francis" could look on Virginia's ratification as a near-disaster. Political disaster threatened also: that same Thursday editor Oswald was charged with contempt of the Supreme Court, for "gross violations of truth and decency," to the anger of Antis, the dismay of Federals. This was no time to give the opposition new ammunition. *"Tyranny!"* cried the Antis. *"Freedom of press will be dead forever, in your new government . . ."*

Thursday evening, the street commissioners went along the line of march, sweeping the pavements clean, clearing stones away, lopping off branches from overhanging trees. Friday July Fourth dawned cloudy but dry. A wind blew briskly from the south. All Philadelphians flocked to their Grand Federal Procession.

It was a prodigious enterprise, vast, immense, incredible. Five thousand citizens (one out of every eight persons in the city) marched, rode, or were carried through the streets that day, and hundreds of others manned the ships in the harbor. The ten largest of these ships, gay with pennons and flags, lay at anchor in a line, in midstream. From the masthead of each an enormous white streamer whipped in the breeze, with the name of a ratifying state sewn in gold letters. Other ships at the wharves dressed their spars with bunting, and the man-of-war *Rising Sun,* flying flags of France and Spain, our foreign allies, lay close-to, off Market Street wharf. Overnight, the ships had been made ready, in the dark maneuvered to their anchorages.

And overnight, almost, the labor of thousands of artisans had wrought such images as men had never seen. No European courtly pageant this, with royalty condescending and nobles riding aloof, but a sudden exhilarating outburst of free people, all of one class, Americans in their brave new world exhibiting the simple ways of their own lives—exhibiting how proudly!

At the very dawn, bells of Christ Church began to peal, the man-of-war *Rising Sun* fired ten-gun salutes. For hours the exuberant din continued. Nine marshalls with white plumes in their hats, General Mifflin their chief, bellowed through speaking trumpets at Third and South Streets, "the place of general rendezvous," where marchers, floats, devices and machines assembled. The procession was to begin at the symbolic hour, nine o'clock. While bells clanged and big guns exploded, the whole south end of the city boiled in a confusion of plunging horses, dust, and shouting men.

Then out of confusion came spectacular order, as the procession began to move. First marched twelve axemen in long white cloaks, bright caps and black belts: they were the lictors, who go before, the heralds of freedom. Next rode the First Troop, Philadelphia City Cavalry, splendidly mounted and garbed. Then came the symbol of American Independence, a staff, crowned with a liberty cap, streaming a long silk flag which said "Fourth of July 1776" in big gold letters. Colonel John Nixon rode straight with eyes front, carrying the staff—the same John Nixon who had stood on the State House Observatory platform twelve years ago and read the Declaration of Independence for the first time aloud to the people.

Only twelve years of history to celebrate—but with history the parade commenced, and as each unit moved into place, the noisy jam in South Street subsided to patient waiting. After Colonel Nixon the artillery company dragged cannon; then came Convention Delegate Thomas FitzSimons on the very horse General Rochambeau had ridden at Yorktown. He represented the French Alliance. "Sixth of February 1778" said the gold letters on his white silk flag. A corps of light infantry followed, then Delegate George Clymer, well mounted, carrying a staff of olive and laurel, symbolizing the treaty of peace with England. His flag read "Third of September 1783." Independence, Alliance, Peace with Victory, these were the three dates of America's existence, the three major events in national history.

And Washington was the national hero. On horseback, Colonel Shee held another flag, "Washington the Friend of his Country." A troop of horse as mounted honor guard rode after.

So much for history. A herald next appeared, proclaiming a New Era with trumpet and verse. "The crimes and frauds of anarchy shall fail," the verse declared. Dr. Franklin, President of Pennsylvania and Delegate to the Convention, was intended to be the herald. But the famous philosopher was eighty-two years old, and sick in bed. His son-in-law Richard Bache rode in his stead.

Afterward came a flag symbolizing the Federal Convention, and music— a band playing the *Grand Federal March* Alexander Reinagle had hastily composed for the parade—and then loomed an astonishing sight, symbol of the new Constitution itself.

It was a huge bald eagle, the tremendous FEDERAL EAGLE, frightening, enormous, a juggernaut. The bird's great head rose as high as the second story of houses along the route. Even the heavy wheels of the wagon that bore him were taller than a man. The Eagle towered thirteen symbolic feet above his perch, stretched thirteen feet from beak to tail. On his breast were thirteen silver stars in a sky-blue field, between his feet a shield of thirteen stripes, red and white. In the talons of his right foot he grasped an olive branch, in his left a tight bundle of thirteen arrows. The wagon under him was thirty-three feet long. Six white horses strained to draw it. The Eagle swayed and nodded on heavy springs as he rumbled along, quite as if he were alive.

Perched high on the back of this imposing creature were, surprisingly, three justices of the Supreme Court of Pennsylvania, in their scarlet robes and heavy curled wigs. Chief Justice McKean held a pole with the Constitution framed, a flag which said "The People" streaming from it, a liberty cap on top.

For blocks, people could see the Eagle bobbing along. When it drew near, crowds standing on the ground and footways were dwarfed. They had to look up, even to see the talons. The proud head of the bird soared majestically far above them in the sky.

On and on the procession went, over its three-mile course, winding up and down streets and out to the fields. It took three hours to pass by a given point, six hours for the last marcher to reach the end of the route. From 9:30 till 3:30, spectators thronged the walks, hung out of windows, crowded onto roofs. Eighty-eight separate units of marchers gave them floats to look at, scenes, spectacles, visions, tableaux. As each unit passed along Fourth Street it received a military salute from a company of Continental troops drawn up in review.

After the Federal Eagle marched a whole corps of infantry, dressing smartly. Then ten men arm-in-arm bearing flags of the ten ratifying states. After them rode consuls of foreign nations, in ornamented carriages. Then a happy sight; people laughed to see. It was the Admiralty Court: the little Judge trudging along in his long trailing robe that dragged on the stones, his tiny face peering merrily out from his wig. On one side his Register marched, on the other his Clerk. Hopkinson had to scamper at times to keep up. Behind him strode his Marshal, Clement Biddle, hoisting a brightly-silvered oar in his hands.

The port wardens followed; then a tableau of an Indian making peace with the white man. More soldiers, and suddenly Hopkinson's second triumph, a structure even higher than the Eagle, THE NEW ROOF, or GRAND FEDERAL EDIFICE. It was a handsome open domed temple, drawn by ten white horses, a uniformed dragoon astride each with the standard of a state. The dome was supported by thirteen columns carved in the Corinthian style, ten of them complete, three (Rhode Island, North Carolina, New York) unfinished. Atop the dome was a cupola, atop the cupola twenty-six feet in the air rode the buxom figure of the Goddess of Plenty, her cornucopia full of good things. She smiled and waved to the crowds below. Ten men sat in chairs in this temple; they were the people at large to whom the new union was committed.

In four days and nights the Carpenters' Company had constructed their

Grand Federal Edifice, carved its Corinthian capitals with acanthuses, shaped its dome and the graceful cupola, its abundant cornucopia. Proudly the Company marched behind it, 450 architects, builders, masters, journeymen, apprentices—followed by the Company of Saw Makers and File Cutters.

Then came the Agricultural Society with floats on which farmers plowed, sewed, and milled; then the Manufacturing Society with combing and carding machines, looms, spinning machines, cutting, printing, and stencilling machines, all mounted on wagons, all being operated as they passed, by workmen who briskly turned out actual cloth. Members marched afterwards with the flag of American manufactures. "May government protect us," the flag said. The Marine Society strode six abreast, shipmasters holding spyglasses, sextants, charts, quadrants, one a globe. Agriculture, Manufacturing, Commerce—these were the "interests" of America, the plough, the loom, and the ship.

Of them all, the ship had most to say, for to Judge Hopkinson's rapid design the boat builders on the ways had constructed his third great marvel, the Federal Ship *Union.* At eleven o'clock Monday morning they had started, by Thursday evening they had finished this splendid apparition—a ship thirty-three feet long, fully rigged, decorated with fine carvings, handsomely painted. Her frame was the actual captain's barge of the *Serapis,* captured long ago in North Sea waters by John Paul Jones in the *Bonhomme Richard.* Ten horses drew her, representing the Ten States; and a canvas, painted to resemble the sea, hung down from her water line, concealing the wheels of her carriage. She mounted twenty guns, was manned by twenty-five uniformed officers and men. As they moved along, they hoisted sail, received a pilot, trimmed sheets with each change of course, fired her guns, heaved the lead line, finally cast anchor. Everyone was enchanted.

The Pilots of the port followed with a small boat of their own, shearing alongside the *Union* early in the procession to put a pilot aboard, coming up again at the end to take him off, all "with the strictest maritime propriety."

And after the Pilots came the Boat Builders, drawing a third wonder: the *Union's* barge, her oars manned by six small boys clad as bargemen, a seventh as coxswain. And the Builders were not finished yet. They had created still a fourth unit, a float mounting a complete tiny boat yard, with men at work. During the parade, these workmen built, calked, and sanded a thirteen-foot vessel. Sailmakers, Ships' Carpenters and Joiners, Rope Makers, Ship Chandlers, merchants and merchant traders marched along in great bodies in the wake of the Builders.

Plough, loom, and ship were not all of America. Forty-four companies of trades and crafts drew floats or marched in huge corps of artisans, hundreds in some groups, displaying placards and flags as they trudged along, mottoes, liberty caps, and laurel. Brewers, striking a blow for American beers against foreign wines, lettered their dray with the legend, "Home Brewed is Best." Over a glistening silver urn, Jewellers proclaimed, "The purity, brightness, and solidity of this metal is emblematical of that liberty which we expect from the New Constitution." Bakers baked bread on their float, tossed warm, fresh loaves to the crowd. Cordwainers made shoes. The Chair Makers' "Federal Cabinet and Chair Shop" produced chairs; the Painters' Company ground and milled colors. Carvers and Gilders displayed an elegant federal edifice of their own, with companion busts of Washington and, of all people, Phidias. (Phidias was the "most eminent of ancient carvers," they explained.) Blacksmiths hauled a complete shop on wheels, the fire at the forge burning brightly. As the parade moved they actually beat swords into plough-shares and sickles. Coach Makers turned out wheels, trim, and harness under a hopeful motto, "No tax on American carriages." Potters fashioned cups, bowls, and mugs on their wheel, baked them in a kiln. The Bricklayers' Company carried a flag, picturing the new Federal City arising in a forest. Under it was the brave free sentiment, "Both Buildings and Rulers are the Works of our Hands."

The Printers, too, as at Charleston, put a complete shop on wheels, presided over by one of the city's publishers dressed as Mercury, with "real wings" on his head and feet. All along the route another printer (it was Melchior Steiner, the German, from his shop in Race Street "zwischen der Zweiten und Dritten-strasse") printed and threw to the crowds the *Ode* Hopkinson had somehow found time to finish:

> Oh! for a Muse of fire! To mount the Skies
> And to a listening world proclaim,
> Behold! Behold! an Empire rise!

and another poem in the German language as well. Ten times "Mercury" attached one of the *Odes* to a carrier pigeon which promptly mounted from his winged cap and flew off, bound for the capitals of each of the ten states in the Union, even the furthest distant.

Finally, after the guilds, came the officers of government—state and local; then another band of music, and sixty men representing the city Night Watch, some of whom chorused for the Ten States, "Past ten o'clock, and a glorious starlight morning!" Next the lawyers in one band, the doctors in another, followed by all the clergy, arm-in-arm, the Episcopal bishop, the Roman priest, all the Presbyterians, the Lutherans, the Methodists, Rabbi Cohen of Congregation Mikveh Israel; the university and school students at the very end, and the companies of county militia.

Out to the big open fields northwest of town the procession travelled, to the meadow of "Bush Hill", old Andrew Hamilton's great house. Today the meadow was christened "Union Green." Here, a five hundred-foot circle of tables stood waiting, under gay awnings, lined with full hogsheads, tuns, butts, and barrels. The ship *Union* navigated neatly to the center of the circle, dropped her anchor. The Grand Federal Edifice was brought up next to her, the Federal Eagle lumbered to a perch nearby. Chief Justice McKean and his two puisne justices gratefully clambered down from their lofty pinnacle on the Eagle's spine, the Goddess of Plenty made her laborious descent. Horses were led off to the Schuylkill bank far from the crowd, for a period of quiet and rest.

Human celebrators were allowed no such pause. It was near four o'clock when Delegate James Wilson mounted the porch of the Edifice, to deliver the oration of the day. Seventeen thousand people milled about as he spoke.

Mr. Wilson was an earnest Scotsman, as thoroughly Scottish as old Andrew Hamilton himself. He peered near-sightedly through his thick spectacles; he raised his voice over the heads of the throng. His oration was elegant, learned, full of wise Scottish precepts, innocent (as always) of grace or wit. Happily, it was not long. When he finished, the military fired salutes, everyone fell to eating and drinking. In good American liquors—porter, beer, cider— ten toasts were offered, one for each state. Every toast was announced with a fanfare of trumpets, proposed with a speech by a Federal leader, concluded with ten rounds from the cannon, which the guns of *Rising Sun* far off in the river echoed on signal.

By six o'clock, Union Green was cleared. The Grand Federal Edifice and the Federal Ship *Union* were dragged down to State House Yard, now the hall of the Constitution as well as of Independence. They stood there for days, mementoes of the festival. (No one left word of what happened to The Eagle.) That night all the ships in the harbor made a brave illumination, shooting off rockets, hanging their spars with lanterns, flambeaux, and flares. Wonderfully that night, to prove Heaven was on the Federal side, an Aurora Borealis danced for hours, turning the north sky to bright day.

And that night, Francis Hopkinson composed a description of his Grand Federal Procession for the newspapers. The day had been a glorious success. It had displayed all of free America at work. Well might George Washington say to LaFayette, "there never was so much labour and economy to be found in the country as at the present moment." Hopkinson was proud of his New Roof, erected over arts, crafts, and professions alike. Not a single accident had marred his great pageant.

But the artistic genius inhabiting little Judge Hopkinson was a mischievous sprite. It could not be suppressed. Tired as he was, an irresistible hilarity seized him. When all his writing was finished, he took a fresh sheet. Secretly, he composed a lively parody of his own parade, an *Account* of an imaginary show by the Antis on July 5, rivalling the Grand Federal Procession. Their chief marshal was clad in a robe of paper money, a fool's cap on his head, he bore a wreath of hemlock in his hand. The procession mounted to its climax, a boy leading a skunk on a leash. Antis trudged along, "Little Francis" wrote, to the music of the "Dead March" from *Saul*.

Of course, the judge never published his parody. Every Federal paper in the country reprinted his real account, though, and his *Ode;* soon a book edition was published. Readers from New Hampshire to Savannah marvelled at his prodigies. It was the mightiest of parades.

Indeed, it was almost too much. Philadelphia's extravaganza was a procession to end all processions—the perfection of art, the ultimate in spectacles. More would be anticlimax. More would certainly be unwise, for pageants are magic only when they touch the heart. Even the headiest Federal recognized the impulse to march about in pageants was almost spent.

But not entirely. One last indulgence was left in the New Roof men. What Philadelphia could do, New York could do better. New York Federals determined to prove it. Their city might not be the great metropolis Philadelphia was, but they had Congress there, and all the foreign diplomats; they were the national capital. And New York Federals sorely needed a celebration. Their state convention was sitting in Poughkeepsie. *Pokepsie, Pokypsee*—everyone spelled the town differently. And everyone had different notions of what the convention would do. It had met four weeks ago, Antis had a clear majority. They elected Governor Clinton president, they controlled all committees. Yet the Federals were persuasive, a middle party of moderates emerged, surprisingly the convention deadlocked. No one knew how the vote would go. "They may possibly adjourn, which is the best expectation I can form," a Federal Congressman wrote. Chancellor Robert Livingston argued, cajoled, orated in his pompous self-important manner, John Jay and James Duane supported him, Alexander Hamilton gave his earnest speeches which, as he said, confounded but did not convince. The real work was done off the floor, in personal conversations. Governor Clinton was "very violent." Justice Yates of the Supreme Court, Mayor Lansing of Albany (the two Delegates who had walked out of the Federal Convention in dissent) were his chiefs of the Anti forces. With them was a formidable merchant, and landowner of the City, Melancthon Smith. News from Poughkeepsie was vague and disturbing when it came down river. In spite of the Ten States already under the New Roof, the Antis might keep New York out, in regrettable isolation. People in and out of convention talked of dividing the state in two parts, north and south.

The Federals resolved to have a pageant, even before the convention acted. They might influence the undecided at Poughkeepsie; and many of them, reported the French Minister, hoped by a great display to persuade Congress to settle on New York City as the capital of the new union. Congressmen held aloof. New York would have to join the nation before she could become the capital. And as for these parades, "I dont know but we are in danger of running into excess in regard to processions," sober Mr. Otis of Massachusetts remarked. The members of Congress declined to march. Still the Federal committee went ahead. They chose Wednesday, July 23, for their fête, a day on which, unhappily, rain fell in torrents.

In New York City lived an experienced pageanteer, Major Pierre Charles L'Enfant, hero volunteer of the Revolutionary War. L'Enfant, son of a French court painter, had come to fight for liberty in America at his own expense, when twenty-three. As engineer officer he was wounded, captured, and exchanged. He painted pictures, drew maps, designed medals; in the sorrows of Valley Forge he sketched pencil portraits to amuse the soldiers. After the war he planned and staged a great spectacle, the public party given in Philadelphia by the French Minister, the Chevalier de la Luzerne, to celebrate the birth of the Dauphin of France. Recently he had built the reredos of a leading church in New York, and had been earning a decent living designing rooms for a number of the city's rich merchant families. The soldier gallant and able engineer had changed gradually into a man of tinsel arts and decoration. He was a curiosity, L'Enfant—but he belongs high on the list of French gifts to America. Soon he would remodel the New York City Hall to receive the new President and Congress, and finally, as the crowning expression of his ingenuity, taste, and imagination, would draw the plans for America's capital city, Washington, which stands today peculiarly his monument.

Yet nothing even L'Enfant could think of could surpass Judge Hopkinson's marvels. New York's pageant was only a gaudy replica on a smaller scale of Philadelphia's elaborate show. There were the same scenes of shops and artisans trundled on wheels, the same farmers, merchants, mechanics and seamen. They all appeared, and marched, in spite of the rain. Tin-Plate Workers constructed a Federal Edifice entirely of tin, on ten tin pillars. Furriers exhibited a real live Indian, swathed in native furs—he sweltered patiently in the damp July heat. Tailors carried a monster flag of sky-blue silk, with a design that fairly startled New Yorkers: life-size figures of Adam and Eve, naked but for fig leaves, reclined in a sylvan landscape. Under them a motto read, "And they sewed fig leaves together"—the relevancy of which to the New Roof the Tailors left to everyone's imagination. Brewers paraded a three-hundred-gallon ale cask, with a boy of eight gambolling on top dressed as Bacchus, in tight-fitting flesh-colored silk hung with hop vines and barley. The boy quaffed beer from a silver goblet, and had a high time "drinking and huzzahing the whole day with the greatest cheerfulness." Inconspicuous among the faculty and students of Columbia University strode Professor Noah Webster.

Antis ridiculed the whole spectacle. They acknowledged the Federals "made a very pompous appearance," were "regular and decent," but they laughed at the parading to and fro, the walking up and down. "The poar *antis* generally minded their own business at home," said a newspaper writer; "others, who were spectators at an *awful* distance, looked sour as the Devil. As for the *feds,* they rejoiced in different degrees—there was the ha, ha, ha! and the he, he, he!"

The procession had only ten divisions, instead of Philadelphia's eighty-eight, yet it marched from eight in the morning till five in the afternoon, in the rain. It began with trumpets and fanfare, then came Christopher Columbus on horseback, and all the rest. But if his show was small, L'Enfant could at least claim the greatest of all federal ships. In his parade was launched the frigate *Hamilton,* thirty-two guns, a model of a man-of-war on a twenty-seven-foot keel, her galleries, rigging, and decorations perfect, manned by three dozen men. The bowsprit figurehead was a carved image of Alexander Hamilton, holding the new Constitution aloft in his right hand.

Unfortunately, just as the ship was launched, the arm of the figurehead broke off, the Constitution tumbled ignominiously into the mud. Antis nearby yelled and hooted. "Gentlemen, there is certainly room for amendments!" someone shouted.

The frigate proceeded, nevertheless, went through elaborate maneuvers of trimming and tacking, received a pilot from a small craft on her weather quarter. As she passed by the Battery Castle a Spanish packet in the harbor fired a thirteen-gun salute.

The whole procession moved out to "The Fields" (City Hall Park today). There L'Enfant had devised an elegant pavilion, under which tables were placed. Six thousand people sat down to dine. Bullocks were roasted, toasts were drunk. The pavilion was an exquisite dome surmounted by Fame proclaiming a New Era. Congressmen, who had refused to march, appeared at dinner—except North Carolina delegates, whose state had not ratified. The French Minister twitted the Delegates at being part of the show in spite of their reluctance. They insisted they were not present in their official capacity, but only as individuals. It was a foolish distinction, the diplomat thought.

And indeed, there was something a little foolish about the whole New York performance—not L'Enfant's part, that was elegant. But the propaganda value of pageantry was waning. The Poughkeepsie convention ratified three days later, by a slim five votes. Yet it was an Antifederal victory, for along with ratification New York sent out a call for a second Federal Convention, to rewrite the Constitution. In New York City the Potters, incensed at the fun an Antifederal editor had made of their part in the procession, formed a gang, broke his windows, hacked at his press and carried off his type.

But in Philadelphia, the great procession had won the people. For months,

Federal hats were sold, Federal toys and Federal furniture became almost an art form. A *Federal Minuet* was composed and dancing masters instructed pupils in its figures; Federal Punch was the drink of the year. The New Roof had still to be made weather-resistant, but by pageants the Great Controversy had been closed. The two national political parties, united now in support of the general federal edifice, prepared to conduct their lesser differences forever under the same shelter.

A free people is a disputatious people; the structure of liberty provides for political conflict, party is an attribute of self-government. To many, the essence of America's new-modelled Constitution was what the Bricklayers of Philadelphia had said: "Both Buildings and Rulers are the Works of our Hands." Whose hands, whose buildings, was a further question, to which partisan politics would supply different answers, in conflict, as the institutions of ordered liberty under law were shaped and developed. Hopkinson's enlistment of artisans and craftsmen in service of the New Roof signified the broadening of the base on which government rested, the enlargement of the numbers of citizens to whom political expression was given, from whom parties and factions would be drawn. This, too, would be "the work of our hands," under a Constitution which gave more people more opportunity to participate in self-government, on a larger scale of nationhood, than any other in the world. Many years later old John Adams wrote, "You say, 'our divisions began with federalism and anti-federalism.' Alas! they began with human nature; they have existed in America from its first plantation."

7

The Case of
the Innocent Blacksmith

In The Pennsylvania Academy of The Fine Arts hangs a painting, heroic
in size and richly warm in color, generally called "Pat Lyon at the Forge."
It is the work of Sully's son-in-law, John Neagle, his finest work, begun
when he was not yet thirty years old, fully five years in the finishing. It is
the work which made John Neagle's career, placed him in the forefront of
American art. "Pat Lyon" is one of the famous *genre* paintings of American
history. And though it is impossible to talk to young artists of today, our busy
and emancipated self-expressors, about *genre* paintings, for they scorn them,
there are still some of us left who enjoy anecdote, and scene, and sentiment;
and for those who look far back into the past, before the days of photography
and rotogravure, such paintings can be delightful. They furnish bright vistas
into former times. We look at them, and say to ourselves, this is the way
life was in the long ago.

When the portrait "Pat Lyon at the Forge" was first exhibited, it was
promptly hailed as a superb achievement. Even so formidable an authority
as *Godey's Lady's Book* pronounced Mr. Neagle a young man "of no common
genius and skill," while a fellow artist and professional critic, less concerned
to seem proper and knowledgeable, described the portrait as "one of the

213

best, and most interesting pictures in the . . . exhibition of the National Academy at the Arcade Baths."

"The picture is remarkable," this critic wrote, "both for its execution and subject. Mr. Neagle of Philadelphia has established his claim to a high rank in his profession, by the skill and knowledge he has displayed in *composing* and *completing* so complicated and difficult a work." The figure, he continued, "stands admirably"; the dress and expression of the head are "truly appropriate"; "light and the indications of heat are managed with perfect skill"; and "the *arm* is a masterly performance."

All this you can see today as you come up the main staircase into the Rotunda of The Academy of The Fine Arts, in Philadelphia. The blacksmith, glowing with color, is almost the first thing to catch your eye. You can see it also in Boston, for young Neagle executed this painting twice. The Boston Athenaeum portrait, now on loan to the Boston Museum of Fine Arts, is the earlier version. Neagle finished it in 1827; in 1828 the Athenaeum bought it from Patrick Lyon for $400, and Lyon at once commissioned Neagle to do a second one. This second, the Philadelphia painting, is more carefully worked, richer in detail, tells its story more fully. The forge and the tools of the smith's trade are rendered with literal exactness. It was this portrait that Pat Lyon kept hanging in his own parlor, and which at his death was deposited by his executors in The Pennsylvania Academy.

It is good to look at, "Pat Lyon at the Forge." The skillful blacksmith has paused a moment in the midst of noisy labors, rested his fire-blackened hand upon his hammer, turned to look at his visitor. The apprentice boy at the bellows seizes the opportunity to take a welcome rest. Outside, the cupola of the gloomy Walnut Street Prison rises against a cloudy October sky. Inside, all around the shop are hammers, awls, tongs, the paraphernalia and tools of the artisan. The fire gleams here red against chimney bricks, there blue against cold metal: Neagle was using arsenic trisulfide colors, for the first time. They served him well. Pinned to a drawing board is a mathematical diagram, from Euclid, Book I, proposition 47, the general proof of the Pythagorean Theorem.

We cannot doubt as we look upon him that Pat Lyon is a master craftsman in his trade, a very Tubal-Cain himself, "instructer of every artificer in brass and iron." No more can we doubt that John Neagle is likewise a superior artisan in his craft. We are struck with the sense of intense activity arrested only for a moment; but even more we are struck with the tribute art has paid to genius, aesthetic understanding to mechanical perfection. In the figure of the blacksmith we behold the confidence of science, the dignity of labor, the pride and significance of the guildsman. The painter has abundantly understood his subject, abundantly met its demands upon his techniques.

And a good thing it was. John Neagle needed every ounce of his skill and training to perpetrate this illusion. Any painting, of course, is an illusion. But "Pat Lyon at the Forge" is more than that, it is a masquerade. No employment is so exacting of the artist as an untruth, and there is a basic untruth in this work. It took all Neagle's highly developed professionalism, his keen sense of craft, and his genuine sympathy with Pat Lyon as well, to conceal it. Even then, if we take a long look, we may wonder that a blacksmith should labor over his hot forge in a fine white broadcloth shirt, in street shoes, with brightly polished buckles. . . .

John Neagle seemed a sober, earnest, thoughtful black Irishman, his strong bony face and rugged jaw, his deliberately courtly manner the very essence of integrity. And true it was that young Mr. Neagle would brook no trespass upon his art. He was a man of firm professional principles, completely serious about his work, completely dependent on it for his living, too. But he was full of fun. An unhappy boyhood dominated by a stupid foster father had taught him how to dissimulate, so he won your confidence easily; but with relish he would then write down all your foibles, hand them to Mr. Dunlap or tell them to his friends.

Not that there was any malice or ill-humor in young Neagle. He was the kindest, the happiest of men. But he was mischievous, along with his cheerful disposition. He had just what Pat Lyon needed in the way of temperament. And he had all the skill Pat so much admired. His marriage a few months earlier had brought him even closer into Sully's fold; he had just returned from a long visit to old Gilbert Stuart up in Boston, where (though Stuart, that ancient monolith, had treated him like a child) he had luxuriated in long discussions on the arts and skills of painting with the great master, talked hours on end as he worked on his own portrait of those familiar features. Stuart had scoffed at Neagle's reading, scorned his lessons in Reynolds' *Lectures.* "You may elevate your mind as much as you can," the old man had told John Neagle. "But, while you have nature before you as a model, paint what you see, and look with your own eyes!"

It took strength of character for young Neagle to disregard the advice of Gilbert Stuart. It took supreme self-confidence, too. Only a fine craftsman could resist the temptation to paint what he saw, and rise above that to paint what he wished others to see. Craftsmanship demanded the most careful preparation. First, Neagle had Pat Lyon sit for an ordinary fifteen-dollar bust portrait, head and shoulders, the sort of parlor portrait artists made their living at, a good likeness—reddened nose, blue eyes, sandy hair, an unsightly wen on his right cheek. As a painter, he must become familiar with these features, deft and sure in rendering. Then he planned his picture: he made a quick small wash drawing on a piece of paper eight inches by six inches. "The first thought sketch for P. Lyon's picture," he labeled it. Here was the blacksmith standing full length in his forge, the apprentice, the cupola of the jail. Soon he was carefully measuring all Lyon's hand tools, studying their various shapes and attitudes. And colors: on a small piece of coarse scrap canvas, ten by eight inches, he made another compositional sketch, applying pigments heavily, thickly. On the back of this second exercise he wrote an inscription: "The original study in color by Neagle for the large picture of Pat Lyon, the blacksmith. A rapid sketch for arrangement and general effect, Philad., Penna."

But these little planning-studies only hinted at the problems he would have when he tackled the life-size painting. One October afternoon he induced a young man about town, notorious for his great muscles and feats of strength, to accompany him to his studio. "Mr. George Hernisen came to show me his athletic arm as a model for Lyon's," he recorded. Then he made a third preliminary version, twice as large as the others, on a piece of canvas eighteen inches by thirteen. This he painted with great care: he modeled the arm, made the face a likeness in drawing and color; he painted thinly, in bright oils.

Finally, he was ready. He bought a large canvas, nearly eight feet by six, from the widow of an English painter, Robinson. (Robinson was a miniaturist; what he was doing with a canvas the size of a bed sheet no one bothered to explain.) He stretched it on his easel, he prepared to begin his work of creative imagination.

Now had John Neagle painted what he saw, the real Pat Lyon of 1826, his portrait would have shown a prosperous Philadelphia businessman, large, sturdy, full-fashioned, his ruddy countenance the product equally of a strong mind and a taste for strong beer. Mr. Lyon, fifty-seven in 1826, his arm no longer athletic, had not been at his forge for many years. He was "possessed of an ample fortune," had been "long withdrawn from the occupations of trade." He was known all over the city as a designer and hydraulic engineer, for Patrick Lyon was America's foremost manufacturer of fire engines. No less than eight of the fire companies of Philadelphia manned huge engines that had originated on his drawing board, had been cast and machined in his factory; and his engines had been bought in other cities all over the country.

Even through the depression of 1820, his factory kept going. He was down to six employees, business was bad, but he angrily rejected every suggestion that the government should protect him from foreign competition, by tariffs. "Heretofore I have manufactured to the amount of 10000 $ per annum and now not one half," he wrote for the Census of 1820, "and the reason why, there has been a depreciation in the demand and very unexpectedly—and I manufacture cheaper and better than the articles I manufacture can be imported. I do not want any additional duty laid for my protection." He signed his statement boldly, "Patrick Lyon Engineer."

And being Pat, he took advantage of slack trade in the depression year to go back to Europe, learn all he could of new methods and products. His name was well known in England; his story was often told, he still had relatives there. A book of Charles Lamb, the gentle "Elia," had been dedicated to him. With sober Scottish attention, Pat visited foundries and forges and brass borings. When he returned, he proudly announced that his fire engines were "far superior to any imported or being made here," his garden watering engines "the most complete and effectual ever known." And then he created his masterpiece—the extraordinary engine of The Diligent Fire Company, at Eighth and Market Streets, envy of every volunteer in the city. The Diligent Engine was famous. It had chambers nearly ten inches in diameter, was the most powerful pump in all America yet made no noise in working, could discharge 240 gallons of water a minute, through the largest nozzle ever bored.

Lyon's factory prospered again, became a busy industrial establishment in the subdivided economy of American artisan enterprise. The Pat Lyon John Neagle saw in 1826 was a man of property, a man by modest standards wealthy. He owned his dwelling house in Walnut Street, as well as the tavern next door where he spent many lonely hours of his widowerhood. He owned the old Southwark Theatre, profitably leased in offices to a number of tenants. He still owned the building on Dock Street where his first smithery had been; it was rented out. And he had a number of buildings where his second forge used to be, in Library Place, an alley running down from the State House Yard. The shop was let now to a spring-coach maker. He had three thousand dollars in United States loan certificates, owned good mortgages, had a fat bank account, some canal stocks, other money out at interest. He was a Mason, an Episcopalian, a member of St. Andrew's Society.

In his hall stood an eight day clock, his bookcase contained a hundred books, his parlor walls were decorated with a series of steel engravings portraying the lugubrious fate of "The Lost Child." Pat Lyon was, in short, a success.

And being a success, he could tell his story over again. It was a famous story, almost a legend, the history of the Innocent Blacksmith. Thirty years had seen changes in America—wholesome changes, developments he had hoped for—some he had helped bring about. Now, with death nearly upon him, he could say once more the things he had said then, when no one would listen. That was why he commissioned young Neagle to do the painting. His story was worth a masquerade. He hesitated a long while, even after he had made his agreement with Neagle. Pat knew he was good; but Mr. Otis, an established professional artist, once Neagle's teacher, warned

Lyon such a work as he wanted done would take a long time, and Neagle was inexperienced. He might not succeed, Bass Otis said. Neagle pled for himself; he convinced Pat finally, by his enthusiasm, his understanding. The project was begun.

There must have been a scene: the ambitious painter starting a prodigious work, the subtle engineer hoping so much from this canvas. I imagine it taking place in Lyon's home, for the forge itself, the tools and the smithery were long since gone. Perhaps Neagle brought along his small canvas for his final compositional sketch; in fancy I can see Pat resurrect from some musty closet the old leathern apron he had not worn for so long, take off his coat and his stock, open his shirt, roll up his sleeves, strike a pose with his hammer at the kitchen table, begin to tell young Neagle what it had been like to work at a blacksmith's forge. It is easy to imagine him forgetting to remove his fine shoes with their shining buckles, easy to imagine the artist noting their sheen and glimmer, faithfully painting them in. . . .

"I am closely engaged *Night & Day*," wrote John Neagle, October 7, 1826, "and doing my utmost on Pat Lyon's picture."

Pat Lyon had been younger then, in 1798, than John Neagle was now, yet those long fall days when he sat alone in the Walnut Street Prison, racked with hunger, bearded and filthy, were as fresh in mind as this morning's breeze. He remembered unspeakable scenes in the prison: hungry, wretched people, some as innocent as himself, others foul and desperate criminals by their own boasts. He remembered how men could starve for week after week, yet not die; how they could lie entirely conscious in mind yet too weak in body to prevent rats from chewing at their flesh.

Unforgettable pictures were engraved on Pat's mind—of a boy in a frenzy of hunger gnawing the plaster on the walls; of gaunt prisoners shackled together without strength enough to stand as they passed water; of depraved, unnatural characters strangely untouched by hardship or suffering, supported in their evil by some unholy strength denied the innocent.

He remembered those who had died. And still, after so many years, he felt an old thrill of angry amazement that others should care so little. His adventure was an insult to the very name of freedom: he had been thrown into jail, for no other reason than that he was a foreigner, a blacksmith, and "a *clever, ingenious* man."

It had happened back, as Pat put it, "in the Presidency of John Adams, whom God preserve"—back in the patrician days of America, days of the Federal Court in Philadelphia with its levees, receptions, balls and theatres, days of elegance and splendor. Every man, said the patricians, was governed by "a passion for distinction." Mr. Jefferson might complain of aristocratical notions, monarchical tendencies, the arrogance of wealth; patrician America feared still more the "artificial democracy" which the French had suffered with all its horrors in their revolution, feared the levelling philosophies, the excesses of unlettered humanity, "the irregularities of the passions." With fastidious distaste, patrician America looked upon the masses to whom liberty had been granted, common people in senate and drawing room, workmen studying in higher schools, artisans in clumping boots and crude homespun, gathering at polls.

In the national Congress, one Representative in the midst of debate spat tobacco juice in the face of another, his victim turned on him with a hickory stick. Rough and rowdy rantings of Republicans mocked the courtesies of statecraft, replaced the genteel exchanges of polite orators in gentlemanly disagreement. Patrician Samuel Coates, philanthropist and Quaker merchant, drew his elegant plain clothes about him: *"Our Democrats (I rather call them Demi-rats) are continually striving to sap the foundations of the federal Ædifice . . ."*

Rich and class-proud merchants would hire the best blacksmith, in this free land of America, 1798, would boast about the work he did for them. But which of them would concern himself when even the best blacksmith was clapped unjustly into jail? American liberty was for gentlemen—gentlemen of trade and finance, of medicine, gentlemen of the clergy, gentlemen of the law. What rights did a blacksmith have in patrician America, which the *gentlemen* who ran the Bank of Pennsylvania couldn't take away from him?

Particularly, when the blacksmith saw through them? Pat had said from the very first who had robbed the Bank—that Isaac Davis did it, though he didn't know his name. "The stranger," he had called him. And he had said the carpenter Robinson, and the cashier Jonathan Smith probably knew something about it. Yet the gentlemen of the Bank threw Pat in jail, and they kept him there week after week, kept him there even after Davis confessed and returned the money—most of it. Davis, the real criminal, the Bank let go. He went scot free, to build a new life for himself in another city. People regarded him with a sort of affection. He had done an amazing thing: stolen $160,000 right under everyone's gaze. No one looked on Davis with hate, mistrust, suspicion; Davis spent not an hour in jail. Even his uncle, Judge Benjamin Brannan, respected gentleman of the bench of Delaware County, who lied and cheated to get Davis off, suffered only a mild legislative rebuke. He stayed on the bench. And the guilty Davis, whom the gentlemen of the Bank said was "from a good family, of Chester county, amiable, and respectable," stayed free.

But Pat Lyon, blacksmith, stayed in prison. "The law must take its course," the gentlemen directors of the Bank voted—at the same meeting they decided they were "in honor bound" not to prosecute Davis. They had "pledged their word," they said. But they prosecuted Lyon. Pat languished in the horror of his airless damp cell, endured the loss of friends, suffered public contumely and slander, he floundered in a swirling eddy of accusation, gossip, mistrust. From this, even his complete innocence afforded no protection.

Yet patricians spoke the language of liberty. Theirs was the lexicon of revolution. Newspapers, public men, preachers were forever prating of liberty here, tyranny abroad, even while they ignored an innocent man in their own jail, suffering under their very noses a tyranny worse than any King George III could inflict, on even the humblest of his subjects. Pat Lyon was in jail, simply because he was in America. And America was in its 1790's.

They were horrid years, the 1790's—when class, caste, and clan engulfed the individual, the very instincts of society were coarsened, ideals of justice were captured by a faction. They were years of restless immigration, of rivers of people flowing westward, of wars on land and sea and in the farthest forests, years of desperate measures to preserve the structures of power. Pat was a foreigner, a Britisher, an "old country man." No foreigner could expect justice in patrician America: the Alien and Sedition Laws had seen to that, just a few weeks before Pat's arrest.

The people's leaders—Dr. Leib, Mr. Dallas, Col. Miles, other admirers of Vice President Jefferson—had warned all spring and summer when Congress passed these acts that they were unconstitutional, they would destroy liberties of native-born as well as aliens. Pat Lyon, blacksmith, had paid scant attention. He knew the great charters of American liberties, Penn's Frame of Government, the Declaration of Independence; he had read Alexander Hamilton's call for "mechanical volunteers" from the old world to profit in America's new free society. But in Walnut Street Prison he learned America's fear of the foreigner, her dread of European ideas, and of European men.

They were years of death in Philadelphia, the 1790's, black years of foul pestilence, coming every autumn year after year in some mysterious way to fill the city with the stink and fright of dying. What the Yellow Fever was, no one could explain; but not a soul who lived through the 1790's in the Delaware Valley could ever forget the appalling scenes of the Great Plagues, as the old century closed—scenes of humanity corrupted, the city falling apart again and again, society demoralized by a fantastic savagery of nature.

Plagues brought fire, crime, riot, desperation in their wakes. Gangs of thieves terrorized the stricken city in 1798, pillaging houses and shops, roaming deserted streets at night, boldly robbing living and dead in broad daylight. "Watchmen be on your Guard!" cried a newspaper. "Some villains are luking about the city . . ." Men of Southwark, the Northern Liberties, the crowded dockside of the town itself, formed citizens' bands, "patroles" to police the "almost defenceless and deserted city." When a cannon boomed,

volunteers rushed to Potters Field to join in the hue and cry against marauders, "frustrate the machinations of those wicked incendiaries . . ."

Business ceased, grass grew up between paving stones, citizens fled, more
than 40,000 of them, someone estimated. The air was filled with hordes of
insects—mosquitoes, grasshoppers, flies. The ground crawled with ants and
cockroaches, myriads of black crickets, whole fields of cabbages and potatoes
were devoured by pests, crops failed, apple worms bored in the hanging fruit,
fresh cider was acrid with their taste. Cats, rats, and dogs were sick or lay
dead in the street. Such dogs as survived, people noted, were "pensive and
dejected," they ran madly about. Dust lay over everything, blew in clouds
up the streets, death and desolation overwhelmed the senses.

Death, and desolation, had confronted Pat Lyon from his very first hour
in America. No one had ever come to these shores with higher hope, nor
better preparation. Born in London, of Scottish parents, Pat had been at the
age of eleven apprenticed to a blacksmith. His tutelage over, he was admitted
as journeyman; at nineteen he went to the forge of his uncle in Edinburgh.
There he worked for six years, became a Master. In 1793, he was twenty-
five years old. And in 1793, Britain declared war against the people of Revolutionary France.

The world has ever been the Scotman's oyster. To and fro over the globe
Scots have roamed, avid in commerce, frugal, honest, zealous in religion,
tough individualists, notably industrious, lovers of liberty. Appalled at this
war, of an Empire they regarded as alien against a freedom they regarded
as sacred, hundreds of Scotsmen looked westward across the ocean for opportunity, wealth, adventure, in the rising republic of the New World. Pat Lyon
heard the call. A ship brought him to Philadelphia—in the very height of
the Great Plague of 1793. All around him that first day citizens were
alarmed, sickened, and dying—victims of the hideous Black Vomit. The
sturdy young blacksmith was untouched. He survived this plague, and the
next year's too. He set up in business at Lombard and Dock Streets, he
worked hard at his forge. Pat had learned well what his uncle had taught
him. He knew Euclid, and Newton, understood the principles of design; he
invented a novel method of cold-boring brass with a hand tool he contrived.
During his first years in America he introduced into his new country no less
than twelve brand new kinds of iron manufacture, including hydraulic
engines.* He made a name for himself with his skill. On July Fourth,
1795, he and Mistress Ann Brimley stood up before Dr. Abercrombie in

---

* The word "blacksmith" was much broader in meaning then than now, and people
also used the word "whitesmith," which meant an artisan who finished and polished
iron and metal pieces. Pat was both blacksmith and whitesmith. Chief Justice Tilghman
described him as a "remarkably ingenious whitesmith."

Christ Church and were married. Next year came a daughter, Clementina.

But death spared no one, these plague years of America. In the spring of 1797 little Clementina died, aged nine months. And that fall, when the Yellow Fever returned, Ann Lyon was stricken. She lasted but a few days; Pat buried her next to his daughter in St. Peters Churchyard. So hurried was the sexton in the mass of plague deaths that he mixed up the names in his book. "Sept. 7," he wrote: "Clementine Loyons, wife of Patrick Loyons —decay."

In 1798, his little family destroyed, Pat was alone in America, a widower at twenty-nine. His business prospered, he worked long hours, with the finest skill; but he was silent, withdrawn. He was also something of a character. Already the city told an anecdote about him—how Mr. Fox the Bank president called him to open an iron chest. The lock was ingeniously contrived, there was no key. With one hand, Pat picked the lock and held up the lid. The other hand he extended to Mr. Fox and murmured his fee for his service: ten dollars. Mr. Fox indignantly refused to pay any such price for two minutes work, whereupon Pat let the lid fall, and the lock bars sprang once again into place. The banker was chastened. He asked Pat again to open the chest, which he did right enough, but this time as he extended his free hand the price had gone up. He demanded twenty dollars—and got it, so the story ran.

His pride in his craft, and the science of his craft, his pride in his knowledge and his works, was something magnificent. He had another vanity, a curious one: he fancied himself a physiognomist. He could tell a man's character, he swore, simply by looking him steadily in the face. He had studied the system of Lavater, that huge three-volume work translated from the German, *Essays on Physiognomy for the Promotion of Knowledge and the Love of Mankind. With Plates.* Pat mastered the book, and the art. He was rarely deceived by a countenance. "It is the deepest knowledge I know of," he wrote.

But nothing—not his skills, his sound reputation, his thriftiness, his faithful performance of contracts, not his physiognomy—could help him when the Bank hurled him into jail. Nothing counted, in a society which drew a firm line between a gentleman and a blacksmith. In prison he saw, finally, that his story was more than a personal disaster. It was full of significance for the whole country, symptom of a disease far worse than the Yellow Fever.

In prison, Pat commenced his book. He told his entire strange adventure, just as it happened, in the most circumstantial detail: how people talked, how they looked, who he was, where he had come from, what he had done.

"It is an observation I have long made, that the great when they have power, will often make a wrong use of it, and that those who are inferior in rank, have very little chance of justice when opposed to them . . ."

The blacksmith became an author. In his prison cell, his pen scratched away industriously.

"To confine, deprive men of liberty, destroy character, wantonly, with a numerous variety of et ceteras, on mere paltry, and vague innuendos or suspicions, is a cruelty perhaps not sanctioned in any other country but this, which should be the grand emporium of liberty . . ."

It was awkward, this job of writing. His hands were more used to hammers and augurs than to quills. Slowly, meticulously, in his large round letters he shaped each word:

"And what a horrid thing it is for an innocent man to suffer for another's guilt . . ."

The great robbery was discovered on Sunday morning, September 2, 1798, in the very height of the Yellow Fever plague.

The Bank of Pennsylvania just three weeks before had moved into The Carpenters' Hall, comely red brick pile off Chestnut Street: clerks and tellers labored at their ledgers in the very chamber where the First Continental Congress had sat back in 1774—a room twice as big now (because a partition had been removed) and twice as handsome, as in those old days when it had echoed the voices of American patriots proclaiming American liberties. Carpenters' Hall was a rental property of The Carpenters' Company, fit place for great affairs of commerce. The Bank of Pennsylvania was getting adjusted to its new, spacious quarters. A guard, Cunningham, slept upstairs, two night guards each with a dog patrolled the tiny yard outside.

The chief teller was sick of the fever, most of the officers had fled the city, Charles Biddle the Bank's notary was gone. Cashier Jonathan Smith and the first teller, an earnest young Quaker named Thomas Annesley, were obliged to do most of the Bank's work. They soaked their clothes in vinegar, smoked black segars, took all the wisest precautions against infection. On Saturday, September 1, about four in the afternoon, Cashier Smith handed Annesley one of the two keys of the cash vault, put the other in his pocket. Everything was in order; they closed the vault, then closed the Bank. Each took his key away with him—it was their custom—and left the guard Cunningham in charge.

Annesley went bustling about the city, for with Mr. Biddle away he had twenty-two notes to protest, and wished if he could to catch people before they deserted to the healthy country. This business of notes was unfamiliar to young Annesley. He had seen only a few endorsers that Saturday afternoon when he found he had forgotten some necessary forms of protest. Sunday morning, about six o'clock, he went round to the Bank to get them.

It was daylight, the night guards had gone, Cunningham should have been about. But Annesley found the front door locked fast. He walked around to the back, thinking he might find Cunningham there. Instead, he found the large back door ajar. He pushed through into the banking room. It was empty. The double doors of the cash vault stood wide open.

Annesley ran back outside, around the building to the front door and pounded on it with all his strength. Cunningham stuck his head out of an upper window: "Come down!" Annesley cried to him. "Come down! And see what condition the bank is in!" Cunningham came down, opened the front door to Annesley, together they inspected the vault. The guard "tore his hair," Annesley related, "and said he would be suspected. He appeared mad or insane. He was exceedingly agitated." But Cunningham kept his head better than young Annesley imagined. He urged the teller to go quickly for Mr. Jonathan Smith. The cashier was with his family out of the city, he said: Annesley could find him on the Lancaster Turnpike, beyond the Schuylkill. Leaving Cunningham on guard, Annesley set out, the only way he had, on foot. Not till he had spent many fruitless hours did he discover Smith was not on the Lancaster, but on the West Chester pike, seven miles south of the area he was searching. It was mid-afternoon before he returned with the cashier. Much later, Annesley would reflect on the misdirection Cunningham had given him.

At the Bank, Cashier Smith sent for President Fox. Together they examined the vault. They found a shortage of $160,000. It was the greatest bank robbery America had ever known.

President Fox acted with speed and firmness. He took Cunningham with him to a magistrate nearby, soon they returned. Cunningham had a paper in his hand. It was, he told Annesley, a warrant for the arrest of Patrick Lyon the blacksmith; would Mr. Annesley please to go with him to Lyon's shop, to serve it? Once again, Annesley accepted Cunningham's word without question. The two men walked down Front Street to Lombard, to Lyon's forge; they found it closed. A neighbor said Pat had not been around for several days. Then they went to the house Lyon owned. No one answered their knock. Thomas Annesley bent down, he later testified, "and saw a cobweb in the keyhole of the door."

It was not strange to find anyone gone, these days. Fully three out of four Philadelphians had fled the fever. But the Bank had a special interest in Patrick Lyon, for he it was who had made the doors and locks of the cash vault, set them just a fortnight ago. President Fox remembered the things Lyon had said then, how the locks were poor, would protect nothing. And he remembered Lyon's rough manners, his independent ways. He was an old-country man, not many years in the city. Mr. Fox jumped at once to the conclusion that Lyon could have done this job.

He would have to have done it Saturday night, for everyone knew the money was in the vaults when Smith and Annesley locked up, at four o'clock

Saturday afternoon. Mr. Fox was determined to find Lyon. He set police machinery in motion, deputies were sworn in and went riding off into Jersey in search of the missing blacksmith, magistrates' warrants were circulated among all his acquaintances—they charged him with robbery, they described him as a fugitive. A reward was offered. Governor Mifflin was informed of everything late Sunday evening, for the Bank owed the Commonwealth a payment of $80,000 interest, and this robbery was a matter of state.

Samuel Fox was praised by the Governor, the newspapers, and the legislature for his prompt and vigorous measures to apprehend the criminal.

Of all these transactions, of the great robbery itself, Pat Lyon knew nothing. On Saturday, September 1, he was in the swamps around Lewes, Delaware, 150 miles away, absorbed in a personal tragedy of his own. It had happened in this wise:

A year ago, in the spring and summer of 1797, Pat had forged two iron doors and fitted locks for the Bank, then in Lodge Alley, at the direction of the carpenter Sam Robinson. At that time, he had told Robinson the doors were badly designed, the locks insecure. They were nothing but old rim locks with the latches taken out, locks proper for ships' cabins or room doors, perhaps, but never for bank vaults. Early in '98 Pat went to see Jonathan Smith and Samuel Fox himself, and told them, too, how unsafe the doors and locks were. They paid no attention. He was doing some work also for John C. Stocker, magistrate in Lombard Street and director of the Bank, the man who had first recommended him to the Bank for his skill. He liked Mr. Stocker; he told him his concern over the vault doors. The magistrate thanked him for the information.

Then the Bank directors decided to move. They would erect a new building of their own, rent Carpenters' Hall while construction was going on; meanwhile until Carpenters' Hall was ready they expanded into the young ladies' boarding house next door to them in Lodge Alley. In the first days of August, 1798, the fever severe, "citizens removing with precipitation in all directions," Pat was forging some iron work for the Bank in preparation for these moves. Suddenly he was ordered to stop it. An attempt to rob the vaults had been discovered on Saturday, August 4; the directors in alarm decided to abandon Lodge Alley at once, and remove to Carpenters' Hall even though the remodelling they planned there was not yet finished.

It was following this decision that Sam Robinson drove up with a dray to Pat's forge, bringing the same two iron doors with the old rim locks and keys: he desired the blacksmith to reverse the hinges and refit the locks, so that one door would be an inner, the other an outer door for the new cash vault. "The business was urgent," Sam Robinson said, "and I told him so."

Pat had a more significant piece of work on hand, the problem of devising a hydraulic engine for Mr. Cramond the merchant. He put off starting on the doors till the next day. When he finally did get to work on them, Robinson came back, this time accompanied by "a young stranger"—whom he did not introduce. The stranger examined the locks with care, while Robinson complained of the delay. The Bank wouldn't hire Lyon again if he took so long with things, he warned. Pat said plainly he didn't care, and in the hearing of the stranger he told Robinson once again that the doors and locks were not fit for a bank.

"Damn it," said Robinson, "they will make a shift."

Pat gave the men something to drink, and they went off. In a few minutes the stranger came back, alone. Pat was talking with a young woman at his door, the stranger wandered into the forge where the locks were lying. Pat paid no attention to him, except to remark as the young man was leaving that he would have to work all night since the Bank was in such a hurry for their doors. The stranger answered, he would see all banks damn'd before he'd kill himself in this hot weather. Then he disappeared.

Next day, Saturday, Pat took the doors to Carpenters' Hall, where he hung one and fixed the lock to it, but the other he had to take back to his shop to cut a mortice in it that would allow it to pass the lock-box on the wall, as it closed. The lock for this outer door lay around Carpenters' Hall all Saturday, Sunday, and Monday. Anyone could have picked it up, or made an impression from it. On Monday, August 13, Pat completed this work. That week he did a couple of odd jobs for the Bank, altering lamp irons, mounting lamp posts. It was all finished by the 16th, nothing had gone wrong. The Bank had not been particularly fair: they had hired another smith to fit the doors of the book vault adjacent to the cash vault, without telling Pat. It was not proper treatment. But Pat had done his job. He handed in his bill, eighteen pounds, eight shillings, nine pence ha'penny, and got back to the fascinating problems of Mr. Cramond's hydraulic engine.

It was a pretty little thing. If Philadelphia regarded Pat Lyon now as "a very worthy honest blunt spoken man, industrious and thriving," it was because all objects he turned out, from fire engines to fine locks, were pretty little things. Only the Bank's work had failed to meet his standards. But even with Mr. Cramond's engine on his mind, Pat watched the advance of the fever worriedly, brooding over Ann's death just the year before, wondering every day if he should leave the city.

On Wednesday, August 22, he walked down Market Street to the Ferry, to buy some fresh Jersey peaches. As he passed the waterfront tavern at the ferry wharf, he glanced in. There was the carpenter Sam Robinson at the front window table, drinking beer sangaree* with the young stranger who had come with him to the forge. Innocently, Pat strolled in to join them. "I never saw two such men so much alarmed and confused in my life, as they were," he wrote. His physiognomist's skill told him his unexpected presence unnerved the carpenter and the young stranger. They collected themselves ("got the muscles of their faces composed," was the way Pat put it) and Robinson exclaimed:

"Mr. Lyon! What brought you this way? Are you not afraid? The yellow fever has broke out here!"

"Are *you* not afraid?" Pat rejoined.

"Mr. Lyon," asked Robinson, "do you mean to go out of town?"

"I don't know," Pat answered. "Do you?"

Robinson had not decided. Then he changed the subject. The Bank, he said, wanted an iron bar for one of the doors of Carpenters' Hall.

"Damn it!" the stranger suddenly snorted. "There will be no occasion for that."

Now Sam Robinson and Pat Lyon were good friends. They "never met without asking each other to drink," Pat recorded. But this time the carpenter offered him no civilities. Pat said casually he was always ready for any tasks the Bank had for him; after a few more remarks he left the bemused men, went over to a peach boat, bought his fruit, and returned to work.

"Jamie," he said to his apprentice, "I saw Robinson and the stranger that was with him when we were doing the iron doors, at Market-street ferry. They seemed to be in deep study. I don't think they are after any good."

That week he finished Mr. Cramond's engine, he made a little piece for Mr. Dobson the printer, then he found no more work left to do, with the town all disorganized by fever. The disease attacked next door to his house; Pat locked it up (that cobweb in his keyhole had ten days to form) and moved into his forge with his apprentice boy. He decided to take Jamie and go elsewhere for a few weeks, to seek what business he could find, then come back when the fever was over.

First, he took stock of himself and his worldly goods. He had been in Philadelphia only five years, yet already he owned a house full of furniture and a shop full of tools—beautiful tools, unmatched anywhere in America. His winter wood was laid in, Jamie McGinley was a skilled, loyal, earnest, intelligent apprentice. And he had money, $1,400, in the Bank of North America. Figuring everything together, Pat Lyon was a substantial citizen, for a city mechanic. So he did what any substantial citizen ought to do in

---

* Beer iced, sweetened with molasses, garnished with nutmeg. Don't try it.

a Yellow Fever epidemic, even a lonely widower. He made his will. First, Pat wrote, he wished to be "buried in as frugal a manner as possible, consistent with decency." On his headstone he wished a verse to be inscribed:

> My sledge and hammer's both declin'd,
> My bellows too have lost their wind;
> My fire's extinct, my forge decay'd,
> And in the dust my *vice* is laid;
> My coal is spent, my iron's gone,
> My nails are drove, *my work is done.*

Then, all his wealth was to go to his father, Patrick Lyon of London, smith; if his father was dead, then to his mother; if his mother was dead, then to his sister Jane; if Jane was dead, to his uncle John Craig of Aberdeen in Scotland, scrivener. To his brother James who lived in America (last Pat heard he was in New York) he left nothing. Three good friends— Captain Richard Guy the bricklayer, the stonecutter James Farquier, Thomas Dobson the printer—Pat named executors.

That took care of everything. If the fever should claim him this time, at least people would find his affairs in good Scottish order. Pat was ready to leave town. But where to go? One day he rode out to Thomas Leiper's estate near Chester, but Mr. Leiper was away. There would be no work there. Another day he walked up into Bucks County, but that was unsafe. He thought of Boston, where a new bank was a'building, but from the papers he learned the fever had struck Boston too. He considered South Jersey, where he had friends. With the family of his apprentice boy, the McGinley's, Pat discussed the whole problem at dinner. Finally, he decided on the Capes of the Delaware. On Tuesday, August 28, he procured passage. He packed some provisions, his clothing, a few dollars in cash, and a bottle of rum. With Jamie McGinley he boarded a shallop bound down the river.

That was fully five days before the robbery.

It was no easy trip. The little river shallop was a leaky old schooner, her sails patched with pieces of aprons and checked shirts, her jib made fast by a woollen stocking, her halyards spliced with so many knots they could scarcely pass through the blocks. Yet her captain, Edward Collins, who had his new bride aboard, astonished Pat by assuming "more dignity, more importance, and more affectation than the commander of a first-rate man of war in his Britannic majesty's navy."

Jamie McGinley, a sturdy youngster of nineteen, was in high spirits the first two days. It was a lark to be sailing down the great river, even in this fantastic old tub with its egregious captain. Pat, too, enjoyed the voyage, as the beamy shallop lumbered along close-hauled against the hot, dry south wind. Thursday, the third day, young Jamie fell ill. A bad storm rose, heavy swells rolled up the bay, the schooner creaked and pitched against head winds. But Jamie's trouble was not seasickness. Pat had seen too much of the Yellow Fever to mistake it. With no medicines on board, far from home or from help, he grew frantic. Jamie sickened alarmingly—the youngest, the strongest were well known to be the swiftest victims. Friday he was too weak to stand. Pat held him in his arms lest the waves wash him overboard, cradled him at the gunwhale as he groaned, sighed, threw up black vomit and blood. All night, he lay over Jamie protecting him, warming him in his chills, breathing in the stink of his fever.

Saturday, September 1, the schooner put into Broadkill Creek, whose torturous channel proved too much for the amazing Captain Collins. Soon he ran her fast aground, in the sticky tidal mud. It was ten in the morning. Disgusted with the foolish Captain, knowing that every turn up Broadkill Creek led them farther from Lewes town, Pat took Jamie, strapped all their gear on his own back, and waded ashore. There was no landing here, no road, only swamps, blinding salt-flats, and woods. They would have to ask directions. Jamie seemed stronger, but he reeled like a drunken man, stared vacantly about him. Slowly they walked across a salt marsh, coming by and by to the house of a Mr. Fisher—who gave them fresh cider to drink, told them of a tavern a few miles farther on.

Through swamp and reed marsh and damp cedar woods they followed a faint path. Jamie grew weaker, he staggered blindly from tree to tree, fell over roots, his feet dragged, "the leaders of his neck were become so weak," Pat observed, "that his head was like a ships mast, having lost all her braces."

Clouds of mosquitoes and sand flies rose at every step, the brackish cedar swamps shimmered in heat, strange white fog-patches lurked in every shade. Stay here, Pat told Jamie, or come on slowly if you can; he would hurry ahead to the tavern and order dinner for them. He lowered Jamie to a moss bank under a cedar.

At Cornelius Fleetwood's tavern, Pat engaged a room, stowed his luggage, then he retraced his steps. Jamie was still where he had left him, fast asleep, burning with fever. Pat gathered him up in his arms and carried him two miles to the inn.

When Mrs. Fleetwood set dinner before them, Jamie was too weak even to take a dish of coffee in his hands. Pat made some excuse to the hostess— he dared not say the boy had Yellow Fever, or she would surely turn them both out. After dinner he put Jamie to bed, and walked the seven miles into Lewes to seek medicine and advice.

At Lewes that evening—the very evening the Bank back in Philadelphia was being robbed—Pat met old acquaintances. Philadelphians scattered to the four winds when the fever came. Suddenly he was no longer isolated; he was back in his busy world of work and contracts, of finely fashioned iron, steel, and brass, of fellow craftsmen. He supped with Captain Learmonth, a river pilot; afterwards he looked up the blacksmith Joshua Hall, who agreed to take Jamie in his forge as apprentice, promising Pat a small sum for the boy's loan. Cannily, Pat said nothing of Jamie's fever. He spent the night at Elliot's Inn, arose the next morning (Sunday, September 2), shaved, breakfasted with the Elliots, bought half an ounce of "the bark" (quinine) and started back to Fleetwood's tavern.

Seven miles on a hot humid day in rural Delaware was a two-hour journey, at best. The lane divided outside Lewes, Pat asked directions of a Negro. But these "Moors" of Sussex county, part Nanticoke Indian, spoke a strange unintelligible language; soon he found himself six miles inland, the wrong way, at Indian River. Tortured with anxiety, tortured with the heat, Pat was "like a person distracted." From farm to farm he plodded, asking directions. Finally he reached Fleetwood's. Jamie lay "in a shocking situation." There was no further chance of concealment. Pat walked and ran the seven miles all the way back to Lewes, for two doctors.

Now medicine was no exact science like the blacksmith's skill, no mathematical formula to be solved by rule, drawn up in mechanical form, then forged with precision. Dr. Wilson said Jamie had *synochus icteroides,* the Yellow Fever. Dr. Little said no, it was not that, but a strange sort of nervous fever of entirely different nosology. Pat didn't know. He asked both doctors to treat the lad. Dr. Wilson was gentle, modest, understanding, sympathetic—as he drew blood in great quantities, administered clysters and violent mercurial purges. He recommended hot vinegar baths, he came again on Monday. Dr. Little prescribed herb tea.

But Dr. Wilson was right. Poor Jamie lingered in horrible torments of fever, and torments of purging and venesection, two days and nights. The Bilious Remitting Yellow Fever was frighful to watch—the delirium, the sighing, incontinent faeces, stinking black vomit, the shrinking flesh, the putrid yellow color, the burning fever, the shaking chills. Pat bathed his boy in steaming vinegar, stood by while the doctors let more blood, fed him Dr. Rush's Mercurial Sweating Powders in molasses, performed the intimate offices of a nurse. On the morning of Tuesday, September 4, Jamie died.

Pat was appalled. For nine months, Jamie had been his only "family," a happy enthusiastic lad, entirely devoted to Pat and his teachings, full of grand plans for his own future. "It is wrong to reflect," Pat wrote soberly, "but the loss I sustained by the death of this promising youth, I am certain I shall never retrieve."

Mournfully he hired a neighbor to make a coffin. With his own hands, he laid Jamie in it, buried him in Squire Hazard's burying ground, scarcely able in a sudden weakness to follow his boy to the grave and "sigh a last farewell to his departed spirit."

People shunned him now: he had nursed a fever victim. All Fleetwood's customers fled the tavern, scholars deserted a school house nearby. Four long days, till September 7, Pat remained a virtual prisoner of poor Jamie's disease, lonely, sad, separated from every human contact, entirely isolated from the Bank's questing messengers.

Then he went to Lewes. He had not enough money to pay Mr. Fleetwood his bill of six pounds. Instead, he left his watch as security and promised full payment next time the innkeeper came to Philadelphia. At Lewes he fished, saw his friends, he stayed at Captain Learmonth's house. He found business—the kind of business a smith could do, repairing guns, coffee mills, wagon wheels, little things of that sort.

One day he went on board the British frigate *Hind* which in company with an armed brig lay off Lewes trying to raise the sloop *Brack* sunk there some time before. Lewes people regarded the British vessels with grave suspicion. They wondered how many good Sussex County men would be impressed into His Majesty's Navy before the fruitless salvage operations ceased. But Pat spent a happy afternoon with the armorer and a group of officers, calculating how to build a diving bell in case the wreck could not be raised. He told them of spherical formulae, neat mechanical jointures, intricate problems of forgings, ingenious designs, he recited the account of the Great Lord Bacon, the whole history of *campana urinatoria*, diving bells, that fascinating problem of pressures resisted and air trapped in balance, Dr. Halley's treatise, William Phipps' celebrated bell, and the work ten years ago of the famous Smeaton . . . Pat stayed so long he missed the barge for shore. Night fell, luckily some ship's officers lingered in Lewes through the evening, and Pat returned on the pilot boat that brought them out. He came back just in time, his friends said, to avoid being seized and articled on the *Hind*.

Pilots, passengers, every vessel brought news of Philadelphia. One pilot, Sam Edwards, said a bank had been robbed; Pat thought at once of Sam Robinson and the stranger at his forge, of their beer sangaree together at the Market Street Ferry. Gossip reaches last the one whose name it soils. Not till Monday, September 17, did Pat learn there was suspicion against him. He learned it from Mr. Hunter, who had brought his wife down to Lewes. Now the Hunters were his oldest friends; they were Scots, with whom he had first lived when he came to Philadelphia, before his marriage to Ann. It was good to see them. They talked of many things: of acquaintances who had died, of young Jamie, of the robbery. Pat told his suspicions of Robinson and the stranger. Hunter mentioned a lot of people had been questioned, he spoke in a rambling way, he was sorry so many innocent men were suspected. Pat found his manner strange. Finally, he saw what Hunter was driving at.

"Am I suspected?" he asked bluntly.

Reluctantly, Hunter admitted that he was.

"Why didn't you say so sooner?" Pat demanded.

He was startled at the news, and offended. Dozens of people could swear to his innocence, testify where he had been, and when, everything he had done since he left Philadelphia August 28. Young Jamie was gone, but there was Captain Collins of the schooner, the Fleetwoods, Captain Learmonth, Mr. Elliot the innkeeper, Squire Hazard, Dr. Wilson, Dr. Little, practically all the people in and around Lewes. . . .

Fever or no fever, he would go up to Philadelphia at once, to clear his name. He said so to Mr. Hunter, who advised him strongly to do just that. Captain Learmonth endorsed the advice.

But how to go? By now, Philadelphia was a closed port, a city besieged. For fear of the fever, vessels would sail no further up stream than Wilmington. Pat found a ship for the Brandywine at once, September 18; on the 20th at dawn he landed at Wilmington.

There he was stranded. No coach would go north, nor was Wilmington safe, for the plague was as bad there as at Philadelphia. So Pat decided to walk. It was early morning; if he walked steadily all day he could reach the city by nightfall. He begged a chew of tobacco—everyone knew there was no better preventive against the Yellow Fever than chewing tobacco—he took off his coat, he started up Brandywine Hill.

Shortly, he met a Philadelphian who told him an unsettling story. They were saying around the city that a river captain confessed he had borne a smith and his apprentice downstream, that the smith had a red pocket-book chock full of bank notes. Pat was astounded. Captain Collins was "a poor, silly ignorant creature," but if he could fabricate a story like that, how could Pat refute it? Just saying he had never carried a pocket-book in all his life would convince no one.

He bought a biscuit, and three peaches, he walked on. The sun was high now, but not oppressive, the temperature that September 20 reached only 78 degrees. At Chester he met Curtis the potter, who tried to persuade him not to go on. The real criminals had been taken, he said. This was encouraging. Pat ate his biscuit, had a drink, and pushed ahead. The way was dusty with people, everyone had some bit of news about the robbery. Plainly Curtis was wrong, the criminals had not been captured, Curtis was only trying to protect him. Squire Robert Wharton passed him, in his fine coach; he had taken his family to the healthy country, and was riding each day into town.

John Haines the saddler galloped past—not till next day did Pat learn that Haines had been named High Constable. At Darby he stopped in a tavern for some ale. Finding a barber in the house, he had himself shaved.

He trudged on across Darby Creek, up the crowded pike to Cobbs Creek, crossed by the Blue Bell Tavern, went through Paschall Village and King-sessing, late in the afternoon he reached the gardens and floating bridge at Gray's Ferry. He paid his toll, walked the undulating length of the bridge which sank into water above his shoe tops every time a coach or wagon crossed, plodded wearily along the new Federal Road to Irish Lane.

Here, if he angled left he could reach the inn at Lebanon on the southern edge of the city. But if he turned sharp right, he would be going away from town but he could reach, down in The Neck, the country home of Alderman Stocker. Now Stocker was a proper magistrate, and he was Pat's friend, for whom he had worked, he was a respected merchant, and a director of the Bank. He could see Mr. Stocker, clear his name, spend the night, go back down the river without ever entering the feverish city. Pat turned right, walked southward, came about seven in the evening to the drive leading from Moyamensing Road to Mr. Stocker's summer residence. He had walked more than thirty miles since he stepped off the boat that morning at Wilmington.

Mr. Stocker was not at home, but was expected shortly. Might he have some refreshment? Pat asked. At this, the servants fell to quarreling among themselves, they would bring him nothing. Nor would they let him in. Pat lay down in the tall grass in front of the house to wait.

Soon night fell, damp and cold. The sweat dried on his body, his clothes clung to him in clammy chill, an ague spread through his tired muscles. By and by, he pulled himself up, started back toward Irish Lane and the inn at Lebanon. At a turning in the lane he met two chairs bound for the mansion house. He waved at them, the drivers reined up.

"Is that not Mr. Stocker?" Pat asked.

"Yes," said the Alderman.

"Don't you know me?" Pat inquired.

"Is that Lyon?" Stocker asked, from the depths of his two-wheeler.

"It is," said Pat.

"Who took you?" was Stocker's first question.

No one had taken him, Pat answered. He hadn't wanted taking, he had come of his own accord.

Where had he come from? Stocker wanted to know. From Wilmington, Pat said. He had come to clear himself, as he understood he was sent for. He had been waiting at Mr. Stocker's house for some time, he added. Then he resolved to learn the worst. What charge had been laid against him? he asked.

A serious charge, Mr. Stocker replied. And he would be glad if Lyon could prove his innocence. Pat answered firmly, he would have little trouble doing *that*. Then he asked if he might stay at Stocker's for the night.

"No," said Mr. Stocker.

Well, Pat persisted, could he bed in his stable, on the hay?

"No," Stocker replied.

Then could he lie down on the floor? Pat asked humbly, hoping he would not have to go into the feverish city.

"No," said John Stocker.

So the tired smith said he would find a tavern, and would come again before Mr. Stocker at nine the next morning. He stepped back, the chairs proceeded on their way, Pat walked the two long miles up to Lebanon, in the dark.

At Lebanon Inn* he came across three friends, Tim Bingham, Mr. Brierly, John Saunders. They gave him supper, made a bed for him on the floor, they discussed the robbery, and Pat's situation. He told them his suspicions— that Robinson and the stranger had done the deed. He must not say these things, Tim Bingham warned. He must prove his own innocence; if he could do that, he ought to be satisfied. Pat spent an uneasy night.

Next morning, stiff and sore, he rose early, went to his house down Lombard Street to get a fresh suit of clothes. As he left his front door he met a friend who said Magistrate Jennings had a warrant out for his arrest. Pat walked at once over to Mr. Jennings' office at Fourth and Union. By order of Jonathan Smith, cashier, Jennings had indeed issued a state's warrant, but, he said, he could not detain Pat because he did not just then have the warrants in his possession. Pat asked permission to get breakfast; Magistrate Jennings readily granted it, remarking since he had been so honorable as voluntarily to come 150 miles to answer a charge, he certainly could be trusted to have a meal. He urged him to go see the Bank officials—they had fled to Germantown, where they were carrying on business during the plague.

But Pat had not strength enough to walk to Germantown. It was seven miles. And he feared to take a carriage, for Yellow Fever victims were constantly transported in every kind of vehicle. Instead, he walked back to Lebanon Inn, feeling "very faint and low." Here he took breakfast with John Saunders—his last meal for many weeks—and though trembling with chills and aching at every step, he trudged down Irish Lane to Stocker's house.

From the beginning, the hearing at Alderman Stocker's was a sorry business. A considerable crowd of people stood about; they were the alderman's

---

* The site today is in South Street, near 10th. Lebanon was never a separate village, only a small settlement on the south edge of town.

relatives from town out here to escape the fever. As Pat turned into the gate, Mr. Stocker mounted his horse, called out "Lyon, I will be back directly!" and rode off. Young Anthony Stocker told him coldly to wait for his father's return.

For two hours, Pat sat on the piazza, tired, sore, apprehensive. Everyone left him strictly alone. Alderman Wharton rode up, strode into the house in his bully-boy fashion, but neither he nor anyone else deigned to notice Pat's existence. Finally, Stocker came back, accompanied by Mr. Fox, president of the Bank, the cashier Jonathan Smith, and to Pat's surprise John Haines the saddler, who was now revealed to be the newly appointed High Constable of Philadelphia.

When after his long wait Pat was at last conducted into the front parlor, he stood before not merely Magistrate Stocker, but the highest officials of the Bank, the imposing Robert Wharton, and the principal officer of police as well. No one stood beside Pat to advise him, no lawyer at his elbow to explain that Stocker was a city magistrate who could not legally act out here in the country. These men were not bothering with niceties of the law. They were all against him—Pat needed no counsel to tell him that.

Yet he knew these men. Haines the saddler was a nobody, a cheap politician, toady to the great. The sour Jonathan Smith he had often seen at the bank. Stocker he had thought was his sincere friend. Everyone knew Mr. Fox to be honorable and just, a philanthropic, unselfish, patriotic gentleman. And Robert Wharton was a hero.

All Philadelphia loved Squire Wharton. He was of the great Wharton family, here since William Penn's time, but he was also of the people. From "a decided distaste for learning" he had gone into trade, and now his grain and flour business was one of the successful mercantile establishments down on Front Street. Two years ago a great strike of merchant seamen had paralyzed the city, throwing the waterfront into confusion. Alderman Wharton personally led eighty men, armed with sticks of wood, against a gang of three hundred strikers, and though knocked down four times he had sprung up again and against heavy odds he quelled the riot.

Wharton was a man of courage, certainly. No one doubted it. Just this month when the jailer and his deputies had all fled the Walnut Street Prison as the Yellow Fever struck, Squire Wharton had personally taken charge of the jail, and brought in his own deputies. He was spending all his time there now, running the prison with his bluff hearty good humor and sportsman's enthusiasm.

And the city was talking again about the kind of man he was, for three days ago another riot had risen, crested, and shattered on his sturdy person. Some convicts in the feverish jail overpowered Dr. Benjamin Duffield on his rounds, seized the keys of their chamber, poured out into the courtyard, knocked down the turnkey Evans and another keeper. Wharton, hearing the noise, grabbed his fowling piece and ran from his office into the courtyard. A prisoner was at that moment lifting an axe to dispatch the unfortunate Evans when Wharton shot him down. Evans leapt up. With another guard and a Negro prisoner he rushed to Wharton's aid; they seized more guns; firing into the crowd they hit two mutineers, and by the use of the bayonet succeeded in driving the prisoners back into their stinking chamber. Thus, John W. Fenno wrote in his *Gazette,* "the designs of these most abandoned wretches have been happily frustrated"—and thus Robert Wharton was once more the savior of Philadelphia.

From such a man, could not a just hearing be expected? Pat hoped so. Alone, certainly very tired and apparently sick, he needed someone of sense and courage, someone who knew men, to appeal to. Pat Lyon, self-made artisan, could scarcely understand a rich and privileged gentleman confessing to "a decided distaste for learning"; but in Squire Wharton's robust activity, his quickness to command, there was something a blacksmith could like.

Alderman Stocker opened by asking where Pat had been. Easily, exactly, he answered. He told of his voyage down the bay, the illness and death of young Jamie McGinley, his stay at Fleetwood's and at Lewes, his friends with their names and circumstances, Hunter's bringing him news of the robbery, his decision to return, his arduous trip back. The men listened silently. They gave no sign of belief. Not till much later did Pat hear Mr. Wharton say, "Lyon gave a history of where he had been, *but told such a straight and well-connected story that I was sure he was guilty.*"

Truth was no defense against suspicion. As soon as questioning began, Pat realized that, and he knew a sudden fear. These men were surly, rude, contemptuous when they questioned him; they were scornful of his work, of his manners, of his plainness. They were the law: before them, he stood branded, convicted, marked forever as a man who had been suspected, summoned, interrogated. His good name was destroyed . . . Pat grew faint. Detail after detail, they went over his story, seeking to trap him, getting it all down on paper. Relentlessly, the questions continued. Then suddenly Smith the cashier spoke, his voice full of Pat's guilt, spoke of locks, vaults, of a cellar door. Pat could not follow him. A miasma clouded his brain. He reeled and staggered, nearly fell; he was pale, and dizzy, he trembled as with the ague. Hoarsely, he asked for water.

Everyone saw the blacksmith's illness, saw him faint when Jonathan Smith pressed his question. To everyone, it was a certain sign of guilt. Stocker sent for wine and water. Pat drank deeply. It revived him. His fainting spell passed, but in the faces of the silent men about him he read his fate.

Questions went on. Pat told of his suspicion of the carpenter Robinson and the stranger, he explained the details of his work on the doors and locks, he alluded to the other smith whom the bank had hired to set the book vault next to his doors. They scarcely listened to him. Stocker turned to confer with Mr. Wharton. Wharton observed, in a voice for all to hear, that Lyon had been "extremely minute in his narrative." This, he said to Stocker, together with "the import of his examination and the embarrassed situation he appears in, would, if I were magistrate, induce me to commit him."

Having said which, Mr. Robert Wharton left the room.

Stocker then addressed Mr. Fox, president of the Bank. He had "a secret conversation" with him, after which he faced the blacksmith.

Now Pat had not known enough about the law to ask for the charge against him to be read, or demand that the information on which he was charged be heard under oath. Nor did anyone present bother to inform him of his rights at law, those proud American rights so explicitly stated in state and federal constitutions: no warrant to seize any person shall issue, *but upon probable cause, supported by oath or affirmation.* The only thing that impressed Pat Lyon was that these men, ignorant of science and craft, could not understand why it had taken a skillful smith from Thursday to Monday to fix the iron doors and set the locks. He had kept the locks so long he must have intended and committed some part of the crime, they said. He had not even kept the locks, he had left them at the Bank. He tried to explain, but none of them would listen.

"I found," Pat wrote, "I was in the hands of those who were not the most intelligent of mankind—rich, but probably connected with Gotham."*

"Mr. Lyon," said Justice Stocker, "I am very sorry: but I must be under the disagreeable necessity of committing you to prison."

With "all the entreaties he was master of," Pat protested his innocence. He was an honest man, the son of an honest man; he begged Mr. Stocker to reconsider. Stocker answered that he had proof against him—proof he did not disclose—and he set bail at $150,000. The constable, he told Pat, was waiting.

Yes, thought Pat, and the Yellow Fever in the jail, and ruin, disgrace, and despair. He was to be committed, an innocent man who had come a long journey and told the simple truth, to a prison where riot raged and a foul disease beset the convicts, where Robert Wharton reigned as warden, heroic little king of an obscene little kingdom, the same Wharton who had judged Pat Lyon's story "so straight and well-connected" as to be certain proof of guilt.

---

* That is, fools in a city of fools. Pat's writing is full of the antique legend and lore of England. The story of deceitful Gotham goes back to the thirteenth century. It had nothing to do with the city of New York, in 1798. Not until 1807 did Washington Irving in his *Salmagundi Papers* apply the name *Gotham* in satire to New York: when he did, the appellation took hold at once, and has stuck ever since.

Ordered into a chair with Haines the oily constable, Pat was driven to the Walnut Street Jail, where he was delivered to Philip Edward, the keeper. He was locked in the storeroom, alone, and left to wonder if he would ever come out of that dismal place alive.

The Walnut Street Prison to which Pat Lyon was thus confined—on no legal warrant, on no oath to support a warrant, and by a magistrate sitting outside his jurisdiction—was one of the boasts of Philadelphia. No Newgate or Fleet or Marshalsea, this; no sink of depravity. Here, Mathew Carey wrote, no one was confined merely on suspicion or for want of friends, to be in evil surroundings rendered obdurate, wicked, ripe for rapine and spoil. Here the profligate and abandoned were reclaimed, made useful members of society.

Such idiotic tributes were written only by men who had never stepped inside the great prison. Pat Lyon with a simple breath could have blown away their roseate fantasies. At best, the Walnut Street Gaol was a hideous place; under the genial Robert Wharton it became a fantastic horror.

The law by which it was governed had been drawn in the spirit of generous humanity. Prisoners waiting trial—those presumed innocent until declared guilty—were to be separated from convicts who had been tried and sentenced. Every inmate was to be furnished with suitable bedding, shaved twice a week, given a haircut once a month; he was to change his linen once a week and "regularly wash his face and hands every morning." So the law read, and it prescribed a wholesome diet: Tuesday, Thursday, Saturday a quart of Indian meal made into mush for each inmate; Monday, Wednesday, Friday a pound of bread and a quart of potatoes, Sunday a pound of bread and a pound of coarse meat made into broth. On paper, the jail looked to be what Caleb Lownes claimed it was, in a book he wrote describing it: a model corrective institution.

But Squire Wharton was none of your sentimental humanitarians. He ran the jail as he knew how to run everything, with club and musket. The law's diet he paid no attention to, he fed his convicts every day on "good beef and soup," even lived on it himself, though from prisoners waiting trial (as Pat was) the beef was withheld. A man had to be proved guilty to get enough to eat in Wharton's jail. The rule of shaving he blandly ignored, and all the rest of the law's provisions for the treatment of prisoners. When attorney Joseph Hopkinson asked Mr. Wharton of the prison, "Is it a cleanly, wholesome place?" Wharton responded, "Indeed, Mr. Hopkinson, if you was there, you would be lousy in a quarter of an hour!" The crowded courtroom roared with laughter at Squire Wharton's sally. None of them had ever been inside his prison.

Yet Wharton was a hero, and the very week Pat went to prison, when

Mayor Hilary Baker died of the fever, Robert Wharton was chosen Mayor. It was the first of his fifteen elections to that office. The robust Wharton's "decided distaste for learning" did not prevent his serving more years as Mayor than anyone in Philadelphia's history.

Pat, of course, had never read the law concerning the jail. His treatment did not surprise him; what else was to be expected from the gentlemen who had imprisoned him with no regard for truth, decency, or civil rights? His cell—the storeroom—was twelve feet by four. There was a fireplace but no fire, and no bed, only boards to lie on. They gave him a single blanket. A barred window looked up Sixth Street, Pat could see the noble tower of Independence Hall a block away. His door was of iron, with a small grating set in it. The rods of this grating were exactly (someone measured them) an inch and three-eighths apart.

Pat was hungry when he went in. That breakfast at Lebanon Inn had been his last meal. The turnkey, the only person who came to his door, was a Quaker named Lewis, a man whose heart, Pat remarked, "was not of the dove kind, but rather in kind more like to a lapstone." He asked for something to eat. Lewis brought him a bowl of rice soup, rancid, stale, made of spoiled rice. It stank. Pat could scarcely look at it without retching. From hunger and fatigue, he began to feel sharp pains in stomach and bowel. He was drawn double. He offered money for something nourishing, protesting he could not swallow the putrid soup. The keeper Lewis smoothly answered, if he didn't eat the soup he could do without food altogether, and took the loathsome stuff away. For twenty-four hours, Pat was given nothing else. Soon Lewis was dead of the fever. "I am apt to think he did not leave too much humanity behind him," Pat remarked.

Day after day passed, and Pat remained in his solitary confinement. Occasionally a keeper would come to his door, and hand through the inch-and-three-eighths grating slices of thin dark bread, and the long spout of a tea kettle from which Pat might suck molasses water. Once the spring-coach maker, William Lace, came to see him. Wharton made a spate of objections, finally he permitted Lace a short visit. But the coach maker came down with the fever, and for many days could not return. John Saunders of Lebanon brought provisions, wept to find Pat in the predicament he was—tears, Pat wrote, were "the most impressive language to show the finest feelings of human nature." Saunders begged Pat to keep his spirits up; he went off sadly, in a few days he was dead. For a long time, no one else came at all. To pass the lonely hours, Pat tried "natural harmony"—his name for whistling and singing. This did bring him attention: two guards appeared with pistols and sticks, growled if he didn't stop his noise they'd clap him in a dungeon.

From his high window, he could call out to passers-by on the street. Once when he had gone several days with no food at all, he spied a friend, cried to

him, tossed him a dollar and begged him to send some meat. The friend disappeared with the dollar, but no food came.

As the fever grew worse in the jail, and guards died, the saintly Moravian
cooper, Peter Helm, came voluntarily to take charge of the makeshift in-
firmary for plague victims, in the east wing. Helm was long practiced in
philanthropy, a person of infinite goodness who in his time had moved the
roughest men to compassion. Though busy with the sick and the dying, he
found time to visit Pat in his cell. Wharton ordered him not to do it again,
Helm serenely disregarded his orders. He began to bring food each day for
Lyon; except for a few times he would find it still lying on the guard's desk
at the end of the day. They had forgotten about it, the guards would say. But
even Wharton's guards dared not defy Peter Helm's well-known piety and
charity. Though they refused to open the door for Pat to be fed, they could
not stop Mr. Helm from climbing up to the storeroom, despite Mayor
Wharton's orders. Did he wish for anything? Helm asked. Pat wished for
everything, but what he begged for were books. Helm brought him a Bible,
and a volume of Burns's *Poems, Chiefly in the Scottish Dialect.* Pat read till
he was weary, paced his cell till he was tired, expecting every day the real
thief would be discovered, and he be released.

Days passed into weeks, and still he remained in the storeroom. From
starvation his belly pains increased till be could neither stand erect nor lie
straight out. His breast swelled, and though his beard grew luxuriantly, all
the hair fell from his head. He had no change of clothing, not even of under-
clothing. No water was given him to wash in, no waste was removed from
his room. The stench grew appalling. He was dirty, lousy, sick, and forlorn.

Convicts who had been tried, found guilty, and were serving their sentences had water, food, clothing, company, even work to do. They could walk
in the large green yard, talk to the great Robert Morris and other inmates
of the debtors' prison whose Prune Street grounds backed up to theirs. But
Pat remained alone in his dark, foul-smelling chamber, denied any visitors
who could not show a pass from two of the inspectors of the prison—and
Wharton was the only inspector to be found in town. Wharton formed the
habit of stopping by Pat's grill every now and again, in a taunting voice
urging him to confess, to acknowledge his guilt and enjoy the easier lot of
convicted felons. "I knew and felt my innocence," Pat wrote, "and that was
my grand, great and substantial support."

It was Helm who brought him a newspaper carrying Governor Mifflin's
proclamation of a thousand dollars reward and complete amnesty for the
return of the stolen money. The Bank advertised an additional reward of its
own. It was Helm, too, who brought him news that the Bank had sent a representative to Lewes, and found Pat's story correct in every detail, except one:

he had forgotten to tell them at Stocker's about going aboard the British frigate *Hind*. President Fox had been impressed with this report; he sent Helm a letter with a twenty dollar note in it. The twenty dollars were to be spent for necessaries for the prisoner, Mr. Helm was to enquire if Pat knew anything of the robbery. Pat told again about Sam Robinson, and the stranger.

The reward brought John Haines to Pat's cell, for repeated visits. If Pat would tell him his suspicions, he kept saying . . . Pat would not—not to Haines, for him to get the reward. Soon William Lace was back again, recovered from the fever, though he had lost his daughter. He found Pat emaciated, weak, ferocious looking with his great beard and bald head. Every day, he applied to visit him, once or twice a week he was given permission. Lace, Pat trusted. But others who came he suspected were spies for Wharton ("I tried many schemes to extort a confession from him," the Mayor testified). To these, he would only repeat his complaints: he was not being fed, had no fire to warm him, no bed to lie upon . . .

Suddenly, on the thirty-first day of his confinement, he was taken out of his cell, John Haines drove him down to Mr. Stocker's counting house, for another hearing. Pat cleaned up as well as he could, after a month in the same clothes. His appearance he knew was shameful, no razor had touched his beard since that half-forgotten day when he had stopped in Darby to be shaved, his hands were grimy and black, his shirt and trousers stank horribly. He could not stand up straight, for his pains. At Stocker's, Mr. Fox walked into the room before the hearing began. He nodded coldly to the shaggy blacksmith, then unwittingly he indulged in a piece of exquisite cruelty. He turned to Stocker and described in sumptuous detail a notable dinner he had lately eaten at Germantown. Pat listened incredulously. They kept him standing all the while till they were done "unfeelingly trumpeting to each other in common though exulting language, the glorious gormandizing." Then they turned and engaged him in a long conversation on lockmaking.

Pat answered briskly, explained about wards, springs, rims, frames, latches, notches, levers; he reminded them of his warnings that the vault locks were not safe for a bank. But the real issue was not the vault locks at all, he told them. Anyone could open those. The real issue was, how did the criminal get into the banking room in the first place? How did he open the back door of Carpenters' Hall?

They had no answer for him. Lyon was a clever, ingenious smith, Mr. Fox said, who could have done the robbery. And Stocker refused to set him free. He was no longer a magistrate, he explained to Pat. He had just been elected to the state legislature; he had not the power, even if he should discover the will to release him. Pat looked at him squarely. "Mr. Stocker," he said, "I have acted as a gentleman since I was put in prison, but now I can restrain my temper no longer. Never more will you hear a civil answer from me!" Constable Haines conducted him back to jail.

William Lace the spring-coach maker had made Mr. Stocker's fine coach. When he heard from Pat the details of his second examination, before a man not even now a magistrate, Lace went to talk with Mr. Stocker. If there had been any wrong done Lyon, Stocker said, he had the law open to him. The coach-maker asked the merchant, how did one do this thing, hire a lawyer, place himself in view of the mysterious science of the law? Stocker recommended a Quaker attorney, John Hallowell. To Friend Hallowell, Lace went at once, paid a fee, made arrangements. On October 29, with his son to drive and accompanied by Peter Helm, Lace called for the blacksmith at the jail.

Pat was shaved, finally, given water to wash in, and fresh clothes. In two chairs he and Peter Helm, William Lace and his son set out for "Mount Pleasant," the country residence of Mr. Justice Shippen on the cliffs above the Schuylkill, three miles from town. As puisne justice of the Supreme Court, Shippen would hear his plea on a writ of *habeas corpus*. No unauthorized or foggy jurisdiction this, no possibility of anyone claiming he had no power, or had been misunderstood; Shippen's very presence was authority itself.

Outside Mount Pleasant, Pat met John Hallowell, told him his story—as much of it as he could in a moment. Fox, Smith, all the Bank party came up and were filing into Shippen's drawing room.

Mr. Justice Shippen, ancient relic of provincial aristocracy, a descendant of William Penn himself, was seventy years old now. More than forty years ago he had been judge of vice-admiralty under the British crown. His daughter Peggy had married Benedict Arnold. With fastidious elegance he had lived his full measure of joys and sorrows. An age had heaved in turmoil, revolution had spilled around him, Edward Shippen had preserved with aloof dignity and genteel demeanor the colorless neutrality of his cold nature. His self-possession caused him to appear quiet, kindly, serene; people thought him fair. Hallowell pled that Pat's commitment had been irregular—he had not been charged on oath, or before a qualified magistrate. The ancient relic leaned forward. "I advise you not to insist on that exception, Mr. Hallowell," he said, "for even if it were well founded I should grant time to the prosecutors to procure a legal commitment."

It was Hallowell's only plea. For the Bank, William Rawle, a Quaker who had spent the years of the Revolutionary War in England, afterwards come to Philadelphia and risen to the first place at the bar, presented a case showing probable cause: Lyon was, he admitted, 150 miles away when the robbery occurred, but still he was an "ingenious, clever man" and he could have manipulated locks. He was observed, that Saturday night of the weekend he worked for the Bank, to labor far into the night at his smithery. (He had cut that mortice on the outside door, Pat remembered. Would they have thought it better if he had gone to Israel Israel's tavern and spent the night in drinking?)

And he had tried to throw suspicion on others, the carpenter Robinson, and "another gentleman." Justice Shippen interrupted; he asked about these two men. The Bank directors declined to give the name of the other, they did not wish "to expose the blameless to slander." Mr. Fox announced he knew both Robinson and the stranger, entirely respected them, reposed unlimited confidence in them. Furthermore, they had come forward and given a wholly satisfactory account of where they had been when the robbery took place. (Well, Pat thought, had he not given an even better account, with an abundance of witnesses?)

Rawle cited Jonathan Smith's suspicions of Pat, he read out Pat's repeated statements that the locks were not safe, he made it all seem a plot, a damning conspiracy. Yet Shippen was old in the law. Add it all up, the only case the Bank really had was suspicion, possibility, that reiterated phrase, *"a clever, ingenious man ..."* Still, the Bank was a semi-public institution, whose payment of $80,000 to the Commonwealth was a matter of grave importance— to Shippen, to the bibulous Governor Mifflin, to every citizen. The robber must be apprehended. Shippen called Mr. Fox to the stand for a final question. Perhaps something lay behind this prosecution that had not yet come out . . .

"Mr. Fox," the justice asked, "have you ever had a former acquaintance with Lyon?"

In his even, deliberate tone, Fox replied. "I have often heard of him," he said. "He has made me a smoke-jack for the use of my house, which answered very well, and he did the work of the Bank before I was elected president. The first job he did for the bank under my direction was his opening an iron chest. . . ."

From what had been related to him, Mr. Justice Shippen said, the Bank's suspicions appeared to be grounded on experience. He could not take it upon himself to discharge the prisoner. He reduced bail to $6,000, but he sent Pat back to prison.

Now bail of $6,000 was far easier to raise than $150,000; but to his amazement Pat found that none of his friends would come forward as sureties. Jonathan Smith the cashier had gone in person to each one of them, warned them not to go his bail. He was "sure Lyon had a hand in the business," he said. When taxed with this slander, Smith blandly admitted it: he had wished to protect the innocent, he explained, he did not wish to see anyone dragged down by Lyon's criminal acts.

The weather turned cold and damp, Pat lay helpless in his storeroom, unable now to care for himself. A jailer was finally persuaded to light a fire in his cell. Then in a few days Pat was transferred to the east wing. They needed the storeroom for another prisoner, the guards said. He was housed with convicted thieves and vagrants, though company, even of the most depraved, was a blessed relief. He recovered a measure of his health in these new surroundings, he occupied his time talking to convicts of the New Testament; he succeeded in getting paper and ink, he began writing his book. When he was allowed to walk in the yard with the others, by his great physical strength he protected the youngest prisoners from the bullying of the guards, and the attacks of vicious inmates. Pat recorded what he saw with a pitying eye. "There is not a better school for villainy anywhere, than the convict-yard of Philadelphia prison," he observed sadly.

General Washington came to town in November. The sounds of salutes and parades, the huzzahing of crowds floated from Independence Hall Yard into the prison. Then on the twentieth of November came the news that the mystery of the Bank robbery had been solved. The real criminals were a young man named Isaac Davis—that stranger who had been so friendly with Sam Robinson—and the guard Cunningham, who slept upstairs in the Bank. ("He tore his hair, and said he would be suspected," Thomas Annesley had said. "He appeared mad or insane.") Cunningham had died of the Yellow Fever; Davis had confessed to the theft, returned the money, had been permitted to leave town. The papers were full of the story, and full of praise for the Bank officers for their part in catching the thieves. Mayor Wharton was asked if he had any hand in it; he modestly admitted he had made certain efforts toward securing the return of the money. . . .

At once, Pat prepared for his release. Davis, the very man he had first accused, the "amiable, respectable young gentleman" of Chester County, in whom President Fox "reposed unlimited confidence," was now revealed to be deceiver, dissimulator, and perjuror as well as thief. The Bank was remarkably tender of Davis's feelings, especially considerate of his uncle, and his family. In his statement, Davis entirely cleared Pat Lyon, made it plain no one but himself and the guard Cunningham had been involved. Yet toward Lyon, President Fox was obdurate. So was the cashier Jonathan Smith; so now was even Mr. Stocker. After the hearing before Shippen, Stocker was observed to grow vehement. "Every second word he said Dam him, we will keep him there: He has threatened to flog us—we will keep him there, while he can stick together!" President Fox agreed. Davis said he didn't know where Cunningham got the false keys; *perhaps* the dead guard had got them from Lyon. The days wore slowly on, Pat remained in prison.

Finally, on December 14, he was taken before the whole Supreme Court sitting in banc. Now this was three weeks after Davis had confessed, and the Bank had its money back; there was no shred of evidence or testimony to connect Pat with either of the acknowledged criminals, there was Davis's statement exonerating him. And the directors, as "men of honour, who had pledged their word," had permitted Davis to go off. But they persisted in their prosecution of Lyon.

Fox, Smith, Sam Robinson, John Haines all appeared against him, before the Supreme Court. William Rawle was their counsel. Attorney General Jared Ingersoll himself conducted the case for the state. He conducted it so well, that even though Pat could say to them, I told you long ago, three months ago, who the real criminals were, and now you know I was right— in spite of this, the justices *en banc* bound Pat over to the Grand Jury on the charge of robbing the Bank. They reduced bail to two thousand dollars. This Pat could raise, and on December 15 he left the jail, a prisoner at large, having been in confinement since September 21.

"I went and saw several old acquaintances," Pat wrote, "and they gave me something to drink."

The Bank was not yet through with him. Cashier Jonathan Smith attacked Pat's honesty in public. "He may think himself damn'd lucky to have got off so easy," Smith snorted. It was partly a cover-up; everyone knew young Isaac Davis had been courting the sister of Smith's wife, had seen the cashier himself with Davis, "jaunting about the city" on many an evening. Mr. Stocker likewise was apprehensive. The Supreme Court had been specific in its criticisms of his conduct that first hearing, had said in no easy terms that an action of trespass lay against him, for sitting outside his jurisdiction, failing to draw proper warrants, take sworn testimony. Mr. Stocker introduced in the legislature, and had it passed through, a resolution commending the officers of the Bank and Mayor Wharton for their efforts in apprehending the criminals, getting back the money, and in particular for pursuing Pat Lyon to his refuge in distant places, for he was suspected. This resolution, a comment by the legislature on the guilt of a person still to be tried, shocked even the Bank's lawyers. It is a unique and embarrassing record in the history of American law.

But Stocker's day was over, and Smith's, and the day of the gentlemen of the Bank. However much influence they might have with magistrates and judges, they had none with the people. The January Grand Jury refused to indict Pat Lyon.

These were the days and months Pat remembered always. And what followed next he remembered, too: the years of disgrace, of poverty, years of misery, not from guilt of his own, but from malice of others, the persistent enmity of gentlemen, secure in their place, their living. A man's reputation was made, not by innocence and excellence, but by words. The Bank spread a constant word of Pat Lyon: he was a jail bird, he was an *ingenious* man.

Seven years, he had scant work, few commissions, he depended on the charity of friends, seven years in every competition for hydraulic engines his very name was enough to ensure his bid would be rejected. "He lost his trade, tools, &c during his imprisonment," the Bank was informed, "and the imputation cast upon his character is, likely, to affect him for life."

It was a defeat more thorough, more crushing, than ever the Yellow Fever, or the poverty of his first years, or the competition in his trade. Pat read his Bible in lonely despair, he reflected on the trials of Job: "Terrors are turned upon me; they pursue my soul as the wind; my welfare passeth away as a cloud . . ." And he reflected on his situation. Now a Scotsman may be no war-charger, his neck clothed with thunder, who saith amidst the trumpets, Ha Ha!—but a Scotsman is such a fellow, when he sees his welfare passing away like a cloud, as will likely rise up. Pat Lyon, with the weapons he could find, fought back.

There was old Mr. Bailey, and his son Robert: Francis Bailey had been printing in Lancaster before the Revolution, he had come to Philadelphia when Congress returned, he was well-known to be opposed to the Federalists' government. To Mr. Bailey, Pat took the book he had written. A lawyer went with him, J. W. Condy, another man of big affairs who had no love for the rule of the rich and well-born, no love for Mayor Wharton, either. From now on, Pat would have a lawyer at his elbow, in everything he did. A few weeks after his release by the January Grand Jury, his book was offered for sale: *The Narrative of Patrick Lyon, who suffered three months severe imprisonment in Philadelphia Gaol; on merely a vague suspicion, of being concerned in the robbery of the Bank of Pennsylvania: with his remarks thereon.** It was a powerful, shocking narrative, Philadelphians read it with genuine surprise, and with genuine dismay. As a writer, Pat was not skillful; but he told his tale with such attention to detail and incident, with so many conversations recorded, so many scenes in the prison described, that no one could doubt its authenticity. And the passionate resentment of the innocent blacksmith, evident in every sentence, spread shame in the city. His book was a plea for brotherhood, equality, humanitarianism, addressed to citizens who cherished those ideals in name, but had abandoned them in practice.

Another weapon was by and by put into his hands, the new spirit in American law. In 1800 came "The Great Subversion"—the election of the

---

* Philadelphia: printed by Francis and Robert Bailey, at Yorick's Head, No. 116, High Street. 1799. The Baileys' Memorandum Book, in the manuscript division of The Historical Society of Pennsylvania, reveals that 193 copies were delivered to Patrick Lyon or to people he designated, and 500 copies, with the plates, to "J. W. Condie." The Baileys, father and son, were not book-sellers. Plainly, Jonathan Condy used Pat's book in his political efforts during this year and next, while Pat apparently sold his copies through booksellers. Those delivered to Pat appear to have been bound copies; those to Mr. Condy are noted to be "in sheets."

Democrat-Republicans; in 1801 began the Presidency of Thomas Jefferson. Pat's prospects improved. A blacksmith had his place in this new scheme of things, and had able defenders. For notable lawyers, leaders in their profession, were decidedly weary of the domination of courts by one group, weary of the continual introduction of more and more of the English Common Law into American jurisprudence. Many of them were weary of the Common Law itself, with its antique doctrines of power and property. Now this new spirit in the law had its radicals, who made a mighty attempt to impeach the Federalist judiciary, an attempt which mostly failed; and it had its advanced intellectuals, who embarked on a program to eliminate entirely the English Common Law from American states. Led by the remarkable DuPonceau, these intellectual giants of the bar sought to give a permanence and special quality to the spirit of the American Revolution, by confining all law administered in courts, specifically to the law which had been enacted by legislatures. The people should *make* their laws, DuPonceau declared. It was their right, it was the meaning of the "liberty" the Revolutionists had fought for, that people should be governed only by laws they agreed upon, never by alien codes or rules, applied by judges whom the people had not elected. The extraordinary movement in favor of "statutory law and no other," like the radicals' impeachment of Federalists, for the most part failed, too. But even in failing, both movements made themselves felt, in court decisions, in lawyers' pleadings, in legislatures everywhere. Though the radicals disappeared, and the advanced and scholarly intellectuals gave up, they supplied a yeast in the ferment of legal reform that was spreading through the land. Between the old Common Law pleaders, the Middle-Temple men of the Revolutionary decades, and the radicals and intellectuals of the dismal 1790's, stood those other lawyers, whose training and experience was entirely American, who were as responsive to the bold freshness of a DuPonceau as to the Common-Law learning of a Shippen, and whose careers boiled up in this ferment of reform to produce ultimately a law which was, for the first time, American.

It was William Lace the coachmaker who first interested Mr. Secretary Dallas in Pat Lyon's cause. Mr. Dallas, Lace told Pat, "is the honest man's friend, and an excellent expounder of the law, and though he may have enemies, merit always causes them; yet he is I believe a just and worthy lawyer." It was little enough to say. Alexander James Dallas had just completed the third volume of his *Reports,* the most important record of federal and state court cases in progress in America; and he had published his greatest achievement, his *Laws of Pennsylvania,* a scholarly work of legal history and commentary, more substantial than any other American had ever produced. Dallas had never had a large share of the court business of the Philadelphia bar; the few famous pleaders of the Old Law monopolized that. He had been

Secretary of the Commonwealth since 1791; Governor Mifflin, for all his charm an indolent, indulgent man, had let him pretty much run things in the state; Governor McKean, full of years, had been happy to follow his lead.

Most useful of all, from Pat's view, Dallas was a Scotsman, trained in Edinborough (though born in the West Indies), and thoroughly acquainted with artisan mechanicks of the old country. President Jefferson appointed him Attorney General of the United States for Pennsylvania, in 1801, but the new position did not prevent him from taking private clients. Jonathan Condy saw to it that Mr. Dallas read Pat Lyon's *Narrative*. It made good Jeffersonian reading. The two Democrat-Republicans interested others. There were long delays; finally in December term of the Pennsylvania Supreme Court, 1805, before justices Yeates and Brackenridge, came Patrick Lyon, represented by A. J. Dallas, Joseph Hopkinson, J. W. Condy, and Moses Levy; and came also the respondents Samuel Fox, Jonathan Smith, John C. Stocker, and John Haines, represented by William Rawle, Jared Ingersoll, and old Judge William Lewis. It was an extraordinary assemblage of talent, a field-day at the bar. Judge Lewis, with his everlasting cigars, his acid tongue, his slovenliness, his sour manner, had been the teacher of the largest number of the lawyers in Philadelphia practice. Courts, when he appeared, set a table for him at the fireplace, that his cigar smoke might go up the chimney rather than fill the room.* On Pat's side were the leading Jeffersonian Democrats of the city; Hopkinson's grace and facility in pleading; fat, jolly little Levy's famous wit; Mr. Condy's skill in examination buttressing Dallas' unmatched learning in the law.

Dallas was trying something brand new, the first time it had been tried in Philadelphia, the first time but once in our jurisprudence.** On behalf of his client, he was accusing officers of the bank, the police, and the county, of malicious prosecution—that willful destruction of reputation under the mask of justice and public spirit, by which, Blackstone wrote, the noble proc-

---

* Judge Lewis was a tall thin stooping man with a remarkably long and high nose on which he wore thick spectacles. Long after they were out of fashion he persisted in dressing in knee breeches, and a powdered, tied wig. He was nervous, restless, a vehement speaker who fairly danced about as he delivered his famous orations; he had a faint hesitation in his speech: "clear" he pronounced "cul-lear," "plain" became "pul-lain." Binney adds, in his vivid description of this significant teacher of America's most notable Bar, "He smoked cigars incessantly. He smoked at the fireplace in Court. He smoked in the Court Library. He smoked in the street. He smoked in bed; and he would have smoked in church . . . if he had ever gone there." (*Leaders of the Old Bar,* p. 41.)

** That once was a tiny matter, a suit involving two pigs. You can find it in Addison's *Reports,* the case of *Kerr* v. *Workman,* 1795. If you can find Addison's *Reports.* It is a hard book to come by. Dallas knew the case, and alluded to it.

esses of the law "are sometimes made the engines of private spite and enmity."

The bank's lawyers were not insensitive to all that had been going on, nor were they unaware they had a poor case. On the eve of trial, Jared Ingersoll, Judge Lewis and William Rawle met together, all three signed a joint letter addressed to Samuel Fox and the others. "Gentlemen," they wrote: "The difficulty and importance of the suit brought by Patrick Lyon against you and Mr. Haines will require all our labor and powers to defend you against the strenuous and artful exertions of your opponent. We consider it proper to make a suitable arrangement in respect to our compensation before the trial comes on and we conceive ourselves entitled to a previous fee of Drs 200 each and an equal sum in case our efforts in your favor should be successful." The bank paid.

It was a famous trial, a long and bitter one, faithfully taken down in characters by another old country man, Thomas Lloyd, America's master artisan in shorthand, formerly reporter of the debates of the United States House of Representatives. Justice Brackenridge, a Scotsman born, asked frequent questions, Justice Yeates scarcely looked up from his endless writing of notes.

Pat knew the moment he stepped into court that things were going his way. The jury was drawn from artisans like himself—a sugar refiner, a wire worker, a soap boiler, a bricklayer. He wished things to be fair: when Mr. Condy caught President Fox in an error, Pat bade him desist, whispering: "Do not let him swear, it is too bad, we will manage it another way, and Mr. Fox will not expose himself to a perjury." But when Condy found Mayor Wharton smilingly asserting the conditions of Pat's imprisonment had been easy and normal, that he had been fed regularly and well cared for, Pat permitted the incisive Condy to expose Wharton's blatant falsehoods and boorishness with no mercy.

The trial was packed with incidents dramatic, appealing, distinguished by long eloquent orations of all the counsel, concluded with a careful charge by Justice Yeates; after the fashion of the day the jurymen were ordered to deliver their verdict the following morning.

When the jury came in with its verdict in favor of an award of damages to Lyon, "an universal clamor of exultation took place," Thomas Lloyd wrote, "among the audience, the most numerous the reporter remembers ever to have assembled in that court room."

Pat Lyon won his victory in 1805, after seven years of disgrace, and he enjoyed every fruit of the vindication of his honor and his name. He rose once more in his profession, he wrought mechanical inventions of uncommon art and beauty, the legend *"P. Lyon fecit"* was a guarantee of excellence. He trained many young men in his shop to take the place of poor Jamie Mc-Ginley, taught them Euclid and Newton and the ideals of craft work. He married again, raised children, buried his second wife, became at length a man of wealth.

But always he remembered, always he told others, the battle he fought had been a needless one, a battle forced upon him by the suspicion of one class of men for another, a battle hard to win because those who controlled the agencies of freedom were unwilling that its benefits should spread to all men equally regardless of place or connections.

In the quarter-century that had passed, Pat had seen liberty extended in America, even to some degree in Philadelphia. But he had seen, too, the persistence of the old barriers between men of science and men of affairs, between the learned artisan and those who reaped the harvest of his art. He had observed how little the legal forms of freedom in a state could mean when not supported in the hearts of men by love, or by a pervading attitude of respect and brotherhood. The Democracy General Jackson was talking about in 1826 was not entirely the sort of democracy that could be enacted by legislatures or ruled on by courts.

It was the sort that could come only when banker, lawyer, judge, blacksmith, shipwright and farmer knew no distinctions of class or honor among themselves. It was the democracy of craft, of calling.

"It has been my chief study," Pat wrote, "to fulfill the station which I believe nature intended me for, in, and on all my transactions in life. A disinterestedness, which has been often an injury to me, but which I have invariably pursued in spight of the false shew, glare, glitter, and splendour of the world: an open plainess, an honest bluntness of speech, which as my feelings dictated: were involuntarily spoken. These are pleasant, soothing reflections to me. They quiet the corroding irksomeness of care, and give a delicious composure at night to the wearied body. And when those *gentlemen,* who are so great in the world's eye, leave this world and the bell tolls their funereal knell, honours they cannot rationally boast of, and all their grand speculations die with them: while on the other hand, *my* works will be durable and ornamental, and probably *my* works and *my* principles, may not so soon be forgotten, as those of the *gentlemen* above alluded to."

It was at least a hope. Pat saw in his own life part of the solution of the problem America had set for itself. For he saw that free laws must beget and nurture free citizens—that though the essence of freedom lies in law, the future of freedom lies in men—men committed to, determined toward, that freedom which the law fosters.

America was producing other craftsmen who thought as he did. Soon another blacksmith, Elihu Burritt up in New England, while he worked at his forge would become a remarkable linguist, master of more languages and literatures ancient and modern than any other scholar in the New World, honored by universities in Europe and America alike, yet a man bold enough to turn down a professorship at Harvard and remain a blacksmith, preaching the gospel of craft to Europe and America. And a young Bowdoin poet named Longfellow was beginning a whole poetic career celebrating in verse

The nobility of labor,
The long pedigree of toil.

Pat was by no means alone. He knew that his experience had become a Romance, had even entered into children's books and chap books as a moral tale. Yet it was a piece of reality, of American life, something which he and the free men of his adopted country could use.

And thus it was, in the Presidency of a second, far-different Adams, in a far-different America, that Patrick Lyon turned to John Neagle and said, "I wish you, sir, to paint me at full length, the size of life, representing me at the smithery, with my bellows-blower, hammers, and all the et-ceteras of the shop around me." And being Pat, he added:

"D——THE EXPENSE! DO IT YOUR OWN WAY, MR. NEAGLE, TAKE YOUR OWN TIME, AND CHARGE YOUR OWN PRICE. BUT PAINT ME AT WORK AT MY ANVIL, WITH MY SLEEVES ROLLED UP AND A LEATHERN APRON ON. I DO NOT DESIRE TO BE REPRESENTED AS WHAT I AM NOT. DO NOT PAINT ME AS *A GENTLEMAN!*"

8

The Mammoth Cheese

Ladies of Cheshire Town bustled everywhere that summer. They were locusts come in June, noisy as August in the trees. They climbed to cabins high up in the back-growth of balsam and spruce, strode down through the sugar-bush on the Berkshire spurs, they called at all the homesteads in the valley, at the church, at every house in town. Gathering suddenly in kitchens, they held brisk crowded conference, as suddenly disappeared. Past ripening wheat they sped on foot to every farm, quizzing, prying. *"Your Swiss-brown heifer, will she come fresh by mid-July?"* *"Your other cows, how much do they milk?"* Farmers had scarcely time to snort *"None of your business, sister!"* before the ladies were off again, beyond the knee-high corn rows.

At dawn, chores still undone, farm wives on buckboards met together, spoke knowingly of curds, of earning, of rendling; they exchanged receipts, recited old grannies' tales of the wonders of rennet, how and when to use it, its mysterious properties. Rennet was delicate, precious: *"Keep your rennet in a goat skin."* *"We always use a calf's stomach."* *"Nothing but a goat skin will do."* *"Any leathern pouch——"* All day at kitchen tasks they talked, evenings they were out again, peering into barns where Cheshire husbands were busy with sun-down milking. *"Will your milkers hold up when the heats come on?"* *"This black, you won't dry her up before August?"* Even staunchest Republicans might envy the courage of one Federalist citizen: *"Sister,"* he said darkly, *"you are not about the work appointed to you!"*

But they were. Elder Leland had appointed the work, and whatever Elder Leland appointed, the goodwives of Cheshire Town were not going to shirk.

Berkshire people truly loved Elder John Leland. They loved his joyous piety, his news of nations and great men; they loved his astonishing sermons sparkling with stories so hearty they roared off in merry laughter before they recollected they were in God's house.

A singular man, John Leland. Everyone agreed. But "among his other singularities," one worshipper wrote stoutly, "he is singularly pious." Through all his noise and fun, his extravagance, his earthy personal jokes, there shone a bright commanding power, even a vision. He was warm, sometimes he was wise, he was evangelical.

His evangelism was Republican. That, Cheshire people loved most. It was what they most needed. All other towns in Massachusetts were Federalist. Everywhere in this most Federalist state of the Union, Thomas Jefferson and his Republican principles were detested—everywhere, except in the "town" of Cheshire.

Dairy farmers of Cheshire, nestled far out to the west in the Hoosick Valley under the green slopes of Mount Greylock, highest point in the state, were out of step with Massachusetts, very much *in* step with their lively minister. The "town" with its two villages, Cheshire and Stafford's Hill, settled by Baptists come up long ago from Rhode Island, was overwhelmingly Republican, pro-Jefferson, anti-Adams, anti-Federalist.

It was a great moment for Cheshire folk in the winter of 1792 when they secured for preacher in their little church a man not only Republican, but a leading Republican—a man from clear down in Virginia, near neighbor to Monticello, actually a personal friend of Thomas Jefferson. Elder Leland was a friend of James Madison, too, and James Monroe, a true Republican to preach Jeffersonian doctrine here in Cheshire hills as formerly he had preached through the War of Independence to mountain folk in Virginia. He was the evangel of equality, and liberty, and Jefferson's Statute of Religious Freedom.

Nine years Cheshire had rejoiced in Elder Leland, nine long years of Adams and Federalism. Republican farmers cherished his stories of Jefferson, stories that always ended with firm pronouncements: Jefferson was "patriarch of liberty, a man of the people, defender of the rights of man and the rights of conscience, the greatest statesman the world has ever produced!"

And now in 1801, Thomas Jefferson was finally President. The little mountain congregation when the glad news came stood alone in Massachusetts, vindicated in its faith. The victorious parson was beside himself. "Now the greatest orbit in America is occupied by its brightest orb!" From his pulpit he looked down on good Mary Smith, fattest, jolliest farm wife in the whole Hoosick valley. A sunny smile spread over Elder Leland's face. "Thomas

Jefferson," he cried, "not only completely fills the Presidential chair—like Polly Smith, he slops over all around it!"

Jefferson had not won election at the usual time, in November, 1800. He had tied in electoral votes with his fellow-Republican Aaron Burr. All through February the House of Representatives balloted day and night to make a choice. Nowhere in the nation was the daily post-rider awaited with more passionate interest than in Cheshire. At the last moment, Burr men gave up. Jefferson was inaugurated on time, with rowdy hilarity a new American era began.

Massachusetts Federalists sneered at the rift in Republican ranks, as they smarted at the Republican victory. "The Great Subversion," they called it. Accounts came northward of Jefferson's regrettable plainness, his unsuitable simplicity: how he would have no parade or procession at his inaugural, but merely put on his hat against the brisk March weather, and with a few friends trailing after walked in an ordinary way from his boarding house over to the Capitol and strode into the Senate chamber. He swore his oath of office, he read his speech (a bit awkwardly, people said) seated in a chair on the dais. Then he got up and walked home again.

It was heady news for Republicans everywhere. General Washington, and after him John Adams of Braintree, had conducted the Presidency with high, stiff dignity, pageantry and pomp. Mr. Jefferson strolled among the people as if he were no one at all. He gave up the state coach with its six horses and outriders in livery; he rode his own saddle mount alone through the capital city. Sometimes, Cheshire heard, he even wandered through the stalls on market day himself, a basket over his arm, buying groceries for the President's mansion.

"We are all Republicans, we are all Federalists," he had said in his inaugural. "Every difference of opinion is not a difference of principle." He meant to quiet faction, bring peace after the stormy election. But to Federalists his very simplicity was a difference in principle. His easy democratic manners were vulgar, they said, unseemly in a President. With only eleven slaves in the mansion, a French cook, an Irish coachman, how could he maintain the style of the head of a nation? Federalists resented his abolishing state levees at the President's house; criticized his dinner parties at which guests from all classes mingled together. They were appalled at his "open house" reception on the Fourth of July when he welcomed high and low alike to the White House: throngs of exuberant farmers and "mechanicks" tramped through the great East Room and stood with muddy boots on the furniture.

Jefferson was the people's President. He was degrading the nation, Federalists complained. They told of his receiving the British Minister at the White House clad only in slippers, pantaloons, and house coat—a vile partisan story. The President's small clothes were not very clean, they whispered.

Massachusetts papers reprinted and Federalist orators cried out the sharp, barbed attacks. They carped at every new appointment: Jefferson was ruining the Navy, he was bringing that atheist Tom Paine back from France.

Elder Leland heard all the bitter outcry, all the harsh critics. He had warned of them: "Expect to see religious bigots, like cashiered officers, and displaced statesmen, growl and gnaw at their galling bands, and, like a yelping mastiff, bark at the moon whose rising they cannot prevent!" He knew his loyal Republican Cheshire people needed answers to the Federalists, ammunition to strengthen their arguments, a project to refresh their Republican faith. It was hard to be the only Jeffersonian community in the state, the single pocket of political difference . . .

As he looked over the plain country faces in his little clapboard church, John Leland had his curious inspiration. These were farmers, mechanicks; these were Jefferson's people—simple, ordinary, hard-working. They had only one distinction, one single claim to fame: Cheshire folk made excellent cheese. Cheese-making was an honorable calling, a worthy employment. Why should not Cheshire Republicans make a gift to the President, a community gift, an amazing, striking gift, something peculiarly their own—a gift of cheese? Why should it not be the greatest cheese ever seen in all the world?

No better celebration could any people make, no better testimony of affection give, than a supreme achievement of what they did best, their everyday art and craft. Federalists spoke of dignity: what dignity could be more imposing than the dignity of toil?

Suddenly, from his pulpit, Elder Leland was talking about cheese. Cheese, and freedom. Cheese, and dignity. Cheese, and Mr. Jefferson. He described to his startled congregation the fame and honor they could win if they made a gift of cheese to the President; he spoke of the joy Jefferson would take in so warm, so simple a tribute, and of the lesson to Federalists that the Presidency itself was no cold remote sovereignty wrapped in velvet and awe, but an office belonging to the people, emanation of their liberty, part of their daily lives. Elder Leland warmed to his subject. The people of Cheshire were as good as committed.

First, the church ladies organized, planned, began their busy campaign. By mid-June, all Cheshire buzzed with the project. Federalist canards were forgotten in the Hoosick Valley, men joined the ladies in meetings, the whole town massed together to fashion the great Republican cheese.

Town meetings were called, committees formed. This largest cheese ever made, Cheshire decided, would be pressed from one day's total milking, contributed by every one of the 186 farmers in the "town." Every farmer would make a gift of his milk, every Cheshireman would share in it alike.

"Federalist cows will be omitted," local wags joked. They said it again and again. A community project needs a community joke.

A day must be chosen—carefully, with Yankee caution, Yankee speculation, thorough Yankee debate. Almanacks promised good weather for late July, grass and clover would be in vigor, the milking season at its height. But would late July be too late for curing the cheese? Cheese-makers were consulted. Make it as early as possible, they said. Who knew how long a big cheese would take to cure? Who knew even how big the cheese would be?

July 20 was fixed. On that date, every farm wife would bring all the curds from her last night's and early morning's milking to a central place, where the whole town would gather to practice the ancient rural art of pressing—on a scale never witnessed before.

Day after day, four weeks and more, preparations went on. A new careful census was taken of all the cows in Cheshire and Stafford's Hill, the ladies asked all their prying questions over again: *"How many milkers have you three years old or more? How many are fresh, or will come fresh by July 20? What exertions can be expected of each?"*

It was asking a Yankee farmer to state his net worth, his whole wealth. Reluctantly at first, Cheshiremen gave out their secrets. Then willingly, then proudly. The list of milking cows mounted to more than a thousand.

"From meadows rich with clover red
  A thousand heifers come . . ."

If each cow gave twelve pounds of milk—even on a poor day they should do at least that—the result of more than a thousand milkers would be an enormous production. an unheard-of giant of a cheese.

It would also be an engineering marvel. The Committee of Management was staggered. They reckoned, and measured: Cheshire's rule of thumb said ten pounds of milk made one pound of cheese. But a thousand cows, curds from more than twelve thousand pounds of milk—how did a man figure on a volume such as that? How big a cheese hoop would be needed to press the huge mass? How much pressure must the screw-press exert? How could any press so large be built—of what woods, and how bound about to withstand the pressure?

Captain Brown's son Darius Brown was a skilled blacksmith, a mechanical genius, the "engineer" of the Hoosick valley. He could build anything. Elder Leland recollected his mathematics. He calculated, he estimated the volume, reckoned pressures, strains, moments of force, weights here, resistance there, reinforcement, iron bindings . . . He came up with a figure.

No cheese hoop so big had ever been seen, or even heard of. Anywhere.

Elder Leland listened to practical men, experts full of facts, of knowledge.

He admitted the problem was grave. But it was not impossible: what good Republicans wanted badly enough to do, they could surely devise a means to accomplish. The means seemed to be up to him. John Leland considered.

Basically, a cheese hoop was nothing but a vat with holes in it, surmounted by a screw-press. It was not unlike any other pressing machines, a cider press, grains, a moulding press . . . Cider. Apples were bulkier than milk curds. And certainly heavier. And more resistant. . . .

Darius Brown had an uncle, Elisha Brown, a good Republican, a church-goer. In his orchard on the edge of Cheshire village, Farmer Brown kept a cider press. It was known miles around for its uncommon size; it was an enormous device, well-mounted. It was so large, indeed, that the weight on its screw totalled 1,450 pounds. Now could that press be used for a cheese? Leland took Darius Brown the blacksmith to Uncle Elisha's orchard to have a look. Then he went back to his ladies.

His ladies raised money for materials, hard Yankee cash. And under Leland's direction Darius Brown fashioned for the cider press a stout cheese hoop of oak, six feet in diameter, twenty-one inches deep, bound around with iron bands forced and bolted in circles, surmounted by an overlapping rim. This rim or gunwhale was removable: it would hold the top curds when they were laid into the hoop for pressing, then be discarded as the press descended. The design was magnificent. Even skeptics conceded it might work.

Next to Elisha Brown's orchard lived Farmer John Wells, Jr., whose wife Frances Wells was the best cheese-maker in Cheshire. All the ladies ac-knowledged her. Indeed she was, the ladies usually added, the best in all Massachusetts, and did not that mean all America, all the world? She was chosen to supervise everything about the milking and pressing; other ladies skilled at cheese were named to assist her. At once, Mistress Wells and her assistant ladies bethought themselves of the quality, as well as the quantity, of the curds to be brought in on pressing-day, July 20.

So much could happen to spoil the cheese, to sink it, or split it, joint it, to funk it with slip curds. Farmers must not drive their cows too far if the day came on hot: that would heat the milk too much in the udders. Or the milk could be agitated almost to churning if farm wives had to carry it long distances in their milking pails.

Mistress Wells wrote out everything she knew: careful instructions about that one day's milking. She sent her directions to everyone. In hope the curds might be reasonably uniform in size and consistency, she gave par-ticular instructions about "earning" or "rendling" the milk, about when to use the rennet (only after the milk had cooled a bit from the udders), about adding a pinch of salt and what that would do, or cold spring water, about how long to let the milk stand in "earning," how long after using the rennet the curd could be expected to "come." She described the delicate stage between "slip curds" and "solid curds": do not "gather" too soon, she warned. And farm wives must cover their buckets while bringing curds to Elisha Brown's orchard, to keep out flies, gnats, mites, all the small folk of summer.

Cheshire studied Mistress Wells's directions. This pressing would be tricky business.

Beyond the green hills, the rest of Massachusetts lay idle in summer doldrums and the gloom of Federalist defeat. News of unaccustomed excitement up in Cheshire crept over the mountains, down to Springfield, Stockbridge, Worcester, to Boston, down rivers to Rhode Island and Connecticut. Visitors from Federalist cities wandered up the Hoosick valley in summer dust to grin at the lively rustic revel—more and more visitors as the date for pressing drew near.

July 20, Cheshire Town made holiday. The morning came on hot and bright, the sun was still low in the east when families began to appear at Elisha Brown's cider mill. They arrived on foot, by horse, in wagon, in buckboard, in carriage and cart. Women proudly displayed their curds, delivered them to the long table under the apple trees where Mistress Wells and her assistant ladies stood waiting. The high rich smell of worked milk settled thickly over everyone; men prepared for their heavy labor; wives set shrilly to their tasks.

Hour after hour the moist curds were sorted, broken up by busy hands, thoroughly mixed, salted, seasoned with herbs and spices, then piled high on the table. They rose in white sticky mountains where green young apples hung down—massive heaps of dampness, more curds than ever seen before. Ladies reached higher than their heads to the tops of the piles. Men lined the huge hoop with cheesecloth. Everything was ready. Finally the ladies pushed the heaps of damp curds into measuring bins.

It was the last step before pressing. The whole crowd fell silent as Elder Leland rose to pray. Of John Leland, of the farm people, of the whole busy scene in the orchard, a Federalist visitor sneered:

Then Elder John, with lifted eyes,
  In musing posture stood,
Invoked a blessing from the skies,
To save from vermin, mites, and flies,
  And keep the bounty good.

Leland wound up his prayer in verse, the "lining-out" of a hymn. Everyone joined in. When the "amens" brought the orchard at last to silence, Mistress Wells gave the signal; Cheshire folk cheered, as women with arms bared and heads wrapped in white napkins seized wooden scoops, plunged them into bins, drew them out laden with curd and handed them up to the rim of the hoop, where men standing on a platform dumped the white pasty stuff into the big vat, and smacked it down with "beetles." High on the scaffold stood Mistress Wells, sharply inspecting every scoopful. She stood there for hours. She made certain the men packed all the curds tight, left no holes or air pockets, squeezed in each scoopful and beetled it down hard.

More and more families arrived, more and more produce was paddled into the machine. Finally it could hold no more. Even Mistress Wells was satisfied: curd rose in a smooth-paddled white rounded heap above the detachable rim. It made a bulging moist globe, glistening dead-white like a winter moon at midnight. But still the people came. Fourteen hundred pounds of solids had been beetled in, three hundred pounds were left over. One day's milking in Cheshire had yielded far more poundage than even the highest estimate had bargained for.

The hoop was full, the time for pressing had come. Skirts of cheesecloth were pulled tight over the hoop and its contents, the cheeseboard braced firmly beneath. Men clambered up to the big heavy beam of the cider press, grasped the crossbar, began to turn the enormous screw. The press creaked ponderously downward, wooden threads screamed. When the three-quarter-ton weight reached the vat, the top curds stood firm under pressure. The anxious crowd smiled. So far, so good.

Grunting, grasping, men leaned on the turnbar with every ounce of strength. Townsfolk watched the iron bands of the hoop straining outward, till iron could strain no more. They studied every rivet, every jointure. The huge globe flattened its bottom against the bending cheeseboard.

Then everyone cheered; for foaming whey suddenly bubbled over the brim, and a moment later began to ooze damply through the holes in the hoop. The press had done its job. Darius Brown's hoop had stood firm.

Elder Leland asked God's blessing again. He dedicated the cheese "to the honor and fame of Thomas Jefferson," he led the whole concourse of people in another hymn. All Cheshire and the horde of visitors ended the holiday with a community picnic under the apple trees, in full view of the cider mill and its sodden burden.

Eleven days, the Cheese remained in the press. Men sent in relays tightened the screw; every day townspeople trooped out to the orchard to see the wonder, check the oozing of the whey. Finally the moisture stopped. The Cheese, Mistress Wells pronounced, was tight and dry. Cheshire Republicans stared at it proudly. They were content. Its strong sweet smell clung to everyone's clothes, whey soaked the ground around the press, all manner of insects crawled in the sticky grass, rose in thick clouds to buzz among the spectators.

But Mistress Wells was far from through with her work, or her worries. The Cheese was too big to be turned, as ordinary cheeses had to be. The single pressing would have to do for it, and a long curing must follow. For the curing, Captain Daniel Brown offered his dairy barn. He was Farmer Brown's brother, father of the blacksmith Darius, proud to take part in this family affair. On the twelfth day, July 31, Cheshire gathered again, made a brave procession to move the Cheese a full mile to its new home.

The move was a difficult, risky feat. First, men released the turnbar and laboriously wound up the heavy screw, hoisting the massive weight to the top of the column. Next, iron bands were severed, the enormous hoop dismantled. Working swiftly against the heat, men pared the Cheese evenly all around, shaving off marks of the oaken boards and prints of the cheese-cloth, while Mistress Wells supervised. At last, Cheshire could behold its creation in full glory. Elder Leland took charge of the painting: he covered the entire surface smoothly, thickly with a bright red wax. And Leland chose the motto it would bear: "REBELLION TO TYRANTS IS OBEDIENCE TO GOD"— Jefferson's motto for the state of Virginia.

No wagon in Cheshire was safe for the weight of the Cheese, nor indeed could it travel on any wheeled vehicle, for bouncing and jolting could split it apart before it had firmed. The ingenious Darius Brown built a long low sled on runners, hitched six horses in pairs to draw it. Gingerly, straining and puffing, men inched the great sphere on its cheeseboard over to the sled. Their feet slipped on the whey-soaked grass, townsfolk trembled to watch. When it was safely on the flat-bed, Elder Leland lined out a hymn to the tune of "Mear":

> To Father, Son, and Holy Ghost,
>   The God whom we adore,
> Be Glory, as it was, is now,
>   And shall be ever more.

He exfloriated in fullsome prayer, while the hot sun beat down on the dripping wax. At last he was done; heads snapped up and the whole town paraded merrily with the Cheese to Captain Brown's dairy barn.

A Federalist from Stockbridge stood amazed to watch the "ludicrous procession, in honor of a cheesen God." What shocked him most was the spectacle of Elder Leland, "an Ambassador of God, running and puffing with a cased Flag to ornament and grace the idolatry." When the Cheese, sled and all, was safely installed in the cool dairy barn, the Wolcott brothers, Moses and Freelove, gave a great feast in their Cheshire Tavern next door with roasted whole lambs and last year's wine for everyone.

The Cheese settled down to its hidden inner mysteries of curing, the good folk of Cheshire patiently waited till it should ripen. They contrived a method for weighing it, on August 20. With pride, they learned they had fashioned a monster of 1,235 pounds. Of the curds left over, they had three additional undoubtedly Republican cheeses of seventy pounds each.

To Federalists, even as the huge cylinder lay there in Daniel Brown's cooling house, the Cheese became a hateful thing, a partisan issue, an object of ridicule. In consequence, it became famous—even before it began its journey to Washington. Leland was "Jacknips" to Federalist versifiers, Cheshire Republicans were "Jacobins," rural clowns. Jefferson, whom Federalists had already dubbed a usurper for his victory over Burr, they now attacked as a crude simpleton, a bumpkin fit to receive gifts of ripe cheese.

From Jefferson's own writings, the great Cheshire Cheese received its famous name. The doors had scarcely closed on Brown's dairy shed when a Federalist in the Northampton *Hampshire Gazette* wrote caustically of the huge globe, called it THE MAMMOTH CHEESE. He meant to be biting, to ridicule. But the name stuck; it came to be used with pride. All America knew of the discovery, far out west in Ohio country, of the bones of an enormous prehistoric beast of the elephant family, the *Mammoth*. Mr. Jefferson had written learnedly of these bones (along with Indian aborigines, Salt Licks, and the Natural Bridge) in his famous little book, *Notes on Virginia*. Anything Jefferson wrote was Republican property, fair game for Federalist sneers—even the Mammoth. Recently the busy artist Charles Willson Peale had excavated in the mountains of New York an entire skeleton of another huge prehistoric beast. He reconstructed it; the "Great American Incognitum," he called it. But others quickly dubbed it "the Mammoth." A new word entered the American language. The word originally had been Russian, *Mamanth,* the extinct Siberian elephant. Federalists took it over now as a term of derision. "THE MAMMOTH CHEESE" became a political cry.

In Philadelphia, a baker advertised "Mammoth bread" for sale, at which a Federalist newspaper chortled, "We suppose that his gigantic loaves were baked at *Salt Lick,* and perhaps may form a great rock bridge, or *natural* arch between the mouth and maw of a voracious republican." From a Connecticut village someone wrote, *"What are the Mammoth squashes, pumpkins, peaches, Ec. to the* MAMMOTH RADISH!" He described a scarlet radish grown in his village, three feet around and six feet long, weighing twenty pounds. In elaborate fantasies, Americans poured out their joyous enthusiasm for bigness, superlatives. "Mammoth" became more than a word, it became a symbol. Long before Leland reached Washington with his Cheese, President Jefferson was hailed in sour Federalist papers as "The *Mammoth* of Democracy."

Republicans were delighted. They contrived telling jibes of their own, laughed at the "Cheese Plot" which struck fear to Federalist hearts. "The

Cheshire Cheese has not yet been seriously represented to be in itself a violation of the Constitution," one Jeffersonian gleefully observed, "but presenting it to the President is thought to be inconsistent with the monopoly of a federal market." The "cheese plot" of the ladies of Cheshire, he added, was far more frightening to Federalists than the Whiskey Rebellion had been in their own administration.

Leland's plan had been to cure the big Cheese over winter, then send it down river in spring floods, by ocean, bay, and Potomac packet boat to Washington. But public excitement was too high to be sacrificed to a long winter's wait; Darius Brown's sled suggested a quicker method. Late in November, the snows came. Leland was ready; the time for the great journey was at hand. Horses were hitched up, The Mammoth Cheese started on its odyssey.

No one could figure out a way to letter the Jeffersonian motto on the red wax. This happy proposal, alas, had to be given up. Instead, the committee decided, they would tell Mr. Jefferson they had intended to stamp his words about the circumference, but so much had they suffered from President Adams's tax stamps on paper, that they had been obliged to refrain. They sent the Cheese in "plain Republican form" instead.

Fred Dunham, teamster of Cheshire, drove the sled with its precious burden lashed on the flat bed due west across icy mountain roads to the river landing called Hudson, New York. Here the Cheese was pried off its sled (where it had lain since July 31), transferred to the freeboard of a sloop, and sailed down river to New York City. At the Albany Wharf it was exhibited to the public on December 6. Elder Leland, meanwhile, with Darius Brown, had proceeded by stagecoach from Cheshire to New York City, stopping frequently to preach his Republican mission of democracy. "The Mammoth Preacher," he was called.

In New York City, so great were the crowds who flocked to the Albany Wharf, that a promoter offered a thousand dollars to keep the Mammoth Cheese for two weeks more and charge admission to view it. Elder Leland refused. Instead, he found the sloop *Astrea,* Captain Rogers, making ready for the Chesapeake Bay ports of Maryland. He and Darius hired men, loaded the Cheese on deck. Captain Rogers stood down the coast in a wintry breeze clear to the Capes of Virginia, then up the long reach of Chesapeake Bay— a two weeks' hard voyage in a coaster. On December 20 the *Astrea* reached Baltimore. Rogers tied up at Smith's wharf—Smith was a leading Republican in Baltimore, his relative Robert Smith already in the President's cabinet as Secretary of the Navy.

The whole Maryland city surged down to Smith's wharf to see the wonder. An English visitor followed the crowds with growing amazement. "The taverns were deserted," he wrote, "the gravy soup cooled on the table, and cats unrebuked revelled on the custards and cream. Even gray-bearded shop-keepers neglected their counters, and participated in the Mammoth infatua-tion." Elder Leland grinned cheerfully at the crowds. Every day when they were largest, he preached Republican sermons. Then he set about finding transport to Washington City.

There would be no difficulty, a Federalist remarked: the Mammoth Cheese was "strong" enough by now to *walk* the whole forty miles to the capital! Baltimore Republicans paid scant attention to partisan slurs. While Darius Brown rested over Christmas, and the Mammoth Preacher preached, enthusi-astic Marylanders provided four horses richly caparisoned, and decorated a wagon. Fred Dunham arrived overland from New York. He managed the eight reins expertly, Darius Brown rode in the wagon bed with the Cheese. Elder Leland sat proudly on the box, bowing and waving to everyone as he and his treasure were driven down the turnpike to Washington, December 29.

People cheered him, or jeered and hurled jibes. Goodnaturedly, he an-swered.

"Any skippers in your Cheese?" happy citizens called.

"Maybe a couple of Federalists got in!" he shouted back.

In Washington, he kept his great Cheese out of sight for two days, while he thoughtfully sent Jefferson a copy of the address of presentation he had written, that the President might have time to prepare a suitable answer.

Then, on New Year's Day in the Morning, 1802, beside Dunham on the box with Darius Brown at the tail gate and attended by a large cheering company a'foot and on horse, the Mammoth Preacher was driven with his Mammoth Cheese on its gaily painted wagon up to the front door of the White House.

President Jefferson rose at dawn, as usual. He spent the early hours of that New Year's Day writing private letters. The Mammoth Cheese was about to be presented, he wrote in one letter. "It is 4.f.4½ I. diameter, 15 I. thick, and weighed in August 1230 lb. . . . It is an ebullition of the passion of republicanism in a state where it has been under heavy persecution."

Cheering, shouting, the noisy crowd of Republicans could be heard far off as they came up the drive to the north portico. The President waited for them at the main door of the White House, chuckling at the specacle. In the midst of the throng high above the heads of cheering jokesters that odd original John Leland could be seen, grinning happily at everyone as the wagon threaded its way in the chill morning air among people in the yard. Finally it stopped directly before the President.

Elder Leland took his position in the wagon, standing alongside the huge red Cheese. In his bubbling bright noisy way, he delivered his speech in behalf of the town of Cheshire. He connected the Cheese to the Constitution, to free elections and free religion; he exhorted the President to "defend *Republicanism*, and baffle the arts of *Aristocracy*." And he presented the Cheese as the labor of "*Freeborn Farmers*, with the voluntary and cheerful aid of their wives and daughters, without the assistance of a single *slave*."

Jefferson accepted the present in a graceful speech. Of all citizens, he observed, farmers were the "most interesting, to the affections, the cares, and the happiness of men." And he said what pleased Leland above all: The Constitution's most precious provisions were "the right of suffrage, the prohibition of religious tests, and its means of peaceable amendment."

Many willing Republican hands helped the White House staff through the laborious job of unloading the Mammoth Cheese and trundling it into the mansion. President Jefferson himself directed its placement in the East Room. From noon on, every New Year's Day, inhabitants of Washington City customarily paid calls at the White House. This day the whole city trooped in. People found the President in merry countenance. He served cakes and wine, invited everyone to go into the East Room. "Walk into the Mammoth Room to see the Mammoth Cheese," the Mammoth President said.

It was in good shape for its age, one visitor wrote. The President was "highly diverted with the present curiosity." That day, and all the next, visitors from everywhere crowded in to see "the New England Mammoth."

But two days were enough. The President of a nation had matters to attend to; huge throngs pushing through his house made work impossible. Sunday, January 3, before a crowd of people shouting advice, the glistening crimson behemoth was removed from the East Room, wheeled out the stately front entrance, loaded again on the Cheese Wagon, paraded down the long muddy mile of Pennsylvania Avenue to the fine new Capitol building. President Jefferson himself followed after it, to a joint session of the two houses of Congress. It was his first attendance there since his inauguration. In the well of the House of Representatives, members beheld the shining giant Cheese; galleries were filled with ladies and gentlemen looking on. The Speaker of the House presented Elder Leland to the Congress, and the gay Sunday assemblage. His surroundings by no means awed John Leland or subdued him. He stared down at the Mammoth Cheese from the dais, he smiled back at the galleries, he grinned at the Congressmen. And with all the mammoth extravagance of his now well-known manner, the Mammoth Preacher began to preach.

He shouted, he whispered, he made jokes, he laughed at them heartily himself. He called for freedom of worship, he cried down aristocracy. His sermon was on his favorite theme, Thomas Jefferson; his text: "*And Behold! A greater than Solomon is here!*"

The President concealed his embarrassment, Federalists winced in pain, foreign diplomats, unused to hearing God addressed in this friendly, jolly fashion, scarcely knew whether to bow their heads in prayer, or clap their hands for a circus turn. Republicans for their part were delighted—delighted with Leland, delighted with the Mammoth Cheese there before them in the well of the House. For days afterwards, Republican papers were laden with tributes, celebrations, poetic effusions:

Most Excellent, far fam'd and far fetch'd CHEESE!
 Superior far in smell, taste, weight, and size
 To any ever form'd neath foreign skies,
And highly honour'd—thou were made to please
 The man belov'd by all—but stop a trice!
 Before He's praised—I too must have a slice.

On Monday, January 4, Leland called again at the White House, to say goodbye. Jefferson handed him two hundred dollars—why, he never said, and since Leland not once ever mentioned the money, no one else can surely explain. (It was not, incidentally, price-current for a cheese. At going rates per pound, the monster would have brought only $136.) Probably, in view of their acquaintance in past years, Jefferson wished to make a donation to Leland's Republican efforts in Massachusetts; and surely from long experience he knew the expense Elder John would be put to on his homeward journey.

That homeward journey was a triumph. The Mammoth Preacher stopped everywhere, carried his message of equality and enthusiasm to huge crowds who gathered, laughing, cheering, to hear him. His work for American freedom was just beginning. The Mammoth Cheese made Elder John Leland a national figure. To common people—artisans, farmers, mechanics, laborers in every village, county, and city—he took his warmth, his pride, gave them a sense of belonging, a sense new in America's political spirit.

While the Mammoth Preacher went cheerfully on his serene way with his adventures of life, the Mammoth Cheese in its red waxen splendor remained where he had put it, in the well of the House of Representatives chamber. It remained here, incredibly enough, day after day, week after week, into months and seasons, sessions and recesses, one year, another year, and on, and on. A curious fetid odor hung in the House Chamber, soon it spread through the whole capitol building, penetrated the whole American government. Clothes and draperies, and the very air the candles in chandeliers burned, smelled of the mouldering Cheese. Mrs. George Washington Parke Custis came in from Mount Vernon to see the noisome marvel. The fine new legislative chamber, Mrs. Custis had heard, with the Cheese in its center, looked like nothing so much as a great oven waiting for a Mammoth Apple Pie.

War in Europe, Napoleon's conquests, the Embargo, the Louisiana Purchase—one after another crises rose up and passed. In the press of great affairs, Republicans lost something of their original rude enthusiasm, and they grew accustomed to the musty, yeasty scent pervading the halls of Congress. Somehow, just the right occasion for cutting the Cheese never seemed to arrive. No one knew quite what to do with it. Attendants dusted it every day, clerks and pages stepped around it on their busy errands, visitors with kerchiefs pressed to their noses gazed solemnly on its deepening damp redness. Congressmen debated high matters of state in its insistent presence. It puffed up; by and by someone had the wit to cut sixty pounds out of the middle, where decay was the worst. Air in the House chamber for a while was noticeably fresher.

In 1804, another national election swept up the country in heady partisan excitements. Congressmen were preparing to adjourn to take the hustings, when the Baker General of the Navy surprised them. On the eve of adjournment he sent over to Capitol Hill a "Mammoth Loaf" of bread. It was to be eaten, he said, with the Mammoth Cheese for a feast on the final day's session.

A merry Cheese Party was held, the hardiest Republican members actually took slices from the huge three-year-old ball and made a brave show of eating them. It was a cheerful partisan picnic, but it made no more than a dent in the Mammoth Cheese. More was served at a Presidential reception in the House chamber, in 1805, after Jefferson's second election—served "with a hot punch," one guest recorded. The punch must have been hot indeed, and well fortified, to compete with the mouldering, maggoty monster.

Finally, some time after 1805, the remains of the Mammoth Cheese disappeared entirely. No one knows how: faint traces of a legend tell that during the recess of Congress the last of it was unceremoniously dumped into the Potomac—simply carted off down Jenkins' Hill and heaved in the river by Capitol workmen, who (not unreasonably) were heartily tired of having it around.

Whatever the manner of its end, that end was a mercy. Its symbolic mission had long since been accomplished. The Mammoth Cheese had dramatized, for all the people, their share in a free government. Federalist slogans, of rule by the rich and well-born, by merchant and professional classes, of vote by the owners of property, Federalist tenets of class and caste, were fading from political life. The Cheese had sped them on their way. The Presidency was the most eminent office in the land, it comprehended the nation's dignity and sovereignty; but still the Presidency was an office bestowed by the people themselves, the highest emanation of their political wills. Elder Leland, through his homely adventure, had demonstrated how even the Presidency, how freedom itself, in a free land belonged to every citizen, every man alike. Liberty was a birthright, not a privilege. To Elder John Leland, it was a birthright to be hymned in cheese.

9

The National Guest

Once Upon a Time—that is the proper beginning of a tale, and this is a tale from history—once upon a time, we Americans entertained a National Guest. And so abundant was the outpouring of our spirit on that occasion, so vivid, so romantic the event in the history of empires, that The National Guest is part of our national folklore. Even now, people retell the story, even now at each retelling there is someone with a fresh episode, a footnote, a tiny fact to garnish the tale a'new.

The time was many years ago, a troubled time, a sad time, Americans stood in sore need of inspiration. A sharp depression began in 1819; it plunged the nation into gloom. Foreign trade all but ceased, people were restless and hungry, the political party of old Mr. Jefferson had exploded into factions and fragments; uninhibited enthusiasts were trumpeting a Manifest Destiny, clamoring for Cuba, for Mexico, for Oregon, for uncharted lands in Western prairies and vast plains; slavery was an angry, acid issue that stretched the idea of union to the breaking-point. The vitality of the Revolutionary movement in America seemed spent, young literary figures were already turning from old-fashioned themes of the new free man in the new free state, to write of the beauties and orderliness of Nature, the decadence of cities and civilized life.

America in short was old, and tired, and in dismal case. The Missouri

Compromise of 1820—the Compromise . . . Once, people said, our leaders fought for the right, persisted till they won. Now, the rule is compromise, give in, trim, palter, till right itself erodes away . . .

Then came LaFayette.

Who it was who first thought of inviting LaFayette to come back to America, no one could ever remember. For once the idea was suggested it gripped the whole nation like a happy adventure, became everyone's idea. LaFayette was a European, but he belonged to America, and to liberty. As the 1820's brought the fiftieth anniversary of one Revolutionary event following hard upon the heels of another, invitations sped across the ocean from all the cities and states of the land, imploring the General to come and take part in the celebration.

Jefferson still lived, and old John Adams, and here and there other ancient relics of the famous congresses and assemblies of the Revolution. But they were civilian heroes, not military, and they were political figures. LaFayette, beloved friend of Washington, was above politics; and he was the only surviving Major General, the last of the great leaders of the Continental Armies.

The last? No! exclaimed a South Carolina newspaper. You have forgotten General Sumter, still living among us down here at the age of ninety. And a Wilmington paper proudly proclaimed Colonel Allen M'Lane of the famous Delaware Regiment was vigorous at eighty-one. Every state, every town suddenly rediscovered heroes of the Revolution, local symbols to vie with LaFayette for notice. But they were always colonels like M'Lane or like Sumter state militia officers. Only the famous French Republican was a genuine Federal character, a Continental officer. "One of our Fathers," the Choctaw Indians called him. All Americans felt the same way. LaFayette was the shining symbol of American Independence, and every discovery that historical enthusiasm produced served only to whet the people's appetite for one more glimpse of the glittering Frenchman.

LaFayette suddenly gave an unintentional fillip to American ardor for his visit. In December, 1823, President Monroe delivered his striking message to Congress, proclaiming his republican doctrine of the end of European colonizing in the Americas, the unity of all the New World in separation from the Old. British opinion casually claimed for British statesmen the credit for Monroe's vigorous policy, and European opinion generally was haughty, condescending. But LaFayette, leader of two revolutions himself, publicly hailed the Monroe Doctrine as "the best little bit of paper that God ever permitted any man to give to the world." It was "a manly message," he said. America was "the protecting genius of the rising republics of both Columbian continents" against the hellish Holy Alliance, and counter-revolutionary corruption in Europe.

LaFayette's bold words sent a thrill through America. The clamor for him to come back rose to a universal appeal; Jefferson hoped for his "restoration to those who love you more than any people on earth." LaFayette talked it over with Albert Gallatin, just then retiring as American Minister at Paris; finally he agreed he would accept an invitation if the Americans should send one. Gallatin brought the news with him when he came home, and in the spring of 1824 the invitation was dispatched—the most remarkable invitation ever offered to a private person by any government.

For Congress passed a resolution imploring LaFayette to accept the hospitality of the nation, and directing the President to send a naval vessel to bring him. President Monroe himself wrote a personal letter full of the affectionate words of an old friend, and proposed to send a fine new U.S. frigate as soon as LaFayette would make ready.

The frigate LaFayette declined. It would seem too ostentatious. But the invitation he accepted, and at once he was deluged with letters from American cities and towns requesting him to stop by. He answered them all, cheerfully promising to come—to New York, to Boston, to Philadelphia, to Charleston, everywhere. But unaccountably he delayed starting, month after month. No one knew why. Then one day he confided to a mercantile friend that he had debts amounting to a hundred thousand francs, which had to be paid before he dared leave the country. Since the death of his wife Adrienne—"the Angel who for thirty-four years has blessed my life"—his estate, LaGrange, belonged not to him but to his children. He had no right to mortgage it, and he had no other assets. His friend told the new American Minister, James Brown; promptly Brown joined with a visiting businessman from New Orleans, and a Dutch banker, to raise the money and make a loan to LaFayette that would pay his debts.

No obstacle now remained. LaFayette, though immensely popular with the French people, was out of favor with the Bourbon court of Louis XVIII; his title "Marquis" had long since been stripped from him, he had just been defeated for reelection to the National Assembly. His place in France seemed gone, his influence at an end. This was the ideal time for a trip. On July 12, 1824, with his son George Washington LaFayette, his secretary Levasseur, and Bastien his valet, he stepped on board the American merchant vessel *Cadmus* at Le Havre. Troops of King Louis brutally rode down the crowds that had gathered to cheer him. The scene of LaFayette's parting from France was made violent by the Bourbon tyranny he had so long opposed.

Forty-seven years before, when he first crossed the ocean as a youth of nineteen, Marie Joseph Paul Yves Roch Gilbert du Motier, Marquis de la Fayette, had found the long tiresome ocean voyage abominable. "We mutually sadden each other, the sea and I," he had written. But now, past sixty-six, he radiated health and good will. Nothing could tire him or bore him, nothing wear out his abundant energies. LaFayette was straight and vigorous, "of fine portly figure, about 5 feet 11 inches high." His long earneset face showed nary a wrinkle in its angular planes, his big dark eyes were clear. He limped, from a bad fall down the grand staircase at LaGrange several years before, but he was still graceful in his movements, alert and spirited. "LaFayette is the only person in France whose health, and opinions, are unchangeable," a vistor remarked.

America awaited the *Cadmus* with passionate interest. Newspapers filled columns, even pages, with accounts of LaFayette's campaigns in America and his life afterwards, his imprisonment at Olmütz by the Austrians, his long steady advocacy of republican liberty through Revolution, Terror, Napoleonic Empire and Bourbon reaction in France. They republished everywhere the acts of Maryland and Virginia which made him and his male heirs forever citizens of those states, and therefore of the United States. They recalled his youthful appearance, and his red hair never powdered. "How far the ravages of time may have encroached on those majestic features," one editor wrote, "we are left to conjecture." In advance, the best portrait painters were engaged to take likenesses of The National Guest, and effusions of verse and poetic anagrams on his name were in endless supply. Every major city expected him; it looked as if the General would have to spend years going to all the places he had promised.

The *Cadmus* had a quick passage of thirty-one days, and as she stood up past Staten Island toward New York harbor, huge crowds lined the shore, guns boomed from Fort LaFayette, small craft in great numbers sailed out with cheering people aboard, and a strange floating castle named *Nautilus*, belching black smoke, moved in the water alongside. The *Nautilus* was the first steamboat LaFayette had ever seen, and through the tears streaming down his face he studied her curiously.

On the steamboat was a young man named Tompkins, son of the Vice President, who informed the General that in spite of the enormous crowds, his reception in New York would be delayed until tomorrow, for this day was Sunday. To LaFayette, free-thinker and deist, the postponement seemed pointless, but he made no protest. He crossed to the formidable *Nautilus* and was landed on Staten Island where Vice President Tompkins received him at his farm home. Just after he landed a summer shower burst in fury on the city and Staten Island, but wonderfully the rain passed around Tompkins's farm, leaving LaFayette bathed in sunlight, and afterwards a glorious rainbow arched across the Narrows from Fort LaFayette to the Battery.

Next mornng at ten o'clock no less than six of the big awkward steamboats puffed over to Staten Island to convey the Marquis to New York. The vessels were dressed with gay flags and bunting, on the deck of each a band blared noisily and committees of busy citizens milled about. As the flotilla steamed up the Narrows, guns boomed from the forts, throngs waved and cheered, and the West Point band played "La Marseillaise," that French Revolutionary hymn which LaFayette had not heard in France since the Bourbon Restoration nine years before.

The Marquis—he was "Marquis" again in America—stood at the quarter rail with Vice President Tompkins, weeping as he embraced old friends. He received the committees, and recognized comrades-in-arms from the dim past. "Do you remember me?" palsied old men in their eighties would ask. "Do you know who I am?" Marvellously, LaFayette remembered. He knew them, and they were enchanted. He bubbled with talk through his tears, he waved to the shore, and to the hundreds of small craft darting about in the fresh breeze.

Thirty, forty, fifty thousand people, nobody knew for sure how many, gathered on the streets and rooftops of New York that August day. LaFayette still did not realize what was coming. He gazed at the multitudes with misgivings. Shall I be able to get a hack to a hotel? he asked on board the steam frigate. His hosts only laughed. At the Battery landing, three thousand troops were drawn up, headed by the "Guards of LaFayette," each man wearing a portrait of the Marquis on his breast, and over his shoulder a silk bandolier labeled "Welcome LaFayette." A carpet stretched from the wharf clear through to the courtyard of Battery Castle, where LaFayette took refreshment at tables laid in the open air. Then, with the reception committee, the Marquis reviewed the troops. He was still, after all, Major General LaFayette, senior commissioned officer in the United States Army.

Limping on his cane, in simple nankeen trousers and a plain blue coat, his hair no longer red but a blonde wig now, the old man walked slowly down the lines of soldiers. The enormous crowds looked upon a legend. In American minds, LaFayette had always remained the boy of nineteen, the heroic youth who gave up his ease, spent his whole fortune to cross the sea and fight for liberty; the support, almost the son of Washington; the spirited leader of Yorktown; the gallant lad wounded at the Brandywine. This lame old man was a grotesque travesty of youth and brilliance. Nothing about him suggested the slim, vital hero, the glittering romance. But as LaFayette turned his face toward the crowd, as he smiled through his tears and bowed, the people cheered and wept, too, and took the old man to their hearts. "He limps from his wound at Brandywine," they said—and the story went through the whole country. LaFayette would never be able to convince Americans that he had merely fallen down stairs.

The General entered an open barouche drawn by four gray horses, and at the head of a long cavalcade drove through the thronging streets the slow mile to City Hall. People hung from windows and railings, from casements and chimneys and dormers and roofs for a glimpse of the hero. LaFayette suddenly realized what it was going to mean to be The National Guest. He bowed and smiled, he managed more tears; at City Hall he shook hands for two hours with hundreds of people in a great press.

There were speeches, a banquet, toasts; cannon roared; in the evening an "illumination," fireworks, elaborate decorations on all the public buildings, huge paintings of LaFayette and Washington on long paper strips with lanterns burning behind them—"transparencies" they were called. From Castle Garden a balloon representing a knight in armor on a spirited steed rose to the heavens, and New Yorkers danced in the streets.

Late that evening LaFayette disappeared. He stole away from all the noise and speeches to call on the widow and son of that other vivid youth of the Brandywine battle, his friend in adventure and arms, Alexander Hamilton. New Yorkers learned of the visit, and loved him all the more.

Four days the banquets, fêtes, entertainments, receptions, speechmakings went on. Old veterans turned up every hour, demanding "do you remember?" Samuel F. B. Morse (who in after years would invent the telegraph) painted a noble portrait which the City Council had commissioned. LaFayette was given little rest and less privacy. It was an ordeal, but he stood it marvellously, seemed genuinely to enjoy every moment, was always ready with a brief speech, a quick accurate memory, and the affecting tears of joy which he could produce at will. Then he departed for Boston.

George, Levasseur, and Bastien were not sorry to go, for Miss Fanny Wright had turned up in New York. Miss Fanny Wright was that most formidable of females, an English modernist reformer. A year or so before, she had visited LaGrange, upset the entire household there, and while it is *unlikely* her relationship with LaFayette had ever advanced beyond the stage of republican friendship, it was painfully evident that Miss Fanny Wright was *prepared* to offer much more. She was, indeed, appallingly amiable. LaFayette was not unaccustomed to receiving the attentions of earnest females, who fell into the emancipated error of believing that an abundance of intellectual energy was one of the aspects of feminine charm. He handled such problems with a casual tolerance; he was incapable of unkindness. Miss Fanny Wright installed herself hopefully in his life, even planned to cross the ocean with him. In this, fortunately, she was forestalled. She came by an earlier passage, began in America her endles speeches and writings. She was, wrote Philip Hone, a "female Tom Paine." And to face it squarely, she was boredom in British bombazine. Happily, if the Marquis would not send her packing, the valet Bastien could. It was pointed out to Miss Fanny Wright that Americans had as yet by no means accepted her easy view of the relations appropriate between the sexes, that her unconcealable presence in LaFayette's entourage would be an offense to every proper citizen, and a serious embarrassment to the National Guest. Miss Fanny Wright accepted her dismal defeat. She set out Westward with Robert Owen instead, to add her energies and talents to his founding of the ideal community, New Harmony, Indiana, and as La-Fayette turned Northward for Boston he could sigh with true Gallic gratitude that he was delivered at last from his determined British adorer.

His trip was a triumphal progression. In a city carriage, escorted by the Mayor and aldermen, by the LaFayette Guards and the Horse Artillery, accompanied by hundreds of citizens on horseback, he proceeded up the Post Road. Every hamlet turned out to see him. At New Rochelle he shook hands with a host of waiting citizens. "Do you remember, General, who began the attack at Brandywine?" LaFayette remembered: Maxwell's Jersey brigade. He had not known it forty-seven years before, an inexperienced youth seeing his first battle, still unable to understand English. He had read it in later times. But his answer was right. "I was *with* Maxwell!" cried the old veteran. At the state border Connecticut troops took over, and a ceremony was held under a triumphal arch. "Sir, America loves you!" said the speaker. "And Sir," LaFayette answered, "I truly love America."

Town after town delayed his progress. At night he left his open barouche and tried to sleep in a closed carriage as the cavalcade plodded along. But even in the darkness crowds huzzahed and militia boomed salutes. LaFayette appeared: people had waited all day and late into the night to see him; he would not disappoint a single American. He was The National Guest, with ten million citizen-hosts.

For a few hours after midnight the big caravan rested at Bridgeport, but by dawn Revolutionary veterans and ordinary citizens were clamoring to look on LaFayette, shake his hand and test his memory. At New Haven the governor met him. There were more troops to review, more speeches, more artillery salutes, more veterans. LaFayette wept and smiled; he recognized and called Colonel Talmadge by name before he was presented, even though forty-four years had separated them. George, Levasseur, and Bastien were exhausted, but the happy Marquis showed no fatigue. He noticed everything, he relished each episode. Not a person worked along his route in New England those late summer days. The coachman at one change of teams said to his horse, "Behave pretty now, Charley, behave pretty! You are going to carry the greatest man in the world."

By torchlight at night, through gay crowds by day, the long slow train of carriages moved on toward Boston. At two o'clock one night they reached Roxbury, where a shower of rockets split the dark heavens and Governor Eustis, attended by a host of militia and citizens each with a torch, escorted the Marquis to his home nearby. Two hours he slept; then as the sun rose guns boomed and bands played, and The National Guest looked out to see his old Light Infantry Fusiliers drawn up on the lawn—The Marquis's Own, with the uniform, even to the red and black plumes, which he himself had designed. He woke his son George and Levasseur. "My brave Light Infantry! Exactly like that were they uniformed! What courage! What willingness! And how I loved them!" The Marquis ate an enormous breakfast and set jauntily on his way at the head of his Fusiliers.

Boston was New York all over again—indeed, even more, for Boston had a special claim on The National Guest. It was a Boston merchant, Thomas Perkins, who had conveyed George Washington LaFayette to America while his father lay imprisoned in Olmütz, cared for the boy as he came of age here in this city. Her son thus in safe hands, the lady Adrienne had thought herself free to take her two daughters, make the sad journey to Austria, join LaFayette in his grim barren cell for the years of his torment. Perkins's kindness LaFayette had never forgotten. Adrienne's coming to Olmütz, he had written long ago, "probably safed my life." Boston to him was the symbol of qualities generous, unselfish, everything compassionate in America's nature.

All the bells pealed, every gun boomed, through packed narrow streets the cavalcade inched forward under huge decorated arches on nearly every corner. Three thousand school children dressed all alike waited on the Common; and here at Boston began LaFayette's trouble with wreaths. From now on, everyone seemed to want to press a wreath of laurel or entwined blossoms on his head—and a wreath is a sore trial to a man who wears a wig. The Marquis learned to ward them off, receiving them graciously in his hand.

Boston's celebration lasted five days. He called on former president John Adams, who had long been part of his life in America and France. Adams was eighty-nine now, and hideously frail; but that wit still sharp and mind still alert were reminders of a greatness that once had been. The Marquis sat in John Hancock's pew in Brattle Street Meeting House; he joined in target practice with a Guards company and before an enormous throng shot perfectly, shattering the target. He attended every function—morning, afternoon, dinner, and night—he handled huge crowds with engaging candor and obvious delight. "How well he speaks English!" someone exclaimed. "And why should I not," LaFayette answered, "being an American just returned from a long visit to Europe?"

From Boston he went up the coast through arches and crowds and parades and militia reviews into New Hampshire. He slept briefly in a bed which Washington had slept in, he received thousands of people, he travelled by night; suddenly he was back in Boston. He breakfasted, he held another reception, then he set out again through Cambridge and Lexington and Concord (young Oliver Wendell Holmes saw him, and young Ralph Waldo Emerson); with relays of horses he galloped his barouche to make his schedule now to Worcester and Hartford, then by steamboat down the Connecticut

River bound for New York. The National Guest was finally so tired that he fell asleep on board the steamboat, even while cannon on the bank thundered salutes and a band on the deck over his very head blared forth its sprightly airs.

A little sleep restored the General. This was a campaign he was making, a compaign of refreshment for himself, for Washington's memory, for liberty in America and everywhere. He would meet all its rigors cheerfully, with no stinting. September 6 the side-wheeler reached New York. It was LaFayette's birthday, his sixth-seventh. A great crowd met him at Fulton's Ferry, followed his carriage to the City Hotel. That night a birthday banquet was held in Washington Hall, and for two weeks more the city, with seemingly inexhaustible resources and obviously unquenchable delight, celebrated his presence. Then New York staged a last great party in Castle Garden, "the most magnificent fête ever given under cover in the world," a newspaper happily proclaimed. At two in the morning The National Guest boarded a steamer for Albany. Everyone who could crowded aboard, far more than safe. No one slept; at Tarrytown the overloaded steamer went aground. LaFayette stood at the rail during the ticklish operation of getting her off, and told George how high on these very banks many years before he had gone with Washington to take breakfast at Mrs. Benedict Arnold's, and discovered the most odious treason of modern times.

Up and down the Hudson he went, attended by an enormous throng; then through Jersey where he called on Joseph Bonaparte, Napoleon's brother; finally to Philadelphia, scene of so many of his memories. Here was the most extravagant fête of all. His guards were liveried in the old buff and blue of the Continental Army; 15,000 thousand mounted men rode after him, and after them a great procession of 150 groups drawn from every profession and trade in the city—apothecaries to weavers—each with its float and banners, all testifying to the growth and prosperity of this New World Republic LaFayette had helped to make free.

The talents of the artist Sully, the sculptor Rush, the architects Strickland and Haviland, had produced mighty arches and brilliant transparencies. Sully took a portrait, which would hang forever in Independence Hall; and to that place, old Andrew Hamilton's State House now suddenly held in higher reverence, thousands crowded every day to shake hands with The National Guest. All the hours he could stay awake he was pressed upon by people. Every house, every shop was decorated; illuminations beamed in every window. America had never seen such a display. One citizen, writing over the signature "A Presbyterian," objected in the papers. "Let our joy be moderate, and it will last the longer," he enjoined. The Marquis was shown to every Revolutionary veteran for many miles around, he was received by every organization and taken on tour of every public institution. In the midst of the ceaseless bedlam he learned, in that surprising way he had of quiet conversation in the noise of a crowd, that Hannah Till, the freed colored woman who had cooked for him and for Washington, was still living, now over a hundred years old. He made Chief Justice Tilghman and the banker Nicholas Biddle take him to her dismal hovel. When he learned that "Aunt Hannah's" home was mortgaged, he arranged to have it paid off.

Philadelphia occupied him for a week. The National Guest was beginning to wonder when it would all be over, when the excitement would die down. There was no sign of it yet: Wilmington, New Castle, Baltimore all received him, and by now freight vans were needed for the gifts people had pressed upon him. At Fort McHenry the Baltimore committee had set up Washington's old headquarters tent for LaFayette, and gathered much of the old camp equipment under it. The whole company wept as LaFayette went from trunk to writing desk, from piece to piece of Washington's command camp sobbing, "I remember! I remember!" Five days Baltimore kept him; then he drove to Washington City—the federal capital he had never seen.

At the White House President Monroe and the cabinet received him. They were plainly dressed, as if they were but ordinary citizens. George and Levasseur were astonished, but the Marquis was pleased. "You see?" he demanded of his son. Eliza Monroe, who had contrived so much to save him from the guillotine in the Terror long ago, was sunk in a sad illness, confined to her room upstairs, but James Monroe was still the warm-hearted, enthusiastic, eruptive friend of old. He had wanted him to stay at the White House, he told LaFayette, but the people would not have it. No one person, not even the President, could be host to The Nation's Guest. The city had prepared a suite for him at Gadsby's Hotel. But, Monroe added, your plate will always be laid at my table whether you come or not. And always, it was.

At Gadsby's, LaFayette was quartered near General Andrew Jackson, and the two old soldiers became fast friends. Curiously, a friend of longer standing, John Quincy Adams, was locked in a political duel with Andrew Jackson in the Presidential election going on. Enthusiasts tried to draw LaFayette into the party struggle. With supreme tact he eluded them, and remained impartial. It took constant watchfulness. At Washington also he was snubbed by the French Minister, who used the pale excuse that news had just come of the death of Louis XVIII. LaFayette made no mourning as Louis gave way to Charles on the Bourbon throne, and he paid no heed to the Minister's slight. But Americans resented the calculated affront; and with loathing they learned that no French paper was permitted to give any news, even to mention LaFayette's visit to America. British papers were full of sneers at the whole affair, which they described as "effusions of democratic twaddling." One London paper snorted, "What demigods revolutionists think each other!" But soon the British editors changed their tone. Even the England of George

IV could be impressed by the abundant, extravagant spectacle in America. We have, said the Edinburgh *Observer,* "like all mankind, been struck mute as it were, by each successive gushing out of the contagious and unpurchased homage of ten millions of free people."

As soon as he properly could, LaFayette went down the Potomac by steamer to Mount Vernon. Cannon boomed in slow measure, bands played a dirge as he set out. In Alexandria he broke his river trip to greet a great crowd. This was Washington's county town; a mighty triple arch, its center span sixty-eight feet wide, soared over the broad main thoroughfare, rechristened Washington Street. A live bald eagle chained atop the lofty center arch spread its wings exactly on cue as The National Guest passed beneath. Here in Alexandria lived Mrs. Henry Lee, impoverished widow of Washington's cavalryman "Light Horse Harry" Lee, LaFayette's brilliant companion in the Virginia campaign. The National Guest rode through the throng to her modest house, spent precious moments in her parlor. Mrs. Lee presented to him her youngest son, Robert E. Lee, a youth of eighteen just now appointed to be a cadet at West Point.

Music accompanied him back to his steamer, somber stately hymns, and the people with him murmured quietly on deck as the craft moved down the broad Potomac to Washington's landing. Here at Mount Vernon, where he had bade his last farewells to his "beloved General" in 1784, LaFayette on this October Sunday in 1824 went alone into the tomb and knelt a long while at Washington's sarcophagus. For the childless Washington, the fatherless LaFayette, the tender bond between them had been a warm and wonderful outpouring of affection. LaFayette kneeling at Washington's tomb was the last testament of love, and in the pathetic scene the whole American nation renewed its faith in its origins.

George Washington Parke Custis gave a well-meaning but tiresome, ornate, and decorated speech, and he pressed upon LaFayette a ring with a lock of Washington's hair in it. LaFayette could scarcely answer. "I pay a silent homage to the tomb of the greatest and best of men," he stammered, "to my paternal friend."

From Mount Vernon the Marquis proceeded to Yorktown. And here, more than anywhere else in America, the past came alive, for the village of Yorktown, forty-three years after the battle, was still in ruins, still as the armies had left it following that autumn day when the British regiments had marched out and stacked arms as the bands played "The World Turned Upside Down." Yorktown had been *his* campaign, *his* achievement, severest test of his skill in command; victory had been *his* victory, a Major General proved at twenty-four. Now the day was October 19, anniversary of the surrender. Virginia's governor, Secretary of War John C. Calhoun, and Chief Justice John Marshall received LaFayette; all about, American troops were encamped as if they had but that day taken the village. Washington's headquarters tent had been brought down and erected on the very spot where it had stood during the last days of the seige; and that irrepressible ancient Colonel M'Lane of the Delaware Regiment seized a tall cornstalk, clambered up on a crumbling parapet, and merrily challenged everyone who passed with the passwords of forty-three years ago.

LaFayette was installed in Governor Nelson's ruined house, which had been Cornwallis's headquarters. A great banquet was held, LaFayette adroitly caught another wreath just as it was descending amid oratory onto his head; candles on the tables were, wonderfully, some which Cornwallis had left in the house forty-three years before, and which had just that morning been found amid the rubble in the basement.

Richmond was next; Edgar Allan Poe saw him there. Then Monticello— where one cold November morning, escorted by four hundred troops and followed by the usual enormous crowd, The National Guest was driven up the winding mountain road to the stately entrance of the mansion. Everyone stood back silently as the Marquis stepped from his carriage and began limping on his cane toward the white portico. Faster and faster he went, hopping, almost running, his eyes on the bent, gaunt figure of Jefferson waiting between the tall columns. Suddenly the venerable apparition tottered down the steps, and in a shuffling gait, his arms spread wide and thin strands of white hair blowing in the wind, ran as an old man could run to meet his friend of so many years. "As Jefferson!" cried LaFayette. "LaFayette," whispered Jefferson. They fell into an embrace, and the huge company was still as the murmuring patriots supporting each other disappeared into the mansion.

For a week, LaFayette stayed at Monticello; then four days with Madison at Montpelier, where the little statesman at seventy-three was bright, and the famous Dolley, only fifty-seven, was charming. The Virginia interlude was more joy and peace than one man might hope for in a single lifetime.

Back at Washington City, LaFayette was ready to rest. Indeed, he was ready to go home. Two months of energetic American hospitality was enough, ten weeks of celebrations and speeches and wreaths, ten weeks of being The National Guest. But America was just beginning. His friends demanded he stay till Congress meet, and at Gadsby's was a trunkful of invitations to visit other cities—the South, the West. LaFayette had no choice. As long as he was a symbol of liberty, he would stay.

A man of wit and humor, which LaFayette was not, a man of imagination, would have called an end. But LaFayette was governed by his emotions, not his intellect. As the years had multiplied, he had become more and more a mirror of his "paternal friend," a second Washington in type. Like his beloved General, he took his ideas from others, and preserved all the strict conventions of his earliest beliefs. He was not a man of original or creative mind, he was a man of character—pure, generous, and innocent in heart, inflexible as Washington in his steady though limited purposes, resolute, and physically strong. He had to be.

On Friday, December 10, two thousand people crowded into the House of Representatives to see Congress receive him. "General," cried the Speaker, Henry Clay, at the peroration of a ringing address, "You are in the midst of posterity!" LaFayette responded in simple words of gratitude. Not for himself, but for all Revolutionary veterans, for all fighters everywhere in Liberty's cause, he accepted America's honors. And he finished, "No, Mr. Speaker. Posterity has not yet begun for me—since in the sons of my companions and friends I find the same public feelings which I had the happiness to experience in their fathers."

When he withdrew, Congress considered his poverty, and recalled the immense personal fortune he had spent for American freedom. Cheerfully the Senators and Representatives voted him a princely gift, in partial repayment: they presented him with two hundred thousand dollars of cash, and a whole township of public lands. Immediately, The National Guest began planning how to spend the bounty: $2,000 to French refugees in England, $400 to other refugees from political tyranny, Spaniards and Italians in London, something to Frenchmen in America, something to relieve the poverty of Revolutionary veterans, a part to pay his own obligations, part to free an old American militia general from debtor's prison in Vermont.

On New Year's Day, 1825, Congress tendered him a state banquet at Williamson's Hotel. Even Monroe came; it was the first time in history a President had dined officially outside the executive mansion. Then late in February, LaFayette commenced his great journey—to the South and West, and all around the new country which had not even been America in Revolutionary times, a journey of five thousand miles by a carriage Mrs. George Washington Parke Custis had presented him, and by horse and steamboat through the wilderness of a continent. He planned an unbelievable itinerary, and he made a schedule, for he was to end his great circle tour in Boston on Bunker Hill Day, June 17. No American thought it could be done.

First South to Fayetteville in North Carolina, the port city named for him. Then through swamps and marshes to the spot on South Carolina's coast where in June, 1777, he had first set foot on American soil, and spent his first few days in Major Huger's house; then West through the pine lands and mountains—Dragooons sounded their bugles all the night long to guide the procession, and a chorus of girls singing hymns and strewing flowers conducted them into Camden, where LaFayette laid the gravestone of Baron DeKalb, the effervescent old German who had crossed the ocean with him in '77, and who had bled to death here on the field of Camden in 1780.

To Columbia where both the Pinckneys met him, and young Huger who had tried to rescue him from Olmütz; then with Huger to the Izards' and Charleston's three-day fête in the rain; on South by steamboat to Beaufort and Savannah and Georgia's celebration; afterwards overland by a wretched wilderness trail, so bad that LaFayette was attacked with vomiting and a fainting illness, through the Creek Indian country of Alabama. For the moment, America lost sight of her National Guest. Then he emerged at Montgomery, telling of Indian ball games and wild yelling dances. One member of Governor Pickens's reception committee tumbled into a well as he listened. Down the Alabama River by steamer to Mobile; from Mobile the whole party, its freight vans and Mrs. Custis's carriage were loaded on the steamer *Natchez,* to go by sea to New Orleans. For the French Republican, this still French-speaking city staged its greatest carnival. The *Cabildo,* or city hall, was his palatial residence. LaFayette responded with his simple charm and gratitude, but he made his hosts uneasy when he insisted on receiving a delegation of Negroes who had fought with Jackson in 1814, and he refused to look upon the spectacle of human slavery.

From New Orleans the travellers, a party of two dozen now, began the long voyage up the Mississippi, with frequent stops and frequent celebrations, and the kind of gifts frontiersmen could give—animals and skins, wild birds, fossil bones of the prairies—all of which would be enshrined in the second-floor library room at LaGrange. Missouri and Illinois received LaFayette, St. Louis and Kaskaskia, newest and oldest settlements of the wild interior; then the steamboat paddled up the Cumberland to Nashville, where Andrew Jackson waited on the wharf. The Hero of New Orleans showed to the Hero of Two Worlds a brace of pistols. Do you recognize these? he asked. "Yes," LaFayette answered. "They are the ones I gave to General Washington in 1778. And am satisfied to find them in the hands of a man so worthy of such a heritage."

Steaming up the Ohio late one night, the vessel suddenly shuddered with a mighty blow, and a great tearing of wood. A snag had caught her bows, and rapidly she began to sink. LaFayette dressed serenely. At the last moment he limped back to his cabin to seize the snuff box he always carried; it bore a miniature portrait of Washington on it. He was lifted into a lifeboat and rowed to the Kentucky shore. In the darkness, rescue operations proceeded. The row boat plied back and forth; finally everyone had been landed but George Washington LaFayette. The National Guest, weeping genuine tears of alarm now, stumped up and down the muddy shore peering into the darkness, crying *"George! George!"* The row boat made a last trip to the foundered steamer, finally returned with the missing passenger, soaked but alive.

All the fifty people were saved, but morning presented a bizarre spectacle. Governor Carroll of Tennessee was barefoot and had lost his wig, everyone was in outlandish dress; Mrs. Custis's carriage was gone. But LaFayette was positively gay at the thought that six hundred unanswered letters had sunk to the bottom of The Beautiful River.

Two steamers hove in sight before noon and rescued the stranded travellers. They proceeded to Louisville, crossed to Indiana and back again, then inland to Lexington and Frankford. Fêtes and banquets waited them everywhere, and national figures—General Harrison, "Old Tippecanoe," was their host at Cincinnati. The party disembarked finally at Wheeling, journeyed over-land through Uniontown into the mountains of Pennsylvania where Albert Gallatin lived at his seat "Friendship Hill," and where he presided at a stupendous forest meeting. Northward from Gallatin's through Pittsburgh to Erie and a banquet in a tent made of sails from the ships Commodore Perry had captured; then through town after town of New York State, day and night, with crowds everywhere who had patiently waited long hours for The National Guest. At Buffalo, old Red Jacket, Chief of the Senecas, greeted him; here was a true enemy, who had fought savagely with the British in the Revolutionary War. But Red Jacket showed him a fine silver medal Washington had conferred upon him in '92, told of his friendship for the Great White Father of them all.

Of course LaFayette was conducted to Niagara Falls; and his journey Eastward was over the finished parts of the Erie Barge Canal, scheduled to be opened in a few months as one of the new wonders of America. The canal trip was broken by receptions, speeches, processions. Once, as the barge passed under a bridge, a young Indian, naked to the waist, dropped down to the deck and demanded of the startled company, "Where is Kayewla?" LaFayette, hearing the name the Oneidas had given him back in '78, went forward. "I am Kayewla," he said. "I am the son of Ouekchekaeta," the young brave announced—Ouekchekaeta, Chief of the Oneida Long House, who had returned to LaGrange with the Marquis so long ago, and had travelled through France as the noble savage come to life. Kayewla talked for two hours with the warrior, gave him a handful of silver dollars; then the young Indian leapt ashore as nimbly and abruptly as he had arrived.

At Waterloo a cannon burst while firing a salute to The National Guest, and killed the militia captain manning it. LaFayette learned the widow was in desperate poverty; secretly he sent a cheque for a thousand dollars for her relief.

From Albany without a stop LaFayette's carriage galloped eastward two hundred miles through the Berkshires to Boston again, where he arrived just in time for his appointment. The hardy old campaigner had covered his wild-erness trail of 5,000 miles through fifteen states in one hundred days. He himself had become an American wonder. He was the only news story that whole spring, the only national issue. So absorbed in his progress were all readers that one editor, lacking any real story while LaFayette was in the

Alabama Indian country, invented a fictitious reception at Caracas and wrote in elaborate detail of a mythical visit the General had made to see Bolivar in Venezuela and present to him the ring with the lock of Washington's hair.

Reality was more colorful than any journalist's hoax. June 17, 1825, was the fiftieth anniversary of the Battle of Bunker Hill, and to the scene of the fighting all of Boston, all New England had come. Forty survivors of the Battle were carried first up the hill; then limped LaFayette; then seven thousand men marched in column while a great multitude stood chanting the spare Puritan melody of the "Old Hundred:"

> For why, the Lord our God is Good,
> His mercy is forever sure,
> His truth at all times firmly stood
> And shall from age to age endure . . .

Daniel Webster delivered his noble oration, his sonorous periods rolling down the hill and over the upturned faces. He ended with an apostrophe to The National Guest: "Heaven saw fit to ordain, that the electric spark of liberty should be conducted, through you, from the New World to the Old . . ." LaFayette laid the cornerstone of the new monument. And that night at the Jubilee Dinner he gave a toast: *"Bunker Hill*—and the holy resistance to oppression which has already enfranchised the American hemisphere: the next half-century Jubilee's toast shall be, *to Enfranchised Europe!"*

Once more he visited old John Adams at Quincy; quickly he made a circle through Maine and Vermont where people demanded him. That meant he had visited every one of the twenty-four states, had seen and been seen by more Americans than anyone in all history. On his way back he stopped at Brooklyn to dedicate a library for apprentices. Briefly he lifted a six-year-old boy in his arms, kissed him, and went on. The boy was Walt Whitman.

New York again, and West Point where Cadet Robert E. Lee saw him once more, and Philadelphia, and the Germantown battle ground, and Brandywine field, and Lancaster and Wilmington to see Mr. DuPont, son of his old friend, and Baltimore and Washington, and finally the sadness of farewell. John Quincy Adams was the new President. He took LaFayette into the White House for a few days' rest, until a fine new naval frigate was commissioned. The frigate was christened *Brandywine*—"the name of a brook instead of a river, of a defeat instead of a victory," LaFayette wrote, moved even by this last gesture, "solely to recall my first battle and my wound."

Once more to Monticello, where LaFayette, Jefferson, Madison and Monroe all joined in a last reunion of the elder statesmen of republicanism; then he spent his sixty-eighth birthday at the White House where Adams broke the tradition that the President should never propose a toast—and proposed *The*

National Guest. The next day the whole city turned out, silent and sad, the cabinet stood by with bowed heads, and President Adams in the rotunda of the White House wept as he delivered an eloquent farewell speech. LaFayette read his answer; at the end he looked up from his manuscript for his last words. "God bless you, Sir," he said to Quincy Adams, "and all who surround us. God bless the American people, each of their states, and the Federal Government. Accept this patriotic farewell of an overflowing heart; such will be its last throb when it ceases to beat."

The little President, usually so austere and reserved, dissolved entirely. He opened his arms, and LaFayette embraced him. *"Adieu! Adieu!"* wept the American President. "Good-bye, good-bye!" sobbed the French Republican. As LaFayette was conducted to his carriage, Quincy Adams turned and disappeared inside the White House. He hurried up the great staircase, and on up the small stairs to the third floor, and through a trap door up a ladder and out onto the parapet, where no President had ever been seen before, and certainly none has even been since. Below him, cannon roared in a twenty-four gun salute, flags were dipped everywhere in honor, and LaFayette was driven off to board the *Brandywine.* The Marquis turned for his final sight in Washington: the sight of his friend the President, another in that long succession of his friends who had been and would be Presidents of the American Republic. John Quincy Adams, quite out of breath, stood all alone atop the high peristyle of the White House, waving his handkerchief, waving until the carriage disappeared from view.

For LaFayette, his year in America had been a return to glory. For the whole people who loved him, fêted him, celebrated his visit and paid him such tribute as a free people could, his coming had been a renewal of liberty, a quickening of the spirit which he and Washington together had symbolized, and on which the nation itself had been founded.

No one man had ever given America more. To no one man had America ever had such opportunity to show the fullness of its gratitude. We had begun to believe in America that we enjoyed our country and our freedom, "by right of *possession,*" a Philadelphia editor wrote. But LaFayette's visit had reminded us that freedom is never won save by the sacrifices and exertions of *men,* that no nation is ever built at less than the highest price.

February 11-23, 1861

10

Twelve Days to Destiny

The President of The United States was a pitiful old man. He was seventy. "I at least meant well for my country," he told Congress. The remark was an embarrassing whimper. "Buchanan has a winning way of making himself hateful," someone said. To the cartoonist of *Harper's Weekly,* the ineffectual old President in the White House was America's great iceberg, slowly melting away.

The Secretary of State was a trembling old man. He was seventy-nine. Fifty-six years he had held public office, a fixture on the national scene. Every American knew the stern lines of his face from copperplate engravings, knew his sharp tongue from the hustings. He was contentious, outspoken, sturdy, a forthright blunt man of virtue, of undoubted courage. Now he trembled. "I am frightened, sir," Secretary Lewis Cass confessed. "I am frightened . . ." Abruptly as 1860 drew to a close he handed the President his resignation, finally left public life forever.

The senator from Kentucky was a desperate old man. He was seventy-four. Once, he had twinkled when he talked, delighted the pretty young ladies around him. "My first marriage was for love," he would say, "my second for money, my third for position. What more could I ask?" Now, old Senator Crittenden was somber. He sought other old men, sought out that witty ancient John Tyler of Virginia, President twenty years ago, six presidents back. On Tyler, on everyone who would listen, he urged his compromise

284

plan, any compromise plan. With tears in his eyes he told young ladies now of his two sons divided—Tom for Union and the Constitution, George for the South, for secession.

The Commanding General of the Army was an angry old man. He was seventy-five. He asked the President for guns and troops to man the nine federal forts in the South. Buchanan refused: all but two of the forts were soon gone. "Old-Fuss-and-Feathers," General Winfield Scott, was a national hero, almost a national monument. He was large as a monument, imposing, this gouty gargantuan. People listened to General Scott, respected him. He had commanded in Mexico in 1849, in the Western Indian wars in '32, had commanded even half a century back, a lieutenant at Niagara in 1812. Somewhere in his massive, mountainous body he still bore two British bullets from that ancient, forgotten action.

What with dropsy, vertigo, rheumatism, arthritis, plain fatigue, Scott was helpless physically. He could scarcely manage his three hundred pounds of hurtful thick flesh decaying, his awkward long frame six-feet-six-inches lame. Never since Mareschal de Saxe had a nation's first general been so unmilitary in his person. Scott lived with remarkable elegance: dining was a fine art, a ritual lasting hours through mid-day, sleeping afternoons was release from every burden. And dressing each morning was an exquisite's triumph of taste. He dressed his vast bulk in fine-tailored blue wool, gold braid, gold buttons gleaming, a plume in his hat. When he walked with two aides from his porch to his carriage, he was a grand parade in himself. Small boys gathered in the street every morning to watch. But he lived in his mind only. He could no longer sit a horse, not even sit much at his desk. He ran the army lying on a huge sofa in his office.

Still the quick mind housed in that pendulous, quivering old body retained all its sharpness, all its brilliance in the arts of war, its high moral power. Concerning the unknown president-elect from down-state Illinois, the new Republican Party's new leader of whom such bizarre things were said, General Scott asked only one question: "Is he a *firm* man?" When assured Lincoln would do his whole duty, "in sight of the furnace seven times heated," Old-Fuss-and-Feathers said thoughtfully, "All is not lost." He began preparations for keeping peace and good order at the inauguration, called up two companies of flying artillery, announced he would organize the militia. What militia? someone murmured. If he could find no one else, Scott thundered, he would swear himself in as constable, go out patrolling Washington streets in person!

It was a wildly comic picture: the angry old elephant of elegance, stern black little eyes glittering in his swollen warty face, masquerading as police constable, teetering ponderously up Capitol Hill, thin mouth drawn down in perpetual petulance, silky white sideburns blowing. . . .

What of the Electoral College meeting? Scott was asked. February 13, Congress would assemble to count the electoral votes, declare Lincoln and Hamlin elected. Washington talk ran high: an outbreak would occur, Congress would never make its count, never be allowed to meet. The sofa creaked as the old general hauled himself angrily up. "I supposed I had suppressed that infamy!" he roared. "I have said that any man who attempted by force or unparliamentary disorder to obstruct or interfere with the lawful count of the electoral vote for President and Vice-President of the United States should be lashed to the nozzle of a twelve-pounder and fired out the window of the Capitol! I would manure the hills of Arlington with the fragments of his body, were he a senator, or chief magistrate of my native State! It is my duty to suppress insurrection—my duty!"

Old-Fuss-and-Feathers. No one doubted the awesome old man knew his duty. But he, too, was frightened. He sent off a letter to Lincoln. He had news, he wrote, of "a wide spread and powerful conspiracy to seize the Capitol." He expected it. He had six hundred men, he needed ten thousand. He couldn't get them. Every department was filled with traitorous clerks. They had already stolen government funds. They would quickly surrender every building to Southern insurrectionists.

Traitorous—the word was used freely now. Americans no longer spoke easily of Northern and Southern, describing a difference in policy. They spoke of treason and traitors, insurrection, rebellion, of liberty, oppression, of fighting for freedom. In the White House, Buchanan said sadly "I am the last president of the *United* States." Scott was prepared for the worst.

So were others. Charles Francis Adams wrote Governor Andrew in Boston his dour prediction: revolutionists would seize Washington City by force, before March 4. Attorney General Stanton told Senator Sumner it was "hardly possible" the government would still be in Washington for Lincoln's inauguration. But General Scott was a doughty old ruin. In public, he exuded confidence. "While I command the army, there will be no revolution in the city of Washington!" he roared. "I'll plant cannon at both ends of Pennsylvania Avenue, and if any should raise a finger I'll blow them to hell, sir! to Hell!"

Old men's threats are empty threats, an old man's confidence idle boasting.

The President-Elect of The United States, preparing to join this regiment of senescence, was a young man. He was fifty-one, a man born to no tradition, untried in administration, only once in national office and that briefly, a man almost unknown on the national scene. Far west on the Illinois prairie he had been saying nothing public, doing nothing public since his nomination in May, his minority election in November.

His days were crowded with office-seekers, party leaders; patronage was his biggest problem. Should Greeley's or Seward's faction have the New

York jobs? Must he take Cameron into the cabinet to please the Pennsylvanians? Or should he cater to Chief Justice Read? The South was falling off from the nation, the North distintegrating in splinters; at Springfield the President-Elect went on endlessly conferring with supporters, ambitious new leaders of the tiny new party.

For twelve years, Walt Whitman wrote—Taylor, Fillmore, Pierce, Buchanan—for twelve long years the Presidents of The United States had been "deformed, mediocre, sniveling, unreliable, false-hearted men." Smarting words, a poet's harsh judgment; brooding over the collapse of the nation, Whitman could say it, troubled people believe it. To the waiting country torn apart, Abraham Lincoln seemed, alas, no more than just another President.

His last days in Springfield, Lincoln spent simply, quietly, a little sadly, as if some mystical forsense had come to him that once he left home for Washington and the Presidency, he would never again return.

Twice in the weeks since election he had been visited with a vision. Looking into a mirror, he beheld himself reflected clearly, at full length, but with two faces—one of them pale as death. During busy days crowded with conferences he brooded over his vision, discussed it with his wife. It meant, said Mary Lincoln, he would be elected to a second term in the White House, but would never live to complete it.

Nights he could not sleep. He was alarmingly thin: in less than a year he had lost fifteen pounds, dropped from one eighty to one sixty five, little enough for his towering frame. In brisk winter darkness he took long walks alone through the streets, abstracted, silent, absently carrying papers and letters in his hand. To Springfield folk he looked strangely different: he had grown a beard. He would never say why; in November he started it, by February whiskers wreathed his chin entirely. That beard softened the rugged architecture of his face, gave a new quality of repose to his "sallow, queer, sagacious visage."

As winter advanced, Lincoln spent days putting his papers in order. He burned hundreds of old files and letters, took a gripsack full of manuscripts to a neighbor. He sold back the German newspaper he had bought a year ago, the *Illinois-Staats-Anzeiger,* to its editor Theodore Canisius. He and Mrs. Lincoln held a public sale of most of their furniture, advertised it in the papers: "Parlor and Chamber Sets, Carpets, Sofas, Chairs . . ."

They packed their clothes and household goods in trunks and boxes, gave their yellow dog "Fido" to a neighbor, sold their horse and buggy, sold the cow they had kept in the back yard for milk, made arrangements to rent their house.

The night of February 6, between seven and midnight, they held their final public reception. The modest residence on Eighth Street thronged with friends, seven hundred of them and more in the evening cold, paying respects. Lincoln stood near the front door, his oldest son Robert by him. Mary Lincoln received in the parlor, attended by four of her sisters. After that final reception, the Lincolns left home entirely, moved for the few days remaining to rooms in the Chenery House, Springfield's leading hotel.

The day before his departure, in the afternoon, Lincoln strolled down the street and climbed upstairs to his office, where he sprawled on his big sofa and talked away the time with Billy Herndon, his law partner of sixteen years. They talked of their clients, of Herndon's drinking, of a hundred things. Finally Lincoln roused himself, picked up an armful of books, the two men walked down the stairs together. Outside, the President-Elect of The United States looked up at the sign above the street door. "LINCOLN & HERNDON," it read. "Let it hang there undisturbed," he told Billy. "If I live I'm coming back some time, and then we'll go right on practicing law as if nothing had ever happened."

Abruptly he added: "I am sick of office-holding already, and I shudder when I think of the tasks that are still ahead."

Monday, February 11, dawned dreary and cold. Rain was falling; it threatened to turn to snow. At the Chenery House, Lincoln was up and dressed before daylight. He busied himself in simple tasks: with his own strong hands he roped up the heavy trunks, labeled them with hotel cards on which he wrote in his clear, slanting script,

A. Lincoln
White House
Washington, D.C.

By and by the landlord's daughter came in, watched him as he worked. She asked for his autograph; he handed her one of the Chenery House baggage labels he had written. The dawning hours moved on; a little past seven o'clock a drayman whipping and shouting backed his team up to the hotel with an omnibus. Lincoln helped him load the trunks. Mary came, and the three boys. They all piled into the omnibus to ride with their bags to the Great Western depot.

Around the ugly little brick station, nearly a thousand people shivered in the freezing rain. The few who could crowded into the dingy waiting room, the rest stood patiently on the tracks, around the train. A stubby locomotive, its name "L. M. Wiley" boldly lettered on the cab, panted like a breathing creature, a head of steam already up. Hitched behind its wood-box tender were two coaches: a baggage van, a single new passenger car. Engine and coaches glistened brightly with new-varnished orange panels, brown trim; soggy flags and streamers once gay and cheerful drooped everywhere, damp red-white-and-blue bunting sheathed the polished sides of the new car. This was the special train, due to leave Springfield at eight o'clock precisely.

Soberly, Lincoln shook hands with his townsmen in the waiting room. He bade goodbye to his wife, kissed his two smaller sons Willie and Tad—at General Scott's orders they were to follow by a later train, meet him next day in Indianapolis. The crowd fell back, made a path; at five minutes to eight he and his party slowly filed out of the station.

Soot and smoke from "L. M. Wiley's" bulging stack hung in the air, drifted damply down on everyone. Lincoln passed among the people. They murmured, they called to him, his neighbors; briefly he grasped the nearest outstretched hands. His ancient beaver hat, worn bare of nap, towered over the crowd, his old coat, ridiculously short, looked more like a sailor's pea jacket than any other kind of a garment. Awkwardly, he climbed up to the rear platform of his train. The crowd gave him three cheers. He turned toward the people, took his hat in his hands. A look of sorrow came over his face. He was silent a moment; then as the locomotive bell on "L. M. Wiley" rang out and the conductor was reaching up to pull the signal cord, Lincoln began to speak. Umbrellas tilted back, people looked up to see him— snow whited beards and bared heads of men in the crowd.

"Friends," Lincoln said, "no one who has never been placed in a like position, can understand my feelings at this hour, nor the oppressive sadness I feel at this parting . . ." He spoke of his love for Springfield and her people: "Here I have lived from my youth until now I am an old man. Here the most sacred ties of earth were assumed; here all my children were born, and one of them lies buried. To you, dear friends, I owe all that I have, all that I am. All the strange, chequered past seems to crowd upon my mind . . ."

He spoke of burdens ahead. "Today I leave you. I go to assume a task more difficult than that which devolved upon General Washington . . . Let us all pray that the God of our fathers may not forsake us now."

And simply he said to his weeping townsfolk, straining to catch his words, "Friends, one and all, I must now bid you an affectionate farewell."

The train bell clanged again, "L. M. Wiley" hissed and snorted, the four big drive-wheels began to turn. Abraham Lincoln had left home for the last time.

Inside the Presidential coach, friends and official guests carefully chosen for the journey settled down noisily, happily. Lincoln picked his way among them without speaking. The coach was richly luxurious, as handsome as taste and craft could make it. The carpet was soft underfoot, dark woodwork gleamed with carvings and scrolls. Sidewalls under windows were deep crimson plush; between windows, panels of royal-blue silk were pierced with thirty-four gold stars, for the thirty-four states. Red-white-and-blue hangings from sills and finials swung with the train's motion, velvet tassels from the center lamps danced in rhythm. Forward in the car, two American flags of glistening new silk stood crossed in their standards.

In his old clothes, Lincoln looked out of place, a crude stranger in the parlor. He reached the front of the car, disappeared inside the private stateroom, folded his tall form awkwardly on the velvet plush cushions, sat there alone. A young journalist aboard—Henry Villard, of the New York *Herald* —came in before Springfield was gone, asked Lincoln to repeat the farewell speech he had given. Lincoln took Villard's pad and wrote out his words, as nearly as he could remember. Villard prepared to wire them East, first words of the Lincoln Legend. No one would ever forget the scene, it would be part of American lore. Years later, people would cherish those farewell words, *what he said at Gettysburg . . . what he said at Springfield . . .*

Villard went back to the others, the President-Elect kept to himself in his stateroom, slouched in his seat as he stared out the window into the driving rain. East from Springfield broad flat prairies of the Sangamon lay gloomy in the dull winter damp, level fields were bare, barnyards deep in mud. At every rural road-crossing, men, women, children stood uncovered, sat in buggies, stared at the swift train, its orange-and-brown colors like an oriole the only brightness in the flat drab winter landscape. "L. M. Wiley" slowed and tooted for each station, every platform was flag-draped, thronging. Past Lincoln's window, villages rushed by as if they were moving, the train standing still. Buffalo, Lanesville, Illiopolis—he knew people in each one, farmers, millers, blacksmiths, prairie people, *his* people . . . A cheer briefly heard, a sudden sight of handkerchiefs waved, hats thrown in the air, and he had left another Illinois town behind him. Soon he passed out of Sangamon County. Niantic, Harristown . . . at Decatur the train paused. He appeared on the back platform, made his first little talk. Behind the crowd he could see a long line of saddle horses tethered. The whole town was here, people of every age. They cheered and yelled; they were old friends.

This was Lincoln country. In carnival spirit prairie folk came paying tribute to one of their own. Not everyone could love a prairie, those vast treeless stretches, green summer heats punishing, winters endless and drab, harsh winds never ceasing, sudden cruel storms, searing droughts. The prairie was flat, unrelieved. Lincoln once had said it: "as unpoetical as any spot on earth." But it was homeland, where

. . . memory will hallow all
We've known, but know no more. . . .

They were his words, a poem he had written years ago, best forgotten as poetry, perhaps, but part of his prairie life. Always, the prairie "aroused feelings in me which were certainly poetry. . . ."

Over the prairie the train-of-cars rushed on, sometimes as fast as thirty miles an hour. It sped through well-loved towns, Cerro Gordo, Bement, Ivesdale, Sandorus, Tolono . . . Beside a trestle stood a farmer with a shotgun. Smartly, he presented arms as "L. M. Wiley" puffed by with the coaches, flags flying, bunting streaming.

At Tolono, Lincoln gave his final talk to Illinois. "I am leaving you on an errand of national importance, attended, as you are aware, with considerable difficulties. Let us believe as some poet has expressed it, 'Behind the cloud the sun is shining still.' I bid you an affectionate farewell." At Danville, he reached down to touch hands reaching up to touch his, while "L. M. Wiley" backed and switched. Another car was inserted here, a car with Governor Morton of Indiana and his party.

Noon, at the little village of State Line, the train drew up for dinner. The crowd pressed wetly about Lincoln as he struggled through to the station where tables were set. This was his last sight of Illinois. From now on, people thronging to see him would be his countrymen, but not his neighbors. They would come more in curiosity, less in friendship. "I find myself far from home and surrounded by thousands I now see before me who are strangers to me," he said that afternoon, in his first platform speech in Indiana.

Eight o'clock, to early afternoon—so short a time to come "far from home." The thought was still with him at two o'clock, on the back platform at Lafayette: "When I came to the west some forty-five years ago, you completed a journey of some thirty miles which you had commenced at sunrise, and thought you had done well." Now, only six hours, far from home, among strangers . . .

Between stops, Lincoln returned to his lonely stateroom, his pensive sadness no match for the gay mood of the crowds, no match either for the merry company on the train. His son Robert, seventeen, was full of laughter, free of care, happy to be released from his Harvard term. That diminutive athletic youngster Colonel Ellsworth could never be sad. Scarcely older than Robert, proud in his bright Zouave uniform, he was the very picture of boyish vigor, youthful strength. Young Villard, the busy secretaries Nicolay and Hay were sprightly companions. Judge Davis's enormous fat bulk seemed to fill the whole car where he sat. Hulking Ward Hill Lamon, Lincoln's long-time friend, "as tall and strong a man as there was in Illinois," rarely sat down at all. He strung up his banjo, sang Negro songs. Governor Morton of Indiana, when he made his way back through the rolling, jerking train from his car to visit Lincoln, found a lively scene in the elegant private coach. The escorting party completely filled it: the four army officers sent by Scott to guard Lincoln, officials of all the railroads the train would pass over—twenty-two railroads, nearly two thousand miles—Governor Yates of Illinois with his people, Norman Judd the state Republican chairman, Springfield friends

Lincoln had invited at random, the journalists, W. S. Wood the railroad superintendent from New York who was managing the entire trip.

All through the noisy car the work of politics went on. Every station produced telegrams, messages, produced throngs of people too, crowding to see the somehow disturbing countenance they had known only through photographs.

Photographs, telegraphs, railroads: these were the new tools of Lincoln's America, the subtle, speedy instruments of his political career. Railroads had been his way to wealth: he was a railroad lawyer, a "chalked-hat" man, he travelled on an annual pass which conductors signified by sticking a white-chalked ticket in his hatband. Lincoln had seen railroads change the life-stream of prairies in his time. He had watched all their improvements— although the new sleeping berth Mr. Pullman designed for the Chicago & Alton was never long enough for him to stretch out full length. The network of American railroads would be vital to the nation if war came, these very railroads, over which his train was rolling. . . .

The journey from Springfield to Washington could have been accomplished in three easy days' travel, a plan Lincoln would infinitely have preferred. But no President, no President-Elect could follow his own bent alone. Washington had travelled about the country as President; ever since, the progression in public, the presentation of the spectacle and the man, had been a tradition of the Presidency. The country demanded a glimpse of Lincoln, this rich Western lawyer, this obscure rustic, this eloquent spokesman of the New Whigs, this man of whom so much had been said—so much good, so much startlingly bad. Some had talked of him as if he were an animal in a zoo: "An African gorilla," ungainly and gloomy; "the Republican clown from the West" with the manners of a flatboatman; a low vulgarian jokester, a giant full of bony corners. Years ago, Edwin Stanton of Pittsburgh, now Attorney General, had travelled out to Cincinnati to argue a case against Lincoln. At the first sight of his opponent, "all there was of him," towering like Saul head and shoulders above the Israelites, Stanton had searched his zoological lexicon. "That giraffe!" he exclaimed, that "gawky ape," "long-armed baboon!" In a few months, Edwin Stanton would be the baboon's Secretary of War, but at his first acquaintance with Lincoln he had called him "a low cunning clown."

Republican leaders wanted Lincoln to be seen, wanted the people to know him. A year's work of vilification must be undone. And so this zig-zag trip, this long way round, through Indiana, Ohio, stops at county-seat towns and all the large cities, east to Pittsburgh, back into Ohio for Cleveland, then Erie and lake ports of New York, past forty platforms crowded with people to Buffalo, along the canal cities to Albany, down the Hudson to New York City, across Jersey to Philadelphia, out to Harrisburg, back to Philadelphia, finally Baltimore and Washington.

Everywhere celebrations were planned—receptions, picnics, parades, as if February were spring in the land. Addresses by five governors were scheduled, special sessions of five state legislatures, everywhere state militia units were togged out in new uniforms, new equipment, as much as to say "we are ready." Americans prepared a greater outpouring, even, than they had accorded the Prince of Wales on his tour a few months before—but with this difference: now that the South had risen in open hostility, all the celebrations in the North had the air of a theatre company playing with false heartiness the last week of its engagement.

The whole enterprise of the trip, said one Ohio paper, was "in extremely bad taste at this time." Seven Southern states had already seceded, more were prepared to go. Government forts, buildings, arsenals, arms had been seized, a convention held, a Confederacy formed, a Constitution adopted. Just as Lincoln started East, the telegraph clicked out the news that Jefferson Davis was named President of "The Confederate States of America"—Davis, a man Lincoln's age, but a soldier, a statesman, senator, one-time Secretary of War, famous everywhere, well-respected. Who could say as much for Lincoln?

In Washington, old men desperate pushed through Congress conciliations, appeasements; in the West, young men high and hot gathered in strength, organized, drilled in arms. "Do you believe, Mr. Lincoln, that if the Republicans elect a President they will be able to inaugurate him?" someone had talked last autumn. Lincoln had answered: "I reckon, friend, that if there are votes enough to elect a Republican President, there'll be men enough to put him in."

There had been votes enough, because the Democratic Party had split wide open. Now there would be men enough. The train sped East: Democrats, Republicans, Old Whigs, Know-Nothings, Constitutional Unionists, every American on the route looked at the lanky angular figure with the sad, bearded face, heard the soft words gently offered, tentative words of hope and patience, heard the sudden flashes of homely humor. On the twelve-day trip, Americans began to know the man, began to separate Abraham Lincoln from the exotics of zoology.

All during last summer's campaign, Lincoln had kept silent. Tradition demanded it: no Presidential candidate must appeal for votes, seek the office. The party platform spoke for him. Lincoln resolved to preserve his silence till inauguration day, March 4. Then he could speak with authority, speak for the whole people, from the highest office in their gift. Not from any premature word of his would the South be urged headlong down its separate road, the North take further umbrage, its tempers aroused. Yet now for twelve days at every whistle stop he must speak: speak counsels of delay, hesitation, state issues but avoid them, test, try, and listen; as he, being looked at and questioned, could in his turn look, and ask, measure the wills, sound the depths of the nation. In these twelve days, he must make more speeches, to more people, than anyone had ever made in all history in that length of time—address crowds, banquets, legislatures, assemblages, address them, but say nothing. "I wish this thing were through with," he muttered.

The train rattled on through the flat Indiana counties with their names from America's past—Tippecanoe, Boone, Marion. Finally at five o'clock it rolled into the sprawling railroad yards of Indianapolis, first big city of the tour, the first reception.

An immense crowd was waiting. Soldiery fired a thirty-four gun salute, Governor Morton gave a welcoming address; the President-Elect was escorted to a carriage which a group of young men exuberantly seized by the hubs and carried a whole block before they hitched the horses up. A long parade led Lincoln under fine arches, past decorations, to the Bates House. He pushed through crowds up the steps to the doors; he disappeared. Soon he emerged on the balcony, to look down over twenty thousand shivering people in torchlight below.

They roared to see him; they were friendly, warm. Lincoln forsook his caution, broke his long silence. "It is your business to rise up and preserve the Union and liberty," he cried. No state could coerce the Union, no state had "a mysterious right to play the tyrant." And he made one of his questionable jokes: states' rights men, he said, seemed to think the Union "no regular marriage, but rather a sort of free love arrangement, to be maintained only on passional attraction." His words were abruptly sectional, far from conciliatory. No one had heard him speak so strongly before. But when he left the balcony for the parlor of the Bates House, he changed his tone. To the Governor and legislature, he gave soft words, warned of "professed lovers of the Union" who viewed the South with spite and venom. He was all conciliation, that moment. And he ended with the same quaint phrase he had been using all day from the train: "And now allow me to bid you farewell."

Next day, Tuesday, February 12, was Lincoln's birthday, his fifty-second. Indianapolis all morning was a confusion of conference and celebration. Eleven o'clock, Mary Lincoln arrived from Springfield with Willie and Tad, just in time to board the special before it pulled out at noon for Cincinnati. Now, the whole family together, the trip could begin in earnest.

East from Indianapolis the train had a heavier locomotive ("L.M.Wiley" was left behind) and four passenger coaches, the three new ones filled with Ohio Republican leaders. Superintendent Wood had taken every care. The line ahead had been inspected and cleared; a pilot engine went first to cover the route. "It is very important that this train should pass over the road in safety," Mr. Wood's laconic instructions inanely announced. "Red is the signal for danger . . ." He made a strenuous schedule: platform appearances all afternoon, speeches off the cuff, that evening a second great fête in Cincinnati, a second major speech, a huge reception, a serenade. "Welcome to the President of Thirty-Four States," one banner in Cincinnati's streets proclaimed. "Honor to a President, not to a Partisan," read another. Lincoln spoke gravely that evening. He pointed across the Ohio River: there were Kentuckians, "friends and brethren," he called them. He wanted what was right for both sides of the river, he said. His task was to call the people, North, South, everywhere, to their sovereignty. "*My* power is temporary and fleeting. *Yours* is as eternal as the principle of liberty . . . . If the people remain right, your public men can never betray you . . . ." In the midst of the gay yelling throng he was somber. "In a few short years, I, and every other individual man who is now living, will pass away . . ."

Early next morning Norman Judd, political mentor of the President-Elect, was in his Cincinnati hotel room. Secretly, a special messenger arrived, unobserved by the crowds. The young stranger introduced himself as agent from Pinkerton's detective agency. Judd, counsel for a railroad himself, knew all about Pinkerton and his famous work; his own railroad (the Rock Island) was a chief supporter of the agency. The stranger brought reports with him, too alarming for the telegraph, full reports from Pinkerton's own hand: a plot against Lincoln was borning in the city of Baltimore. Suddenly, Norman Judd and Superintendent Wood realized Baltimore was the one city which had wired no plans for a reception, sent no official invitations. Yet there was no possible way to reach Washington by rail, except through Baltimore. To the two worried men on the special train, the very word *Baltimore* became a symbol of disaster, a sinister threat.

Judd and Wood resolved to keep the news secret. They talked softly together as the train rolled its busy, punctuated way through Ohio all the third day to Columbus. At Columbus, the telegraph brought better news. Congress had opened the Electoral College ballots, nothing had happened. A hundred plainsclothesmen patrolled galleries and corridors, no outrage interfered while Congress proclaimed Lincoln and Hamlin elected. True enough, a representative from Virginia arose on the floor to threaten secession of his state, denounced the spectacle of Lincoln's trip, cried out against "the forms of an imperial court which attend the progress of the Republican president-elect."

On the special train, no one was conscious of the forms of an imperial court. They were conscious of the American people, surging strongly, noisily around a new chief, waiting hopefully the words of a leader. Lincoln gave them words of his faith, words of belief in their sovereignty: ". . . . *as eternal as the principle of liberty . . . If the people remain right, your public men can never betray you . . .*" but no words of passion, no leadership.

At the Ohio capital the whole city turned out, the legislature sat to be addressed, thousands of hands stretched forward to be shaken. At first, Lincoln reached both his hands down from a stairstep for the crowd to grasp. Soon his strength gave out. He retreated a step further, contented himself with smiling, looking, waving, nodding from the staircase. Only Ward Lamon's huge form kept the crowd from crushing up to him.

The third day had been hard on the President-Elect. He had a cold from his back-platform speeches in the rain, he was tired, his throat burned, he was hoarse. The *Ohio State Journal's* editor described him addressing the legislature: "Tall, kindly, amiable . . . as he speaks, the greatness and determination of his nature are apparent . . . He looked somewhat worn with travel and the fatigues of popularity, but warmed to the cordiality of the reception. . . ." "Mine," Lincoln told the legislators, "is such a task as did not rest upon Washington." And he struck his most conciliatory note: "there is nothing going wrong," he said, "there is nothing that really hurts anybody." Far different from his "rise in mass" speech at Indianapolis, "there is nothing going wrong"—the soft words fell hollowly as the Confederacy was forming, as Buchanan was uttering forecasts of doom from the White House.

East of Columbus, the excursion moved on toward Pittsburgh, avoiding Wheeling in the northern spur of Virginia, pausing at each crowd, taking on more cars at Steubenville with Pennsylvania party leaders, more newspaper representatives. The locomotive was forever loading water, and firewood; sometimes passengers clambered onto the tender, helped the firemen feed logs to the fire-box. Along the red clays of the river Ohio, through fog-gray forests and dripping mountains to Pittsburgh, Lincoln knew he had left the prairies at last. Elsewhere the country wondered at his speeches, what they meant, what foreboded. "No crisis but an artificial one"—strange words, unrealistic, unsettling . . . Democrats seethed angrily, editors in the South ridiculed the rail-splitter and his words; one eastern city paper pictured Lincoln as singing, "I'll put my trust in Providence, and let my whiskers grow!" The *New York Herald* published Villard's stories, but with no editorial approval. What would Lincoln say when he reached the East? the *Herald* asked. "Will he kiss our girls, and give a twirl to the whiskers which he has begun to cultivate? Will he tell our merchants groaning under the pressure of the greatest political convulsion ever experienced in America, that 'nobody is hurt' or that 'marching troops into South Carolina' and bombarding fortresses is 'no invasion'?"

"Lincoln is a Simple Susan," an angry Republican declared.

Young Villard heard all Lincoln's speeches, recognized their vagueness, the puzzlement they caused. He found himself quickly weary of Lincoln's anecdotes, his way of skirting an issue by telling stories, jokes, never answering directly. Still, he wrote, Lincoln was a man of undoubted power, immense character, talent, "so conscientious, so earnest, so simple-hearted . . . Tremendously rough, and tremendously honest."

Lincoln had no time for reflection, nor any reserves of strength—up each day before dawn for back-platform appearances, tested till long in the evening with parades, receptions, crushes, addresses, his voice giving out, his coughing spells frequent, his cold worse. Still he smiled and joked with the crowds, told his homely stories, everywhere summoned tall men to the platform to measure heights with him, back to back. Everywhere he presented diminutive Mrs. Lincoln, laughing as he introduced her. "I wanted you to see the long and short of it," he said. He had no time to rest, plan for the grim future, take thought. Once in the midst of bonfires, oratory, cheers, parades, a cannon fired its salute too near the train, shattered a window, showered Mrs. Lincoln with glass. The mishap was a frightening reminder of violence; to Judd and Wood it spoke of Baltimore ahead. At every major stop the train seemed to grow. More cars were hitched on, more state leaders, more journalists.

Politicians, Lincoln left to his staff—to Norman Judd, Ward Lamon, Judge Davis, Nicolay and Hay. Most of the time he sat alone in his stateroom, or chatted with Mary and the boys. Journalists wrote of his loose shambling gait, his nondescript clothes, his quaint way of ending every appearance with that too-stately phrase, "I must now bid you an affectionate farewell." Robert delighted the journalists; he quickly became their favorite. "Prince of Rails," they dubbed him. At one back-platform, the crowds called on Robert for a speech; the young Harvard student was startled, embarrassed. "My boy Bob hasn't got in the way of making speeches," Lincoln smiled to the crowd. His younger sons Willie and Tad had a merry time with correspondents, with crowds, with everyone. Writers had not missed the warm sight of Lincoln romping in the Cincinnati hotel with Tad, trying to coax him to go to sleep. The two youngsters had a favorite game: they would greet new arrivals on the train with the bright enquiry, "Do you want to see Old Abe?"—then point out Ward Lamon, and hide to watch the visitor's discomfiture.

Mary Lincoln mystified the journalists. She mystified everyone, this quick, busy, bustling little person, quaint, unexpected in what she said. When people were presented, she would greet them with the question, "How do you flourish?" The surprising phrase became a byword for the moment through the country. "How do you flourish?" ladies grinned at each other on the streets of New York. And Mary would answer the writers' inquiries with the improbable announcement, "We are pleased with our advancement." Journalists saw strange traits in Mrs. Lincoln, which people at large did not learn of.

The people were delighted with her: she remained in the background, as an American wife should. At one stop, they called for her to come out. He doubted, said Lincoln, if he could induce her to do so; "in fact," he added, "I never succeed very well in getting her to do anything she doesn't want to do"—exactly the sort of thing an American husband ought to say.

But what ought a President-Elect to say? Making speeches with nothing at all really in them, Lincoln told Lamon, was the hardest work a man could do. At Pittsburgh he finally did say something real. He spoke on the tariff, a controversial issue; it was meant to be a definitive speech, carefully prepared, announced far in advance. Pennsylvanians waited it with the deepest interest. Tariff was the plank which had won them to the Republican Platform, the policy by which Pittsburgh expected to become the industrial center of the ironmonger's dreams. Lincoln's speech was protectionist: he hoped, he said, "adequate protection can be extended to the coal and iron of Pennsylvania, the corn of Illinois, and the 'reapers of Chicago' "—it was general in its terms. Pittsburgh editors wished it had been firmer, more specific. They were surprised to hear Lincoln say he did not know the details of the tariff bill now before Congress. Why didn't he? They all knew its details, the bill had been argued continuously through three successive sessions, three years and more, Republican Senator Morrill was its advocate. Should the President-Elect not know it, know it thoroughly? Still, Pennsylvanians liked the man they saw, and heard. He was moderate, he was cool; he spoke for the Union. At Erie, he appeared with an American flag in his right hand, used calm words, urged patience, forbearance, pled for patriotic adherence to the Constitution. An Erie editor found him much better-appearing than he had expected: "There is a blending of gravity and goodness in his look, even when his face is in repose, which wins confidence and affection, and satisfies one of his fitness for the great office. . . . When he smiles he is handsome, and when he bows he is graceful, notwithstanding the bow is a peculiar one, and the form that bends is not of graceful mould."

At Pittsburgh, it rained. At Cleveland, it rained. At Erie, it rained. But everywhere people jammed sidewalks, roared greetings, cheered the train. Horace Greeley appeared at one stop, in his curious clothes, his odd myopic stare. He boarded the train, lectured Lincoln brisky all the way to the next stop, there disappeared, convinced the President-Elect was sound on the issues he had covered. At Westfield, New York, Lincoln made his usual friendly little speech, then he said suddenly to the crowd, "I have a correspondent in this place, and if she is present, I should like to see her."

"Who is it?" someone yelled.

"Her name is Grace Bedell," Lincoln answered.

An eleven-year-old girl was carried to the platform. Lincoln explained, "She wrote me that she thought I would be better looking if I wore whiskers."

He looked down at the girl. "You see, I let these whiskers grow for you, Grace." And he kissed her.

Buffalo was the half-way point. Here lived the last previous Whig president, Millard Fillmore, a neat genial little man still only sixty-one, popular, pleasant, happy in his second marriage, and in his avocation—which was to be chancellor of the University of Buffalo. (Fillmore had been able to come back home from the Presidency, go right on practicing law "as if nothing had ever happened.") He waited at the station for Lincoln; a wild scene of near-riot ensued. Crowds broke through their barriers, the two public men were in danger of their lives. "The Pass of Thermopylae was a memorable performance, but it was no such jam as the Pass of the Central Depot," the *Courier* declared. Order was restored, President Fillmore received the Lincolns, entertained them in his fine home for dinner. At Buffalo, the whole party rested over Sunday. Tad and Willie played leapfrog with the hotel owner's boy in the lobby. In a happy, homely moment, the President-Elect joined them in their noisy game.

Monday the second week began its relentless schedule. In a new private car (because the track gauge was different), the same car recently used by the Prince of Wales on his tour of the country, the Lincoln entourage travelled through New York State—Rochester, Syracuse, Utica, Albany— among huge crowds as telegraph wires from Montgomery, Alabama, told of the inauguration that day of Jefferson Davis as President of the Confederacy. At Montgomery, people had danced on the Stars and Stripes underfoot as a granddaughter of President Tyler raised the strange new flag of the South. That day, Mary Lincoln decided she had seen enough of her husband's shabby coat and worn hat. Mr. Wood was keeping the telegraph humming with arrangements, Norman Judd was receiving constant coded messages from Pinkerton and General Scott, but into their busy load Mrs. Lincoln thrust firm orders to be despatched. At Utica a new broadcloth overcoat was pressed upon Lincoln with wifely determination, and a new hat. He looked "fifty per cent. better," a journalist wrote. At Albany, Lincoln appeared on the steps of the capitol for a short speech. "I have neither strength nor voice to address you at any greater length," he said. Before the Governor and legislature that evening he observed, "It is true that, while I hold myself, without mock modesty, the humblest of all individuals that have ever been elevated to the Presidency, I have a more difficult task to perform than any of them."

High water and ice in the Hudson prevented crossing by the rail ferry at Albany, so the special train made an unexpected detour north to Troy, the nearest train bridge. Bob Lincoln rode the locomotive cab part of the way from Troy down the majestic Hudson; his father appeared for talks at Poughkeepsie, Hudson, Peekskill. Skaters in gay colored costumes on the frozen river waved and cheered as the train passed. At three o'clock on Tuesday, February 19, ninth day of the trip, the party reached New York City. A great parade began at the depot; Lincoln entered the barouche recently used by the Prince of Wales. Crowds were enormous—but there was something reserved, even cold in their manner, and oddly few women were in evidence. New Yorkers were not friendly. They came to see but they came with "significant and solemn curiosity."

Strong Republican organizations thrived in New York State, and lively units of the "Wide-Awakes"—young Republicans banded together for political or military service. And there were Unionists a'plenty. But New York City, bound with the South in a network of trade and credit, was resolute against war. Mayor Fernando Wood, self-contained, elegant, a thoughtful-appearing man rumored to be corrupt, known to be anti-Lincoln, even proposed the city secede from the state and the Union, follow its own destiny as a free city in the world of nations. Lincoln expected little friendship here, no cordial support.

He stepped from his carriage at the Astor House, unfolded himself on the sidewalk, looked around. And he did a regetttable thing: he stretched—luxuriously, stretched his arms and legs. It was a thoughless act, in the circumstances crude. New Yorkers were offended. Lincoln turned to survey the unfriendly crowd. He was composed, looked calmly at the silent people. He made a few quiet remarks: "I have nothing just now to say that is worthy of your attention." Inside the hotel, he found the Republican Clubs of New York City waiting. He addressed them with a wit and charm they had not expected; they were reassured. But still he said nothing significant.

Conferences occupied the whole evening; next morning Mayor Wood received the President-Elect in City Hall, made a precisely proper address, no warmth in it, no word of approval. Lincoln responded with dignity, serenely. He acknowledged that only a minority of New York City citizens supported him, he made no effort to win people. He spoke soberly of the Union, of its future. At a long reception afterwards, standing by a bust of Washington, under a portrait of Senator Seward, he greeted people with such jollity, such flashes of comedy, that Mayor Wood was in continual laughter. That night with Judge Davis and two ladies, the President-Elect went to the opera, where Verdi's *Masked Ball* was given its second performance. Lincoln was tired, and evidently bored with the unfamiliar entertainment. The audience gave him a long hearty ovation, the cast saluted him with anthems, but New York society did not fail to observe he wore black gloves instead of the white fashion dictated. "The Undertaker of the Union," someone sneered. Mary Lincoln meanwhile held a reception at the Astor House. A scant hundred guests appeared. Mrs. August Belmont caused a note to be published in newspapers and magazines: she had *not* called on Mrs. Lincoln during her stay in the city, Mrs. Belmont announced.

At breakfast with the richest merchants in New York, someone proudly told Lincoln he would not meet so many millionaires together at any other table in the nation. To this egregious remark Lincoln (himself so often accused of poor taste) responded pointedly that he, too, was a millionaire— he had received a million votes in the November election.

That day, the cheerful Hannibal Hamlin turned up, a merry hulking bull of a man. He and his pretty young wife told of many adventures on the way down from Maine: how at New Haven the Vice President-Elect had actually toppled off his back platform while shaking hands, and had to run hard to catch the moving train. Hamlin was a tonic: bursting with animal vigor, enormously likable, loud, hearty, a master politician, with his striking swarthy good looks and boyish way of exhibiting his physical strength; he could take some of the burden from Lincoln. At a great dinner, with the Hamlins present, Lincoln confronted oysters-on-the-half-shell for the first time in his life. "Well," he said, "I don't know that I can manage these things, but I guess I can learn." A midnight serenade was scheduled; Hamlin took that duty on himself, appearing on the balcony, drawing a gasp from the crowd. So dark was Hamlin in complexion, that though his lineage was descent from the earliest Puritans of Plymouth, on first sight people always thought him Negroid.

Lincoln was tired. He went to bed, slept through the din and the singing while Hamlin made the crowd roar with his bright sallies and jokes. In his own room, Norman Judd secretly received Kate Warne, female operative of Pinkerton's agency. He studied her factual reports of a Baltimore plot, heard her own first-hand information. Pinkerton would meet the President-Elect in person in Philadelphia, Kate Warne told him.

Everything was sour about the New York visit—everything, except hats. Mr. Knox the hatter called on the President-Elect at the Astor House, presented him with a soft wool hat, inscribed "Abraham Lincoln." In less than an hour Mr. Leary, whose hattery was actually in the hotel building at the Astor, sent up the best of his manufacture, a beaver, in a proper box. Lincoln put both hats in his luggage, grinned amiably to the hatters. "They mutually surpass each other," he said.

On Thursday, the eleventh day out of Springfield, the whole party crossed by ferry to Jersey City at eight in the morning. Immediately the atmosphere was friendlier, Lincoln easier. He spoke as he boarded the train, again at Newark, twice at Trenton to the Democratic legislature. "If the ship of state should suffer wreck now," he said, "there will be no pilot ever needed for another voyage." Then he crossed the Delaware. At four o'clock he was in

Republican Pennsylvania, in the Republican city of Philadelphia. Here crowds roared approval, the city bubbled with enthusiasm. He gave his best little talk that evening: all his political struggles had been in behalf of the teaching that had come forth from the sacred walls of Independence Hall, he said. "May my right hand forget its cunning and my tongue cleave to the roof of my mouth if I ever prove false to those teachings." Then he stood shaking hands for two hours among a great noisy press of Philadelphians in the Continental Hotel.

At the height of this reception, young Nicolay pushed through the throng and whispered to Lincoln: Norman Judd must see him at once, on a matter of the utmost urgency, of the utmost secrecy. Lincoln nodded, even as he shook someone's hand. He moved a step or two, gradually edged his way toward the end of the lobby, a person at a time, speaking to people as he went. Then he disappeared quickly up a back staircase. In Judd's room a stranger waited. Allan Pinkerton the detective had kept Judd advised constantly by telegram and messenger; now he had come himself. He spoke with the burr of his native Scotland. To Lincoln he revealed for the first time what Judd already knew, the grim details of a plot to burn railroad bridges, sink the Havre de Grace rail ferry, blow up the train, assassinate Lincoln as he passed through Baltimore.

"But why? Why do they want to kill me?" Lincoln asked. Pinkerton told him of fanatics in Maryland, of his own spying there, of local troops and bands resolved to block passage, so "no damned Yankee could ever get through to sit in the Presidential chair." The three men talked gravely in Judd's room. Late in the evening, Frederick Seward, son of Senator Seward who Lincoln had already announced would be Secretary of State, reached Philadelphia from Baltimore. He came secretly; he bore urgent letters, one from his father, one from General Scott. They too had learned of the danger in Baltimore, learned it was too great to guard against. Local authorities were secessionist, would not cooperate; fifteen thousand men were organized to prevent Lincoln's passage, do him violence, fire the train. Plans must be changed.

Frederick Seward, his father's letters and General Scott's burning in his pocket, had endured the long tedious ride on the train-of-cars from Washington. Now he found Chestnut Street surging with people, bursting with music and hurrahs. Torches and flambeaux lighted the city, as if it were midday. At the Continental Hotel he entered an indescribable Bedlam. Assassination would be so easy. . . .

Young Seward struggled through the clutching hands, roaring voices, pressing bodies, up to the head of the main stairs. He opened the first door he came to, found himself in a roistering crowd of merry youths. One of them recognized him, stepped forward with a greeting—young Robert

Lincoln. Robert listened to him briefly, went to find Ward Lamon. (It was Robert's choice; he should have found Judd. Lamon was the last person to let in on a plot, a state secret—excitable, romantic Lamon, all too devoted, too likely to erupt into action.) The huge Lamon bent down to hear Seward's whispered message, took him to the President-Elect's bedroom, where he could wait secretly.

Seward waited a full hour and more. It was midnight before Lincoln came in, entirely calm, completely at ease. He greeted the young man pleasantly, quietly, took Senator Seward's letter, and Scott's, read them deliberately through. While the noise of the crowds rumbled up from the Continental lobbies, young Seward added to what was in the letters. He spoke for his father, for Scott too. They both urged him to say, as Judd and Pinkerton said, Lincoln must change his route, change his time schelude, come in secret to Washington some way unannounced.

Lincoln thanked the young man for his pains, asked if he had found a room and bed for the night. He would give no answer, not till the morrow, he said. Frederick Seward's countenance fell. Lincoln smiled at him kindly. "You need not think I will not consider it well," he assured him.

Next morning—Friday, February 22, twelfth day out of Springfield, Washington's birthday—Lincoln rose early. At six o'clock cannon boomed and bands played, he raised a flag over Independence Hall—a flag with a brand new star in it, a thirty-fifth star for the thirty-fifth state, Kansas, admitted that day to the trembling Union, a Union still, at least in name, "Bleeding Kansas" a memory of strife. After his sleepless night, the grave dangers before him, Lincoln yet could feel deep emotion at being in Andrew Hamilton's old State House, in the Hall where the Union itself had been formed, the very room where Independence had been declared, the Federal Constitution fashioned. He spoke of the principles of that Declaration, the "promise that in due time the weight would be lifted from the shoulders of all men and that all should have an equal chance." There were freedoms more vital than any system, any government. There was a principle at stake. Could the Union be saved without giving up that principle? If it could not, he said, "I would rather be assassinated on this spot than surrender it!"

His sudden melodrama, his sudden public mention of assassination, made Frederick Seward gasp. The young man rushed away, he sped back to the hotel before the crowd moved. Lamon met him, whispered to him Lincoln had agreed to change his plans. He would slip through Baltimore earlier than announced. Seward must got at once to Washington, tell his father, Scott too, in strictest secrecy. Let Senator Seward know when to meet him, only Seward, and Washburne of Illinois . . . Judd had been up all night making private arrangements with the railroad men. Lincoln heard the plans; he ordered that Mrs. Lincoln be informed.

Learning of the plot, learning that Lincoln would travel without her, Mary Lincoln went almost to pieces. She finally consented to the arrangement, on one condition: Lamon must accompany her husband. Young Seward went off South with his news, Mary Lincoln with every strength she could call on put herself in good order. She held her head high on her tiny body, sat straight, looked firmly about her at cheering Philadelphians as the whole Presidential party moved in a fine open carriage through the streets and over the Schuylkill Bridge to the West Philadelphia station, where they entrained for Harrisburg. No inkling of anything wrong leaked out to the people.

In Harrisburg, Lincoln spoke to big crowds, in the afternoon addressed the legislature. Afterwards Governor Curtin gave a large state dinner at the Jones House. The President-Elect was tired, tense, oppressed by the secret adventure before him. Suddenly he found that his son Bob to whom he had handed his most precious gripsack (the one containing his inaugural address) could not tell him where it was. He had mislaid it. Lincoln exploded in temper. It was the only time the whole trip he lost control, one of the few times in his public life anyone saw his great angers. With Bob and Lamon, careless of his safety, he strode to the hotel baggage room, turned over every piece of luggage himself, finally they found the satchel. Lincoln grasped it firmly. It would not leave his hands again, he said darkly.

Before dinner was over, Lincoln was called from the table. He went to his room, changed into a travelling suit; he put on the old short overcoat he had worn leaving Springfield, the coat that looked so much like a sailor's pea jacket. He donned the soft felt hat Mr. Knox the hatter had given him in New York. The hat was strange on his head; he had always worn a beaver stovepipe before. He looked "like a well-to-do farmer." He grasped his satchel; he and Lamon went alone down a back stair, left the Jones House by a back door. A carriage was waiting; they were driven to the railway station. Here a locomotive with one coach, no lights burning in the dusk, moved out as soon as they were aboard.

All telegraph wires in and out of Harrisburg had been silenced. The ghost train rattled through the night, unexplained, unsignalled. Trainmen working Main Line evening traffic were startled, alarmed: an engine unlighted, one car, no orders, no shuntings to the shoo-fly. Through German farm towns, past the bright lights of Lancaster station, down hill to Coatesville, through the steel mills, the towns of the Welsh tract—Bryn Mawr, Haverford, Bala Cynwyd. . . . In the dark car, windows curtained, Lamon set upright, alert, bristling with arms: two horse pistols, two large knives, a brace of Derringers. Lincoln was still. At West Philadelphia Station they stepped off, Pinkerton met them, a railroad official at his side. He had a closed carriage waiting. Lincoln sat between Pinkerton and Lamon, the railroad official rode the box with the hack driver. The ordinary route between depots was over Market Street Bridge, east on Market to Broad, down Broad to Washington Street and the big barn-like Philadelphia, Wilmington & Baltimore Railway station. The railroad official varied this; on the pretext he was searching for a friend, he had the puzzled driver go up and down side streets, spending time till the train was about to leave. In the dark interior, Pinkerton was full of the day's news from Baltimore: rowdies had climbed aboard Hannibal Hamlin's train, rushed through all the cars, alarmed everyone with threats, foul language. The muscular, hearty Hamlin was unharmed, he had been dissuaded from fighting, he had reached Washington safely. Finally, the carriage ride was over. At the end of the train shed, Pinkerton, Lamon, and the President-Elect of The United States stole onto the last car of the regular nightly New York–Washington train. A woman operative in Pinkerton's agency had engaged rear berths "for herself and her invalid brother." Pinkerton took one, Lincoln closed the curtains of the other, opposite. Lamon sat forward, wide awake. Unknown to them all, Chief Kennedy of the New York City Police was riding in the car, too. He had heard rumors, he was on his way South to protect the President-Elect. Lincoln went to bed.

Half past three in the morning the train reached Baltimore. The cars for Washington were detached, horses were hitched up to pull them one by one on street rails the slow mile through downtown Baltimore to Camden Station. This was the ticklish moment, the most vulnerable point. At Camden Station, Lincoln's car sat more than an hour, waiting the connection from the West. On the platform a drunk sang "Dixie." Train crews went about their noisy tasks, hammering on metal, yelling back and forth. A railroad official whispered into Pinkerton's berth, "All's Well."

Six o'clock on the morning of Saturday, February 23, still not yet daylight, Abraham Lincoln, satchel in hand, stepped off the last car of the train, in Washington City. Elihu B. Washburne, Congressman from Galena, Illinois, was standing on the platform, waiting. In spite of the short coat and soft hat, in spite of the beard, he recognized Lincoln. Grinning, he came up, his hand out in greeting. "You can't play that on me!" he cried. Lamon jerked in alarm, drew back his fist. Lincoln quickly stopped him. "This is my friend Washburne. Don't you know him?" he asked.

"Keep your voices down," said Pinkerton.

The Congressman took them off to Willard's Hotel. Senator Seward, never an early riser, had chosen this morning to oversleep. He joined them, full of apologies, for breakfast. At Willard's the President-Elect was given room number 13. He signed the register "A. Lincoln, Illinois."

The long, strange trip was over. To Mrs. Lincoln, Pinkerton sent a coded wire: PLUMS DELIVERED NUTS SAFELY. She came on with the boys; at Baltimore a large angry crowd milled about her train during its transfer, men swarmed over the tops of the cars like so many monkeys, stamped, hallooed, hurled insults at Mary Lincoln, obscenities, and at Robert when they spied him. One man tried to force his way into Lincoln's private car, John Hay slammed the door, held it against him. Badly shaken, the whole party reached Willard's in the afternoon.

Through the South, a flood of ridicule poured out on Lincoln's escapade by night. Even the North was shocked at the "outrageous romance." Satires, laughing pieces, disgusted comments appeared in the friendliest journals. Sober weeklies regretted the masquerade, "a melodrama out of a two-shilling novel." Tales of his disguise were embroidered: soon everyone said he wore a Scottish plaid cap and long military cloak. The spectacle of Lincoln in a Scottish cap tickled the country's funnybone. "The McLincoln Harrisburg Highland Fling" was pictured by cartoonists. "Lanky Lincoln came to town, In night and wind and rain, sir," was sung to the tune of *Yankee Doodle:* "Uncle Abe had gone to bed, The night was dark and rainy— A laurelled night-cap on his head, 'Way down in Pennsylvaney . . ." Greeley's *New York Tribune,* in an elephantine attempt to be funny, observed "Mr. Lincoln may live a hundred years without having so good a chance to die." Bennett's *Herald* added, the President-Elect "with a most obtuse perception to the glory that awaited him, did not 'take fortune at the flood.' " The *Baltimore Sun,* ignoring the ugly mob scene at the station, announced it would not have been surprised had Lincoln turned sommersaults into Willard's Hotel, finished like a clown with a "headspring" and cried the circus greeting to General Scott: "Here We Are!"

The *Sun* added: "We do not believe the Presidency can ever be more degraded by any of his successors, than it has been by him, even before his inauguration, and so, for aught we care, he may go the full extent of his wretched comicalities."

Never had a head of state reached his capital in more bizarre fashion. But public censure was brief: to Northern citizens, the significant fact was that the head of state had actually reached his capital, unharmed, prepared for duties. What those duties would be, the accelerated pace of events would determine. To the nation, in twelve days, Lincoln had become a familiar figure, untested, still a question mark in the biggest issues, but a real person, no longer a mystery. To Lincoln, the American people had become a present, pulsing reality, the nation of wills and minds he must serve. Twelve days had been preparation, twelve days of conferences, meetings, advices, of hopes, and passions. All through the trip, he had thought of his inaugural address, hidden in that gripsack. Seward had drafted most of it, furnished thoughts, even the language. Others had helped, the Republican Party leaders. Long before he left Springfield, Lincoln had put their words, their wishes into his own cadence, his own forms. Now in Washington, he met with all the old men, Buchanan, Scott, Crittenden, met with subtle old John Tyler of Virginia. On March 4, he stood in their place, alone, ready at last to speak to the people.

He spoke to a people already in arms, spoke in a nobler, stronger voice than America had heard all its years. The words he spoke were Seward's, but he spoke them with the rhythmed accents the world would come to know, to remember, Lincoln's own:

"In your hands, my dissatisfied fellow-countrymen, and not in mine, is the momentous issue of civil war. . . . Though passion may have strained, it must not break our bonds of affection. The mystic chords of memory, stretching from every battlefield, and patriot grave, to every living heart and hearthstone, all over this broad land, will yet swell the chorus of the Union, when again touched, as surely they will be, by the better angels of our nature."

Notes

1. Philadelphia Lawyer

Not long ago a colleague of mine encountered an austerely critical remark on a piece of narrative history, from one of those austerely critical students who always seem to enroll in the course called Historiography. "This document," the student wrote, "has no references at all; therefore the historian can only consider it the product of the author's imagination."

Now "Historiography" may or may not mean what it sounds like it ought to mean; and we are all used to severe young people who enjoy being critical more than they enjoy appreciating the efforts of others. But that student, if he goes far enough, will one day come with the absorbed concentration of the scholar to deal with particular manuscripts and antiquities, as if no one had ever dealt with them before. And then he will learn what is not always evident in history: that any work is a product of the author's imagination. References, however copious, cannot make it less than that.

For the evidences of the past, the "sources," do not limit or restrict the imagination. They evoke it. It is to the imagination that sources speak. History is a product of wonder, and a quest. It is an imaginative art—with its craft and techniques, to be sure; but these serve the wondering, they do not smother it. The wondering is what the writer takes to his sources. It is how he permits them to speak to him, saying more to him of their world than they originally designed to say.

In the case of Andrew Hamilton, the sources have been well-known to scholars for a long time, and in the ordinary ways of scholarship easily available, but very little wonder has been taken to them. Since 1904, when Mr. Livingston Rutherford published *John Peter Zenger, His Press, His Trial,* it has been clear that the text of Hamilton's speech in Zenger's printed-book edition differed significantly from the text given in earlier newspaper printings, and the differences involved points at law. But no one has bothered to study these points, nor wondered what moved the editor to make Mr. Hamilton seem more correct than he was, in conventional terms. (One of the things cut out, incidentally, was Vaughan's language in Bushel's case.) Even the latest editors have not tried to establish the best, most authentic text. Neither has anyone tried the not-too-difficult task of reconstructing Bradley's and Chambers's speeches from the hints given us in the report, after both refused (we are told this) to assist the reporter.

New York lawyers at the time, striving as they were for improvements and regularities in pleadings, were obviously disturbed at Hamilton's performance. A thorough rebuttal of his arguments and careful exposition of the correct

English law was prepared at once, by some one of those lawyers. It appeared in July, 1737, in Keimer's *Barbados Gazette*. The author, significantly, signed himself *Anglo-Americanus*. And this has been entirely within the purview of scholars, because it was promptly reprinted in full by Franklin in his Philadelphia newspaper and Bradford in New York. It was *Anglo-Americanus's* embarrassing candor and correctness which occasioned James Alexander, certainly one of the principal Anglo-Americans in law, to respond with his apologetic defense of Hamilton's pleading, acknowledging his errors. This, too, Franklin printed. The controversy was a brief one, but it displayed Hamilton's contemporary reputation among lawyers, as a lawyer—when even Alexander whose cause he had pled could apologize for him in public (making no mention, of course, of the skill with which the Philadelphia Lawyer by circumventing the law had prevented the disclosure of the principals in the libel.) Indeed, it is entirely clear that both in New York and Philadelphia (and in London as well, judging from the observations of one *Indus-Britannicus* in his *Remarks on the Trial of John Peter Zenger,* ca. 1738) Hamilton, far from winning plaudits or fame as a learned attorney from his pleading, caused lawyers a considerable amount of distressful annoyance for having undermined much of what they had been struggling to achieve.

Other sources unfolding for us Hamilton's actual career in its true dimensions have likewise been readily available: the legislative and administrative records of Pennsylvania and Delaware, election records of Philadelphia, the many survivals of the Keithite struggles, several bibliographical studies of law libraries of contemporaries, the Penn–Logan correspondence, various publications resulting from Hamilton's own busy public and private controversies. From New York records it is clear Alexander had won the city voters; plainly the jury Mr. Hamilton addressed was of Alexander's partisans, who needed no persuading but only a justification at law for the defiance of the Governor they unquestionably intended—that, and a way of avoiding exposure of Alexander. A manuscript memorandum book of Mr. Hamilton exists; and frequently, incidental records of significance turn up. On the 150th anniversary of The Philadelphia Bar Association, 1952, which the Hon. Bernard G. Segal, Chancellor, turned into a memorable scholarly occasion, The Historical Society of Pennsylvania exhibited the Freedom Box presented to Hamilton by New York City; The Rosenbach Foundation displayed unique Hamilton–Zenger items; so did The Free Library of Philadelphia from its Hampton L. Carson collection; and Mr. and Mrs. Joseph Carson from their private collection showed Hamilton's manuscript account of his fourteen years as recorder of Philadelphia. His salary had never been paid him; on his death in 1741 his son-in-law William Allen (also his successor as recorder) presented his account for collection.

With all this material, there should be no mystery about Hamilton. Yet mysteries have been made, and a legend. Sober historians still write of him as if he were a towering professional figure, standing alone, a giant in legal scholarship and learning. "The eighty-year old Nestor of the American bar," says the leading text in Colonial history, and the legend is met with everywhere. The real man in his real dimensions, with all his tough Scottish vigor, his contentiousness, his rigidity and schemes, his undeniable charm and imposing personality, is lost in the legend.

It is by now impossible to persuade the Philadelphia Bar Association that Hamilton was far from the knowledgeable and experienced lawyer that his

New York colleagues and adversaries were, that what he did in Zenger's case ran counter to the best legal thought and standards of his day. In Philadelphia it is universally believed that Hamilton's 1735 trip to New York and his victory was the episode that gave rise to the familiar phrase "as smart as a Philadelphia Lawyer." Unfortunately this too is legend. That epithet, as near as research has been able to find out, arose after 1800, in Jeffersonian struggles. Its first known use was in 1803, when it was "a Yankee phrase." Twenty years later it was still Yankee: "The New England folk have a saying, that three Philadelphia lawyers are a match for the devil himself."

Some scholars believe they can trace some such saying to a slightly older time, that perhaps it arose among British seamen in Post-Revolutionary days when Philadelphia proctors in admiralty got them out of difficulties, or protected American seamen from British impressment. "To puzzle a Philadelphia lawyer" seems to have been in general use in England in the 1830's, as a common phrase describing a difficult problem.

It is not to be imagined, of course, that members of the Philadelphia Bar themselves coined the cherished epithet, or immodestly preserved it; yet phrases similar to the Yankee and English aphorisms did have a wistful sort of currency in the Quaker City during the first half of the nineteenth century, after Philadelphia had ceased to be the national capital and New York City had surpassed it in commercial and financial importance. Peter Stephen DuPonceau, David Paul Browne, and Horace Binney all speculated on its origin, in the practice of city lawyers travelling circuits.

But there has never been found any reason at all to think that it, or any other characterization of the Philadelphia Lawyer, was associated with Hamilton's 1735 Zenger adventure, until a century and more afterwards, when someone made an irresponsible assertion, and others began endlessly to repeat it—as historical writers will. But the legend has become ineradicable, I imagine; and in our time Philadelphia Lawyers have become such fellows as a mere antiquarian could never hope to persuade.

The trouble is, of course, that historians who have written of Hamilton have not been lawyers, and lawyers when they have gone to the story have not been seeking history. They have been seeking a hero for their guild. And that is what they have made out Hamilton to be. Even legal historians (there have been a few) have fallen into a particular difficulty, for they have written of separate bars in each colony without comparing one with another, or wondering very deeply about Inns-of-Court training. I don't like to complain, but here are two examples: Mr. Hamlin in his excellent study (*Legal Education in Colonial New York*) writes of the New York bar as a group small in size; yet everything he exhibits makes clear that it was a large group of lawyers for any city of 8,000 people—it would be large for such a city today—and was far advanced in English training and practice over Philadelphia's, Boston's, or Charles Town's. Mr. Richard B. Morris (*Studies in the History of American Law*, 2nd ed., 1964, p. 66) also describes these three dozen practicing attorneys as a bar "extremely limited in size," and he permits himself this remark: "The outstanding attorneys in the middle and southern colonies received their legal education at the Inns of Court. Among them may be mentioned the distinguished Andrew Hamilton of Philadelphia." Hamilton, of course, received no education at all at the Inns. Bradley and De Lancey did, but Hamilton, Alexander, and Chambers had all been called *per favor* to the bar.

A later generation, the Revolutionary lawyers, true enough contained many American barristers of the Inns, from the middle and southern colonies—a little more than seventy in all. But the British part of their training was opposed to Hamilton's sort of law, and his antagonism in *Zenger* to British rules made him in Revolutionary times a retrospective hero not to those who advocated English Common Law, but to those who advocated its abolition.

What lawyers have done, journalists have out-done in fashioning the Hamilton legend. Journalists have celebrated the Zenger case, as if it were in every modern way the achievement of freedom of the press. There is a sort of infectious enthusiasm which those words "freedom of the press" carry with them as a contagion, and journalists are swift to host the virus. Mr. Vincent Buranelli (*The Trial of Peter Zenger*, N.Y. 1957) with some justice presents James Alexander rather than Morris, Smith, or Van Dam as the leader of the anti-Leislerian faction; but he goes much beyond existing historical evidence when he describes Alexander as "editor" of Zenger's *Journal*, even calls him "the first American editor to practice freedom of the press systematically and coherently, and the first to be justified legally . . . ." which is (to say the least) reading a great deal back into the record. And he adds, "The defense of Zenger's person was a defense of Alexander's philosophy of journalism." It is an extravagant remark. Alexander's motives were far less elevated, and far more exciting, than that. Yet Mr. Buranelli will have it that this Jacobite riser of '15 was charged with a mission of pure endeavor: "For [Alexander] this Scottish immigrant of the eighteenth century taught his adopted land the first law of sane journalism: that the news is to be reported on the basis of factual accuracy, and that censorship of the authorities is to be resisted as far as is consistent with national security and the interests of society."

Much as I am attracted by the admirable Alexander, I cannot find him concerned with sane journalism or factual accuracy in his partisan writings on the Governor, nor with national security (what *nation* does the enthusiastic writer have reference to?), nor any interests of society other than the special interests of his own mercantile faction in the struggle for the trade of the port of New York.

Historians should be used to journalists, and not overly surprised to find them going too far. But one journalist's production on the long shelf of Zenger literature is an outlandish example of enthusiastic irresponsibility, by a man who should have known better. That severe student in Historiography would notice it contains ten undoubted documents. But alas, it is not to those documents that the journalist's imagination has been alert. The book is entitled *Anna Zenger, Mother of Freedom;* it was published by a reputable house in 1946; the author was Kent Cooper, who for many years headed the Associated Press. Mr. Cooper was a professional journalist of the first rank and the highest standards, conspicuously able and successful. Personally he was a lively individual with many interests, and he wrote other books. But his "novelized biography" as he calls it —the regrettable word "novelized" is his—of Anna Maulin, the wife of the printer Zenger, purporting to persuade us it was she who wrote the things Zenger printed, is a monstrous production. It is full of black villains surrounding a shining heroine, written from an evident ignorance of New York in the 1730's and, one would think, an ignorance of human beings of any time. From regard for Mr. Kent Cooper, I wish his book had never appeared.

It will always be a mystery to me how certain men busy with big affairs, full of responsibility and integrity in their professional dealings with others, can regard the past and human beings in the past as trivial matters, fit prey for games, speculations, and irresponsible inventions. Mr. Cooper was by no means alone: Dr. Sigmund Freud of all people was willing to deal irresponsibly, as if it mattered to no one, with Leonardo da Vinci on evidence so slender as to be almost nonexistent; there is a faint possibility he may even have misbehaved to some degree in this fashion at the behest of William Bullitt, regarding Woodrow Wilson.

Burton Alva Konkle's *Life of Andrew Hamilton* (Philadelphia, 1941) in spite of the high hopes and aspirations of the venerable author, is a thin production, of meager usefulness, best forgotten. Mr. Konkle, himself a New-Light Presbyterian, could not accept the simple fact that Hamilton was a deist. Spirited, informed accounts of the Zenger case recently are in Richard B. Morris's *Fair Trial* (New York, 1952) pp. 69–95, and Helen Hill Miller's significant book of studies, *The Case for Liberty* (Chapel Hill, 1965) pp. 29–66. The rest of the bibliography is extensive; one of the most recent lawyers' celebrations is an article by Mr. Walker Lewis of the Washington, D.C. bar, "The Right to Complain," in the *American Bar Association Journal*, XLVI, no. 1, January, 1960. And certainly there will be others. But I fancy it will be a long time before a scholar unimpeded by legend will write the whole story of the common law in the colonial outposts of empire, how migration of Scottish rebels after 1689 and 1715 affected it in Hamilton's and Alexander's time, how the Newcastle Whigs succeeded in using it as an instrument of colonial development and imperial domination, how it developed last in the Quaker colonies, and how Mr. Hamilton's various career in Scotland, Virginia, Maryland, Delaware, Pennsylvania, New Jersey and New York fitted in to this history of pleadings, doctrines, and rulings, of technical legal skills improving, court systems reforming, of political battles won and lost in the new law.

"Trials," Louis Nizer has said, "are the wonderland of the unexpected." Certainly Hamilton's argument against settled doctrine was unexpected that August day in New York. But in the long view of two centuries and more, the most unexpected thing of all about this Scottish wanderer's career, is that it should have been he who built Independence Hall. That building, as much as the Zenger plea, is the improbable legacy he left us as an American character, and the chief reason for his inclusion in this book.

2. Treason in Profile*

Dr. Lawrence Henry Gipson, master historian of our day, has brought to triumphant conclusion his multivolume work of a lifetime in studies, *The British Empire Before the American Revolution*. Scarcely any recent work can match it; for the purity of his scholarship and the clarity of his style, Dr. Gipson is unexcelled, and so is he for his evident humanism, his concern that his study should illuminate our times as well as his. Already his work commands the field of eighteenth-century American history; for a generation hence, much that

---

* An earlier, shorter version of this story was published, under the same title, in *The General Magazine and Historical Chronicle* of The University of Pennsylvania, Autumn, 1956, pp. 1–10.

scholars produce will be merely trying up thread-ends of the huge tapestry he has wrought for us.

And certainly his work will last. For it is narrative history, an account of events that occurred, from thoughtful consideration of the records that survive—one could almost say all the records; surely more than any other single scholar has used. A teacher of mine once observed, "There is a temptation to think of history as something that can be understood, rather than as something that actually happened." What actually happened, is—the research scholar learns this—the hardest of all problems to solve. It is the first and highest calling of the historian. Interpretation is by comparison facile, superficial, and temporary. The interpretation of one generation is bound to be replaced in the next. But completeness and sureness of narrative, from imaginative discovery, is likely to be permanent. Gipson does not force his events of the past to support a personal theory of history, he does not manipulate today's passing fads and fashions of thought to explain the people of long ago. Or of now. There will come a time when Toynbee's *A Study of History* will no longer speak effectively to readers. It is theory, reflection, reason; it is philosophy, not history. It will be read by scholars, not for truth but for symptom and example of our Western intellect in this mid-twentieh century, and our wistful search for meaning beyond meaning. But Gipson's *British Empire* will speak with undoubted authority, then and always, not as theory for our swift day alone but as chronicle and relation of significant episodes, presented with professional skills and professional confidence, a witness of the remarkable professional scholarship of this age which is ending.

Because I admire his work so sincerely, I am sorry to think we may feel differently, he and I, about the traitor of Beauséjour. Of course, any sensible reader confronted with any difference however slight between Lawrence Gipson and me will at once choose Gipson. He would be foolish not to. He can find Dr. Gipson's telling of this story in volume six of his work, the volume called *The Great War for the Empire: The Years of Defeat, 1754–1757.* Chapter VIII of that volume, pages 212–242, is "The Treason of Thomas Pichon." There he will find the man I have called rascal, liar, and rogue handled much less unsympathetically—handled, indeed, as a hard working civil servant, a scholarly theorist of colonial military and economic policy. Similar sympathetic treatments characterize the two monographs on the subject, J. E. Webster's *Thomas Pichon: The Spy of Beauséjour* (1937)—a satisfying work of exploratory research—and the Rev. Albert David's *Le Judas de L'Acadia* (1934).

Other writers have described Pichon as a patriot honestly disillusioned with French colonial management and the French church, sincerely convinced the best future for Acadians lay in a victory of English power. If it had been so, honorable courses more consistent with sincere conviction lay open to him—courses not likely to produce a traitor's revenues, to be sure, but capable at least of convincing posterity. The best defense of Pichon is consideration of his undeniably able book on *Isle Royale;* but he wrote that book long after the fact of his treason, and the results that flowed from it. And certainly it was no statesmanlike discontent with French colonial administration that induced him to spy for the British in later years on Acadian refugees in Pennsylvania, and the Channel Islands. It was money.

As for the difference between Dr. Gipson's view of Pichon and mine, it is actually more apparent than real, I think. It arises from the way an historian, and one who might be called an antiquarian, differ. They differ on how they deal with good and evil. Dr. Gipson's authoritative account is an historian's. He exhibits the imperial significance of the betrayal of Beauséjour, its critical importance in the whole continental struggle; he describes the linkages within French America between Quebec and New Orleans, in the other direction the French need for land linkages between Quebec and Louisbourg for the defense of that bastion from the rear; he reviews the history of the French in Acadia after Utrecht. The war of giants is his theme—that, and the step-by-step fashioning of the British Empire in idea and reality as an instrument of free and prosperous government in a reasonable world.

The historian encounters both good and evil, in the march of events. He acquires a wisdom that accepts both, as parts of the record humanity has left. In the masterwork of Lawrence Gipson, that historian's wisdom is superbly exemplified. "Can anything justify treason?" he asks, considering Pichon—and he reflects for a moment on treasons in our own time. He is not horrified to confront a traitor, nor surprised; traitors have appeared before, they will come again. The British Empire is fashioned of innumerable events, of innumerable kinds. The historian who has written with eloquent self-control of the death of Byng, that tragedy of state still appalling in the telling (and Gipson's telling is skilfully affecting), is not going to be disturbed at the personal corruption of a Pichon.

Self-control is the historian's wisdom. It must not be mistaken for serenity; the indifference and withdrawal characteristic of serenity are not required of him, as he contemplates the play of good and evil in the past. Indeed, I cannot imagine a man could study history serenely. But he can, if he is gifted and perceptive, study good and evil knowing that history goes on—that, as my grandfather used to say to his students, "there never was a disaster in history so bad, that it was not succeeded by one infinitely worse." The historian's skill is to tell of good and evil impartially, disinterestedly, for neither good nor evil is the essence of human movement in time. Each is but an episode.

The antiquarian is interested in that episode. What is the evil history has passed by? What is the good it has swept over? And what are the personal dimensions the record reveals? I hope these are not trivial concerns; any single episode can leave a convincing record of every human element worth a man's contemplating, however swift its moment in hurrying time. But this approach to the past is significantly different from the historian's—different in values. It is one thing, imposing and awesome, to exhibit the succession of events by which Britannia came to rule the waves. It is quite another to reflect briefly on the plight of poor Mme. de Beaumont, who could not even rule herself.

3. "A Certain Great Fortune and Piddling Genius"*

Dickinson College in Carlisle, Pennsylvania, is an uncommonly attractive place, both from the people in it, and from its setting. The old town has changed,

---

* The first version of this article was a lecture delivered at Dickinson College, February, 1960, the annual Boyd Lee Spahr Lecture in Americana. That version was published in the third collected volume of those annual lectures: *Early Dickinsoniana: The Boyd Lee Spahr Lectures In Americana 1957–1961*, Carlisle, Pennsylvania, The Library of Dickinson College, 1961, pp. 41–72.

of course, since the days when James Wilson practiced law there on the frontier of settlement, but not so much as some other towns have changed. And the purple hills of Cumberland County remain much as they were, scarred but not entirely reduced by the great turnpikes and railroads snaking through. Wandering these hills, and Carlisle streets, you can pass by houses James Wilson passed by, and if you are at ease—in Carlisle you are bound to be at ease—a doorway or finial here, a lintel there, a chuchyard near a spire on a hilltop, will give you some sense of scenes past: Washington the President-General arriving here to review troops in '92, before they set out to quell the Whiskey Rebellion (happy memory); or drovers lumbering up with their Conestoga wagons, laying by for a change of teams at the tavern on the Wagon Road West, hopefully chalking up their Pints and Quarts in the Ordinary against their return journey East with hard money in pocket—hopefully, till the innkeeper advises them, "Mind your Ps and Qs."

The instinct of blending old and new is part of the historian's calling. A reasonable adult does not spend his years bothering about old forgotten far-off things and battles long ago, unless he has something of this response which can be quickened by a scene, this reflex of re-creating what has gone—and unless he believes it is intellectually worthwhile. An important part of the content of thinking and feeling of any generation is the thinking and feeling that generation does about its past. Not in every place does the significant past come so agreeably to mind, as in this lovely part of Pennsylvania.

That the college is called "Dickinson" is less the perfection of a tribute to The Pennsylvania Farmer than it is one of those things that happen when someone starts raising money. Dr. Benjamin Rush founded this college. He had visions of a vast endowment from the generosity of benefactors. With all-too-evident calculation, he told Dickinson, who was at that time President of the Supreme Executive Council of Pennsylvania and one of the richest men Rush knew of anywhere, that he intended to name it in his honor—and in honor also of his wife Mary Norris Dickinson, who was certainly the richest women the busy Doctor could have known. The name Dr. Rush proposed was, "The College of John and Mary."

To us, it sounds like a soap opera; to the modest John Dickinson it sounded like a crude travesty of "The College of William and Mary," that already venerable institution in Virginia which commemorated a Stewart sovereign and her royal Dutch husband. He was repelled by the name, he told Rush so. But (as the Doctor well knew) he actually was engaged just then in giving away large amounts of capital for various philanthropic purposes, including education, and Rush was confident his new foundation would come in for some of the bounty. He trimmed the name to the more acceptable form, Dickinson College; and he finally succeeded in extracting a couple of farms from his friend as part of the endowment, and a library of medical books Charles Norris (Mary's dead brother) had owned. He kept trying for more; by and by he did get some other gifts, but in the total very little, far less than a man might think just as a return for the honor of a name.

Still, the people of Dickinson College have always maintained a polite if bemused interest in hearing news of John Dickinson, and on both occasions when I was asked to give Boyd Spahr's annual lecture, I devoted it to some piece of The Farmer's career.

Mr. Charles Coleman Sellers, historian of art, distinguished biographer of

Charles Willson Peale, librarian of Dickinson College, has general charge of these lectures. The first one I gave, I could never find afterwards. Mr. Sellers recollects that I spoke extemporaneously, which I insist on doubting for it is a practice I never indulge in myself and disapprove of in others. The second, Mr. Sellers politely but firmly demanded I hand him at once, as soon as I finished, fearing I might contrive to lose it as well. I nearly did, for at the outset of my talk all the electrical current at the college unaccountably failed. Those who especially admire John Adams (he has had a very good press in recent years) may feel that in this talk I was shedding more heat than light. Certainly I confess to a heated annoyance with the use that has been made of Adams's late writings and recollections; but my annoyance is more with historical writers than with Adams himself. It adds a very human dimension to his character, to find Adams so bent on self-justification, so determined to discredit Dickinson, so wistfully desirous of enlarging his own rôle as he looked backward to great scenes. Biographers have always missed this dimension. They could have used it; it belongs to biography. Except for Catherine Drinker Bowen, and unfortunately her penetrating, candid study carried him only to 1776, biographers have all treated these self-serving distortions and twistings in his late writings uncritically; they have become Adams partisans, rather than analysts. Adams is worth far more understanding and discriminating treatment than that.

Examples of his distortions of fact are so many, they would make a study in themselves. Even apart from his personal attacks on Dickinson, they provide us with a history that never happened. One letter will make the point. It relates to the independence struggle of the next year (and the next chapter in this book). Adams wrote William Plumer of New Hampshire on March 28, 1813 (*Works,* X, 35) answering Plumer's question whether "every Member of Congress did, on the 4th of July 1776, in fact cordially approve the declaration of Independence." He states, that all who were then members signed it, which was by no means the case; and then he gives an account of the issue of independence which is remarkable for its misrepresentations and twistings. "The Measure had been upon the carpet for Months, and obstinately opposed from day to day," he declares—while the record shows independence itself was debated only twice, June 8–11, and July 1, 1776. His statement could square with the facts, only if we understand him to mean by "independence" a whole congeries of issues such as opening the ports or forming state governments, which in his own mind at the time had been separable (and indeed separated) from independence. But that concession to his words would vitiate his next statements. "Majorities were constantly against it," he adds, which was not true; a majority against independence appeared only once, June 8–11, 1776; and on those other issues, majorities were in favor, not against, all during May. And then he says something that could not be true in a body that voted by colony rather than by head: "For many days the Majority depended on Mr. Hews of North Carolina." Now Joseph Hewes, during April, May and June, 1776, sat alone for North Carolina. His colleague Penn did not arrive till June 24. Had his instructions permitted him to cast the vote of his colony alone, it is conceivable that on some issue he might have settled a 6–6 tie, or a 5–5 tie, by North Carolina's voice. But during that whole period, there was no such vote, nor were his instructions on voting clear to Hewes. Throughout May he received, and announced to Congress, the various actions of his colony as a state government was formed, and by May 20 his instructions had arrived to vote for independence. They would have reached Hewes first, not the Congress; certainly Hewes was best-aware of all members of what was going on in his own state. But Adams invented a pretty tale, about Joseph Hewes:

> While a Member one day was speaking and reading documents from all the Colonies to prove that the Public Opinion, the general Sense of all was in favour of the Measure, when he came to North Carolina and produced letters and public proceedings which demonstrated that the Majority of that Colony were in favour of it, Mr. Hews who had hitherto constantly voted against it, started suddenly upright, and lifting up both his Hands to Heaven as if he had been in a trance, cry'd out "It is done! and I will abide by it." I would give more for a perfect Painting of the terror and horror upon the Faces of the Old Majority at that critical moment than for the best Piece of Raphaelle. The Question however was eluded by an immediate Motion for Adjournment.

John Adams loved to scatter through his memories of his years in Congress moments of high drama worthy of the pencil of "Raphaelle." Historians search in vain for such moments. Joseph Hewes was a thoughtful, hard-working man, and conscientious; he was a leading politician, merchant, and ship-owner of the Edenton community in Carolina (and was the first American to befriend and support John Paul Jones). He was certainly going to abide by the instructions he had received from home, even though he appears to have thought independence at the moment unwise and premature. And certainly the Delegates of the Second Continental Congress were very serious in their work. No one can doubt it, who reads the record. Men working together six days a week, all day, are bound to experience moments of tension, of lightness, of merriness, of deep dismay. But these were informed and knowledgable men. Terror and horror on their faces, occasioned by a reading of dispatches which did not take them by surprise, is not imaginable—however it appealed to Adams as a scene he wished had occurred.

He proceeds to say, "some Members who foresaw that the point would be carried, left the House and went home to avoid voting in the Affirmative or Negative." Adams invented this. Andrew Allen, it is true, did not attend after May 20, and certainly he was a Loyalist after July 1. But he left Congress because of the meeting of the Pennsylvania Assembly, and he did not return because he certainly and openly opposed independence. The only other possibility is Oliver Wolcott, who happened to make a trip home June 28, just before the issue of independence came up for a second time, but his views in favor were well known.

And Adams says, Pennsylvania recalled all her Delegates who had voted against Independence and sent new ones expressly to vote for it, though actually the new Pennsylvania Delegates were not chosen until independence was two weeks old, and Pennsylvania's vote had already been cast by Franklin, Wilson, and Morton—three of the old Delegates. In every statement he made answering Plumer, he was wrong. "There were no Yeas and Nays in those times," he says, though Thomson's records and some few other sources do suggest that the vote of each member (at least in Committee of the Whole) was called for.

Yet it is not John Adams, in his great age, seeking to revise the record in behalf of his own self-esteem that I object to. That is a phase of Adams I rather enjoy. It is a familiar phase, we all know old people who do that sort of thing. Adams withdrew from public life in March, 1801, in his sixty-sixth year. He lived twenty-five years more, dying at ninety-one on the Fourth of July, 1826, the fiftieth anniversary of American Independence, the same day Thomas Jefferson died at eighty-three. In those last twenty-five years, he had no other employments than those he contrived for himself. The considerable energy he had exhibited in his youth and his middle years had long since deserted him; he had been an indolent President, he did only a small amount of executive office work compared with Washington before him and Jefferson after. And the political attitudes and political party he had represented were both thoroughly discredited in his own time. It was not as an elder statesman he remembered, looked back, recalled the exciting events of his triumphant days. It was as a statesman whom the world had passed by. In retirement years, he wrote vivid, pungent, passionate letters, wonderfully revealing, but what they reveal is John Adams, not the events of which he treated. He left us records endlessly charming to a student concerned to know character, and the qualities of his intellect command the most respectful attention as well as the most diligent attempts to understand and properly evaluate the curiosities and impulses of his self-justifications. It was quite like Adams, for example, in that Plumer letter suddenly to beguile us by equating public opinion with what Rousseau called the General Will of All. He always brings us up short with the extent of his knowledge and the depth of his penetration. But historians and biographers both have duties in their callings that require more than the bland acceptance and uncritical recording of recollections offered as truths. Adams' prejudices and petulancies give to the Continental Congress record extraordinary color and surprisingly fresh portrayals. Yet they are the interested and biased jottings of a highly contentious individual, and they should be placed in their proper perspective.

I shall always think it odd of the excellent M. Gilbert Chinard to have called him, "Honest John Adams."

Mr. Lyman H. Butterfield has compared all known texts of the famous intercepted letters, and commented on the episode, *Adams Family Correspondence*, I, 256–57; Adams' *Diary and Autobiography*, II, 174–75; III, 318–19. Allen French has described the publication of Harrison's intercepted letter to Washington, "The First George Washington Scandal," Mass. Hist. Society, *Proceedings*, LXV, 460–74.

4. The Day of American Independence*

There is so much the records do not tell, so much that remains conjectural . . . When exactly was it that President Witherspoon said the colonies were ripe for independence, rotten for the want of it? Can it really be that Adams gave two separate speeches? Why was Hopkinson not present Monday morning? Did

---

* Some of the material, and some of the points of view of this article, were published in three previous attempts to tell the story of this day's transactions: (1) "Speech of John Dickinson Opposing the Declaration of Independence, 1 July, 1776," *The Pennsylvania Magazine of History and Biography*, October, 1941, pp. 458–481; (2) "The Debate on American Independence July 1, 1776," *Delaware Notes*, Twenty-third series 1950, pp. 37–62; and (3) 'The Day of American Independence," *Woman's Day*, December, 1950.

Abraham Clark enter the hall with the rest of the Jersey Delegates? (No one mentions that he did, yet he signed the Resolution of Secrecy that day.) When exactly did the Maryland instructions arrive—"just as we were entering on the great debate," Adams said that night; but does this mean while Hancock was still in the chair, or after Committee of the Whole had been formed, with Harrison presiding? Did the house have to go out of Committee to receive Maryland's official communication, that Paca might read it? Was Timothy Matlack actually present? His position of "clerk" was originally as "Clerk in Chief" to the Committee of Claims (i.e., Accounts); sometimes Delegates called him Commissary or Commissary Clerk. He was paid 15 shillings a day, hired an under clerk for £6 a week (the discrepancy is more apparent than real; the 15 shillings was good Pennsylvania money), and other clerks as well. But some evidences suggest he was, by this summer, actually attending plenary sessions and acting as clerk in more than Accounts functions.

Which day did Rodney arrive? the 2nd, or the 4th? There is still some puzzle over that. When did the rain begin? How long did Dickinson speak? When did he commence? To understand this better, I read aloud the letters from the generals and colonels, slowly, as a clerk might read, and the letters from New Jersey, New Hampshire, and the Georgia credentials for Walton. And I guessed at Clinton's speech. All that is certain about it is that he read the letter from the New York Provincial Congress. I allowed a certain amount of time for the motion, perhaps, by Francis Lee, and the seconding, perhaps by Gerry, but these too are uncertain. If Congress in Committee of the Whole operated in strict legislative fashion, the reading of the order of the day would make unnecessary a motion and a seconding. Here, I was at sea. Then I read Dickinson's speech aloud. It was the best I could do.

For a good many years now I have worried all the evidences of this day, trying to reconstruct what it must have been like to the men present. The writer must see the scene; here there is so much we cannot see. For example, we do not know for sure how the Delegates sat, whether together as colony delegations, or at random about the hall. We do not know if each had a desk before him. We do not know how they voted: did they rise to vote, or raise their hands, or call out their votes orally from their seats? Were Delegates called individually to vote, or did one member as chairman announce the vote of his colony? Was voting the same in Committee of the Whole as in Congress? Already by this summer of '76, the internal development of the administrative institutions of Congress—that Committee of Accounts with its staff, the office of the Secretary, the Committee of Secret Correspondence, the boards and the appointed officers—had proceeded so far, that the peculiar nature of this body was becoming evident. Congress had started out in 1774 with parliamentary proceedings familiar to all Delegates who had sat in Assemblies, but its development was not along parliamentary lines. By the time of the Federal Convention of 1787 it would be clear to everyone that the Congress was not a parliamentary body at all. This makes it all the more significant to wonder, was there a gavel, was there a mace? On two subsequent occasions, when unseemly quarrelings broke out on the floor, there was no mention of the presentation of a mace to keep order, nor was there a sergeant-at-arms to present it. So far as I can ascertain, neither a mace nor any indication of sovereignty existed in the Congress; and these Delegates certainly persisted in thinking of sovereignty as appertaining to their separate colonial establishments, whether the old governments or the new. From all I have been able to learn, I have guessed that the voting was done by a call of each Delegate, and the vote of the colony was announced by the Secretary. But it is only a guess. To see the scene, one of the great scenes of American history, is excessively difficult when we have only hints and suggestions to rely on. The guesses I have made are the products of a good number of years' study, yet I cannot be confident of them, and doubtless there are students of the Congress who may think them too free. Mr. Burnett once told me he would never go so far as I had, in the matter of how they voted. (His Tennessee mountain language was actually more picturesque than that, but his meaning was clear.) He always hoped more evidence would turn up, and I hope so too.

The materials now available are well known to all scholars in the field, except for the Dickinson papers, and perhaps they should have a word here. John Dickinson saved every scrap of paper, all his life. A good many of his out-papers came to The Historical Society of Pennsylvania with the Logan Papers, and the Norris Papers, and the Maria Dickinson Logan Papers. But the vast bulk of what he received, and his retained copies, all tied up in pink ribbands and neatly filed, passed at his death to his daughter Sally, and at her death to his second daughter, Maria, who had married a Logan of Stenton. Ultimately they descended to his great-grandson, Robert Restalrig Logan, Esq. He properly esteemed them, and their importance. There came a time during the Depression when Mr. Logan was briefly very hard-pressed for money to maintain his contributions in support of the many charitable and philosophical causes to which he devoted his unusual talents and his remarkably sweet nature all his exemplary life. At that time, he was induced to sell a few items of his Dickinson inheritance. Among these he sold to Mr. Simon Gratz, greatest of all American autograph collectors, the manuscript of notes which Dickinson held in his hands July 1, 1776, and from which he made his notable speech. Mr. Gratz left his collection entire to The Historical Society of Pennsylvania, which is where I encountered this manuscript in 1939. Meanwhile, Mr. Robert R. Logan, having succeeded in keeping alive the several enterprises he was encouraging, even through the worst of the Depression, sold no more of his Dickinson material, but instead decided to convey all the great bulk of the manuscripts to two institutions equally, for he had an equal interest in them both: The Historical Society of Pennsylvania, and The Library Company of Philadelphia (which included the Loganian Library, of which he was, by an ancient Logan will, hereditary trustee. He was senior heir in the direct line from James Logan, and he had mastered Greek to the degree of comprehension of Hesiod and Homer). I assisted him in searching through his attic at "Sarobia" for every last scrap, opening the amusingly contrived "secret" compartment in John Dickinson's desk, I joined with him in a final visit to Dickinson houses on Jones Neck, in Kent. Mr. Logan had the happiness to know, before his death, that every bit of the Dickinson papers, so long preserved in his family, had at last found its way into public repositories, and would be permanently available to scholars.

When Mr. Leon de Valinger, Jr., the able archivist of Delaware, has completed and published his *Letters to and From John Dickinson,* and when Mr. H. Trevor Colbourn has brought forth his *Political Writings of John Dickinson,* the place of the Pennsylvania Farmer in the generation of leaders of the American Revolution will be better appreciated and better understood, and perhaps then historical writers will place in more just and appropriate perspective the passionately biased evidence of New Englanders, as they deal with such issues as the issue of independence. I hope they may give somewhat more room to the men of peace and reason, who would not willingly join Adams in committing prematurely the lives of citizens to the hazards and obscenities of war—a war for which they knew those citizens to be unorganized, unprepared, and unsupported.

The subsequent history of John Alsop is instructive: he withdrew entirely from public life during the war years, lived quietly in the Connecticut valley unmolested, unnoticed. Around him were a good many others who had contended sturdily against parliamentary measures from the time of the Stamp Act on, but would have no part of the abandonment of lawful government and constitutional processes in 1776. William Samuel Johnson was one of them; he settled not far off from Alsop's retreat. Yet after the war, these able non-combatants who had been neither rebels nor tories resumed with apparent ease their places of leadership in the affairs of the new nation to whose independence they had not originally consented. Dr. Johnson pled the Connecticut cause against Pennsylvania in the Trenton trials, he was a busy and useful member of the Federal Convention of 1787, and became the first President of Columbia College in New York. Mr. Alsop returned to the city after the British left; when the merchants organized the new Chamber of Commerce of New York City and procured a charter from the state, Mr. Alsop was unanimously elected its first president. His daughter Mary in 1786 became the bride of Congressman Rufus King of Massachusetts, and King removed permanently to New York where his father-in-law's substantial position was a great help to him in his public and his private career. Mr. Alsop died respected and honored, late in 1794. One grandson, John Alsop King, became Governor of New York, another became President of Columbia, a great-grandson sat in Congress from New Jersey.

The records, I am sorry to say, do not make clear whether Mr. Thomas Lynch was ever again able to attend Congress, to give that body the happiness of seeing a father and son sitting together as members. It is known that his name was signed, along with his son's, to two communications the South Carolina Delegates sent to President John Rutledge, back home. Neither of these letters would have been written in Congress; they would have been agreed upon outside the session hall by the South Carolina Delegates meeting together. And neither document has survived. They are known only in official copies, so we cannot tell if Mr. Lynch signed his own name, or had Tom Junior sign for him. Benjamin Rush, speaking of a debate on September 5, says "The speakers in favor of the motion were Ed. Rutledge, Thos. Lynch, Jno. Stone," but he undoubtedly meant Thomas junior (just as he meant Thomas Stone, not "Jno."). There is no evidence Dr. Rush ever met the senior Mr. Lynch. He did not come into Congress at all while the elder Lynch was present, and he nowhere mentions or describes him. Apparently he was not one of the several doctors attending Mr. Lynch's case. It is entirely clear that the ailing planter did *not* turn up on August 2 for the occasion of the signing of the Declaration of Independence by the members. That occasion was not regarded as particularly important at the time, though of course it has become of immense importance in retrospect, as Americans have celebrated and avidly collected "The Signers."

Mr. Lynch was so much esteemed, and personally so well-liked except by New

Englanders, his grave illness had been so interesting to all the members and so many had called upon him, that surely if he *had* come again to Congress, some letter-writer would have mentioned it. I fear he did not. And I'm sorry, for by every indication he was one of the most significant men of the First and Second Congresses, and one of the most attractive. In November, Thomas Junior began to convey his father home, along with his mother and sister, his own wife, and all their servants. The journey proved too much for Mr. Lynch. In Annapolis, where they paused, he suffered another stroke. Tom took him to Mr. Paca's house, "Carvell Hall," and there he died. In the next two years, though Tom Junior struggled manfully to discharge all his public work, phthisis made steady progress in his frame. Finally in 1779, he and his wife took ship for France, hoping to find some better climate for him. The ship they sailed in never reached port, the junior Lynches were never heard of again.

Following is a list of the forty-seven men who were in attendance as Members of Congress on July 1, 1776, heard or participated in the debate on Lee's Resolution, and who voted that day on the question determining American Independence:

MEMBERS OF CONGRESS, JULY 1, 1776

CONNECTICUT
Samuel Huntington
Roger Sherman

DELAWARE
Thomas McKean
George Read

GEORGIA
Button Gwinnett
Lyman Hall
George Walton[1]

MARYLAND
William Paca
John Rogers
Thomas Stone

MASSACHUSETTS
John Adams
Samuel Adams
Elbridge Gerry
John Hancock
Robert Treat Paine

NEW HAMPSHIRE
Josiah Bartlett
William Whipple

NEW JERSEY[2]
Francis Hopkinson[3]
Abraham Clark
Richard Stockton
John Witherspoon

NEW YORK
John Alsop
George Clinton
William Floyd
Francis Lewis
Robert R. Livingston
Henry Wisner

NORTH CAROLINA
Joseph Hewes
John Penn

---

[1] In Congress for the first time today.

[2] The New Jersey Delegates arrived in mid-afternoon, or later.

[3] Attended for the first time Friday, June 28, but apparently came in late this day with the other Jersey Delegates. For had he been there alone, he could, by New Jersey's appointment, have acted for the state, and there would have been no need for the second "speech" by Adams.

PENNSYLVANIA

John Dickinson
Benjamin Franklin[4]
Charles Humphreys
Robert Morris
John Morton
Thomas Willing
James Wilson

RHODE ISLAND

William Ellery
Stephen Hopkins

SOUTH CAROLINA

Thomas Heyward, jr.
Thomas Lynch, jr.[5]
Arthur Middleton
Edward Rutledge

VIRGINIA

Carter Braxton
Benjamin Harrison
Thomas Jefferson
Francis Lightfoot Lee
Thomas Nelson, jr.

5. *General Washington and the Jack Ass**

People who have written the most-read books about Washington have not been farmers. In all the vast bulk of literature relating to him, too little has been made of the consuming business of his life, the Mount Vernon farms. There is plenty of material; the various records he left make Mount Vernon one of the best-documented agricultural operations of the eighteenth century. And scholars have published quite a lot of this documentation. But our writers, when they leave the vivid scenes of war and government and go with the General back to Potomac shores and his "office"—where he kept very busy indeed— seem not to esteem the materials they have to deal with, nor find them exciting.

It is too bad. Writers pay due attention to Lincoln's professional life as a lawyer; they seem to have a feeling for it. And the qualities in Woodrow Wilson characteristic of a dedicated teacher give them no trouble. But Washington's farm life has never meant to them what it meant to him. They appear not to think of his life's work as his profession, they will not consider him a man engaged in business. Consequently very little has been caught for us of his striking originality, his creativeness, the lively imagination that dwelt always in his mind—when his mind dwelt on the true calling of his life.

It was not ever thus. Dr. Rush, who knew and admired them both, called Washington a farmer, Benjamin Franklin a mechanic. Heaven, he once wrote, "stamped a peculiar value upon agriculture and mechanic arts in America by selecting WASHINGTON and FRANKLIN to be two of the principal agents in the late Revolution. The titles of farmer and mechanic, therefore, can never fail of being peculiarly agreeable in the United States while gratitude and patriotism live in American breasts." Rush was in this more prepared than we are today, to recognize that Franklin was a superb and ingenious mechanic, Washington an uncommonly able farmer, thoughtful, experimentive, continually searching for new methods, new ideas—a man to whom the word "originality" properly belongs.

---

[4] Franklin's attendance this day is not clearly established. It is probable he attended for at least some of the session. He was present the following day.

[5] His presence is not clearly established, but it is likely.

* A first version of this talk was published as an article in *The South Atlantic Quarterly*, LII, No. 2, April, 1953.

In military and political affairs, Washington's greatness was the greatness of character, not of originality. Only in agriculture was he a radical, a reformer. The awesome stature he attained, even in his own lifetime, as the unique personal symbol of the Republic, never induced anyone anywhere to celebrate him as an innovator. It is military and political affairs our writers give us, and often they write of the symbol rather than the man. General Washington has eluded his biographers; he still eludes historians. He would emerge as more of a person, more of a believable, living, breathing human being, if writers studied his life as a husbandman, studied his mules, and his jack-ass letters.

In our day it is not easy to persuade people of the significance of such matters. I tried. This piece began as an entertainment for the gentlemen of The Philobiblon Club of Philadelphia. Soon I was giving it elsewhere, but always before audiences entirely urban, entirely mechanized and motorized in their daily lives. Farms, and mules, were unrealities to them. They were even jokes. *Jack ass* is a term city folk use often enough, but scarcely ever in referring to an animal. I was in constant difficulties over terminology.

They even use *jack ass* as a single word, *jackass,* which is a lamentable error. The word *ass* has indeed proved susceptible of a variety of uses both grave and merry, suggested by the personality and strong-mindedness of the beast in question. It was so in ancient Rome (*asinus*), it was so in old England (*assa*). But when the word *ass* is used to designate the equine quadruped of the Mediterranean basin, the donkey, or burro, it is a general word, which leaves unresolved the question of the sex of the particular individual. Unlike the word *horse,* which can mean both the general class of quadrupeds *equus* and at the same time a young specimen, formerly a stallion, who has suffered modern improvements to be done upon him, the word ass has never come to indicate a beast tampered with in specific ways.

The male of the species *ass* is properly denominated a *jack ass,* the female in strict usage is a *jennet ass,* or since the word is French, and mispronounced as such, a *jenny ass. Jennet* or *jenny* standing alone is merely an easy though a venerable contraction for *jennet ass.* In General Washington's earliest letters, so little did he or Americans know of the ass, he usually wrote of a "she-ass." By and by he learned the word *jennet.*

Jack ass, therefore, is a designation consisting of two separate words, indicating an ass which is a jack, or uncut male, suitable for the important and significant work of reproducing his species. Or producing a hybrid species, the mule. In the French language, incidentally, a curious confusion can occasionally arise, for in one locality the same word, *ministre,* is used to designate a jack ass, and a minister of state. No less an authority on both these *ministres* than the late President Raymond Poincaré developed the possibilities of this linguistic oddity in a few bright paragraphs.

There is no such thing as a female jack ass. That phrase (it brought me up short one day while listening to lunch-table conversation in the Deanery at Bryn Mawr) is as much a contradiction in terms as if one should say, a female stallion. A jack ass is an ass indisputably male. Mules are similarly designated. A mule possessed of male stigmata is referred to as a jack mule; one with female generative organs is known as a jenny mule, sometimes (confusingly) as a jenny.

The late Chief Justice Walter Clark of the Supreme Court of North Carolina,

Mr. Julian Boyd tells me, was once moved to observe in a decision, "The mule is an animal without pride of ancestry or hope of posterity." To take exception to the learned Chief Justice's language would be very bold indeed, and his was a high court, from which no appeal lies; but I hope it is permissible to remark that many thousands of mules in the United States of America, even in North Carolina, could refer with legitimate pride to their legitimate ancestry, if they stemmed from Royal Gift, The Knight of Malta, or Compound. And as for the second allegation, established facts constrain us to relegate it to *obiter dicta,* for despite the imposing authority of the valuable Chief Justice, mules have actually been known to produce offspring. They are not always sterile.

In justice to the Chief Justice, however, it should be added that their biological abilities in the business of reproduction are so meager that jack mules are usually cut on reaching half or most of their growth, to make them more manageable as draught animals, and to add to their weight—though this last seems to be more a venerable agrarian suspicion than scientific truth.

Among city folk, a popular confusion exists between the *mule* and the *hinny.* The unsophisticated sometimes refer to a hinny as a female mule. This is of course incorrect. The hinny is the (infrequent) biological opposite of the mule. As a mule is produced by a jack ass covering a mare, so a hinny is produced by a stallion covering a jennet ass. (No farmer would ever let it happen on purpose.)

It is instructive to realize how rare a thing a mule actually was in America, before Washington began his notable project. William Byrd of Westover had owned one, fifty years earlier. Mrs. Joseph Carson has discovered a creature named "Tickle Pitcher" advertised for sale in 1756 in the *Maryland Gazette.* Dr. Tilton mentions that some were bred in Delaware in the 1780's; up in Rhode Island a few were raised for export, but the business soon died. Mr. Julian Boyd writes that Thomas Jefferson "evidently had a mule at Monticello" in 1782. That seems to be about all. Whatever started Washington on his adventure I do not know—except for his constant intense desire to reduce the cost and increase the profit of his agricultural enterprise.

That this was his constant and intense desire will be apparent at once to anyone who leafs through the Bi-centennial edition in thirty-nine volumes of *The Writings of Washington.* He will quickly see how the largest bulk of his day-to-day writings dealt with his farms, even during periods of the most critical public issues. Much remains unpublished. In The Library of Congress is the record he made of his conversations with Pedro Tellez, assisted by unskilled translators. At Mount Vernon are records and stud-books, which tell much of the story as the General recorded it. At Mount Vernon also is the mule shed, recently restored under Mr. Cecil Wall's direction.

If the scene of General Washington performing in person the offices of a nurse for poor Don Juan de Miralles as he died, emptying body wastes and vomit, cleaning the patient, giving him medicines, seems uncharacteristic, it is because Washington's life-long poor health and his own constant illnesses are other truths about him which have never entered into our popular legends of the General. He knew everything of the sick room from his own dismal experience. He never threw off the malaria acquired in his youth; it came back on him frequently with its shaking chills and nausea, its blinding headaches. He suffered chronically the sharp chest pains of pleurisy, not unconnected with the tuberculosis that had attacked him at seventeen. His harshly pitted face in his shaving mirror every morning was a reminder of the dread small pox of his boyhood. At twenty-three, with Braddock in the Wilderness, he was "seized with violent fevers and pains in my head which continued for nine days." He never forgot the solicitude with which Braddock cared for him then. As an adult he lived through not a single year without weeks filled with agues and fevers, influenzas, dysenteries, fluxes. At fifty-four, just before the Federal Convention, he was in bed with rheumatic pains so piercing he could not raise his hand to his head. It may have been toxic uremia. In his late fifties and early sixties he was the most sickly of all our Presidents. That somewhat mysterious illness, the "malignant carbuncle," for which Dr. Bard cut him in New York in his first term of office, nearly killed him. People gathered in the streets outside "The Residence," stood every day and all night for a week and a half to learn if the President-General still lived. The hemorrhoids for which Dr. Glentworth cut him in Philadelphia during his second term proved less serious. His teeth were poor from his youth. After all of them had been pulled his facial pains were lessened somewhat, but eating was awkward and difficult; he could find no prosthetic devices to fit him, his gums were raw, talking was sometimes embarrassing. In nothing was George Washington more tested in character than in his struggle, never ending, against illness and pain—this man who could say "It is better to go laughing than crying through life."

Every writer knows that in however orderly a fashion he begins his work and plans his research things turn up by accident. One day I was looking over a bindery order in a library which was then part of my responsibility, thinking department heads might have sent off a rarity or two to be clipped and cropped and bound in unsightly buckram. (It is a thing department heads do.) I stumbled across a much-worn copy of Youatt, *The Horse,* Philadelphia, 1843. Now William Youatt, that uncommonly appealing character, was an Englishman, of course, and his famous book was first published in England. This American edition ten years or so later was not, so far as I knew, a rarity. But I liked the idea of a farrier's treatise being much-worn in a big-city library a century ago, and I studied the volume.

It turned out to be the first of two American editions of Youatt, edited by a certain J. S. Skinner. (His second edition came in 1855, after Youatt's death.) And to the great English horse-leech's authoritative volume on the horse, this American editor of 1843 had appended a considerable effort of his own: "The Ass and The Mule." In preparing his essay the conscientious and thorough Skinner put himself to the trouble of making a journey to the fountain-head of mule culture in this nation, Mount Vernon.

He found the farms in a deplorable state of decay—this was ten years before the valiant Ladies' Association acquired Mount Vernon and commenced their devoted and effective restoration. But George Washington Parke Custis was still living, and he granted Mr. Skinner an interview. Faithfully, the scholar-editor recorded the description of Mount Vernon asses and mules which Mr. Custis gave him, particularly noting details of Royal Gift and The Knight of Malta. These are the eyewitness descriptions I have relied on, in my text.

For in his younger days, as a youth at Mount Vernon, George Washington Parke Custis had known both of the two jacks, personally.

6. The Grand Federal Processions*

A procession is a joy of an instant; it dies the moment it passes, no video tapes or cinématographic recordings call back its wonders and its glories. Like the court masques of Jacobean England, so the exuberant processions of our American ancestors were an art-form we can never realize, nor ever reconstruct. We are not artisans, we are manufacturers. We produce extravaganzas, spectacles, magnificences; we do it with machines, we show them everywhere, we take pride in enormousness, too often we bring forth enormities.

These Americans of 1788 were artisans, men of craft—masters, journeymen, apprentices. They were Alexander Hamilton's "mechanicks," who spent their personal skills on single productions of their craft. The "sub-divided" economy of America was an economy of skilled artisans. That is what Washington meant when he said we had "so much economy" among us. His word was not one of his frequent mistakes in diction. Even the advanced Hamilton's notions of what Adam Smith called division of labor were of the most rudimentary character. Smith had seen such unskilled work as he described, Hamilton had not. His experiment at Paterson, New Jersey, might have come nearer success but for his concept of "labor" as artisan labor. He seems, to his enthusiastic admirers today, to have had a vision he never really had, for when he writes of "labor" he means the craftsman, but his twentieth-century admirers insist on reading it as "the factory laborer." The first "factory," in our meaning of the word, was yet to be formed. It soon would be, by Robert Dyott in Philadelphia; the artisan age was but a brief interlude in our economic history. But that brief interlude had its philosophy, and its poets. Hamilton was certainly one of these. In the artisan's brief day the word "industry" meant diligence, hard work. The word "protection," leading artisans hoped, might come to mean legal shields around craft guilds formed in rigid organizations, as well as its more familiar meaning of national tariffs to price out foreign competition.

And the proposal of a procession meant a splendid opportunity for the industrious artisan to exhibit his skill, and his professional pride in his labor. This day's exuberance was, Carl Van Doren said, "a dramatic epitome of the life and work of a separate state, a symbolic act of faith in the future of the United States." (The Great Rehearsal, 251.)

Mr. Lyman H. Butterfield has pronounced Judge Hopkinson's Grand Federal Procession "the greatest spectacle presented in eighteenth-century Philadelphia." And since Mr. Butterfield himself has described L'Enfant's fete for the French Minister in the summer of 1782 (when the common people clambered to the roof of Independence Hall to stare down at the gentry's revel) I am sure he is right. Everyone else at the time certainly thought so. Mr. Butterfield was brought to consider the Federal Procession from a detailed description Dr. Benjamin

---

* A briefer account of this episode was published in Woman's Day, November, 1951. There, it was distinguished by a handsome, spirited illustration which the skillful Mr. Isa Barnett contributed. He recreated elements of the scene from intensive independent researches of his own, and from his artist's gift of imaginative response, and I am grateful to him.

Rush wrote of it, for the *American Museum*. He has published Rush's happy pages in his remarkable *Letters of Benjamin Rush* (I, 470–477).

Now the good Doctor Rush was, of course, impossibly serious in his eternal moralizing, as tedious as ever Franklin in his *Poor Richard* almanacs, and without Franklin's common wit. But Dr. Rush had something Franklin did not: the writer's eye, the humanist's ear. Mr. Butterfield celebrates these memorable gifts. From Rush's description, we learn many things of the Grand Procession—how the vast crowds fell solemnly silent as the great elements of the parade passed, "for sublime objects and intense pleasure never fail of producing silence!" Rush observed; how the Eagle ("the triumphal car," Rush called it) with Chief Justice McKean holding the Constitution aloft denoted "the elevation of the government and of law and justice above everything else in the United States"; how "the *clean white* dresses" of victuallers and bakers pleased the Doctor's hygenic eye (though keeping those dresses clean and white that dusty, windy day must have been a trick); how people loved the two oxen, decorated so tastefully, plodding so patiently along, and raised an outcry when they learned they were to be slaughtered the next day for the poor.

It was Rush who recorded Judge Peters's joke: Peters was marching with the Agricultural Society, just behind a man sowing grain, when he passed his brother lawyers standing in a group. "We sew, gentlemen," cried Peters to the Bar, "but you reap the fruits of our labors!" It was Rush, who noticed how each marcher's countenance "wore an air of *dignity*, as well as pleasure. Every tradesman's boy in the procession seemed to consider himself a principal in the business. Rank for a while forgot all its claims . . ." One worthy German who had been chosen to carry the standard of his trade, took it home with him, Dr. Rush recorded, told his wife to care for the flag till he should have the honor of carrying it again, or if he should die, to bury it with him in his coffin.

Rush was astonished—everyone was, he said—by the cotton display, the spinning and carding and weaving machines that worked busily as they were drawn by. "On that stage were carried the emblems of the future wealth and independence of our country. Cotton may be cultivated in the southern and manufactured in the eastern and middle states in such quantities in a few years as to clothe every citizen of the United States. . . ." Rush began to speculate about cotton, how it was better than wool, would serve both in summer and winter, moths would not eat it, he said, and America could make it cheaper than any nation else. It was bound to become the uniform dress of every American. "Several respectable gentlemen exhibited a prelude of these events by appearing in complete suits of jeans . . ."

It sorely pained the earnest physician to know that some brawlers were among the great crowd at Bush Hill, and several citizens got uproariously drunk. Temperance was one of the host of causes Benjamin Rush was forever advocating. Beer and Cider, he declared, were the "invaluable FEDERAL liquors . . . companions of those virtues that can alone render our country free and respectable," while "SPIRITOUS LIQUORS" on the other hand were "*Antifederal . . .* companions of all those vices that are calculated to dishonor and enslave our country." He wished the words inscribed on a monument foreiver at Bush Hill.

When I was gathering all I could find of the Grand Procession (I never could find one of those Procession imprints of the *Ode,* nor what became of the carrier-pigeon copies, nor indeed what became of the Federal Eagle) Mrs. Joseph

Carson showed me the issue of Eleazer Oswald's *Independent Gazetteer* of Friday, June 6, 1788. Curiously, this bitterest of all Antifederal editors published in full the account of the Charlestown procession from the *Columbian Herald* of May 29. In an adjacent column, he happened to have standing his paid advertisement for Luther Martin's *Genuine Information,* the most detailed and explicit attack on the Constitution of the whole Ratification Controversy. Mr. Oswald was willing to give Federal news, though he charged run-of-paper rates to his Antifederal companions.

Francis Hopkinson was so unusual an American of his practical, materialistic age, that he seemed to me sufficient justification for the somewhat formless and tandem construction of this piece. These essays are meant to suggest character, more than issues, for character is certainly the ultimate object of the historian's contemplation. Hopkinson was the subject of a thorough study forty years ago by Dr. George E. Hastings (*Life and Works of Francis Hopkinson,* Chicago, 1926). Certainly it is a useful volume, though I find it more analytical than appreciative. No scholar has yet successfully presented the work of that "lost court" of admiralty, in conjunction with similar courts of other states, especially South Carolina. I hope someone will—and will show us the heartbeat of the process of domesticating law in America.

The Hopkinsons were all three remarkable people, in that generation. Dr. Rush knew them, attended them, loved them. (*Vd.* Corner, George W., *The Autobiography of Benjamin Rush,* Princeton and Philadelphia, 1948, pp. 236, 238, 147, etc.) Francis had two sisters. One of them, Elizabeth, married the talented but unhappy minister Jacob Duché, the other, Mary, became the wife of Dr. John Morgan, founder of the first Medical School in America. Their mother left through Dr. Rush hints for us of what sort she must have been. She lost her husband, she survived him many years, living always alone because "she was afraid her love for her children would lessen her communion with God, which she enjoyed in her own house, and alone." Then she lost her children, Mary Morgan, "Little Francis," Elizabeth Duché. The day Mrs. Duché died, Dr. Rush found the mother, past eighty, resigned and composed. She spoke of the loss of all her children: "I must be a crooked stick, to require so much affliction to straighten me," she said.

7. *The Case of the Innocent Blacksmith**

Fred Morrow Fling of cherished memory—you have to have a long memory to know of Fling; ask Nebraskans, the older ones will tell you—Fred Morrow Fling used to define "an historical fact" in this formidable fashion: "an event, episode, or occurrence, testified to by at least two independent witnesses, who are not self-deceived." He was a "scientific" historian. I am not; but I am by way of being an antiquarian, and I have dealt quite often with what scientific historians called in their quaint vocabulary "original primary sources." During the years I worked with Pat Lyon, I kept thinking of Dr. Fling. He would not have liked Pat's story, nor thought it worth bothering with; he would have bade me get on with more important things. But certainly he would have been astonished, even as I, at the abundance of sources. Far more than two independent

---

* A short version of this article was published in *Woman's Day,* July, 1951.

witnesses testify to the events, episodes, and occurrences of The Case of The Innocent Blacksmith. And Fling would have relished the way all the "sources" check each other, add conviction and multiply details at every point, report the same happenings, even the same conversations, attitudes, facial expressions. Pat Lyon's adventures certainly could be; in the hands of a scientific historian, one of the most thoroughly documented stories of the early Republic.

Pat's own *Narrative* is a voyage of discovery for any reader. It is filled with individual American people brought to life, filled with their speech, their clothes, their attitudes, their houses, their down-spouts and chimney jacks, the manner and methods of their travel, their crimes and criminal argot, their pleasures, their fellowship and fears. Not many artisans wrote books. It is a happy circumstance that one of the greatest artisans left a book so contentious and so honest, so completely revealing of himself and his age. I wish someone would reprint it.

Yet the *Narrative* is only the beginning. That famous trial, in which Dallas sought Pat's remedy by a pleading of malicious prosecution, winds in and out of Pennsylvania *Reports,* and the reports of other states too. Officially it was *Lyon* v. *Fox et al.,* but its first publication was a private venture by the master reporter Thomas Lloyd. That busy individual took down in his quick little characters a good many celebrated cases, from Philadelphia clear up to Boston; he published his account of Pat's 1805 trial three years after it closed, as *Robbery of the Bank of Pennsylvania in 1798. The Trial in the Supreme Court of the State of Pennsylvania. Reported from notes by T. Lloyd. Philadelphia: printed for the publishers. 1808.* I have seen two copies with manuscripts of Pat Lyon, Mr. Dallas and other figures of the trial, bound in. The many witnesses giving testimony in court piece out Pat's *Narrative,* depict both the robbery and the Bank's evident malice—"express malice," the law calls it—in detail.

Thomas Lloyd was a curious fellow, highly partisan, by many thoroughly disliked. James Madison said he was indolent, sometimes made up speeches willy-nilly, was "a votary of the bottle." Madison was too severe. Lloyd was not so bad as all that. He had many lapses of attention, but there were times, whole days even, when he reported diligently. He sat, he tells us, "on the Prothonotary's seat at the back of Mr. Condie and Lyon, and had an opportunity of hearing their conversation." (*Robbery,* p. 61, fn.) Mathew Carey, who knew him much better than Madison (they attended the same Roman Catholic Church) described him as "an excellent stenographer as far as taking down notes" but "a miserable hand at putting them in English dress." Carey was right: there is an example here, though in justice it should be said it might as well have come from the lapse of three years between taking down and transcribing, as from being (as Lloyd often was) disguised in liquor. In his published report of the trial, Lloyd records a witness as saying, of Pat in jail, "he had *Dr. Rush* by him, and said he wanted for nothing." That makes no sense at all, and anyway Dr. Rush was nowhere near the jail at any time during Pat's imprisonment. Fortunately, we have another, more complete report of the trial, not in shorthand characters but in an abbreviated longhand. In the Yeates Papers in The Historical Society of Pennsylvania (filed as Miscellaneous Legal Papers—1805) is a manuscript of thirty-four folio pages covered solidly in Jasper Yeates's tiny diamond-clear writing. These are the notes the careful Federalist judge took swiftly down during the long trial. They contain all that Lloyd recorded, though not *verbatim,* and about twice as much more, which Lloyd missed, or omitted. At the same point, Justice Yeates records the same witness as saying, "he had *Rye Mush* by him, and said he wanted for nothing." I found a copy of *The System of Short-Hand, Practiced by Mr. Thomas Lloyd, in taking down the Debates of Congress* (Philadelphia, 1793) and tried to dope out what the symbols for "Dr. Rush" and "Rye Mush" would have been. It did not take very many sips of beer sangaree to make them look pretty much alike.*

The case of *Lyon* v. *Fox et al.* had a long subsequent history. Yeates made full notes of the reargument the following week, on the Bank's plea that a new trial should be granted, because the jury's verdict was against the evidence, the law, and the charge of the court, and because the damages were excessive. (They were $12,000.) Term was drawing to a close; the court entered a decree *nisi,* stayed the proceedings, took the plea under advisement. Next spring, 1806, the case was postponed till December term. Finally on January 17, 1807, the Bank won its motion for a new trial, when Tilghman, the new Chief Justice, in a long and eloquent opinion paying much more than conventional deference to the sanctity of trial by jury, nevertheless concluded that Lyon's was "a cause, which in the hands of able Counsel, is well calculated to surprize the Judgment of a Jury, by enlisting their honest passion on its side." The able counsel, Dallas, kept right on being able, and enlisting all the honest passion he could. The issue was, of course, probable cause: unless the Bank people could prove they had a probable cause for believing Pat guilty, by showing acceptable reasons that persuaded them to think so, the law said they were guilty of express malice. Pat did not have to *prove* malice on their part, the Bank had to prove probable cause, or malice on their part would be assumed. And probable cause was something the Bank never could prove, in spite of the Supreme's Court's persistent efforts to help. The case became leading law on the granting of new trials, as well as on the issue of express malice. Mr. Justice Brackenridge, that sturdy and merry Scotsman, both times on both points dissented, coming near himself to pleading Pat's side of the case. Where Yeates justified the Bank's prosecution as not malicious, on the grounds of Pat's "apparent guilt," Brackenridge insisted on applying a more severe test, and he obliged Yeates to include it in his charge: "I am desired by Judge Brackenridge," said Yeates from the bench, "to state that he would substitute the words 'upon reasonable Ground' instead of 'upon apparent Guilt.'"

Thus the case, new in the legal positions and arguments it raised, opened opportunities for innovation and invention on both sides. It seems odd, now, to think of a time in American law when granting new trials could be used as a partisan device of social control, and when malice, "that bad mind which is

---

* In the interest of that objectivity prized above all things by the sober scientific historian, let it be said that by no means all the differences in *reportage* between Lloyd with his shorthand and Yeates with his quick long-hand *precis,* favor the Judge. For example: Lloyd (*Robbery,* p. 36) reports that Thomas Annesley *affirmed* rather than *swore,* from which we know he was a Quaker, and that he testified: "In 1793, at the commencement of the Bank of Pennsylvania, I was runner; but in 1798 I was employed in the house as first Teller." Yeates' MS notes read simply, "Thomas Annesley: I was employed as first Teller of the Bank from 1793 till 1798." Differences of this character make it all the more regrettable that Lloyd omitted so much testimony and argument—which Yeates summarized.

inferred from the bad act" had never been charged against authority. Dallas and Ingersoll found Pat Lyon's case the chance to start many hares.

So did Brackenridge. Some years later, the able Justice in one of his most remarkable works, *Law Miscellanies: Containing an Introduction to the study of the law; notes on Blackstone's Commentaries shewing the variations of the Law of Pennsylvania from the Law of England* (Philadelphia, 1814), reviewed Lyon's case thoroughly, and summed up the legal issue in conflict as he saw it: was probable cause a question of fact only, or a mixed question of law and fact? Did the lawful commitment by a court, of a person accused, binding him over for trial, furnish the prosecutor probable cause to assume his guilt? This had troubled Yeates and Shippen, too. It came near destroying the ancient presumption of innocence in the Common Law: a man is presumed innocent until proven guilty beyond a reasonable doubt. But courts must be given some presumptions, as well. They must be assumed to have acted honorably, fairly, according to their oaths. Pat had been committed first by a magistrate, second by a Supreme Court Justice, third by the whole Supreme Court in banc. "I participated therein," said Justice Yeates, "and I trust, that we have no Enemies, who will not suppose, that the several Judges acted conscientiously, according to the best of their Judgments . . ." Did these proceedings of lawful courts, committing the accused and ordering trial of his guilt or innocence, constitute probable cause for his prosecution? The Bank said, indeed they did. Yeates agreed. He held, in a telling sentence, "we should think it *hard* indeed, that the Officers of the Bank going on with the Prosecution under our Orders should be subjected thereby to an action for Damages."

Mr. Justice Yeates was one of the Federalist Judges who had just barely survived the partisan impeachments brought against the bench. He would strive till the day of his death for the integrity and dignity of the courts. Brackenridge, himself a Jeffersonian from the Antifederal West, far less wedded to the Common Law than Yeates though every bit as wedded to the Law, took an opposite position, and he developed it through the years. Probable cause was no question of law at all, he said, no question of the integrity of the courts. It was a question of fact only, to be determined by the jury. Commitments, even those by the whole Supreme Court *en banc,* he held, "did not stand in the way of shewing *before a jury,* that notwithstanding all this, no *probable cause* existed; that the *weakness* or wickedness of a prosecutor, and what was more, the *error* of judges in thinking there was probable cause, did not affect the right of Lyon on a trial before a jury to shew there was no *probable cause.* And this doctrine," Brackenridge added in 1814, "I have understood to have been approved by the whole profession."

Spiritually, Hugh Henry Brackenridge, "very Scotch, very Old Country," was a proper descendant of Andrew Hamilton as he sat in Hamilton's State House and made this element of the law, just as Hamilton had made another element, peculiarly American, and an undoubted engine for the protection of the citizen against authority misused. Brackenridge went so far, in one case, as to rule that even a True Bill by the Grand Jury could not be regarded as conclusive showing of probable cause, reasonable cause. It could only go to the mitigation of damages. "I am not to be at the mercy of a judge, or a whole bench, who *at the instance of a prosecutor have thought* there was probable cause. For I cannot sue them; or have redress, otherwise than against him. . . ."

It was novel doctrine; there were those who thought it dangerous, destructive of authority. It was American doctrine, a tiny chink in that mounting structure of a thoroughly American law this second generation of free Americans was building, which was effectively separating us far wider in substantive ways from Britain than the mere Declaration of Independence had separated us, but which has been little noticed by historians. Brackenridge, DuPonceau, Dallas are never remembered for the work which they themselves regarded as their lasting achievement. It is our loss. Brackenridge, instead, is remembered for his happy genius in sparkling literary productions. In his satirical novel, *Modern Chivalry,* a mountebank gives this advice to a scalawag, on being a judge: "It would be a substitute for sense if you could cite cases . . . . gravity is a great cover for stupidity. . . . If you do not take notes, seem to take them, for it is the fashion to be a great note taker. The greatest virtue in a judge is to be a good listener. . . ." In our time, Mr. Justice Brackenridge, the innovating liberal judge, has been obscured by Brackenridge the delightful *farceur* of an all-too-thin period of American *belles-lettres.* It was Brackenridge's own fault. The bubbling comedy of his happy nature was never very deep beneath the surface. That remarkable *Law Miscellanies,* so full of serious matter, is the same book in which the irrepressible Scottish frontiersman warned youthful applicants to the bar to beware of imitating their elders, beware of puppyism, don't wear spectacles just because Wilson, Lewis, Coxe and Wilcox wear them— "on account of the convexity of the visual orb," the Justice said solemnly; particularly, don't smoke segars. There is no hope for young smokers. Every lawyer should discipline himself, should reserve stimulants—"until an advanced age . . ."

Lyon's case was but the first of these developments, the first pleading in malicious prosecution, the first granting of a new trial when the judgment of the jury had been "surprized." "In the case of Lyon *v.* Fox," Brackenridge wrote in 1814 (*Law Misc.,* 438), "a new trial was granted; but on the ground only of *excessive* damages. We heard no more of it; I presume there was a compromise." There was. Tilghman's words in granting a new trial had been warning enough for Dallas. He had won Pat's victory at a moment when courts and banks were at the nadir of their political fortunes, and lowest in public esteem. Now two years later the Supreme Court justices had survived the Jeffersonians' impeachments. Political passions had not been able to defeat them, only age. The formidable Jasper Yeates was gone, and old Shippen, but the new Jeffersonian appointees were showing every bit as much care for the power and integrity of the bench as the Old-Law judges had. Even Brackenridge had proved himself a judge, not a partisan. He had demanded he be impeached too, along with his Federal colleagues. His defiant presence before the bar of the House, his sturdy defense of the independence of the judiciary from political interference, had been a principal weight in the acquittal of them all. Dallas had won his point, established the pleading of malicious prosecution as a remedy, as an effective protection of the citizen against authority. Brackenridge had been with him; but only Brackenridge. The line was too thin, between probable cause as a mixed matter of law and fact, or probable cause as a matter of fact alone. The line was always too thin, between the rights of the citizen and the necessary power to govern. Pushing too far, too soon, he could lose what he had won. Resigning now, he would leave a victory in the records, a precedent.

As for Pat, he had won what was dearest to him, vindication. Compared with this, the amount of money was of no moment. As for the Bank, they were eager to settle. Probable cause in fact they had never really had, probable cause in law, relying on Yeates' ruling, they could never be sure of. To the Bank, the amount of money was of great moment. Dallas convened all the counsel on both sides, set a chair by the chimney for old Lewis with his segars. He did so willingly, there would be other clients, other causes. In the law, one moved slowly, case by case, to build a structure. An accommodation was reached; Dallas, Levy, Hopkinson, Condy executed a release: "I Patrick Lyon, in consideration of full satisfaction to me made, do hereby release and forever quit claim unto Samuel M. Fox, John C. Stocker, Jonathan Smith and John Haines all causes of action, claims, and demands . . ." The matter was left in Joseph Hopkinson's hands, the sweet-natured Hopkinson, whom everybody liked. Pat signed the instrument: "Witness my hand and Seal this Seventh day of March 1807. Pat^k Lyon." At the bottom, Hopkinson made this notation: "The Satisfaction above mentioned was the Sum of Nine thousand Dollars . . ."

The committee of the board of the Bank charged with settling the matter paid over the money to Dallas, who distributed it. And the committee made its report. They were induced to accept the compromise, they told the board of directors, "from a Conviction, that under all the circumstances, it was for the interest of the Institution, and a measure, calculated to produce effects, more pleasing, than was to be expected from a Continuance of the action." On the docket of the Supreme Court, April term, 1807, Dallas entered a discontinuance.

Legal developments growing out of *Lyon* v. *Fox*, and the progress of Brackenridge's doctrine, can be traced sketchily through *Pennsylvania Reports*, much more thoroughly through such old-fashioned volumes as the *American Decisions* series, Yeates's *Reports*, Browne's *Pennsylvania Reports* (supplemented by the same writer's agreeable *The Forum*), and reports such as Barr, Smith, and the like. Brackenridge's able dissent from Tilghman's judgment on a new trial is in II Browne's *Reports* (1813), Appendix, pp. 77–80. ("I would define [malice] to be *a disposition of mind which works a mischief* . . . With regard to *intention,* we cannot search the heart, and where the matter rests upon the want of probable cause, we cannot say what is actually the motive . . . there was proof of other motives than those of public justice. Taking this to be the case, I do not know what damages I would call excessive.") In the same Appendix, incidentally (II, pp. 42,ff.) Browne gives the case of *Munns* v. *Dupont and Baudy,* in the Circuit Court of the United States, Pennsylvania District, 1811, in which Mr. Justice Washington put severe brakes on actions of malicious prosecution in federal (as opposed to state) jurisprudence. By Washington's ruling, the plaintiff in a federal court must prove the malice of his prosecutor, and must prove want of probable cause, too (a strange moment this, when Bushrod Washington requires the proving of a negative). If the defendant merely proves probable cause, no verdict of damages against him can be given, even in cases in which the jury assumes malice. Thus far had federal and Pennsylvania rules already diverged by 1811, and it did not occur to Pennsylvania lawyers and judges to regard the federal courts' decisions as controlling them, even when delivered by the highly-admired Supreme Court Justice Washington on circuit—himself formerly of the nisi prius bench in

Philadelphia, and still celebrated as the very model of an efficient, hard-working judge.

Forty years later, the Pennsylvania requirement on a prosecutor for proving probable cause had gone so far Brackenridge's way that a Philadelphia court defined it as furnishing "a *reasonable* ground for suspicion, supported by circumstances sufficient to warrant a *cautious* man believing the accused guilty." (*LeMaistre* v. *Hunter*, 1851. Brightly, *Nisi Prius Reports*, 494. Italics mine, for reasons which will at once occur to admirers of Justice Holmes.) Of course by now, the whole subject is of historical interest only. Lawyers, after Restatement, are impatient with these out-of-date episodes and forgotten struggles toward fresh principles of justice. If they paid them more attention, they might spread less alarm than some are disposed to, about recent civil-liberties decisions erecting hedges around the activities of arresting officers in criminal cases.

John Neagle's successful career was much noticed by writers and critics of his time, and his two portraits of "Pat Lyon at the Forge" came in for a lot of comment during the nineteenth century. Both paintings were frequently exhibited, and a certain T. Kelly made a not-very-good steel engraving of the Philadelphia version. Neagle's letter of October 7, 1826 ("I am closely engaged *Night & Day* . . . on Pat Lyon's picture") I ran across in some James Barton Longacre papers at The Library Company of Philadelphia.

Mr. Ransom R. Patrick, historian of art, published a painstaking study of the Lyon portraits in *The Art Bulletin*, XXXIII, No. 3, Sept., 1951, pp. 187–92: "John Neagle, Portrait Painter, and Pat Lyon, Blacksmith." In that article he used what I knew of Pat, and in this one I have used much that I learned from him. It was to Professor Patrick that Dean Carl Wittke suggested the Pythagorean Theorem on the drawing board in the Philadelphia version might have been the diagrammatic symbol of Free-Masonry—Pat's calling attention to his membership in the Philadelphia Grand Lodge. It was Joseph Fraser, the excellent and devoted director of The Pennsylvania Academy of The Fine Arts, who pointed out to me that that drawing board is detached from the physical universe, actually floating unconnected in space. Incidentally, both versions of the portrait have been cleaned and restored, the Philadelphia one in 1912, the Boston in 1939. Some of the differences between them may owe more to restorers than to John Neagle.

If Pat's motive in commissioning the painting was to preserve green the memory of his story, he succeeded. Every time the two paintings were exhibited, the tale of the unjust persecution of the innocent blacksmith was retold. There is, oddly enough, a completely different portrait of Pat, by someone unknown; it is a steel engraving, with the legend "Grav'd by J. Akin"—quite a good engraving in the original, which can be seen at The Historical Society of Pennsylvania. A very poor metal cut was made from it for use as the frontispiece of one of the books. The picture shows Pat sitting in a neat, clean jail cell on a fine Chinese Chippendale chair. He is fresh-shaven, handsomely dressed; he holds a pair of calipers and a mechanical design of some kind in his hands. It is scarcely to be thought of as a likeness, any more than the cell can be thought of as that storeroom in the great Prison.

Mr. Eugene Ferguson, historian of American engineering and technology (he is also the biographer of Thomas Truxtun) was at the Smithsonian Institution, one of the scholars who added recent excitements to that now venerable place, while I was working on Pat Lyon. He turned up many fugitive items of Pat's technological achievements for me, and found that characteristic letter Pat wrote for the Census of 1820, about his manufacturing. The late, lovely Jimmy Shields discovered the book of Charles Lamb dedicated to Pat—a mystery to Jimmy, and still to me. Mr. Thomas R. Adams knew I was interested in Lyoniana, and took the trouble to collect and reproduce for me advertisements Pat ran in forty-one separate issues of William Duane's *General Advertiser* (*Aurora*). I have seen one of the children's books about Pat, *The Locksmith of Philadelphia,* revised ed., New York, 1854.

And all around Philadelphia are "original primary sources" to be found. Pat's final will (March 4, 1829; he died the following month) is in the office of The Register of Wills, with the executors' inventory, bonds, and testimonies. Rare old city directories of 1797–1805 locate all the people of the story—where they lived and what they did; church and churchyard records of St. Peter's record Pat's marriages, his losses, his own death at sixty on April 14, 1829. His son, a civil engineer who built a bridge over the Schuylkill, lies in Christ Church yard at Dover, Delaware. Neagle's bust portrait of Pat is in The Historical Society, so is one of the three preliminary sketches of the large painting. The others are in The Pennsylvania Academy and the Boston Athenaeum. Quite a number of letters and papers of Lyon himself and the various lawyers, relating to the trial, have turned up, as well as some letters of Pat relating to his own metal work, in various libraries and collections. In one letter old Judge William Lewis says to a client, 5 May, 1796: "P.S. You know that a lawyers fee is almost universally paid before the Trial." (Gratz MS Collection, HSP.) Descriptions of Pat's fire engines, particularly by rival manufacturers, are to be seen. One is a detailed description of the awesome "Diligent" engine of 1820 in the "Personal Reminiscences of George Escol Sellers," a MS in The American Philosophical Society Library. Sellers's father tried with all *his* ingenuity to invent an "hydraulion" superior to Lyon's "Diligent." He succeeded only in producing his Camel, or Hunchback, a machine which took eight more men than the "Diligent" to run, and in several trials could never match the "Diligent's" performance. The trials were about as accurate as today's measurements of the distance of a major-league home run. They stationed both machines on the same spot, then calculated how high each could throw its stream of water, through various nozzles, over Dr. D. Jayne's Building—the iron and glass skyscraper which still stands in Old Philadelphia. At least, the Jayne Building got its windows washed. Pat Lyon called Sellers' hydraulion a "Double Damned Cholera Morbus Machine."

A lithograph by G. G. Heiss of that famous "Diligent" engine was published by Wagner & McGuigan, Lithographers, in 1836, at the time when John Agnew rebuilt Pat's masterpiece. It has been several times reprinted. Not many of Pat's works, durable and ornamental though he pronounced them, have survived, as he hoped they would. (His principles have proved more lasting even than steel.) So far as I know, only two of his fire engines still exist. They are smaller things than the "Diligent," not particularly remarkable. The last time I saw one of them, it was in the Old City Hall, in the Independence Hall group of buildings. Mr. Audubon R. Davis, Librarian of The Bucks County Historical Society at Doylestown, showed me models there (made about

1915) of the first hose wagon in the United States, designed and built by Pat Lyon for the Philadelphia Hose Company in 1803, and another of Lyon's pumpers. When I spoke on a pleasant occasion to St. Andrew's Society of Philadelphia, Dr. N. E. McClure (then President of Ursinus College) introduced my talk by observing I would describe Pat Lyon, the only member of St. Andrew's Society who had ever been *unjustly* imprisoned. Through Dr. McClure's kindness I was permitted to use materials relating to Pat in St. Andrew's Society's library.

More will turn up, and surely more of the products of his forge will be identified. Mr. M. Joseph McCosker, director of The Atwater Kent Museum of City History, himself an authority on the history of fire-fighting, has shown me a number of pieces in the Museum's collections, which it is certain that *P. Lyon fecit*. Among them I was brought up short to discover the great key of the front gate of Walnut Street Prison—and to wonder with what feelings Pat must have fashioned it, at his forge.

Some years ago when the artist Raymond Spiller was a young first-year student at The Pennsylvania Academy, he spent an hour with me going 'round the permanent collection in the galleries. He passed by the big Neagle, "Pat Lyon at the Forge," without comment. I am used to artists' attitude toward iconography, and *genre* portraits, but I was already beginning to work on Pat's story, and I wanted a reaction. "Don't you like this?" I asked.

"Of course not," he said. "Does anyone?"

"Why not?" I demanded.

"There's nothing right about it," he said. "You take one look at that guy, you can't believe he's any blacksmith."

8. *The Mammoth Cheese*

Mr. Lyman H. Butterfield has written a sprightly account of this episode, in his authoritative study, "Elder John Leland, Jeffersonian Itinerant," *Proceedings of the American Antiquarian Society,* October, 1952, at pages 214–29. To him I am indebted for many details of the story, and for the delightful sense of hilarity with which he relates this and many other colorful moments of the American past. Mr. Butterfield was in turn indebted to another, and so am I; for a few years earlier Mr. C. A. Browne made a sober, earnest investigation of this far-from-sober event: "Elder John Leland and the Mammoth Cheshire Cheese" (*Agricultural History,* XVIII, 1944, pages 145–53).

The town of Cheshire, incidentally, has cast a replica in concrete of Elisha Brown's cider press, which stands idiotically today on Cheshire's green, a memorial to a moment of innocent fame.

It was McMaster who figured out that Jefferson paid more than the cheese was worth—which was quite like McMaster. I'm told that Oberholtzer learnedly disputed McMaster's figures on this calculation, which would have been quite like Oberholtzer. Historians used to have fun.

There is a modest literature surrounding Leland, his tracts, his career. Much of his correspondence has been published, and a volume of his *Writings* appeared in 1845, edited by a Miss L. H. Greene. Those who enjoy primitives, those who are not repelled by enthusiasms, find him an engaging character.

But even they must acknowledge that he was one of those who did most, in the bursting bubbling age of our national inward-turning, to vulgarize religious experience in America and retard the development of genuine theological studies. The American spirit at its most abundant has always been a hindrance to deeper religious evocations.

But not always to political. The expression which the generation of Jeffersonians gave to Mr. Jefferson's ideas, ideals, and visions, may have been a crude expression, sadly coarsening to the best of Jefferson's thought, but certainly that generation vastly broadened the base on which American political liberty rested. Leland, for all his egregious jollity and his lack of built-in safety devices, was one of those who most encouraged the participation in politics of the least-privileged citizens. That they were also the least-prepared for political judgment proved in the long run no fatal impediment to American free institutions. And indeed, the evocation of political enthusiasm was a natural and predictable result of Jefferson's ideas, and Madison's activities in their behalf. So, too, natural and predictable, were the modifications and attenuatings of those ideas into slogans and generalized principles, when they became the possession of masses of people not individually committed to their actual meanings. The most unfortunate result of popular government is popularizing.

For a period, while studying the operations of the Congress and the courts during Jefferson's Presidency, I was continually tripping over contemporary references to the Mammoth Cheese, both in the brief moments of its glory, and in the sad years of its unseemly decay. Finally, I composed a lecture on its history for the entertainment of the members of The Philobiblon Club of Philadelphia, and I found myself giving it elsewhere as well. It grew as I gave it. That Breughelesque scene of the pressing in Farmer Brown's orchard was fascinating to imagine: reconstructing what must have taken place was made easier by several eighteenth-century cheese-making manuals which librarians turned up for me.

The most detailed and useful of these was a delightful do-it-yourself book published (second edition, corrected and improved) at Warwick, in England, in 1787. It is titled *Dairying Exemplified, or the Business of Cheese-Making,* and was written by a certain J. Twamley. For those who have never discovered the pleasures to be found in handicraft manuals from the age of the artisan and guild master, when excellence of the single product rather than machine-produced masses of identical products was the joy and the calling of labor, J. Twamley has many surprises to offer. His account of the *mystique* of rennet, the rich lore surrounding it, and his description of noxious weeds, may strike the reader as the pure creative imagination of a poet, until he learns that such things were "facts" in J. Twamley's day. Many of them are still facts in our day, in the pressing of cheese.

The imposing *Cyclopœdia, or Universal Dictionary of Arts and Sciences, and Miscellaneous Literature,* first American edition in forty-one formidable volumes, is in many ways the finest record of the Age of the Artisan—that unstudied, unregarded period in American social history and economic life which preceded the Age of the Industrial Factory. The *Cyclopœdia* was, of course, patently a steal of the great English prototype, but printers found such stealing profitable business in the 1790's. Volume VII, with an extended essay on how, when, where, and why to make cheeses, had appeared in print (from Dunlap's shop, in Philadelphia) before the ladies of Cheshire undertook their adventure. Perhaps they studied it. I did.

Mr. Saul Rutstein, cheese-master at the Wildstein Cheese Company of Philadelphia, granted me an interview and permitted me to see something of cheese-making today, which assisted me in understanding some of the technical problems of pressing cheeses. Of course, the modern dairyman meets few of the difficulties of the farm wife of the eighteenth century—and is heartily thankful for that.

The end of the Mammoth Cheese is not yet. Soon after I began talking of it, the librarian of the Public Library of North Adams, Massachusetts, offered as a gift (August 25, 1955) to the Chapin Library at Williams College the original letter of presentation of the Cheese to the President, signed by the Cheshire Committeemen: Daniel Brown, Hezekiah Mason, Jonathan Richardson, John Waterman, and John Wells Jr. Bound with it was President Jefferson's reply. Mr. Thomas R. Adams, then Librarian of the Chapin Library, gladly accepted the two letters. Certainly more items will turn up, for quite like the great red-wax monster itself, the story and the memory of the Mammoth Cheese persistently refuse to die.

9. The National Guest*

The visit of The National Guest had been a matter of state, and when it was all over President John Quincy Adams commented on it in his annual message to Congress. "It will form hereafter a pleasing incident in the annals of our Union," he concluded, "giving to real history the intense interest of romance . . ."

He was right. Not merely a pageant, but a whole year of pageants, month after month a whole year of celebrations, parades, extravaganzas, floats, arches, façades; not merely a city but a whole nation of cities, and towns, and villages; not merely one committee, but hundreds of committees, thousands of people planning, managing, arranging—the event stands entirely apart. It is like nothing else in all history.

Young men in vast numbers poured out to join phantom regiments of an army long since gone, struggled into uniforms lovingly wrought from patterns fifty years out of date, drilled, marched, rode, fired antique guns to orders out of obsolete manuals—this, in a land where the professional soldier was all but unknown. Every artist was put to work, every architect, builder, joiner, musician, engraver, every artisan, printer, weaver, dyer, craftsman, every wrangler, surely every farrier. Museums and private collections still retain in their storerooms bandoliers, medals, prints, sheet music, banners, engravings, paintings—survivals of the Year of The National Guest. "Come Honor The Brave" and many more of the songs written to delight LaFayette are valued for the scenes on their lithographed covers. In Chadds Ford, Pennsylvania, the Brandywine Battlefield Park Commission preserves one of the coaches he rode in; and those coaches (there were a great many of them) turn up in the most unlikely

---

* A first version of this address was published as an article in *Woman's Day,* July, 1955.

places. There is a silvered one in dead-storage in a museum in Philadelphia; no one knows what to do with it. There is one on the plains of Nebraska. A catalogue of every item produced during this illuminated year, and still preserved, would be a record of the genius, energy, taste and skills of the second generation of independent Americans.

How much did it all cost? No one can guess, and significantly no one that year or afterwards ever thought to ask. I have found only two financial reports of city committees (more will surely turn up); contributions came in readily, with no complaining.

That the people sustained their enthusiasm so abundantly, so long, is only less remarkable than that LaFayette sustained his, found within himself the resources and willingness to go through it all, that appalling daily schedule, week after week, in unflagging good spirit. The aptness, the tenderness, the transparent sincerity of everything he said, the love he evoked and the love he returned, revealed dimensions in his character and his intellect, too, which France had never noticed, and which America, caught up in stretching her own dimensions, was too busy to apprehend.

I was brought to the retelling of this tale because an impressionable girl of eighteen in New Castle, Delaware, transported by the sudden joyousness of the nation and by her first dawning perception of what America had been, and could be, took an old ledger-book of her father's and began to make a newspaper-clipping album. Diligently, for more than a year, she pasted in the lined folio volume stories from newspapers all over the nation, from Maine to Georgia, from Boston, New York, New Jersey, from the new Western states which Randolph of Roanoke called "those geographical *expressions* beyond the Alleghenies," from neighboring Baltimore and Philadelphia. Mistress Ann Booth had no direct part in the nation's exuberant celebrations. I cannot find that she did more than *look* upon The National Guest from the midst of a crowd. But she collected a remarkable record of American literary effusions, which tells a very large part of this most-journalized event in our early national history. Her scrapbook has come, a charming *ephemeron* of our past, into the collections of Mrs. Joseph Carson. The yellowed pages of half-a-hundred newspapers crackle and crumble, but in their dust is still a sparkle, which I hope may not have lost its radiance.

Mrs. Carson is certainly one of our most original collectors of Americana, and her collecting is animated by her own creative purposes. It was she who urged me to the subject, and encouraged me to study Ann Booth's scrapbook. Otherwise, of course, the writings of Levasseur, LaFayette himself, all the contemporaries who kept diaries or chronicled the days of their years, the records of governments state, local, and national, the letters of major figures and minor, make a vast reservoir of source material from which to draw. The standard biography, Whitlock's, is curiously full of tiny annoying errors; some of them persist in the literature. Professor Gottschalk in his lifetime study has been less interested in this year than in LaFayette's career in France, but his four books are of course masterful. The late Bennett Nolan's two works, *Lafayette Day by Day* and *Lafayette in America,* are careful, reliable, and pleasant to use.

Mr. Nolan defended his spelling, *Lafayette.* Any of the variant spellings is defensible. It is not that LaFayette changed his own spelling, but rather that it is impossible to tell from his handwriting whether he meant that *F* to be capitalized, or the *L,* or whether he meant a space between the *La* and the *Fayette.* By the time of his last visit, Americans were all using the *La* as part of his name, with a capital *L,* whether they capitalized the *F* or not, or made one word or two. Fifty years before, however, people had often referred to him as *de la Fayette,* sometimes merely as *Fayette.* General Washington in his letters used all possible variants. He referred to George Washington LaFayette as *young Fayette, young Lafayette, Mr. George Fayette, Mr. La Fayette,* or simply *Fayette.* For a while, when young George was living with him at Mount Vernon and the Marquis was imprisoned in France, Washington seemed to distinguish between father and son by using some prefix for the father, *Mr. de la Fayette, Mr. LaFayette,* or *LaFayette,* while omitting if for the son: *Fayette.* But he forgot himself continually, and used both forms for both his friends, sometimes in the same letter.

This amusing oddity, of our not knowing for sure the right way to spell or say the name (in strictest usage, the title) of the most exotic of our heroes, has led to some curious results in the American gazetteer. There are eleven *Fayette* counties in this nation, four *Lafayette* counties. Twelve towns are *Fayette* or *Fayetteville,* nine are *Lafayette,* two are *La Fayette.* In four of our states, The National Guest is actually honored by two different towns which use two variant forms of his name, so fortunately the Post Office can index the two towns separately: in Alabama and Georgia, *Fayette* and *Fayetteville* are the county seats of *Fayette* counties, *Lafayette* and *La Fayette* are in other counties far away. In Tennessee and Pennsylvania, *Lafayette* and *Fayetteville* are nowhere near *Fayette* counties, nor near each other. Incidentally, eleven towns and one American county are called *La Grange,* though Indiana and Texas spell it as one word, *Lagrange.*

This piece began as an address to The Franklin Inn, an amiable company of, for the most part, literate (and even a few literary) gentlemen of Philadelphia, upon whom the affliction of the epithet "club" sits lightly. The subject proved, as Mrs. Carson had predicted it would, uncommonly appealing. I found myself talking on The National Guest at colleges and universities, historical societies, libraries, museums. Then came the two hundredth anniversary of LaFayette's birth. That year, The Mount Vernon Ladies' Association of The Union—the gallant, resourceful and hard-working band which first rescued Mount Vernon from decay and for more than a century now has lovingly preserved and maintained Washington's home as he knew it—invited me to address their annual assemblage at the Mansion. To stand in Washington's own parlor, before his own desk, near the key of the Bastille LaFayette sent him, and speak of the remarkable friendship between the two men, that friendship which wrought so mightily in two nations, was an unforgettable experience. To Madame Regent Mrs. Harkness, and her successor Madame Regent Mrs. Beirne, to all the gracious Vice Regents, and to Mr. Charles Cecil Wall the Resident Director, I am grateful indeed for an hour in a glow reflected.

Later, the Pierpont Morgan Library mounted an exhibition of rarities, "LaFayette and the American Revolution," and the address as it is published here was used to mark the formal opening. On that pleasant occasion, I mentioned in conversation my continuing wonder at LaFayette's patience and willingness to endure the rigors of his year as The National Guest. Why did he do it? Why would anyone do it? Mr. Herbert Cahoon of The Morgan Library, who had assembled the exhibition, gave us the answer. He led us all to a case where a book from LaFayette's library lay—closed, to exhibit the binding. LaFayette had stamped his family's coat-of-arms in gold on the leather covers of his books, and along with the family arms he also stamped a device—a "pugnacious device," Mr. Cahoon called it—which bore his own personal motto.

His motto was: *CUR NON?*

10. Twelve Days to Destiny

Miss Norma Cuthbert's *Lincoln and the Baltimore Plot,* making use of Pinkerton's papers, opened up this subject fully, and immense amounts of contemporary materials relating to the twelve-day journey have long been available. Indeed, so complete is the documentation almost hour-by-hour of Lincoln's trip and the country's curiosity, of every city's celebrations and each mile's progress of the train, so abundant are photographic and iconographic remains, that at no time else in his whole life are we able to get so close to Lincoln, and the activities that filled his days.

Still, no major scholar of Lincoln has written the story of this journey. The reason is evident. It is an interlude; it belongs nowhere in a biographical narrative. It falls between chapters.

Sandburg in his masterwork could afford little space for this interruption, this period of no positive action, this indecisive time of waiting. Even less in their briefer works could Thomas, Angle, Randall.

Some day, someone will give us a complete account. In the case of Lincoln, as with Washington, it is a difficult job to separate the historical person from the legend. This is Lincoln before the legend, Lincoln before anyone imagined the qualities he would exhibit, a Lincoln who was not so large in the public's mind as Buchanan, or Pierce, or Fillmore, or Tyler, or Chase, or Davis, or Douglas, or Bates, or Seward. The student must thrust himself backward in time, looking forward to an unknown future, if he would discover what sort the man actually was, and what he faced.

Americans have a reluctance to do so. The very name Lincoln is a distraction from study, a barrier when one tries that thrusting backward-looking forward which is the only path to historical discovery. Every mention of assassination in 1861 is irresistibly a reminder of the tragedy of 1865, and conditioned by a century of romance one cannot entirely obliterate the insistent mysticism, the spiritual overtones and second-sight which so many read into everything Lincoln said.

I was first brought to this subject in 1944, when I had the assignment of opening the papers of Chief Justice Read, which had come to The Library Company of Philadelphia. John M. Read was deeply concerned to learn of Lincoln as a person, after that nomination in May 1860. He wrote widely to the West, asking questions. At his own expense, he commissioned an artist (oddly, a miniature painter) and sent him clear out to Springfield to take a Lincoln portrait. From the portrait, he had Sartain execute an engraving. Read, C.J., did not trust photographs. It was the election engraving. It was before the beard, of course. When the Chief Justice finally met Lincoln, during this trip, the President-Elect looked quite different from the portrait and engraving on which he had spent so much money.

From everywhere Lincoln stopped, Read asked for newspapers. What he learned did not altogether reassure him. What the whole country learned these twelve days had much disturbing in it. Lincoln was caught, momentarily, in a trap where no man could shine. He was obliged to reveal himself very publicly yet avoid decision, shy away from policy. It was a Lincoln trimming, paltering, seeking the way of a master-politician—the way which that past-master politician James Buchanan had failed to find.

Yet it was a very human Lincoln, and around him surged a very human America. Every aspect of his trip was a reminder of crisis. Even the simplest people sensed the awesomeness of impending events; many of them kept records, and sources still turn up—little facts to chink into the structure of the story. Recollections of those not politically involved have the unmistakable stamp of authenticity—recollections such as C. W. Lamb's. As a young man, he was a member of the first train crew. As an old man, forty-eight years later, he told what he remembered of the journey from Springfield to Indianapolis, and a prairie newspaper published what he said: the Keokuk *Gate City Daily*, February 12, 1909, Lincoln's hundredth birthday. Incidentally, L. M. Wiley, for whom the first locomotive was named, was, incongruously, a South Carolina cotton shipper and secessionist, who happened also to be a director of the Great Western Railway Company.

Late in 1960, Mr. Victor Searcher published a book on these twelve days: *Lincoln's Journey to Greatness*. It is a convenient volume to have, but it is a disappointment; it is not the study someone some day will write.

Until a scholar of undoubted authority has uncovered every detail and presented the whole story, we must continue to regret the incidents of the night ride from Harrisburg, while approving the decisions that occasioned it. To hold the inauguration in Philadelphia, as leading statesmen suggested, would have been to acknowledge defeat in advance, and in all likelihood would have lost Maryland to the Union. Once it was resolved to proceed to Washington, only a man of uncommonly trivial nature would have ignored the warnings of danger from the Baltimore rousers, warnings which Pinkerton, Chief Kennedy, Mr. Wood, General Scott, Seward, and Judd were fully justified in taking very seriously indeed.

Trivial, Lincoln was not. A lasting regret remains, that neither he nor those around him had sufficient wit and invention to accomplish the feat without giving it the ludicrous appearance of timidity, and a masquerade.

Index